MA 0713 99

D0298524

Leabharlanna Fhine
MALAHIDE LIBRARY
Inv/03 : 03/1130F Price ε24.57
Title: People's King the tru
Class: 941.084092

The People's King

SUSAN WILLIAMS

The People's King

The True Story of the Abdication

ALLEN LANE
an imprint of
PENGUIN BOOKS

ALLEN LANE

Published by the Penguin Group

Penguin Books Ltd, 80 Strand, London WC2R ORL, England
Penguin Putnam Inc., 375 Hudson Street, New York, New York 10014, USA
Penguin Books Australia Ltd, 250 Camberwell Road, Camberwell, Victoria 3124, Australia
Penguin Books Canada Ltd, 10 Alcorn Avenue, Toronto, Ontario, Canada M4V 3B2
Penguin Books India (P) Ltd, 11 Community Centre, Panchsheel Park, New Delhi – 110 017, India
Penguin Books (NZ) Ltd, Cnr Rosedale and Airborne Roads, Albany, Auckland, New Zealand
Penguin Books (South Africa) (Pty) Ltd, 24 Sturdee Avenue, Rosebank 2196, South Africa

Penguin Books Ltd, Registered Offices: 80 Strand, London WC2R ORL, England

www.penguin.com

First published 2003
1

Copyright © Susan Williams, 2003

The moral right of the author has been asserted

All rights reserved. Without limiting the rights under copyright
reserved above, no part of this publication may be reproduced, stored in
or introduced into a retrieval system, or transmitted, in any form or by
any means (electronic, mechanical, photocopying, recording or otherwise)
without the prior written permission of both the copyright owner
and the above publisher of this book

Set in 9.75/13 pt PostScript Linotype Sabon
Typeset by Rowland Phototypesetting Ltd, Bury St Edmunds, Suffolk
Printed in England by Clays Ltd, St Ives plc

ISBN 0–71399–573–4

For Tendayi and Monica

'He nothing common did or mean
Upon that memorable scene'

Words spoken by Winston Churchill
after saying farewell to King Edward VIII,
11 December 1936

from 'An Horatian Ode' by Andrew Marvell, 1650,
on the beheading of King Charles I

Contents

List of illustrations   xi
List of characters   xiii
Preface   xvii

 1 'Something must be done'   1
 2 'My own beloved Wallis'   18
 3 'The Spirit of the Age'   47
 4 'King to marry Wally'   68
 5 'I had declared myself'   89
 6 'The Battle for the Throne'   111
 7 'The People want their King'   134
 8 'Tell us the facts, Mr Baldwin!'   153
 9 'Cavaliers and Roundheads'   171
10 'Don't abdicate!'   191
11 'Our cock won't fight'   209
12 'God bless you both'   233
13 'Rat Week'   254
14 'We have had such happiness'   273

References   283
Archive sources   335
Bibliography   338
Index   353

List of illustrations

Photographic acknowledgements are given in parentheses. Every effort has been made to trace all copyright holders. The publishers will be happy to make good in future editions any errors or omissions brought to their attention.

1. Edward VIII walking to the Glebe Sports Ground at Abertillery, South Wales, November 1936 (Hulton Archive)
2. Edward with international troops on the Italian Front, 1917 (from F. G. H. Salusbury, *George V and Edward VIII: A Royal Souvenir*, London, 1936)
3. Edward visiting Ontario Agricultural College, Canada, 1919 (*Ibid.*)
4. Edward visiting a miner's home in County Durham, 1929 (Popperfoto)
5. Edward presenting medals to players in a football cup final for unemployed men, early 1930s (Camera Press)
6. Edward receiving debutantes at Buckingham Palace, July 1936 (Topham Picturepoint)
7. Edward with his parents, Queen Mary and King George V, in 1917 (courtesy Al Fayed Archives)
8. The Duke and Duchess of York with their daughter Princess Elizabeth at the Richmond Horse Show, 1935 (Hulton Archive)
9. Wallis Simpson on holiday in Europe in 1929 with her aunt, 'Bessie' Merryman (Urban Archives, Temple University, Philadelphia, Pennsylvania)

10. Wallis at the International Country Club, Wien Lainz, Austria, September 1936 (Victoria & Albert Museum Picture Library)
11. Wallis and Edward in Italy in 1936 (Pictorial Parade)
12. Wallis and Edward on holiday in Yugoslavia, 1936 (Hulton Archive)
13. Winston Churchill in conversation with Prince Edward, 1919 (Hulton Archive)
14. Cosmo Gordon Lang, Archbishop of Canterbury, 1929 (Hulton Archive)
15. Illustration of Stanley Baldwin speaking to the House of Commons, 4 December 1936 (Camera Press)
16. Crowd with anti-Baldwin banners outside Buckingham Palace, December 1936 (Popperfoto)
17. Telegram to Winston Churchill from the son of Sir Reginald Banks, December 1936 (Churchill College Archives, University of Cambridge (CHAR 2/599))
18. Letter to Edward from an anonymous correspondent, December 1936 (The Royal Archives, copyright © 2003 Her Majesty Queen Elizabeth II)
19. Letter to Edward from Harold H. Eastlake, December 1936 (The Royal Archives, copyright © 2003 Her Majesty Queen Elizabeth II)
20. Letter to Edward from an anonymous correspondent, December 1936 (The Royal Archives, copyright © 2003 Her Majesty Queen Elizabeth II)
21. Wallis at Lou Viei, France, after the abdication (Victoria & Albert Museum Picture Library)
22. Edward and Wallis on their wedding day, Château de Candé, France, photographed by Cecil Beaton, 2 June 1937 (copyright © Cecil Beaton Photograph/courtesy Victoria & Albert Museum Picture Library)
23. The Duke and Duchess of Windsor, photographed by Cecil Beaton, 1937 (copyright © Cecil Beaton Photograph/courtesy Camera Press)

List of characters

Principal characters

Edward, Prince of Wales/HM King Edward VIII/HRH The Duke of Windsor, 'David' to his family
Wallis Warfield Simpson/The Duchess of Windsor

King George V
Queen Mary, Queen Consort/widow of King George V
Prince Albert, 'Bertie', Duke of York/King George VI
Princess Elizabeth, Duchess of York/Queen Elizabeth/Queen Elizabeth the Queen Mother
Prince George, Duke of Kent
Princess Marina, Duchess of Kent

Stanley Baldwin, Prime Minister and leader of the Conservative Party
Lord 'Max' Beaverbrook, owner of the *Evening Standard* and the *Express* group
Peregrine ('Perry'), Lord Brownlow, Edward VIII's Lord-in-Waiting
Stanley Bruce, High Commissioner for Australia in London
Winston Churchill, Conservative MP and friend of Edward VIII
Geoffrey Dawson, editor of *The Times*
Major Alexander Hardinge, Private Secretary to Edward VIII
Dr Cosmo Gordon Lang, Archbishop of Canterbury
Mrs D. Buchanan ('Bessie') Merryman, Wallis Simpson's aunt
Walter Monckton, Attorney-General to the Duchy of Cornwall and Edward VIII's advisor
Ernest Simpson, second husband of Wallis Simpson

Other participants

Major Ulick Alexander, Keeper of the Privy Purse
George Allen, Edward VIII's solicitor
Clement Attlee, leader of the Labour Party
Sir Harry Batterbee, Assistant Under-Secretary of State, Dominions Office
Dr A. W. F. Blunt, Bishop of Bradford
Ernest Brown, Minister of Labour
John Buchan, Governor-General of Canada
A. Canning, Superintendent of Special Branch, Metropolitan Police
Neville Chamberlain, Chancellor of the Exchequer
Sir Henry ('Chips') Channon, a socialite of American birth and Conservative MP
Sybil, Lady Colefax, Wallis Simpson's friend and Society hostess
Lady Diana Cooper, prominent member of Society and wife of Duff Cooper
Duff Cooper, Secretary of State for War
Lady Emerald Cunard, Society hostess
Nancy Dugdale, wife of Thomas Dugdale
Thomas Dugdale, Parliamentary Private Secretary to Stanley Baldwin
Thelma, Lady Furness, Edward's lover before Mrs Simpson
Sir Philip Game, Commissioner of the Metropolitan Police
Theodore Goddard, Mrs Simpson's solicitor
Viscount Halifax, Lord Privy Seal and Leader of the House of Lords
Helen Hardinge, wife of Alexander Hardinge and daughter of Lady Milner
Esmond Harmsworth, chairman of the Newspaper Proprietors Association and son of Lord Rothermere, owner of the *Daily Mail*
Sir Samuel Hoare, First Lord of the Admiralty
George and Kitty Hunter, friends of Wallis Simpson
William Lyon Mackenzie King, Prime Minister of Canada
Charles Lambe, Edward VIII's equerry
Lord Linlithgow, Viceroy of India
David Lloyd George, Liberal MP and former Prime Minister
Edith, Lady Londonderry, Tory hostess and wife of Lord Londonderry

Joseph A. Lyons, Prime Minister of Australia
Ramsay MacDonald, Lord President of the Council and former Prime Minister
Harold Macmillan, MP
Violet, Lady Milner, mother of Helen Hardinge
Louis Mountbatten, Edward VIII's cousin and aide-de-camp
Mary Kirk Raffray, Wallis Simpson's old friend and Ernest Simpson's lover
Sir John Reith, Director-General of the BBC
Joachim von Ribbentrop, German ambassador to Britain
Katherine and Herman Rogers, American friends of Wallis Simpson
Hilda Runciman, wife of Walter Runciman
Walter Runciman, President of the Board of Trade
Michael Savage, Prime Minister of New Zealand
Sir John Simon, Home Secretary
Sir Archibald Sinclair, Leader of the Liberal Party
Sir Malcolm Stewart, outgoing Commissioner for the Special Areas
Godfrey Thomas, Assistant Private Secretary to Edward VIII
Eamon de Valera, President of the Executive Council of the Irish Free State
Mrs Freda Dudley Ward, the Prince of Wales's lover from 1918 to 1934
Lord Wigram, Private Secretary to George V and briefly to Edward VIII
Sir Horace Wilson, Chief Industrial Advisor to the Government
Lord Zetland, Secretary of State for India

Preface

In his portrait of Edward VIII in the *Dictionary of National Biography*, the historian John Grigg described the King as a man out of the ordinary, with virtues of moral and physical courage. 'He surely deserves honour', wrote Grigg, 'for the chivalrousness of his decision to abdicate, no less than the perfect constitutional propriety with which it was carried out.'[1] I was startled to read this warm description of Edward at the beginning of my research on the abdication. I had boundless respect for John Grigg, but little at that time for Edward. I shared most of the conventional – and unflattering – opinions about him and Wallis Simpson. My plan was to tell the story of the abdication through contemporary letters and the diaries of the British elite, most of whom regarded his approach to kingship as a threat to the survival of the monarchy. They thought even less of Mrs Simpson, and assumed that she was scheming to be Queen.

But I had barely scratched the surface of my research before I realized that the truth might be different. As I watched a newsreel of Edward VIII's tour of the Welsh valleys in November 1936 – when he urged that 'Something must be done' to find work for the unemployed – I saw a man who was visibly moved by the sufferings of the poor. He brought hope to the valleys, as to the other areas of unemployment he had visited as Prince of Wales, and the whole country seemed to admire and appreciate his efforts. I started to see the story of the abdication on a wider screen: it was no longer simply a tale of royalty and the Establishment, but included the ordinary people of Britain. Indeed, as I was later to discover, it also included the people of the

Empire, across the globe. Edward's sixty million subjects counted as much in this story as the tiny circle of 'Society'.

Shortly after watching this newsreel, while doing some research at the Public Record Office of Northern Ireland, I stumbled – quite by chance – upon the diaries of a middle-aged linen draper in Belfast. The opinions he expressed in December 1936, just after the news of Edward's love for Wallis Simpson had broken in Britain, were very different from those I had found in Society diaries. As far as he was concerned, Edward was a fine King and Wallis Simpson a reasonable choice for a wife. I was fired with curiosity: how many other people had felt like he had? I started a search of record offices all over Britain and found many more diaries written by the general public – by the kind of people 'who lived faithfully a hidden life, and rest in unvisited tombs', as George Eliot put it in *Middlemarch*.[2] Many of them, I discovered, were deeply sympathetic to Edward. Clearly, one's perception of the abdication changed if one looked outside and beyond the usual parameters of study.

Then the Royal Archives offered me access to a set of ten massive boxes, bursting with thousands of letters and telegrams that were sent to Edward during the weeks of the abdication crisis, from people all over Britain and from many other countries of the world. A former Assistant Private Secretary to Edward gave an account of these boxes in a note written nearly ten years after the abdication: 'They contain a remarkable cross-section of public opinion, from all classes, which should be of much interest & value to anyone who in years to come is writing about the Abdication.'[3]

Some of the letters were hostile to Edward, others were written by cranks, but overwhelmingly they offered loyal and heartfelt support to the King. As I sat at a desk in the Round Tower at Windsor Castle, I was often moved by these letters: some were signed by every member of a family, from the smallest children to the grandparents; others were petitions signed by whole streets or by all the people in a café or a shop. Many were written by ex-servicemen, whose loyalty to Edward had been increased by the fact that he had shared with them the horrors of the First World War. With one letter there was a small packet containing one of a pair of four-leaf clovers. The veteran had been sent the clovers while he was serving at Gallipoli in 1915. Although the Allies had suffered a terrible and brutal defeat, with over two hundred thousand casualties, he had survived – thanks, he believed, to the clovers. He had carried them with him ever since, and now he hoped the King would accept one of the clovers 'for luck'.[4]

A striking feature of many letters is the acceptance of Wallis Simpson as a suitable wife for the King. Whereas the social elite dismissed her out of hand, many of the general public welcomed her as someone more like them – someone who came from an ordinary family and had struggled as they had themselves. 'A Commoner has a Soul & is worthy in the sight of God', wrote a woman from Wales, adding, 'It is character that Counts here, & in the Great Beyond, not a Tytle [sic]. The greatest thing in life is love & sympathy, & Your Majesty should be allowed to choose your Queen and help mate in life.'[5] The fact that 'the Lady of your choice having been in a humbler position one time', said the wife of an unemployed ex-serviceman, was an advantage – 'she will know how to help you in doing what you have for the poor. Not like some who has never known what is to want a real meal, the same as I have . . . My wish is you will make the Lady of your Choice our Queen.'[6]

I have quoted from a large number of these letters and telegrams in the book because they offer a unique window onto the attitudes and feelings of ordinary people. Many of the authors were not used to writing letters and had not received much schooling – as one person wrote, 'the writing and spelling is bad but my heart is good'.[7] For the most part I have standarized the spelling and grammar, to make the book easier to read, but some of the idiosyncrasies have been left to keep the flavour of the letters. I have taken the same approach with the letters and telegrams sent to Stanley Baldwin and also to Winston Churchill, Edward's champion during the crisis – 'the ordinary letters from various people all over the country about the King', as a note to Mrs Churchill observed.[8]

*

I am grateful to Her Majesty the Queen for access to the papers in the Royal Archives and for permission to use them. I should like to thank Miss Pamela Clark, the Registrar at the Royal Archives, for her helpful comments on a draft of the book. I should also like to thank Miss

Clark and her team of staff for their invaluable assistance and the warmth of their welcome. I am grateful, as well, to the Churchill Archives Centre, Churchill College, University of Cambridge, for permission to use the Churchill Papers and for the benefit of the expertise of their staff.

I was blessed with many strokes of good fortune in the course of my research for the book. One of these was the timely release in January 2003 of the government records relating to the abdication, which had been closed since 1936. I was honoured to serve as the Historical Advisor to The National Archives for this release, which gave me full access to the documents before they were opened to the public. For this privilege I am grateful to the Keeper, Sarah Tyacke, and to David Thomas. These documents – sprinkled liberally with the words 'Secret', 'Very Secret', and 'Top Secret' – have filled some important gaps in knowledge and have helped me to understand better the relationships between crown and government between the wars. This new information has wonderfully fleshed out the story told in this book. My time at The National Archives was exciting, and it was a great pleasure to work with Clea Relly, Robert Smith, and Stephen Twigge.

Research for the book depended on access to public record collections across Britain, and all of those consulted are listed at the end of the book. I was given generous help by librarians and archivists and should like to mark out two people for special thanks: John Gurney, Curatorial Officer of the Historical Manuscripts Commission; and Carolyn Jacob at the Merthyr Tydfil Public Library. The resources and expertise of the British Library (not least the Western Manuscripts and the Oriental and India Collections) and the Newspaper Library at Colindale were indispensable, as were the books and the wonderful flexibility of the London Library.

I am indebted to the following institutions for their help and for permission to make use of documents in their custody: Amgueddfa Pontypool Museum, and the assistance of Glyn Lloyd; Fototeca Berenson, Florence, and the help of Fiorella Gioffredi Superbi; Birmingham City Archives, where I benefited from outstanding help from Rachel MacGregor; Bristol Record Office, and the assistance of Rob

Petre; Caernafon Record Office; the Syndics of Cambridge University Library; East Sussex Record Office; Gwent Record Office, and the assistance of Luned Davies; the Kensington and Chelsea Reference Library; the Centre for Kentish Studies; the Lincolnshire Archive; Special Collections and Archives at the Sydney Jones Library, University of Liverpool; Mass-Observation Archive, University of Sussex; the London Metropolitan Archives; the Manuscripts and Archives Division at the New York Public Library, with special and much appreciated help from John D. Stinson; the Special Collections of the Robinson Library, University of Newcastle upon Tyne, and the assistance of Lesley Gordon; the Modern Papers and John Johnson Reading Room at the Bodleian Library, University of Oxford, where all the staff deserve prizes; the Public Record Office of Northern Ireland; Somerset Record Office; Staffordshire Record Office at Stoke on Trent, where I was given wonderful help by Liz Street; King's College Library, University of Cambridge, and the assistance of Rosalind Moad; the Archives, University of Wales Swansea; Archives and Manuscripts at the Wellcome Library for the History and Understanding of Medicine; Westminster Library; West Sussex Record Office; and the West Yorkshire Archive Service: Bradford, where I was fortunate to be given excellent assistance by Lorraine Mackenzie.

This book relies heavily on papers that are held privately. Earl Baldwin gave me access to and permission to quote from the papers of Lucy Baldwin, and Lord Crathorne photocopied for me the abdication papers of his mother, Nancy Dugdale. I enjoyed stimulating discussions on various occasions with both Lord Baldwin and Lord Crathorne, who offered new insights into the abdication and a better understanding of the complexities of the period. Lady Mairi Bury kindly allowed me to quote from the papers of her mother, Edith Lady Londonderry. John Simon gave me permission to quote from the Simon Papers; George Trevelyan gave me permission to quote from the Moorman Papers; and Mr P. M. Furbank, the Turing Executor, gave me permission to quote from the Turing Archive. I am also grateful to Robin Dower for the permission of the Trustees of the Trevelyan Family Papers at the Robinson Library, University of Newcastle upon Tyne.

Ted Rowlands has taken a real interest in this book and provided me with information about the history of South Wales. Chandrika Kaul, a historian at the University of St Andrews, shared with me her unique knowledge of Edward's tour of India. Philip Williamson of Durham University has generously shared sources and information, and we have enjoyed discussing the subject of the abdication together. Andrej Olechnowicz, also at Durham, gave me a set of the Hilda Runciman and Trevelyan papers; he organized a conference on 'Manipulating the Monarchy' at Durham University in April 2002, where I had the opportunity to air some of my ideas and to participate in stimulating debate. Barbara Naegele in Ottawa sent me details about Edward's time in Canada. I am grateful to Steve Bailey and to Bill Barrell for information about postage rates in the past. Access to the photographs in the Windsor Albums was provided by the Victoria & Albert Museum, where Martin Durrant was especially helpful. Ann Towns made some excellent suggestions on searching for diaries. Bernard Welchman searched various local archives on my behalf; and Elizabeth Murray, with her characteristic efficiency and reliability, carried out some vital research. At moments of computer crisis I have been expertly bailed out by Alisdair Duthart.

Newsreels are an area of special expertise, and I was fortunate to meet Luke McKernan, Head of Information at the British Universities Film & Video Council, who helped me with all kinds of information. So did David Haynes of British Pathe, who also arranged for me to view numerous Pathe newsreels. Barbara Heavens, Senior Librarian at British Movietone News, answered all my queries and thoughtfully sent me shot lists. At the British Film Institute's National Film & Television Archive, I was ably assisted by Steve Tollervey, Chief Viewing Technician.

Philip Ziegler's brilliant biography of Edward VIII is an essential source for anyone working in this area. I am heavily indebted both to the book and to Philip himself, who kindly set aside some time to talk to me, at my request. At the time I had been concerned about some aspects of the book; I emerged from our discussion thinking more clearly and feeling much happier. I am also grateful to Michael Bloch, whose books have made an important contribution to scholarship on the Duke and Duchess of Windsor. Michael generously shared his ideas with me and also went to considerable trouble to find the print of the image that appears on the jacket. I should also like to acknowledge a debt to Greg King's outstanding biography of the Duchess of Windsor.

Many friends and colleagues helped me with this book. It is a pleasure to thank the kind and generous people who read and offered criticism and comments on the various drafts: Dennis Dean, Gervase Hood, Jackie Lee, and Margaret Wynn. All these readers improved the book immeasurably.

For their interest and encouragement, I am immensely and especially grateful to Monica Ede, Jackie Lee, Elizabeth Patience, and Margaret Wynn. I also thank Barbara Bamber, Dennis Dean, Theresa Hallgarten, Ferelith Hood, Tom Hooke, Lesley Hall, Ornella Moscucci, Jennifer Pader, Tina Perry, Desna Roberts, Sandra Stone, Alfred Thomas, James Thomas, and Joan Williams, and also my colleagues at the Institute of Education, University of London.

I am deeply indebted to Mr Eric Ezra of Moorfields Hospital, who rescued my sight during the final stage of producing this book.

It is a privilege and a pleasure to write for Penguin. I am grateful beyond measure to my editor, Margaret Bluman. She was always willing to read and comment on drafts, despite her own busy schedule. At every stage we discussed the implications of new findings and the way forward. Her advice and guidance were unfailingly right. It is no exaggeration to say that without her involvement, this book would not have been written. Cecilia Mackay is a brilliant picture editor whose detective skills deserve special mention. John Woodruff is a gifted copy-editor who not only picked up blunders but also made important suggestions which have improved the book's readability.

My daughter, Tendayi Bloom, was instrumental in the decision to write about the abdication. I was still wondering whether or not to do so – and talking incessantly about this – when we went together to visit Horace Walpole's home at Strawberry Hill, Surrey. While there, we had a cup of tea in the cafeteria. She told me to look up at the wall – where I saw a portrait of Edward VIII – and observed that I must be destined to write the book because he seemed to follow us everywhere.

She cheerfully accepted the book as a new member of the family circle and came with me to South Wales on a fruitful mission of research. Benedict Wiseman offered useful insights on the politics of the interwar period and encouraged me in my efforts during the long days of writing. His thoughtful gifts of music gave special pleasure to those days. Gervase Hood, my husband, contributed to the book in important ways that are too numerous to list. His loving presence kept me going when I faltered; and his delight at my growing excitement multiplied the joy.

I

'Something must be done'

More than two thousand people were waiting for King Edward VIII at the abandoned steelworks of Dowlais in South Wales on Wednesday, 18 November 1936. It was a damp and chilly day: jackets were tightly buttoned and shawls held close. As soon as the royal car was seen driving up the hill from Merthyr Tydfil, everyone cheered in delight and the Dowlais Aged Comrades' Choir struck up *God Save the King*. Excited children jumped up and down, waving their Union Jacks in a sea of flags. The King – a short, slight figure, with deep blue eyes and a shock of thick, golden hair – stepped from his car, smiling, and waved his hand in greeting. Forty-two years of age, he was sovereign of over 600 million people, the citizens of Britain and its Empire. And today, just ten months after his accession to the throne, he had travelled through the night to visit the people of South Wales.

But once the King had looked about him, he stopped still. He was evidently distressed and stood quietly for a few minutes on the road, his bowler hat in his hand. He was facing a scene of desolation – hundreds of gaunt and weary men sitting on heaps of twisted metal. Their clothes were worn and their boots were broken. Three-quarters of the men of Dowlais were unemployed: once a symbol of industry and prosperity, the Dowlais steelworks had closed down six years before and was now a derelict ruin. The King stood gazing in silence at the wreck of the huge blast furnace; few people, observed a Pathe Gazette newsreel, would ever forget His Majesty's expression at that moment.[1] Then he went slowly among the men, who rose to their feet and removed their caps. Some of them started to sing the Welsh hymn *Crugybar*, and the strains of deep male voices lifted into the air. The

King walked down a gangway into the centre of the works, through the roofless buildings and in the shadow of a skeleton of steel girders. Doffing his hat again and again to the crowds, he turned to the officials walking next to him. 'These steelworks brought the men hope', he said. 'Something must be done to see that they stay here – working.'[2]

The royal visit to Dowlais was just one stop on a hectic two-day tour of the industrial valleys of Glamorgan and Monmouthshire, South Wales. The King had left London shortly after midnight on a special train, arriving in the morning at the tiny railway station of Llantwit Major, a little town on the coast of Glamorgan. Being in Wales in the autumn of 1936 was a powerful reminder to the King of his investiture as Prince of Wales in the summer of 1911, when he was sixteen years of age. 'From Llantwit Major, where I got off the train,' he commented later in his memoirs, A King's Story, 'it is not over one hundred and fifty miles to Caernavon where, one July morning, a quarter of a century before, in the pomp and splendour of the medi-aeval setting of the ancient castle, my investiture as Prince of Wales had taken place.'[3] His style and titles had been proclaimed from the battlements of the castle by Winston Churchill, who was then Home Secretary. This was the start of a steadfast friendship between Edward and Churchill, characterized by mutual admiration and respect. Ever since the investiture, said Churchill, years later, Edward 'honoured me . . . with his personal kindness and, I may even say, friendship . . . In this Prince there was discerned qualities of courage, of simplicity, of sympathy, and, above all, of sincerity, qualities rare and precious.'[4]

The investiture had taken place twenty-five years before. This time, Edward was no longer Prince of Wales but King of Great Britain, Ireland and the British Dominions beyond the Seas, and Emperor of India. And this time, he was not greeted by pomp and splend-our. Instead, he was met 'by humble arches made of leeks from Government-sponsored co-operative farms, and of unlighted Davy lamps strung together by jobless miners.' The people looked thin and weary and were dressed in shabby clothes. Even a King, 'who would be among the last to feel the pinch of a depression', said Edward, 'could see that something was manifestly wrong.'[5]

There was indeed something wrong. Industrial South Wales had been unable to pull itself out of the economic depression that followed the collapse of the New York Stock Exchange in 1929. By 1936 most parts of Britain had recovered from the national slump, and a Government leaflet issued the previous year had claimed that over a million workers had got back into employment and wages had started to rise.[6] But this recovery had not spread everywhere. In South Wales, West Cumberland, Durham, Tyneside and industrial Scotland unemployment was still very high, and desperate families were forced to depend on the meagre dole provided by the Unemployment Assistance Board. King Edward was deeply troubled. He looked upon unemployment 'as the one black spot in the country' and was anxious to help in any way possible, wrote Major Alexander Hardinge, his Private Secretary, to the Minister of Labour in October 1936. Referring to Edward's coronation, which was planned for May the following year, he added that it would give His Majesty 'the greatest gratification' if the celebrations were to coincide with 'a real improvement of the lot of these unfortunate people, whose share in the general recovery has as yet been so very limited.'[7]

Even when their men had been in work, for families in South Wales life was a daily grind. Many of their homes had just two rooms, one bedroom and a kitchen, while some families lived in a one-room cellar dwelling. Almost every home lacked electricity. Water was carried in from a tap in the backyard, and the toilet, which was also outside, was shared by several families. These harsh conditions had been worsened by long years of unemployment. Families could not even afford to buy the coal that lay at the centre of their lives and had to scour the tips daily in search of bits of coal for a fire.[8] Children were dressed in ragged clothes and broken boots, handouts from organizations such as the Mayor of Merthyr Tydfil's Distressed School Children's Fund.[9] Short of money for food and fuel, women were unable to provide their families with nourishing meals. 'Two tin mugs and one plate were the whole equipment of a family of nine', reported the *Evening Standard* in an article on South Wales. 'There was no pot in which to warm the soup. Neither could the neighbour provide one ... Both households had been unable to cook anything at all for months, and had apparently lived on bread and margarine and tea.'[10]

Men and boys with no jobs and no money for hobbies and entertainment spent their days hanging around on the streets.

For many of the rich of Britain, little had been changed by the Depression. The women still organized 'coming out' parties for their debutante daughters, and the men still relaxed in the clubs of Pall Mall. Joey Legh, a royal courtier, lost some money in the Depression, but all he had to do was cut down on domestic staff – 'making do with one footman instead of two.'[11] Even in the Monmouthshire valleys, near the coalfields, there was luxury and splendour. Tredegar House, the glittering home of Viscount Tredegar, hosted an endless round of weekend parties attended by footmen dressed in breeches and powdered wigs.[12] In County Durham, another coal-mining region of Britain that had been hit badly by the Depression, the enormously wealthy Londonderry family enjoyed every luxury at Wynyard Park – just one of their three family seats. At Londonderry House, in London's exclusive district of Mayfair, Edith, Lady Londonderry held massive receptions to mark the opening of Parliament; the guest lists, of about a thousand people, took up nearly two full columns in *The Times*.

It was against this background of extreme contrast between the lives of the rich and the lives of the poor that King Edward's visit to South Wales in the late autumn of 1936 took place. Aneurin Bevan, the radical Labour MP for Rhymney, regarded the visit as patronizing and refused to welcome him. Organizing the visit in 'much the same way as you might to go to the Congo', he thought, was an affront to the people living there.[13] But few people in Wales shared this view. 'Everywhere the people looked delighted and hopeful at his visit', noted his equerry, Charles Lambe. 'They obviously loved and trusted him.'[14] Men, women and children thronged the narrow roads of the valleys.[15] '*Croeso i'r Brenhin*', declared a large banner – 'Welcome to the King'.[16] Colourful flags and bunting hung from shops and homes. 'As everywhere it's the same story, flags waving above the grime and decay, cheers breaking the silence where work hooters have long since ceased to blow,' observed the Pathe Gazette newsreel that was shown in cinemas the following week.[17] 'Surely, something will happen now' was the widespread feeling in South Wales, reported the *Spectator*.[18]

The King's Ministers of Attendance on the tour of Wales were Ernest Brown, Minister of Labour, and Sir Kingsley Wood, Minister of Health. He was also accompanied by representatives of social service organizations, among them the National Council of Social Service, of which Edward was patron.[19] The royal party was met at each stop by local representatives of these and other welfare groups, by town mayors and by the chairmen of urban district councils. Everywhere, groups of ex-servicemen who had served in the Great War of 1914–18 waited patiently to see the King.

The royal courtiers on the visit to Wales were led by Alexander Hardinge. The son of Lord Hardinge of Penshurst, who had been Viceroy of India between 1910 and 1916, he had been educated at Harrow and Trinity College, Cambridge, and fitted easily into the royal household – a closed world of upper-class men and women who shared the same background. They identified strongly with the elite of Britain and knew little, if anything, about the lives of the working classes. As Bevan suggested, to Hardinge and the other courtiers the people of South Wales must have seemed as foreign and remote as the people of the Congo. Hardinge had been a courtier to King George V and had taken part in the unchanging royal circuit of the previous reign: Buckingham Palace in the winter and summer seasons, Windsor Castle over Easter, Sandringham House in the autumn and over Christmas, Balmoral Castle in August, and sometimes the royal yacht at Cowes. He now found himself visiting very different places as Private Secretary to the new king, George V's son.

Charles Lambe was another member of the royal party to South Wales. A tall, good-looking naval officer of thirty-six, he had been appointed Edward's equerry just a few months before, in July. He had been put forward for the post by Lord Louis Mountbatten, his best friend, who was also Edward's cousin and aide-de-camp.[20] Lambe had no experience of the previous royal court and served Edward with loyal and unqualified enthusiasm.

From Llantwit Major, Edward was driven in the royal car to nearby Boverton, where the Welsh Land Settlement Society was developing a cooperative farm on an estate of 650 acres. The King chatted with the settlers on the farm, most of whom were unemployed miners, and many of whom were wearing medals they had won in the Great War. With smiles and handshakes, Edward told them how much he admired their hard work. Then a drive through the rolling countryside of the Vale of Glamorgan brought him to a very different scene – to the Rhondda Valley, the heart of the South Wales coal industry, scarred with slag heaps and idle mines. 'To-day, for miles,' wrote a Rhondda man in 1935,

you see the soft contours of the valleys, gashed and streaked by rows of ugly, drab houses, built anyhow, anywhere, to serve the purposes of those gloomy collieries; the rubbish tips sprawl everywhere, polluting the mountain air with dust and the streams with inky filth.[21]

A small mining town called Dinas was Edward's first stop in the Rhondda. Here, a disused coal tip was being converted into a re-creation ground by voluntary labour. The King sympathetically patted on the shoulder a man who had told him he had been unemployed for four years. To another man, who had been out of work for seven years, Edward said simply, 'I am indeed very sorry for you.'[22]

Soon after, the King was taken to the Pentrebach Preparatory Training Centre for the unemployed, where young men were learning the skills of the building trade. He received a tumultuous welcome. He paused for a moment, visibly moved, and raised his hat in acknowledgement. Lunch was scheduled at the centre. But before sitting down to eat, the King asked to see the men's dining hall. He waited until everyone was seated and then stepped briskly into the hall, where he rapped sharply on the metal wall of the hut. In the tone of an orderly officer and with a broad smile, he asked, 'Any complaints?' This produced a burst of laughter from the men as they sprang up from the tables – laughter in which the King merrily joined. After lunch, he went on a tour of the centre and asked for instructions on how to mix mortar. He picked up a trowel to try it for himself, which delighted all the working men around him, reported the *Merthyr Express*.[23]

The centre of Merthyr Tydfil was the next stop, and Edward was taken to see the Merthyr Maternity and Child Welfare Clinic. This clinic sought to provide mothers and children with extra nutrition and basic medical services. So high was the infant mortality rate in the region that in Abertillery in 1935, more than eleven infants in every hundred had died before they reached twelve months.[24] The Monmouthshire County Health Department reported that eight out of every ten schoolchildren in the area were sickly and that only ten out of every hundred were in normal health.[25] This meant that most of the children Edward met on his tour of South Wales were suffering from some kind of physical weakness.

A major worry at the Merthyr clinic was the rate of death in childbirth, which was high nationally but even higher in areas blighted by long-term unemployment.[26] At the end of 1934 the maternal death rate in the Rhondda was so grim that nearly one in every hundred women in the region lost their lives in childbirth.[27] Every pregnant woman lining the roadside to cheer Edward on his tour of Wales faced this high risk of death. She knew that by the time of the King's coronation next May, she might have lost her life – and left her baby motherless. Such suffering was unnecessary: research carried out in 1936 had demonstrated a clear connection between unemployment and maternal mortality, due to poor diet, fatigue, nervous strain and inadequate medical care.[28]

Edward's next stop at Merthyr was the Ministry of Labour Home Training Centre at Gwaelodygarth, where girls from unemployed households were being trained for work as domestic servants. Their uniform of white pinafores and headbands had been starched and carefully ironed, and their shoes polished to a shine. Then on to the employment exchange in the town, where the King saw men queuing up to register, dressed in threadbare jackets and caps. He went to the front of the queue and spoke to some of the men waiting for work.[29] A visit to an employment exchange had been specially asked for by the King.[30]

The tour continued to Aberdare and Penrhiwceiber, and then to Mountain Ash, where Edward was greeted by the singing of the local choir as he entered the pavilion in the centre of the town. Here, a great gathering of social service workers waited for him. As he stepped forward he was welcomed by thunderous applause, and for a brief moment he was overwhelmed. Then he walked up the steps of the platform and in an impromptu speech, told the audience of seven thousand that

You have made me feel at home in this part of South Wales today, and although I do not now hold the title of Prince of Wales – a title which I held for 25 years – my interest in the Principality will never diminish.[31]

A few weeks later the King received a letter from a woman living in Barry – 'just a "nurse" and young like yourself!' – who said she had had the pleasure of seeing him at Mountain Ash during his royal tour. 'I think you must have felt', she said, 'how sincerely the Welsh people love and admire you.'[32]

In a plain grey overcoat bare of official insignia, Edward's slight frame blended easily into the crowds of working men. Everywhere he went, he mingled with the people, doffing his hat. He got out of his car, reported a letter to the *Spectator* on 27 November, in the heart of a vast crowd, with not more than one or two policemen anywhere near him – 'His utter confidence in the goodwill and the affection of a much maligned people was magnificent.'[33] This display of trust was greatly appreciated by the people themselves. Shortly after the visit, an 'ordinary married woman from the distressed areas' who signed herself 'one full & loyal heart from Wales' wrote a long letter to the King. She had always admired him, she said, 'but lately, especially since your visit here, though I saw little of you myself (how I would love to have been one of those with whom you shook hands), my admiration has grown into the deepest love towards your Majesty.' She planned to go to the coronation in May the following year and would be cheering him with all her heart,

not because of who you are, but because of what you are, in spite of your Kingship. I do not suppose for one moment that you are perfect, no one in the world is, but your humanity & kindly interest in the people has touched me very deeply. You could profess concern & interest & yet stay away, but that you do not do, and may God bless you for it.

'By your stooping to us,' she added, 'you have gained what no other King has ever had, the deepest love & trust of his people . . . we down here in Wales are grateful. I wanted you to know.'[34]

The people of the Welsh valleys had a long tradition of welcoming outsiders who were genuine friends. One such outsider between the wars was Paul Robeson, the Black American singer and actor. While in London in 1929, he had come across a group of unemployed miners from South Wales who had walked all the way from the Rhondda Valley to petition the Government for help. They were singing for money to feed themselves, and Robeson joined the group to sing with them. Afterwards he bought them tickets back home on a goods train, as well as food and clothing for their families. He visited South Wales many times after this, singing with male choirs to support the Welsh Miners' Relief Fund and other causes. He believed there was a parallel between the exploitation of Black people in the USA and the conditions of coal miners in South Wales.[35] In 1936, the year in which Edward became King, Robeson was again in London, winning accolades in the role of *Othello*. But he still managed to visit South Wales and publicly to support the miners' cause.

King Edward's own warmth and concern for the poor marked him out as different from previous monarchs. He had first visited South Wales in 1919, after the end of the war, when he had spent four days visiting slum areas and had gone down a pit. This was the first of his numerous tours as Prince of Wales to the industrial and impoverished parts of Britain. King Edward VII, Edward's grandfather, had shown little interest in the ordinary people of Britain. 'He'd just sit in the open landau, receive an address, snip a ribbon and declare something open', observed Edward many years later, returning 'to dine with his girl friends. He didn't even leave that landau.'[36] David Lloyd George had considered King George V, King Edward VIII's father, to be obtuse about working-class grievances. 'He is a very very small man and all his sympathy is with the rich – very little pity for the poor', he wrote to his wife from Balmoral in 1911, when he was Chancellor of the Exchequer. 'The King is hostile to the bone to all who are working to lift the workmen out of the mire.'[37]

'You seem to us to be about the only reigning monarch who is worth anything at all', wrote a Chester woman to Edward VIII. 'We like you for the concern you have for the welfare of the poorest and most unfortunate of your subjects. No other King has gone among them as you have done, or shown signs of appreciating their distress in the way you do.'[38] A man who had spent forty-five years in the coal mines of South Wales and was now living in Brighton as a 'navvy washer up on washing steps', told Edward that 'No King in History has lived amongst the People as you have.' He himself, he added, was 'one of the Common People & The Commonest of Them'.[39] A woman in Sheffield wrote to thank him for some practical help. 'You once did me a great kindness I shall never forget', she said grate-fully. 'You helped me a great deal when you sent the lady the money towards my teeth. It was and is a thing I shall thank you for all my life.'[40]

Edward's ready sympathy for the sufferings of ordinary people was encouraged by his mother, Queen Mary. The Queen showed a genuine interest in the sufferings of the unemployed, and tried to help individuals and welfare organizations. Under her influence, Edward's brother, Prince Albert, Duke of York, had initiated the Duke of York's Camps in 1921. These were annual events where 200 boys from public schools joined 200 working-class boys at a summer camp for two weeks. The camps gave the different classes an opportunity to meet and mix with each other in an informal atmosphere, and Albert always spent one day with the boys.[41]

George V was kind-hearted, like his wife, but with 'strict views as to the correct conduct of children', recalled Edward many years later.[42] Alec Hardinge, whose post as a retainer to King George required him to live in close quarters with the royal family, felt sorry at times for the sons when they were young. 'At lunch today,' he wrote to his wife in 1925, 'we had one of the King's tirades against the younger generation. My sympathy with his sons increases daily!'[43] Mabell, Countess of Airlie, who was lady-in-waiting to Queen Mary, com-mented that although King George V and Queen Mary were often depicted as stern, unloving parents, this was not the case. It was her belief that they were more conscientious and more truly devoted to their children than were the majority of parents in that era. 'The tragedy', she thought, 'was that neither had any understanding of a child's mind.' George V, she observed, 'was fond of his sons but his manner to them alternated between an awkward jocularity of the kind which makes a sensitive child squirm from self-consciousness, and a severity bordering on harshness.'[44]

Queen Mary was keen to support Edward's efforts on behalf of the less fortunate people of Britain, and before he set off on his train journey to Wales in November 1936, she wished him luck for the tour. The first day of visits to the towns and centres of the valleys was completed by five o'clock, when Edward joined the royal train at Mountain Ash station and was taken to Usk, a quiet rural town. It was here that he and his party spent the night. A special cable had been laid to the King's apartment on the train, reported the *South Wales Argus*, because he wanted to make a telephone call; it was assumed that he wanted to communicate with Buckingham Palace.

Edward had a bad cold and wanted a hot bath. His equerry, Lambe, had to telegraph the local station-master to buy a hip bath in the village, and it was filled with hot water in his sleeper. The local people were delighted that the King had 'a dip in a tin bath such as miners use!'[45] Had the King been willing to travel to Wales in the 'proper royal train', which was fitted out with every kind of amenity, this would not have been necessary – but he had preferred to travel on an ordinary sleeper.[46] As Prince of Wales and then as King, he always resisted special treatment. When on one occasion the royal car was driven onto a station platform, abreast of the train that Edward was about to board, he was furious. 'Why must they do this?' he complained. 'Do they think I can't walk 20 yards like an ordinary person? Oh God! they've got barriers up to keep the crowd back. Who on earth arranged this?'[47] He insisted that when he was travelling through traffic to royal events, policemen should not clear the way for him.

After his bath, the King gave a dinner party on the royal train. It was a formal occasion – short coat and black tie.[48] As well as his ministers and courtiers, he invited representatives of the key Welsh government departments: John Rowland from the Welsh Board of Health and Captain Geoffrey Crawshay, the Commissioner for South Wales. Also invited was Sir George Gillett, the Special Areas Commissioner for England and Wales, whose job – as directed by the Special Areas (Development and Improvement) Act of 1934 – was to alleviate the worst effects of unemployment through regional development in health, housing, social improvement and industry. A more surprising guest at Edward's dinner was Malcolm Stewart, the outgoing Special Areas Commissioner, Gillett's predecessor. He had resigned his post just four days before. His reason, it was said officially, was poor health; but there were grounds to suspect that he had simply despaired of his job. He had published a blistering report a few days before his resignation, which argued that none of the measures provided for by the Special Areas Act made any real difference to the long-term unemployed. It supported hospitals, clinics, sewage disposal, allotments, and schemes such as children's school camps, physical culture and cookery classes. But it did not provide *jobs*, complained Stewart, which was the most fundamental need of the unemployed.[49] This was a major difference between the aims of the Special Areas Act and those of the 'New Deal' legislation passed in the USA in 1933, which also addressed the problems of unemployment created by the Depression.

Next morning, King Edward set out on another fifty-mile leg of the tour, this time through the mining towns and villages of the Monmouthshire valleys. The countryside was bleak and bare. Everywhere, observed the Pathe Gazette newsreel, 'It's a repetition of yesterday's scenes: roads lined by cheering crowds, narrow village streets packed tight with welcoming faces.'[50] In the bitter cold, bunting fluttered over cottages and arched the streets of the route, and streamers bade the King welcome in English and in Welsh. At Brynmawr, a painted streamer strung across the main road read, 'Brynmawr Welcomes Your Majesty and We Need Your Help'.[51]

The royal train took the King to Cwmbran. Crowds were waiting at the station, and as the royal train steamed in they sang '*Mae Hen Wlad fy Nhadau*' – 'Land of My Fathers' – and then the National Anthem. Here the King met a group of twenty-five workless men, several of whom had taken part in a national march of the unemployed to London the previous month. They had trudged from the valleys to Cardiff, then to Newport, Bristol, Bath, Chippenham and Swindon before reaching Reading, Slough and finally London. Like many of the frequent marches of the unemployed to London, this one had achieved nothing. In despair, the unemployed of Cwmbran presented the King with a petition asking for his help to start a sewerage scheme and a plant for the extraction of oil from coal. 'We believe you can accomplish much for the depressed areas by your influence with these recommendations', declared the petition. The closing of various works in Cwmbran, it added,

has rendered 2,250 men unemployed. We, the unemployed of Cwmbran, have been looking forward to your Majesty's visit with the hope that some tangible benefit and improvement will be the direct result ... Our women grow prematurely old and many are broken in the unequal fight against the conse-quences of unending penury ... The bodies of our children are stunted and frail.[52]

The royal car picked up the King at Cwmbran and took him to Llanfrecha Grange, an old mansion converted into a domestic training centre for boys. It was described in the official programme of the royal tour as an experimental venture to 'meet the demand for house and kitchen boys' that had resulted from 'the continued difficulty in obtaining girl domestic servants. South Wales was selected for such a centre because Welsh boys were regarded as particularly suitable for work of this kind'.[53] All the roads to the Grange were crowded with spectators, and the long drive to the mansion was lined with Girl Guides and Boy Scouts, dressed in uniform. The King joked for a while with the trainees and posed for a photograph with them. Then he was driven up the valley to Blaenavon, on the hillside, where over a third of the men were unemployed. The King was officially received near the Workmen's Hall, and the bells of St Peter's Church rang out a peal of welcome. 'It was more like a family party than a Royal visit', said one spectator. Edward shared some of his thoughts on the condition of the valleys with the people of Blaenavon. To an unemployed shop assistant, he said that, 'Something will be done for Wales in general'.[54]

The sprawling hilly town of Pontypool was the next stop. Here, Edward inspected a rally of Welsh Guards Old Comrades and ambulance men. As they chatted, one of them reminded him that they had met previously on the Somme in 1916. As Edward took a salute from the massed groups, he turned and raised his hat, standing to attention. The crowds cheered wildly. It was then time to go with Sir Kingsley Wood to the new Penygarn housing estate, which was part of Pontypool Council's slum clearance housing programme. Housing was a particular interest of the King: he had rehoused many of the Duchy of Cornwall's tenants in Kennington, London, and had improved farm workers' houses on Duchy estates in the West Country.[55] Shocked by the grim conditions of the slums he visited during his industrial tours as Prince of Wales, he had organized a dinner in London to address the issue of poor housing. To this meeting he invited not only experts and philanthropists, but also Ramsay MacDonald, who was then Prime Minister, Neville Chamberlain, who was Chancellor of the Exchequer, and the Minister of Health. Edward later observed that this was very likely the first debate on housing that ever took place under the auspices of the Prince of Wales.[56]

'Terrible! Terrible!' exclaimed the King, when he was told that over a third of the tenants on the Penygarn estate had no job. 'You may be sure that I will do all I can. We certainly want better times brought to these Valleys.'[57] The King was taken to houses that had been carefully chosen by the organizers of the tour: it had been decided in London that the party would 'drive slowly round the Estate stopping perhaps at one or two *selected* houses which The King might enter. These would of course *need to be chosen with some discretion.*'[58] This conflicted with the King's own and clearly expressed wish – that he wanted to see some working-class houses, but 'not only the good ones!', as Hardinge had explained to the civil servant who was drawing up the King's itinerary at the Ministry of Labour.[59] But Edward was not to be fobbed off. He duly visited the selected houses, asking with interest whether there was electricity in the district and if it was going to be installed on this estate. And he then went to a house that had not been specially chosen. According to the local press, it was occupied by a family who had lived there for nine years, for seven of which the man of the house had been unemployed. The King knocked at the door and, when it was opened, asked if it might be possible for him to come in. He was welcomed and ushered in, where he shook hands warmly with the family and chatted with them about their daily lives.[60]

Edward had been visiting the industrial areas of Britain ever since the start of the economic depression in 1929. On all these visits, commented the *New Statesman*, he had 'always shown a welcome desire to look beneath the surface.'[61] In the spring of 1936 he had visited the slums of Glasgow, after a ceremony to launch the new ship, the *Queen Mary*. 'Visiting the slums, HM was really at his best', wrote Hilda Runciman, the wife of Walter Runciman, the President of the Board of Trade, in her diary. She added,

He understands how to do that perfectly. Eg. He knocked at a door & when the woman opened it he said 'I'm the King, may I come in'? And then he asked all the right questions about washing cooking etc. He had told W[alter] that he had seen worse slums in Durham and also that he and his brothers had picked up vermin when doing their slum visiting.[62]

From Pontypool, Edward went to the Snatchwood Junior Instruction Centre, where girls and boys were being given 'useful occupation and instruction during the enforced leisure produced by unemployment' – woodwork for boys, and basketwork and weaving for girls. For several minutes he watched the daughter of an unemployed collier making a brooch in 'petal' work, and was then delighted to be given it as a gift. Noticing that the glass between the girls' workroom and that of the boys was frosted, he asked for the reason – and was told that it was to stop the boys looking through at the girls. 'I see. You want to keep their minds on their work', laughed the King.[63]

Ernest Brown, the Minister of Labour, kept close beside the King throughout the tour.[64] His presence on the royal visit had been objected to by Aneurin Bevan, and he was 'inclined to arouse boos', noted Lambe, the royal equerry.[65] This was because Brown represented the labour policies of the National Government, which was widely

criticized for doing little to address the problem of long-term unemployment. The Government was called 'National' because it was a
coalition and its cabinet was made up of ministers from all three major
parties. But most of these ministers were Conservatives, and by 1936
the policies of the National Government were dominated by the
influence of the Conservative Party.

At one unemployment centre, recorded Lambe,

the King, E. Brown and I went into the cellar where men were repairing boots.
The King left E. Brown talking and, no sooner had he gone, than the whole
party crowded round Mr B, talking rather threateningly.

'I've a wife & 5 kiddies and all I gets is so and so – 'ow d'you expect me to
live?'

He let them have their say & then said 'Now look here you fellows – for
the last 4 months I've been working till 3 & 4 in the morning on your behalf.
Will you please believe I'm doing all I can?'[66]

The men pulled back, presumably out of respect for the King. Let
Brown try going to South Wales 'without the shelter of the royal
purple!' mocked Aneurin Bevan.[67] It was certainly unusual for government ministers to walk among the people, as Brown was required to
do on this royal tour. 'The Ministers are emphatically unable to voice
the opinion of the people', it was observed in a letter to the King,
because 'they never come in contact with them, when they constantly
drive about in cars.'[68]

At Nantyglo and Blaina, where three-quarters of the population
were unemployed, cheering crowds congregated behind barricades on
the coal tips and pavements. It was bitterly cold – the village was 1,400
feet above sea level. When the King arrived at the Miners' Welfare
Institute at Garn-yr-Erw, he was smoking a cigarette and appeared
thoughtful. After meeting local officials, he lingered on to talk with
ex-servicemen. He met an old Welsh Guardsman, a miner, who had
been unemployed since 1929. He was appalled when told that
although the Cwmtillery and Six Bells collieries on the outskirts of the
town were at work, the three pits in the centre of the town were
now closed. One miner who had been working for forty years and

unemployed for nine, said he prayed that the royal tour would bring improved conditions. 'I hope so', answered the King.[69]

The next stop was Abertillery. Through a maze of short streets, the King's car was driven to Rhiw Park where an unsightly slag heap had been converted into a grassy recreation ground for children. Noticing the former president of the South Wales Miners' Federation among the spectators, the King immediately crossed over for a chat. The royal party then went to the club room, which was being used as a children's feeding centre. Here, the King would not allow his arrival to interrupt the meal of stew and pudding. When the children saw him and scrambled to stand up quickly at their wooden benches, he told them at once to 'Sit down and get on with your meal!' He was informed that the menu varied from day to day. A child might have boiled beef, potatoes and haricot beans for dinner one day, with bread, butter, jam and fresh milk for tea; then boiled fish, mashed potatoes and suet pudding for dinner the next day, with bread and butter, banana sandwiches and fresh milk for tea. This was a godsend to the mothers.[70]

The final stage of Edward's tour of Wales was the long run to Rhymney. The old shops of the Rhymney Iron Company by the railway station had been converted into a social centre for the unemployed, to which about two hundred men and women belonged. The men repaired boots and did carpentry and woodwork; they also took part in physical training, sang, listened to broadcast talks, debated, and heard lectures and concerts. Here the King met an old man at work with a saw and, trying it himself, exclaimed, 'You are very lucky if you can use it!' The women did sewing, knitting and crochet. Edward spoke to the men who were responsible for the working of the outcrop scheme, by which unemployed men were able to obtain their coal for tuppence a week. He then joined in the singing of Welsh songs and the classic hymn 'Cwm Rhondda'.[71]

This was the last stop: it was now time for the King to leave South Wales. 'I have seen a great deal,' he said, 'and I must now go home and think of what can be done.' At 3.30 p.m., he boarded his train for London. The echoing cheers of the enthusiastic crowds followed the train as it pulled slowly away from the station.[72]

2

'My own beloved Wallis'

When King Edward returned to London from South Wales on the evening of Thursday, 19 November 1936, he was in high spirits. He went to a dinner party at the home of Sir Henry ('Chips') Channon, an American friend and a Member of Parliament. Channon watched the royal car draw up and Edward emerge, followed by Peregrine Brownlow, his Lord-in-Waiting. At once, Channon wrote in his diary, he could see that the King was in a cheerful mood – 'no doubt a reaction from his depressing Welsh tour, two dreadfully sad days in the distressed areas.'[1] But Edward's happiness was far more likely the prospect of seeing another of the dinner guests – Mrs Wallis Simpson, an American. Although she was married to another man, she was the centre of Edward's life, and he ached for her whenever they were apart. 'My own beloved Wallis,' he wrote in 1935 in one of many devoted notes, 'I love you more & more & more & more . . . I haven't seen you once today & I can't take it. I love you.'[2] He had missed her badly in South Wales, and it was not Buckingham Palace he had wanted to telephone from the train at Usk – it was Wallis.

Edward had found qualities in Mrs Simpson, believed Winston Churchill, that were

as necessary to his happiness as the air he breathed. Those who knew him well and watched him closely noticed that many little tricks and fidgetings of nervousness fell away from him. He was a completed being instead of a sick and harassed soul.[3]

They were not youngsters – he was forty-two, she was forty – and their easy ways with each other reflected a natural and relaxed companionship. But there was a chemistry between them, too, that was electric and seemed to separate them from the rest of the world. Photographed unawares while they were on holiday in Italy, their tender embrace was caught on film. Edward leaned forward to Wallis, pressing his left cheek against her own and possessively embracing her body with his left arm; her face was creased with laughter and pleasure. Edward's behaviour towards Wallis was watched with curiosity by the people around him. 'Every few minutes,' wrote Victor Cazalet, a Tory MP, after watching them at a dinner together, 'he gazes at her and a happiness and radiance fill his countenance such as make you have a lump in your throat.'[4] He was utterly devoted. One weekend in 1936, Charles Lambe noticed that as they came in from a walk in the garden,

The King and Mrs S entered the front door first, and he at once went on his knees to take off her galoshes. As the passage was thus blocked, the rest of us stood contemplating the spectacle, she tickled to death and mildly remonstrative, he, earnest and intent, muttering slightly to himself but oblivious of us.[5]

As the year 1936 neared its end, few people in Britain had even heard of Wallis Simpson; those who *had* heard of her belonged to the tiny social circle surrounding the royal family. She was carefully excluded from the newsreels and from the pages of the press. The only exception was the magazine *Cavalcade,* which in the summer of 1936 defiantly printed photographs of Edward and Wallis on holiday together and made veiled references to their relationship. 'The plain truth', wrote Bill Deedes, later to be editor of the *Daily Telegraph* but then a young journalist, 'is that newspapers showed more deference to the Royal Family in those days ... There was also a far greater distance kept between Royalty's close circle of friends and the rest of us. Gossip was harder to obtain.'[6] H. A. Gwynne, editor of the *Morning Post*, which he described as 'the staunchest supporter of monarchical institutions', sent a letter to the Prime Minister warning that any break in '"The Great Silence"' would deal 'a deadly blow to Monarchy'.

On such 'a delicate matter as this,' he said, 'the Press should follow the Government and not dictate to it.' He warned, however, that some sections of the press, especially the 'sensational newspapers', were getting very restive.[7]

But it was only in Britain, as well as most of the Empire, that the affair between Edward and Wallis was a closely guarded secret. The American and European media were under far fewer constraints than British journalists were. So while the people of Britain remained quite unaware of the King's private life, many Europeans and most Americans were fed endless (if not always accurate) snippets of news. So were Canadians, as many American newspapers were distributed across the border.

In August 1936, readers of American newspapers (and of the British *Cavalcade*) gasped when they saw a photograph of the King and Wallis together on a little boat while on holiday in Yugoslavia. Wallis was tenderly touching Edward's left arm and he, in an open-necked sports shirt, leant towards her attentively. This was just one of many photographs suggesting an intimate friendship between Edward and Wallis. A woman from Edmonton in Canada told King Edward in a letter that 'When looking over the different portraits in the papers of you and your friend Mrs Simpson' she had been delighted by 'your million dollar *smile* with your friend on your Holiday.'[8]

The mathematician and code-breaker Alan Turing, who in 1936 was a twenty-four-year-old student at Princeton University, New Jersey, sent his mother in England some newspaper cuttings about Mrs Simpson. 'I don't suppose you have even heard of her,' he wrote, 'but some days it has been "front page stuff" here.'[9] Such reports never appeared in publications available in Britain. Wholesale distributors of foreign newspapers and magazines, said Deedes, were apprehensive of libel, because Mrs Simpson was still the wife of Ernest Simpson – 'They therefore cut or blacked out passages in overseas publications which could give offence.'[10] References to Wallis were so thoroughly censored that the Labour MP Ellen Wilkinson rose in the House of Commons to ask why American papers and magazines arriving in England had so many paragraphs and pages clipped out.

Wallis's background was markedly different from Edward's. She was born Bessie Wallis Warfield in 1896 in Blue Ridge Summit, Pennsylvania, and grew up in the city of Baltimore, Maryland. The Warfields belonged to one of the oldest families in the state and were proud of being a Southern family – Wallis's grandmother was said to have possessed an undying hatred for anybody born north of the Mason–Dixon line.[11] Wallis was a striking Southern belle, with dark hair, a smooth creamy skin and huge brown eyes. She was of average height but very slim, which earned her the nickname 'Skinny'.[12] Her childhood was a loving one, but it was made difficult by financial hardship. Her father had died just months before she was born, leaving her mother, Alice, struggling to make ends meet. Her uncle Saul, a well-off banker, often helped the family out, but her mother and her mother's sister, Mrs Bessie Merryman, found it necessary for a time to take paying guests into their home – a three-storey brownstone with a weather-beaten façade on Biddle Street in Baltimore. Wallis 'spent her youth in a boarding-house', reported the *Los Angeles Times*. 'Two men of lean pocketbooks rented rooms there by the week and had their meals at the family dinner table.'[13]

When Alice married a man with some money, Wallis was sent in 1912 to an exclusive boarding school; but when her stepfather died the family fell once again on hard times, and she was brought home. Mrs Merryman – whom Wallis called 'Aunt Bessie' – was a constant and loving figure from Wallis's earliest years, and Edward was to describe her later as 'the wise and gentle woman who had raised her from childhood.'[14]

In 1916 Wallis married Lieutenant Earl Winfield Spencer, Jr, a pilot in the US Navy who was known as 'Win'. She soon discovered that Win was prone to bouts of heavy drinking which led to brutal behaviour. Whole days might pass with him speaking barely a word to her, except to accuse her of being a flirt and ignoring him. He started to lock her up in a room while he went out. One afternoon, Wallis recounted,

Win locked me in the bathroom of our apartment. For hours, I heard no sound from beyond the door. Whether Win had gone out or whether he was still in the apartment . . . I could not tell. I tried to unscrew the lock with a nail file, but I had to give up when I found I could not stir the screws. As the afternoon wore on and evening came, I was seized with panic at the thought that Win might mean to keep me a prisoner all night.

Eventually she heard the sound of a key turning in the lock:

But the door did not open, and I was afraid to try the handle myself. When I finally got up enough courage to do so, the apartment was in darkness. I could hear Win's breathing from the bed. The rest of the night I spent on the sofa in the living-room, endlessly reviewing the events that had led to my personal catastrophe.[15]

By morning, Wallis knew that she had to leave Win, and she went to live with her mother. She gave Win one more chance, sailing to the Far East to join him at a naval posting, but realized that he would never stop drinking. She despaired of the marriage, and obtained a divorce in 1927.

While living on her own, she had grown to like Ernest Aldrich Simpson, a shipbroker she had met in New York. Rather tall and with a slight dark moustache, he was much attracted – being himself a serious and prosaic sort of man – by Wallis's fresh and lively spirit. Although a New Yorker who had been born in America, Ernest Simpson was of British parentage and had enlisted in the Coldstream Guards for the duration of the war. In 1928 he moved to London to take over his family's shipping business, and asked Wallis, now thirty-two, to join him. She crossed the Atlantic, and they were married in July. At first they were quite well off, but like many others they were hit by the Depression of 1929, which was a disaster for Ernest's shipping firm and slashed the value of some shares Wallis had been given by her uncle.

She found it difficult to settle down to British ways. American slang, she wrote in her memoirs, was practically never heard in Mayfair drawing rooms – and it was not welcomed. 'When with characteristic impulsiveness I agreed to something with a cheery "O.K.",' she wrote, 'my sister-in-law stared at me with an expression of shock and disappointment that could not have been more in evidence had I dropped an "h".'[16] She was astonished by the deference to titles, which seemed to her 'almost irrational in a country otherwise so democratic. If one was a Lady Vere de Vere there was never any difficulty about opening charge accounts, and salespeople fell over themselves for the privilege of serving a title.' Reading the Court Circular, the daily list of the monarch's official engagements, she was surprised that an entire nation should follow 'with such rapt attention the purely formal goings and comings of a single family'. But her greatest difficulty, she found, was her habit of speaking her mind. By contrast with American women, she thought, English women 'were still accepting the status . . . of a second sex. If they had strong opinions they kept them safely buttoned up, confidences were seldom given or encouraged.'[17] Despite these obstacles, Wallis settled down cheerfully to life in London. She enjoyed organizing their home, especially when they moved to 5 Bryanston Court, in the Marylebone area. Unlike Win, Ernest was steady and dependable, and the couple got on well with each other. In any case, Wallis felt now that she had to recognize the limits of middle age. Sailing back to London from a holiday in the USA in 1933, she wondered with dismay if this would be the last time she would be able to enjoy the feeling of youth. 'I know it really was my swan song,' she wrote to her aunt, 'unless I can hang onto my figure and take a trip before I'm 40 which is only 3 years off.'[18]

It was just a couple of years after her arrival in London and her second wedding, that Wallis first met the Prince of Wales – Prince Edward Albert Christian George Andrew Patrick David, known to his immediate family and friends simply as David. In the autumn of 1930, Wallis and Ernest were invited to a dinner party at the home of the sister of Thelma, Lady Furness, who was Edward's lover at the time. Shortly afterwards the Prince left for a tour of South America, but on his return in 1931, the Simpsons saw the Prince twice, at the home of Lady Furness. In January 1932 the Prince invited them to stay for the weekend at his home, Fort Belvedere, an eighteenth-century folly that was half-castle, half-house, on the edge of Windsor Great Park. By the middle of 1933, the Simpsons were regular visitors at the Fort.

In early 1934, Thelma Furness asked Wallis to 'look after' the Prince for a while, as she wanted to go to the USA with her twin sister

Gloria Vanderbilt. While Lady Furness was away (and caught up in a passionate affair with the wealthy playboy Aly Khan), Edward would call at the Simpsons' flat early in the evening, and Wallis welcomed him with cocktails. Frequently, he stayed on for dinner.[19] Everything was in exquisite taste at Bryanston Court, wrote Edward later, 'and the food, in my judgement, unrivalled in London'. There he met young British and American men of affairs, foreign diplomats and 'intelligent women'. The talk, he said, was 'witty and crackling with the new ideas that were bubbling up furiously in the world of Hitler, Mussolini, Stalin, the New Deal, and Chiang Kai-shek.'[20] When Thelma returned to Britain, she realized with a shock that she had been replaced. From now on, Wallis was Edward's chief companion, with Ernest usually in attendance too. This was the best-known threesome in London, wrote an American journalist, adding dryly that, 'They went everywhere together, and Mr Simpson's deadpan demeanour on these outings inspired the inevitable sad gags about the Importance of Being Ernest.'[21]

A woman who worked as a housemaid at Bryanston Court remembered that just before Princess Marina's wedding in the autumn of 1934, the Prince called for cocktails with Wallis and Ernest before leaving to attend a reception at Buckingham Palace. He left at about 8 p.m.

and returned later and dined with Mr and Mrs Simpson. He left alone at about 9 p.m. and went to the Palace and his car returned to take Mr and Mrs Simpson to the Palace. When the Prince arrived that evening for dinner he was in full Court dress. He wore a sash across his breast and he was wearing a gold garter around his knee.[22]

But increasingly, the Prince and Wallis were alone together. He called upon her during the daytime, recalled the housemaid. 'Sometimes he remained for half an hour, and on other occasions he remained for an hour; they would be alone in the drawing room.' On one occasion 'he dined alone with Mrs Simpson and they both left the flat together in the Prince's car at about 10.00 p.m.' When Ernest returned from a ten-day trip abroad, 'Mrs Simpson had already gone to Fort Belvedere for the weekend . . . I was with her and Miss Burke her maid went with her.' Wallis always addressed the Prince as 'Sir', she added, but on one occasion when the Prince was dining at Bryanston Court, 'I heard Mrs Simpson address the Prince as David.'[23]

One day, wrote Edward in his memoirs, Wallis 'began to mean more to me in a way that she did not perhaps comprehend. My impression is that for a long time she remained unaffected by my interest.'[24] For Wallis, it was not until a cruise with Edward through the Mediterranean in the summer of 1934 on the *Rosaura*, that she knew that she and Edward were in love:

Often the Prince and I found ourselves sitting alone on deck, enjoying the soft evening air, and that unspoken but shared feeling of closeness generated by the immensity of the sea and the sky. Perhaps it was during these evenings off the Spanish coast that we crossed the line that marks the indefinable boundary between friendship and love. Perhaps it was one evening strolling on the beach at Fomenter in Majorca.

'How can a woman ever really know?' wondered Wallis in her memoirs, *The Heart Has Its Reasons*. 'How can she ever really tell?' But she realized that a line had been crossed, and there was no going back.[25]

Other guests on the *Rosaura* were Mr and Mrs Lee Guinness, Lord Hamilton and Sir John Aird. The Prince of Wales and Mrs Simpson occupied two separate bedrooms in the fore part of the ship, while all the other guests slept in the aft or on the lower deck. One of the stewards later stated that he thought it strange that Mrs Simpson should be occupying a bedroom close to the Prince's 'and I was a little nosy':

I mean I made her bed on most occasions and I changed her bed linen about every other day. I watched the sheets but I never saw a mark upon them. Sometimes when I went to Mrs Simpson's bed her maid had already made it. I never knew she was going to make the bed and I don't know what reason she had for making it.

The Prince always had breakfast on deck at about 10 a.m., while Wallis had breakfast in her bedroom, which was always taken to her by her maid. The steward never noticed any endearment between Wallis and the Prince, such as walking arm in arm together, but he often saw them 'sitting alone together and laughing'.[26]

So intimate did they become that they developed a private language in which to communicate their feelings to each other. The most important word in this language was 'WE', which joined the first letters of the names Wallis and Edward. One weekend in 1935, when they were staying as guests of Lord Brownlow at Belton House in Lincolnshire, Wallis sent Edward a gardenia with a note which said, 'God bless WE. Good-night, From Her to Him.'[27] Another important word was 'eanum', meaning something like 'dearest little thing'. In a letter Edward sent to Wallis in Spring 1935, he used both these special words:

My Eanum – *My* Wallis
    This is not the kind of Easter WE want but it will be all right next year . . . I love you more & more & more each & every minute & miss you *so* terribly here. You do too don't you my sweetheart. God bless WE. *Always your* DAVID.[28]

According to Walter Monckton, a friend of Edward's from Oxford days, it was a

great mistake to assume that he was merely in love with her in the ordinary physical sense of the term. There was an intellectual companionship, and there is no doubt that his lonely nature found in her a spiritual comradeship . . . No one will ever really understand the story of the King's life, who does not appreciate . . . the intensity and depth of his devotion to Mrs Simpson.[29]

It seemed to Churchill that their 'association was psychical rather than sexual, and certainly not sensual except incidentally. Although branded with the stigma of a guilty love, no companionship could have appeared more natural, more free from impropriety or grossness.'[30] However, Edward's cousin Louis Mountbatten thought that the chemistry between them was intensely physical. He observed that once their friendship had reached the point where they went to bed together, Edward lost all sense of reason.[31]

Wallis understood some of the reasons why she had fallen under the Prince's spell. Beyond his warmth and charm, she explained in her memoirs years later,

he was the open sesame to a new and glittering world that excited me as nothing in my life had ever done before. For all his natural simplicity, his genuine abhorrence of ostentation, there was nevertheless about him – even in his most Robinson Crusoe clothes – an unmistakable aura of power and authority.[32]

This was an aura that had captivated many other women, too. 'He was the Golden Prince', said Diana Vreeland, a stylish fashion designer. 'You must understand', she added, 'that to be a woman of my generation in London – *any* woman – was to be in love with the Prince of Wales.'[33]

What Wallis understood less well than her own emotions was Edward's love for her. 'Searching my mind,' she said later,

I could find no good reason why this most glamorous of men should be seriously attracted to me. I certainly was no beauty, and he had the pick of the beautiful women of the world. I was certainly no longer very young. In fact, in my own country I would have been considered securely on the shelf.[34]

Edward evidently cared nothing about Wallis's age – it was simply irrelevant to him. But in any case, there is nothing so rejuvenating as the feeling of desire and of being desired. As the romance grew into love, Wallis bloomed and her eyes sparkled. Her previous anxieties about middle age – her dread of the last swan song – slipped away.

Edward looked upon Wallis as the most independent woman he had ever met. 'I admired her forthrightness', he wrote later, in his memoirs. 'If she disagreed with some point under discussion, she never failed to advance her own views with vigour and spirit. That side of her enchanted me.'[35] She was also completely open and honest about her background and never pretended to be anything other than what she was. She never concealed – from Edward or from anyone else – the fact that her beloved Aunt Bessie worked as a paid companion to a rich American woman, even though she was well aware that the idea of working for pay was despised by the English elite. Wallis was never anything but proud of her aunt. In 1930 and again in 1934, Mrs Merryman came over from America to stay with Wallis and Ernest, and in 1936 she travelled once more to London to be at Wallis's side.

Edward was not bothered by Wallis's lack of titles and wealth. He was free of snobbery to a degree that was remarkable, given his background. He came to 'sit in my office and talk to me as an ordinary person would', said the head porter at Bryanston Court.[36] He saw Wallis as an individual woman, not as a member of any particular social group. And she, in her turn, saw him as an individual man – not simply as a king. She was probably the only woman he had ever met, commented Diana Mosley, one of the Mitford girls who became Oswald Mosley's second wife, who

did not feel obliged to behave slightly differently because he was there to the way she would have with anyone else . . . She was always very polite, curtsying, calling him 'Sir', but she always spoke her mind. It must have made him feel that at long last here was someone who treated him as he would have wished.[37]

John Gunther, an American journalist who was a friend of Edward's, made the same point. 'She treated him', he said, 'like a man and a human being.'[38]

Edward and Wallis had many shared understandings in their ways of looking at the world. Like Edward, observed Lord Beaverbrook, the newspaper magnate, Wallis 'showed a liberal outlook, well maintained in discussion, and based on a conception which was sound.'[39] One evening, when Edward invited Wallis and a few friends to dinner at the Dorchester Hotel, the conversation turned to his interest in the new social service schemes for the unemployed. Only that afternoon, he wrote in his memoirs, 'I had returned from Yorkshire, where I had been visiting working-men's clubs in towns and villages.' In the female company to which he was accustomed, he added, the disclosure of such a chore would usually have provoked a response like, 'Oh! Sir, how boring for you. Aren't you terribly tired?' Wallis, however, wanted to know more. 'I told her what it was and what I was trying to do.' She was genuinely interested in how the Prince of Wales went about his job. In addition, said Edward, she was discriminating, with 'an intuitive understanding of the forces and ideas working in society. She was extraordinarily well informed about politics and current affairs.'[40] Wallis admired Edward's concern about social problems. 'I am crazy to hear if you heard the King's broadcast and what you thought of it', she wrote proudly to her aunt,[41] after he had given a speech on 1 March 1936 in which, departing from the text supplied by the Government, he declared his commitment to the welfare of his subjects:

I am better known to you as Prince of Wales – as a man who, during the war and since, has had the opportunity of getting to know the people of nearly every country of the world, under all conditions and circumstances. And, although I now speak to you as King, I am still that same man who has had that experience and whose constant effort it will be to continue to promote the well-being of his fellow-men . . .[42]

They even shared a concern about their body weight. In 1932 Wallis told her aunt that she had recovered some of her 'pep' after an operation to remove her tonsils – 'and the 4 pounds in weight have improved my disposition if not my "behind".'[43] She wrote with some satisfaction in February 1934 that, 'I am feeling very well but am quite thin not in the face but in the figure. Naturally worry over finances is not fat-making. I weigh 8 stone undressed but eat and drink as usual.'[44] Edward, too, kept track of his weight, though he was always thin and light. Right from his teenage years he had worried that he was becoming fat, so he ate frugally and took frequent vigorous exercise. When Edward was nineteen, Winston Churchill wrote from Balmoral Castle to his wife that

He is so nice, & we have made rather friends. They are worried a little about him, as he has become so vy Spartan – rising at 6 & eating hardly anything. He requires to fall in love with a pretty cat, who will prevent him from getting too strenuous.[45]

Edward's size was a constant source of worry to his father, George V, who feared he might 'remain a sort of puny half-grown boy'.[46] He never lost his obsession with weight and exercise. For a voyage to the Far East on HMS *Renown* in 1921, he had a squash court specially built in the ship. He was 'mad keen' on keeping fit, wrote his equerry Bruce Ogilvy, who had to play squash with him every morning.[47] And in Wallis he had found someone with whom he could share this interest:

I'm longing for an eanum letter Wallis . . . Please don't over eat until we can again together or I'm there to say stop or you'll be quite ill I know . . . Oh! to be alone for ages and ages and then – ages and ages. God bless WE sweetheart but I'm sure he does – he must.

Your DAVID[48]

Edward and Wallis had both travelled to many distant and exotic parts of the world. He had visited practically all the major nations of the world except Soviet Russia, while she knew her own country from the Atlantic to the Pacific and had travelled through Europe and Asia – something unimaginable to most Western women at the time. It was not so much that women didn't go abroad between the wars. Upper-class women travelled all over the world, but for the most part they did so as a wife or as a daughter, protected by a man and by his wealth and status. Wallis, on the other hand, had often travelled alone, without much money or any status beyond that of being an American citizen. 'From the first,' wrote Edward later, 'I looked upon her as the most independent woman I had ever met.'[49] Wallis was also quite fearless. After her final separation from Win, at the age of twenty-eight, she left him in Hong Kong and journeyed to Shanghai in China. When she decided to go on to Peking, she was advised by the American Consul against travelling by rail, on the grounds that it would take her through territory made dangerous by a local war. But she went anyway:

The train was late in getting under way. As usual, the aisles were crowded with Chinese passengers, chiefly occupied in eating oranges and spitting out the pips. Seated across from me, the only other Occidental in the carriage, was a rather plump, middle-aged man . . . several times on the way the train jerked to a violent stop; evil-faced men in shabby uniforms and armed with rifles pushed into the crowded vestibules . . . I assumed an air of utter indifference. Nothing ever happened; after a quick look around the soldiers disappeared.[50]

Once she had arrived in Peking, Wallis met an old friend from the USA, Katherine Rogers, who invited Wallis to stay with herself and her husband, Herman.

Both Wallis and Edward understood the complexities of differences between nations and cultures. On his tour of India in the early 1920s, Edward had been aware – and regretted bitterly – that he was given few chances to meet the native people. He complained to Lord Reading, the Viceroy:

The ostensible reason for my coming to India was to see as many of the natives as possible and to get as near to them as I could. At least, I presume it was the main reason, and I looked upon that as my duty. Well, I am afraid that I have not had many opportunities of doing this, either in British India or in the Native States.[51]

Similarly, Wallis realized that because her life in Peking had been limited to the foreign colony inside the walled city, she learned very little about the people and their culture: 'Actually, I never did get much closer to the real Peking than [the] views from the top of the city walls and my occasional encounters with dealers in jades and porcelains and the can-do tailors.'[52]

Well read, interested in politics and independent, Wallis was different from most of the women Edward met at court. Indeed, she 'was a great deal more intelligent than many in the Palace circle,' according to the writer and journalist John Gunther.[53] 'Little Mrs Simpson is a woman of character and reads Balzac', approved the social hostess Emerald Cunard, herself a serious reader.[54] Her appearance, too, was striking. 'Mrs Simpson is quite a different sort of woman', judged the novelist Marie Belloc Lowndes. 'She doesn't pose as being young and in fact must be nearly forty . . . I did not think her in the least pretty . . . She has an intelligent but in no sense a remarkable face.' Mrs Belloc Lowndes was at once impressed, though, 'by Mrs Simpson's perfect figure. She was of medium height, and beautifully dressed in the French way, that is, very unobtrusively.'[55] Mrs Simpson 'looked very well tonight, like a Vermeer, in a Dutch way', observed Chips Channon approvingly one night.[56] The unshowy elegance of her appearance seemed to him far more attractive than the dress of British women. This view was shared by aesthetes such as the Society photographer Cecil Beaton. When Beaton saw a home movie of some of Edward's house guests, he observed that the 'tall, badly or boringly dressed Englishwomen with their untidy hair' were in sharp contrast with 'the neat and perfectly turned out Wallis.'[57] At a photographic session in late 1936, he observed that Wallis was 'soignée and fresh as a young girl. Her skin was as bright and smooth as the inside of a shell, her hair so sleek, she might have been Chinese.'[58]

Since Wallis's arrival in London in 1928 she had developed a style of her own, with an emphasis on simple shapes and clear colours as well as immaculate grooming. No doubt her slim physique assisted this effect. Her favourite designer was Mainbocher, an American who had been the influential editor of French *Vogue* until 1929, when he resigned to open his own *maison de couture* in Paris which soon became known for his stylish, tailored look. Wallis often looked severe, but this was arguably useful for a woman who, in a man's world, liked to be independent. The aggressive behaviour of Win Spencer, her first husband, had given her a keen sense of the need to protect herself – and looking tough would have made her feel less vulnerable. Perhaps she *was* quite tough. Duff Cooper, a friend of Edward's and the Secretary of State for War, thought she was 'as hard as nails'.[59] Meeting Wallis must have been a puzzling if not intimidating experience for Duff, who had a very low opinion of women's abilities. He confided to his diary that Lady Cunard 'hasn't, of course, the faintest idea of what the British Constitution is all about. I suppose very few women have.'[60] He had numerous adulterous affairs with women, but presumably never expected to discuss political matters with them.

Wallis was a survivor in the face of considerable odds, and she was proud of it. When Bessie sent her a letter warning her of the unhappiness that might result from her intimacy with Edward, she reminded her aunt of her ability to weather storms:

As you know people must make their own lives and I should by now nearly 40 have a little experience in that line – as I wasn't in a position to have it arranged for me by money or position and though I have had many hard times, disappointments etc. I've managed not to go under as yet – and never having known security until I married Ernest perhaps I don't get along well with it knowing and understanding the thrill of its opposite much better – the old bromide nothing ventured, nothing gained.

'I might still be following ships,' she added, recalling the bitter experience of her marriage to Win Spencer, who was a navy pilot.[61]

She was also liked and respected by her servants. 'All the maids spoke well of Mrs Simpson', said a kitchen maid who worked at Bryanston Court.[62] Her personal maid, Mary Burke, who went everywhere with her and would have known everything about her, was fiercely loyal. So too was Mary Cain, her Scottish parlour maid, who was 'a confidential servant and she never spoke about her mistress. If anyone spoke about her mistress she would at once leave the room.'[63] According to the head porter at Bryanston Court, 'there was nothing frivolous' about Mrs Simpson – 'She had a sort of command about her.'[64]

But however worldly-wise she was, Wallis had a warm heart and liked to care for people. 'She was so affectionate, a loving sort of friend – very rare, you know', commented Diana Vreeland.[65] Wallis was devoted to her mother and her aunt, with whom she exchanged weekly letters from London, full of gossip and recipes; she also sent cheques home on a regular basis. When Alice was only fifty-nine, in 1929, she suffered a stroke. Wallis rushed home, taking the next boat across the

Atlantic. She stayed as long as she could, until Ernest pleaded with her to return to London. Wallis worried incessantly and wrote to her aunt:

I feel desperate being so far away and knowing she is not getting better and wants and needs me there with her and to think of you having to bear it all alone. I don't think I am much use here as I'm really so sad the majority of the time I'm not a fit companion.[66]

She returned to America in the autumn, but it was a brief visit because her mother had fallen into a coma, and died in November. Wallis was overcome by grief.

Aunt Bessie became even more important to Wallis. Now in her seventies, with an ample matronly figure, Mrs Merryman was loving, affectionate and kind. She lived in Washington, where she was employed as a paid companion to a newspaper heiress. Over the next twenty years Wallis wrote her a stream of letters. 'It was thrilling to hear your voice on Xmas eve. It did make me want to see you so badly', she wrote in 1935.[67] She worried about her aunt's health: 'I am so worried about your blood pressure,' she wrote in 1936, 'and please be sure to do exactly what the doctor tells you.'[68] Edward adored Bessie and delighted in her company. At the end of one of Wallis's letters, he pleaded in a postscript:

Please Mrs Merryman not to be cross with Wallis for writing you [sic] in so long! it really has been quite a busy time with the Jubilee and various ceremonies and social functions connected with it. I wish you could have seen one or two of them . . . Do come over and see us again soon.
EDWARD P[69]

How different was Mrs Merryman from Edward's mother, although they did share a gift for plain speaking. On several occasions Bessie warned Wallis against further involvement with Edward. 'You did give me a lecture,' acknowledged Wallis in one letter, 'and I quite agree with all you say regarding HRH and if Ernest raises any objections to the situation I shall give the Prince up at once.'[70] Similarly, Janet Flanner observed that Queen Mary 'can't make a speech but knows how to speak her mind, and gets to the point without shilly-shally.'[71] But there the similarity ended. Mrs Merryman's kindly behaviour contrasted sharply with the stiff and unbending Queen Mary. So did her comfortable appearance, which was a world away from the very formal dress of the Queen, who was said by Janet Flanner to have resisted

hints from dressmakers, worn her skirts long when skirts were rising, raised hers, slightly, when it was too late; her hats, during her sons' sensitive sartorial twenties, caused them pain . . . She looks like herself, with the elegant eccentricities – the umbrella or cane, the hydrangea-colored town suits, the light lizard slippers, the tip-tilted toque – of a wealthy white-haired grande dame who had grown into the mature style she set for herself too young.[72]

Like her aunt, Wallis was affectionate, almost motherly, towards people she loved. This met Edward's need for emotional warmth. Her care of him took many forms, of which one was a simple domesticity. According to gossip spread by Alice Keppel, who had been the favourite mistress of King Edward VII, Wallis was 'an excellent cook and has sent off the cook the Prince has had for long at Belvedere . . . the Prince talked to her of nothing but cooking for two whole hours at an evening party the other night!!!'[73] She served good food that was simple and nutritious, 'introducing succulent Southern dishes to a people long paralysed internally by boiled meat and suet pudding.'[74] Edward basked in these comforts. One contemporary reported that

she had a delightful way of bossing him around without being boring or coy about it. 'Don't eat that, Sir!' she would say smiling and taking a caviar canapé out of his hand. 'Have this instead?' and she would give him a bit of cream cheese on toast . . .

Wales, who had never been looked after except officially, blossomed and beamed under this fond supervision . . . all of Mrs Simpson's menus were planned with a view to his nervous stomach, which became less and less nervous as one calm meal after another vanished within it.[75]

'I have learned to make that gooey stuff Mrs Bristol puts on the top of her ham. It's made of peaches,' reported Wallis to her aunt. 'I will send the apple recipe on separate cover,' she added, 'as I'm writing from the Fort where there has been a pompous week-end including the King's secretary and wife.'[76] She did not feel comfortable with Alec Hardinge and his wife, Helen, whose extreme formality exemplified the manners of the royal court.

Wallis helped Edward with royal entertaining. 'Have the table moved back as far as possible', she wrote before a dinner party in 1935. She offered advice on the menu: 'I would also have two sorts of cocktails and white wine offered as well as the vin rosé, the servants to service the wine. Also I didn't see a green vegetable on the menu. Sorry to bother you but I like everyone to think you do things well.' She added playfully, 'Perhaps I'm quite fond of you.'[77] When he finally managed to get away from his royal duties for a summer holiday, she wrote fondly to her aunt, 'At last this poor tired King got off.'[78] Edward was equally solicitous about her and found it difficult to separate his own well-being from hers. 'But I do long long to see you even for a few minutes my Wallis it would help so much', he wrote during the days when his father lay dying. 'Please take care of yourself and don't get a cold. You are all and everything I have in life and WE must hold each other so tight. It will all work out right for us. God bless WE.'[79]

Standing by Edward's side, Wallis watched from a window in St James's Palace as he was proclaimed King Edward VIII on 22 January 1936. She tried hard to support him in his work. 'God bless you and above all make you strong where you have been weak', she wrote in a letter, adding that soon she would be happy because 'you would be holding me and I would be looking "up" into your eyes.'[80] Since Wallis was slightly taller than Edward, who was only five feet seven inches, it is difficult to see how she could have looked 'up' into his eyes. But comments like these must have helped him to feel vigorous and manly. Wallis also helped him with those parts of his job that he found wearisome, and many people recognized her usefulness in this respect. At a party, Prince Paul of Yugoslavia went up to Wallis and begged her to persuade the King to telephone his sympathy to the Infanta, Beatrice of Spain, whose second son had just been killed. When the King pleaded, 'Couldn't I do it in the morning?', she intervened firmly – 'No, now, to please me, sir.' He obediently made the call.[81]

Some of the King's friends tried to exploit Mrs Simpson's influence on him. For example, Lady Oxford and Asquith (Margot Asquith) wrote to her at the start of Edward's reign about his churchgoing – or rather his lack of it. 'Actually, he goes quite often to the simple little chapel in Windsor Park,' replied Wallis in his defence,

but I am afraid this does not appear in the 'Court Circular'. As you know he has been going to his country house for weekends since he has been King – this form of relaxation I think he finds essential as he is so accustomed to *air* and *exercise* it would be difficult for him to give it up entirely and I personally feel it makes him more fit for his great task.

But she would urge him, she promised, to show his religious feeling more publicly:

I think however that perhaps if he went to St George's Chapel there would be more publicity – and I heartily agree with you that though he may be deeply religious within himself, the outward expression of this is very necessary to his subjects. I shall try to suggest this to him tactfully – and I am sure he will be only too glad to change his church – for no one is trying harder than he to do all he can for us all.[82]

Lady Oxford was 'full of Mrs S's good sense and good influence on HM', noted one observer.[83] Winston Churchill saw the same benefits. Since the King had met Mrs Simpson, he commented, he looked 'older and harder – a little stiffer perhaps since he became King, definitely more confidence in himself.'[84] Monckton thought so too: 'She insisted that he should be at his best and do his best at all times, and he regarded her as an inspiration.'[85]

But Edward's father, George V, had been horrified by the unsuitability of Mrs Simpson. Edward and two of his brothers – Albert, known in the family as 'Bertie' (and who later became King George VI), and George – had already distressed their father by indulging in relationships with married women. Mrs Freda Dudley Ward, who was married to William Dudley Ward, Liberal MP for Southampton, had been Edward's 'own beloved Angel'[86] from 1918 to 1934. Her place in Edward's affections was then taken by Thelma, Lady Furness. Prince Albert, too, had been involved with a married woman. In 1919, he fell in love with Sheila Loughborough, an Australian-born London Society beauty who was married to Lord Loughborough, by whom she had had a baby boy the previous winter. At this time, Edward and Albert more or less shared the same social circle, and Albert prevailed upon his brother to spirit Sheila away from her husband so that they could spend some time together.[87] George V objected strongly. 'Christ! how I loathe & despise my bloody family' expostulated Edward to Freda Dudley Ward from a sea voyage on 24 May 1920,

as Bertie has written me 3 long sad letters in which he tells me he's been getting it in the neck about his friendship with poor little Sheilie & that TOI et MOI came in for it too!! But if HM thinks he's going to alter me by insulting you he's making just about the biggest mistake of his silly useless life . . . God! damn him![88]

King George decided to tempt Albert away from Sheila with the carrot of a dukedom. 'Now as regards old Bertie & Sheilie,' Edward told Freda,

B talks a lot of hot air about HM making him a duke on condition that his name ceases to be more or less coupled with Sheilie's . . . Bertie may be a Duke now for all I know, as I think that his rather pompous nature makes him want to be one.[89]

On 5 June 1920, Albert was made Duke of York. The next year he transferred his attentions to Helen ('Poppy') Baring, who had the reputation of being 'fast' and fun-loving. He proposed marriage to her while staying with her parents during Cowes week. She accepted, but his mother, Queen Mary, swiftly made it clear that the match was impossible. Six years later, Prince George also fell for Poppy and proposed, but this marriage was not allowed either.[90]

Prince George had numerous affairs and one-night stands with both men and women. 'I was told no one – of either sex – was safe with him in a taxi', said one person who knew him well.[91] One of his lovers was Noel Coward. In 1932 there was 'a scandal about Prince George – letters to a young man in Paris. A large sum had to be paid for their recovery.'[92] He also became addicted to cocaine after an affair with Kiki Whitney Preston, an American woman who belonged to the decadent group of white settlers in Kenya known as the Happy Valley set. To rescue George from Kiki, Edward forced her to leave England in the summer of 1929. He then cancelled a holiday with Freda Dudley Ward so that he could devote himself to the task of curing George of his cocaine addiction, with the help of doctors. He told Freda that he was forced to act as George's 'doctor, gaoler and detective combined'. By the end of the year the worst was over: Kiki was safely abroad, and the Prince was weaned off the drug.[93]

The 'fast' life of these princes was by no means at odds with the customs of the English elite. Despite the strait-laced nature of George V's court, it was perfectly normal for many of the upper classes – married and unmarried – to enjoy sexual relationships with any number of others – again, married and unmarried. Edwina Mountbatten had a number of passionate affairs; but the only time this became a scandal was when a magazine called *The People* insinuated (mistakenly, it appeared) that she was having an affair with Paul Robeson. Edwina's husband, Louis, also had many affairs, with both men and women. Lord Londonderry had affairs with one woman after another. Many of these women were American, including Consuelo Vanderbilt, the heiress who had married his second cousin, the ninth Duke of Marlborough. By another American, a married actress, he had a child who was born just six weeks after his wedding; and his most lasting affair was with yet another American woman, the wife of the Earl of Ancaster.

Bertie settled down finally when he married Elizabeth Bowes-Lyon in 1923. Technically she was a commoner until her marriage to a royal, but as the daughter of the Earl of Strathmore she belonged to one of the oldest upper-class families of Britain. George settled down when he married Princess Marina of Greece in 1934. And in his own way Edward settled down too, when he fell irrevocably in love with Wallis Simpson. But while everybody in Society could understand why Albert had chosen Elizabeth and George had chosen Marina, they were utterly baffled by Edward's choice. 'He is, I believe,' said Robert Bruce Lockhart, a former diplomat who was the editor of the 'Londoner's Diary' in the *Evening Standard*, 'suffering from *dementia erotica*.'[94] Theories abounded of special sexual skills used by Wallis to satisfy the King. It was said that she appealed to a latent homosexuality in Edward, because of her slim, boyish figure. Virginia Woolf wrote in her diary on 27 November that Kingsley Martin, the editor of the socialist magazine *New Statesman and Nation*, had earlier been 'approached by one of the King's circle, was asked to write an article, revealing the facts from the King's side. Then he was told to wait . . . The King's men told him in strict secrecy about the sexual difficulty.'[95] Whatever this 'sexual difficulty' was, she did not explain; most probably she had no idea and was simply repeating some of the gossip that was doing the rounds.

Wallis was seen as simply too lower-class and too poor to qualify for special attention – or, indeed, any attention – from royalty. Edward's adoration only made sense if it was seen as an obsession – as a pathology rather than love. The editor of *The Times*, Geoffrey Dawson, recorded in his private diary on 2 November a conversation about this with Lord Dawson of Penn, the royal doctor who had attended King George V on his deathbed. Lord Dawson, he wrote, 'was interesting on the subject of HM's obsession from the medical point of view. The Literary Society, with whom I dined that evening, was also absorbed in the same subject (to the complete exclusion of literature!).'[96]

An added difficulty for Wallis was her nationality, because the upper class of Britain tended to look down on arrivals from America. 'The Americans are funny,' said Jean, Lady Hamilton, 'titles go to their heads – Society turns them into mere social machines – sort of climbing tanks – funicular tanks . . .'[97] Nancy Dugdale, the newly married wife of Thomas Dugdale, Baldwin's Parliamentary Private Secretary and MP for Richmond in Yorkshire, was dismayed by Edward's 'marked preference for American women as opposed to English women'.[98] Wallis decided that the British seemed to cherish a sentiment of settled disapproval towards anything American. She commented in her memoirs later that 'The only contemporary Americans, outside Hollywood, of whom British women appeared to have heard were named Vanderbilt, Astor, or Morgan. By and large they seemed mildly regretful that the continent had ever passed from the control of the Indians.'[99] Nancy Astor made fun of this attitude towards Americans. She was the first woman to sit as an MP in Parliament and was herself an American, from Virginia. Playing charades during Christmas festivities at Cliveden, her family home, she invented 'an upper-crust British woman with prejudices against Abroad and "Emmericans".'[100] Nonetheless, she objected to Wallis on the grounds of her social inferiority. When Edward invited Wallis and Ernest Simpson to dine at York House in May 1936, Lady Astor was indignant. She told Harold Nicolson that only the best Virginia families should be received at court, and that the effect in Canada and the USA would be deplorable. (Nicolson commented in a letter to his wife that he refrained from the retort that, 'after all, every American is more or less as vulgar as any other American'.)[101]

As well as lacking both title and wealth, and being American, what made Wallis objectionable to the English upper class was that she was divorced. In fact, civil divorce had been legal in Britain since 1858: divorced persons had the right to remarry, and the legally innocent party of a divorce could remarry with the sanction of the Church of England. Some attitudes to divorce in Society circles were enlightened: in 1906 Waldorf Astor had married Nancy Langhorne – the future Lady Astor – who was then a twenty-six-year-old American divorcee with a six-year-old son. Waldorf's father, William Waldorf, had trusted his son's judgement and assured Nancy that, 'If you are good enough for Waldorf, then you will be good enough for me.'[102] But overwhelmingly, divorce was a barrier in public life and court circles.

Wallis had been presented at court in June 1931, but this was allowed only because she had been the innocent party in her divorce. Because of this interdict, 'which rightly or wrongly I regarded as hypocritical,' observed Edward in his memoirs, 'an ever-increasing number of otherwise worthy and blameless men and women were forced to stand apart in a permanent state of obloquy.'[103]

There were mutterings of horror and indignation when in the summer of 1936 Edward took Wallis on a cruise through the Adriatic aboard the *Nahlin*. She was one of several select guests, including Lord Sefton, Helen Fitzgerald, Duff Cooper and Lady Diana Cooper, and Lord and Lady Brownlow, as well as Katherine and Herman Rogers, the friends with whom Wallis had stayed in Peking. The Captain of the ship found Mrs Simpson 'a most charming lady'. This view was shared by a bedroom steward on the ship, who remembered when Mrs Simpson joined the ship in Poland, and her stay on board until leaving at Constantinople three weeks later. 'I have had to deal with a great many ladies in my time,' he said, 'but I never met a more charming lady than she was.' It was a very happy party, he thought. As on the *Rosaura* two years earlier, Wallis's bedroom and Edward's bedroom were in the fore part of the ship, while the rest of the guests had rooms in the aft. After the King and his guests had left the *Nahlin*, said the steward, the crew 'naturally spoke about them'; they had all liked Mrs Simpson. A dining room steward noticed that Wallis addressed Edward as 'Sir', but was not submissive – 'I mean that if His Majesty was speaking to other guests Mrs Simpson would butt in with some witty remark. When at the table I have noticed His Majesty leave off talking to others to answer Mrs Simpson.'[104]

Lady Diana Cooper seemed to resent Wallis's presence. 'It's impossible to enjoy antiquities with people who won't land for them and who call Delphi Delhi', she wrote, snobbishly. 'Wallis is wearing very very badly. Her commonness and Becky Sharpishness irritate', she added, likening Wallis to the social climber in Thackeray's *Vanity Fair*.[105] Diana's hostility may have been fed by annoyance that the King was not paying her much attention on the cruise. As the daughter of the Duke of Rutland and someone who was generally regarded as one of the most beautiful women in London, she was usually at the centre of anything that was going on.

Although the *Nahlin* voyage had been planned as a holiday, Edward also visited the battlefields of Gallipoli and performed a number of royal duties. He visited the King of Greece and the King of Yugoslavia, helping to cement friendly ties between these nations and Britain. While they were in Greece, Sir Sydney Waterlow, the British Ambassador in Athens, was impressed by the bond between Wallis and Edward. He wondered 'whether this union, however queer and generally unsuitable and embarrassing for the state, may not in the long run turn out to be more in harmony with the spirit of the new age than anything that wisdom could have contrived.'[106] Edward also met with Kemal Atatürk, the ruler of Turkey. This was the first time a British king had ever been to Turkey, and the occasion was a great success. On his way home Edward visited Vienna, where he made a point of looking at housing estates for the poor. An Austrian living in London later wrote to a member of Edward's staff to tell him of the King's immense popularity in her country,

for which he has done such a lot. We have the greatest trust in him to prevent another war at all costs and admire his genuine concern for the people and their problems. It really made an impression in Vienna when the King visited the Workmen's blocks of flats with such interest.[107]

Despite her divorced status, her nationality and her lack of the kind of social status that counted in Britain, Wallis had many friends, among them journalists, politicians, diplomats and artists of all kinds. Elsie de Wolfe, a Parisian hostess, instructed her on entertaining and introduced her to fashion designers such as Schiaparelli and Mainbocher. One lively friend was 'Foxy' Gwynne, whom Wallis had got to know in Paris during her stay there years before. Foxy had once been a fashion model and owed her nickname to her red hair. She was later to marry the Earl of Sefton, who was a good friend of Edward's.

An especially close and loyal friend in London was Sybil, Lady Colefax, a pretty and popular social hostess in her early sixties. Many people shared Charles Lambe's view that 'Lady Colefax was nice, intelligent and sympathetic. I felt at ease with her.'[108] Like Wallis, she was a remarkably resourceful woman. After losing her wealth in the crash of 1929, she set up a very successful business in interior decoration, which popularized the vogue for English chintz. When her husband died in February 1936, she had to move out of her grand home, Argyll House, to a much smaller home on Lord North Street in Westminster. But despite the relative shortage of space, money and time, she continued to be an influential hostess. The number of her acquaintances was vast. 'I would so like to ask someone to meet you,' wrote the novelist E. M. Forster to Lady Colefax, 'whom you don't know, but whom do I know whom you don't know, I don't know.'[109] Unusually for a social hostess, Lady Colefax was politically left of centre and usually voted Labour; she invited Labour politicians and their wives to her soirées and was a great admirer of the radical economist John Maynard Keynes.[110]

Sybil did not meet Wallis until the summer of 1935, but they quickly became friends. Not only did Sybil like Wallis, she also approved of her as Edward's companion in life: 'His first great love was always hard and in love with someone else ... His second awful (Lady Furness). Wallis tactful, helpful and wise and I've seen her at it.'[111] Sybil hosted formal occasions for Wallis and Edward. To one dinner at Argyll House she invited Perry Brownlow and his wife Kitty, the Duchess of Buccleuch, Lady Diana Cooper and Duff Cooper, Lord and Lady Vansittart, and Mr and Mrs Artur Rubinstein. It was a summer evening, and through the great double doors, which were open, the guests could see the garden with its spreading lawns and a sea of green trees, lit by Chinese lanterns, 'pale moons of white' floating in the branches.[112] Later in the evening, Lord Berners, Winston Churchill and some other men joined the gathering. Rubinstein played Chopin, which delighted Sybil (Rubinstein did not like playing for social gatherings) but also caused her some anxiety, as Edward was not keen on classical music. Bruce Lockhart wrote in his diary that the 'King sat down on a little stool beside Mrs Simpson. Seemed rather bored, but stayed on.' After he had finished, Noel Coward was asked to sing, which cheered the King immensely – he 'bucked up and looked quite amused. He did not leave till nearly one. Came with and left with Mrs Simpson. Quite unattended. No ADC etc.'[113]

It was by no means unusual at this time for social hostesses to lionize people with a particular claim to attention by Society. Albert, the Duke of York, and his Duchess, Elizabeth (the future King George VI and Queen Elizabeth), were cultivated by Mrs Ronnie Greville, who had a house on Charles Street in London and an immense country estate in Surrey, Polesden Lacey. Here, Albert and Elizabeth spent a part of their honeymoon. Born the illegitimate daughter of a Scottish millionaire brewer, Mrs Greville had managed to put this behind her and establish a position among the elite and many of the royal family. Edward disliked her and thought her behaviour to royalty was syco-phantic. People such as the Coopers and Cecil Beaton held her in contempt because of her zealous pursuit of titles to attend her recep-tions (of sixty-one names mentioned on one evening, over fifty were titled, and on most occasions there was at least one royal). Cecil Beaton thought she was a 'galumphing, greedy, snobbish old toad who watered at the chops at the sight of royalty.'[114] Menus were pre-sented in French, and at one large Christmas party, one of the seven courses was 'Oeufs Duc d'York' in honour of the most important guest.[115] Mrs Greville, like many of her circle, was an enthusiastic supporter of Adolf Hitler. She was fawned upon by Joachim von Ribbentrop, the German ambassador, and was present at a Nazi Party rally in Nuremberg; she was furious at the British Embassy for not sending a representative.[116]

Because of her intimacy with Edward, Wallis was eyed as a passport to the King. 'Of course anyone who can get hold of Mrs Simpson can now secure His Majesty', commented Jean Hamilton enviously in the summer of 1936.[117] Emerald Cunard, an American, was a keen contender for Wallis's favour. She was the estranged wife of Sir Bache Cunard, grandson of the founder of the Cunard shipping line. She was known for her affairs with the writer George Moore and then with Sir Thomas Beecham, the famous conductor, and had a particular interest in the patronage of musicians and writers. By the time Edward had started his reign, Lady Hamilton was observing in her diary that Emerald Cunard and 'all her crew' were 'tumbling after' Wallis. Their nickname, she added, was 'The Royal Racket'.[118] Some resentment was felt at Lady Cunard's determination to win Wallis's favour. At a 'pompous, manqué dinner' at Lady Cunard's in 1936, when she was 'looking like Pavlova in white', wrote Chips Channon, she slipped a crumpled note into his hand for him to read. It was an anonymous missive she had received. It began, 'You old bitch, trying to make up to Mrs Simpson, in order to curry favour with the King.' Emerald was frightened, thought Channon, 'and yet rather flattered. It was in an educated handwriting.'[119]

Wallis fully understood what was going on. 'One gets tired of having people make a fuss over you because they want to see HRH', she complained to her aunt.[120] She knew, though, that it was important not to alienate anyone. 'I have tried awfully hard this year to be nice to the natives,' she wrote, 'answering thousands of notes, going to boring parties.'[121] With wry humour, she congratulated herself on managing to cope so well in Edward's world, given her limited means. 'I imagine anyway I am doing far far better than Thelma on far far less', she told Bessie, referring to Edward's previous lover, Lady Furness.[122] 'I enjoy meeting and seeing all these people', she wrote in another letter, adding that 'some times it seems strange to think of those days of struggle in Earl's Court [an apartment building in Baltimore] and the other flat where mother had the café and was forever working herself to death to give me things.'[123] In June 1935, Wallis told her aunt about a recent court ball at which the Prince had danced with her directly after the opening dance with the Queen. She had been thrilled by Edward's public display of devotion and by the attentions of the court. 'I really know them all now and must say they are grand to me', she reported with pleasure. But she was under no illusions. 'Naturally,' she added dryly, 'only for the duration of my length of service.'[124]

3

'The Spirit of the Age'

Wallis Simpson had never been heard of by the general public in Britain when Edward visited South Wales in November 1936. They knew nothing about the most important thing in his life – the woman he adored. But they *did* know about his concern for the welfare of the poor, which was further demonstrated on the royal tour. It wasn't only in South Wales that people witnessed Edward's ready sympathy with the unemployed of the valleys, for the following week newsreel reports of the royal tour were shown in every cinema of Britain. It had been filmed by all five of the newsreel companies – Gaumont-British News, Movietone News, Pathe, Paramount and Universal. The coverage of the tour was highly sympathetic to the King: it followed him as he walked among the poor, visited their homes, mixed mortar at their instruction, doffed his hat and nodded his head, and showed his evident distress at their sufferings. 'Bringing the whole problem of the Depressed Areas out of the shadows into the floodlight of world attention,' announced Pathe Gazette's *The King Visits South Wales*, 'His Majesty's visit to South Wales is not only a promise of new life but a gesture of sympathy.' It stressed the King's plea for urgent action:

But beneath all this His Majesty saw the disillusion and suffering brought by long workless years. His visit has cheered them as nothing else could. And as he leaves there is a new found faith that some solution will be found. Let no one belittle the magnificent work that is being done by the social services. But social service is not enough. These men want work. New industries must be brought to the stricken areas of South Wales.[1]

Through newsreels like these, people all over Britain were made aware of Edward's visit to South Wales.

In 1934 there were over four thousand cinemas in England, Scotland and Wales, and going to the 'pictures' was the most popular form of entertainment for just about everybody except the very poor (who could not afford the tickets) and the very rich (who disdained it). By the middle of the 1930s, some twenty million people in Britain each week saw the newsreels, which were shown before the feature films. These newsreels gave suburban audiences and people throughout Britain all kinds of new knowledge about their own and other countries. Watching the reports of Edward's visit to South Wales, they learned not only about the latest exploits of their King, but also about the plight of the people living in the Special Areas. This was driven home to cinema-goers by the scenes of unemployed families and pale, thin children against a backdrop of disused pits and grassed-over coal tips. In the middle of these scenes was Edward, his slight but regal figure commanding viewers' attention. Without his visit, newsreel directors might not have sent film crews to South Wales to film this story of human suffering amid industrial decay. Edward had brought the distressed areas into the news.

Edward had been a dominant figure in the newsreels ever since the end of the Great War, first as Prince of Wales and then, when he ascended the throne on 20 January 1936, as King. Audiences saw him on his numerous visits to the industrial areas and the inner cities, touring factories, visiting housing estates, opening hospitals and inspecting lines of ex-servicemen in Britain and in France. Films such as *50,000 Miles with the Prince of Wales* showed his overseas tours.[2] When he became King, commented Sir John Simon, who was then Home Secretary, Edward was the most widely known and most universally popular personality in the world.[3]

His popularity came not simply from his being the newsreels' favourite star. He earned it with his warm personality and genuine concern for people, whatever their background, age or status. He won Charlie Chaplin's esteem by sitting at a party with his host's mother, who was in her eighties, until she retired; only then, remembered

Chaplin years later, did he join the rest of the group and have fun.[4] He was remembered for many such acts of kindness. A woman wrote to the King to tell him that

When you visited Sydney NSW it came to your knowledge that my late Aunt, one of the oldest inhabitants of that city, and who had seen the wedding of your Grandfather, was longing to see you. You caused her to be brought to you, yourself hand her to a seat, and chatted with her for some time. Such kindly consideration will never be forgotten by members of my family . . .[5]

Another woman wrote to express her gratitude to him for 'listening to my appeal re the railway Arabs', who were homeless children living near railway lines.[6] His interest in the poor was especially appreciated. One mother described him as

The man who moved among them with sympathy and with a Christ-like understanding, and in so doing compelled the people to learn of the terrible distress, bravely borne, by the peoples of the distressed areas . . . you had trod their slums, entered their homes, spoken to them words of hope, actions kindly and kingly, such as no High Church bishops, archbishops, and lesser Church lights had condescended to do.[7]

Marcus Garvey, the President of the General Universal Negro Improvement Association, told King Edward that 'the Negro race' regarded him 'as a true friend'.[8]

Edward was no socialist, though. His concern for the poor and his keen sense of social justice were genuine and heartfelt, but he shared the political attitudes of most of the upper classes: he did not support the Labour Party and he did not want to see any fundamental change in the structure of society. He put his faith in David Lloyd George, the Liberal Prime Minister from 1916 to 1922, and then, when the Liberals were no longer a political force to be reckoned with, in the Conservative Party. However, he objected strongly when the Conservative-dominated National Government failed to meet the most basic needs of the poor and the long-term unemployed. Like Harold Macmillan and other Tory paternalists, he felt a keen sense of obligation towards those who were less well off. In fulfilling his own responsibilities, notably for the vast estates of the Duchy of Cornwall in London and the West Country, he sought to act as a fair and decent landowner. His official biographer, Philip Ziegler, records that he invested a great deal of money in new machinery for the Cornish tin mines, and set up a farming concern run on cooperative lines. In London, he regularly visited his estates in Kennington, and the housing in areas of the borough which he owned was much better than in the parts for which the Council was responsible.[9]

He may not have been a socialist, but he was driven by democratic ideals. One ex-miner described him as 'a real democratic King, The Common People's King (as the snobbish aristocracy will have it)'. Using imagery that drew on the experience of his working life as a miner and a washer-up, he told the King, 'You have constantly been mining under the feet of the snobbish aristocracy. You have washed it up and dried and drained it wherever you went.'[10] Edward was seen to share the same concern for the poor as the Democrat President of America, Franklin D. Roosevelt, who had been re-elected with a landslide victory in early November 1936. Roosevelt had promised 'a new deal for the forgotten man' and was the architect of the New Deal, a package of social reforms to benefit the poor and the unemployed. Certainly, the long-term problems created by the Depression were similar on both sides of the Atlantic. Charlie Chaplin's film *Modern Times*, which came out in 1936, drew attention to these problems – unemployment, poverty, strikes and riots.

To many Americans who supported the Democrats, King Edward VIII seemed to display the same qualities as their President. 'You & Roosevelt. What a Democratic combination! What a team!' wrote a man living in Birmingham, Alabama, to the King.[11] An estate agent in Philadelphia told the King that 'you and President Roosevelt are the two Greatest men in the world, you and he believe in the good things for all of us'.[12] Edward himself admired Roosevelt enormously. In 1934 he told the American Ambassador, Robert Bingham, that Britain needed leadership of the kind that Roosevelt was giving to the United States, with the aim of relieving poverty and distress.[13] Edward could be 'a very serious young man on serious questions', said the American writer Alexander Woollcott in 1936, adding, 'That is what will get him into trouble one of these days with the Tory prigs and bigwigs.'[14]

Edward's personality would have been remarkable, observed the historian John Grigg, even if he had not been royal. 'Allied to his princely status it was irresistible.' There was about him, he added, 'the indefinable aura known as star quality'.[15] This 'star quality' shone brightly during a visit to the Home Fleet at Portland in November 1936, in the week before Edward's visit to South Wales. He arrived exhausted. The day before, he had been to the Cenotaph in the morning for Armistice Day, and at the Albert Hall in the evening. He then caught a midnight train to Portland, which arrived in the middle of a storm at four o'clock in the morning. But despite this fatigue, reported a naval commander who was there, the King's words and manner went straight to the hearts of the men.[16] Edward was accompanied by Samuel Hoare, First Lord of the Admiralty, an old friend from Oxford days. He noticed that Edward managed to make every officer and seaman in the fleet feel that he knew them personally. On one evening, at a smoking concert in an aircraft carrier, the underdeck was packed with thousands of seamen. In his long experience of mass meetings, said Hoare, he had never seen one so completely dominated by a single personality:

At one point he turned to me and said: 'I am going to see what is happening at the other end.' Elbowing his way through the crowd, he walked to the end of the hall and started community singing to the accompaniment of a seaman's mouth-organ. When he came back to the platform, he made an impromptu speech that brought the house down. Then, a seaman in the crowd proposed three cheers for him, and there followed an unforgettable scene of the wildest and most spontaneous enthusiasm.[17]

'Here, indeed', observed Hoare, 'was the Prince Charming who could win the hearts of all sorts and conditions of men and women and send a thrill through great crowds.'[18] No wonder that so many people wrote to tell him of their love. 'When I go to the pictures or see your photo in books,' said one woman, 'I have bought them and loved them and you don't know what a sensation I have I almost want to shout out to you.'[19]

This massive popularity with the general public did not make Edward popular with his father, George V. When George came to the throne in 1910, Edward was sixteen. 'To the very natural dislike that a very conventional man often feels for an adolescent,' commented Diana Mosley, 'was added in this case an equally natural grain of jealousy of the physical beauty and winning manners of the Prince.' Many things about Edward annoyed the King, but 'above all his undoubted popularity'.[20] Prince Albert, Edward's brother, noticed this too. 'Papa seems to think that anything you do which he doesn't like has been influenced by Fredie,' he wrote to him in 1920, referring to Edward's lover at the time, Freda Dudley Ward. 'This of course is due to the great popularity which you have everywhere, and Papa is merely jealous.'[21]

Edward had first met the ordinary men of Britain during the Great War, for much of which he served at the front. He joined up as an officer in the Grenadier Guards in 1914, at the start of the war. He had just completed two years at Oxford University and the president of Magdalen, his college, watched his departure for the army with regret:

The Prince, and this is what he would have wished, has suffered the common lot of his compeers. Like two-thirds and more of the men with whom he was up, like ever so many 'second year' men of 1914, he was swept off into the service of his country, and his second year of Oxford has proved his last.[22]

It was a terrible war, most of it fought from the trenches cut deep into the ground of the battlefield by both sides and protected by barbed wire and machine-guns. Many of the soldiers lived in these filthy, rat-infested trenches. Every so often they would be ordered to climb 'over the top' of their trench and advance over no man's land towards the enemy's trench, in an attempt – usually useless – to capture it. On just the first day of the Battle of the Somme, nearly twenty thousand men were killed and nearly sixty thousand were wounded. The death toll was increased by the epidemics that swept through the trenches. From 1916, all able-bodied British men between the ages of eighteen and forty-one had to go into the army, replacing the injured and the dead.

Edward had been determined to fight, but this was flatly forbidden on the grounds that he might be captured by the enemy. 'If I were sure you would be killed, I do not know if I should be right to restrain you', said Lord Kitchener, the Secretary for War. 'But I cannot take the chance of them ever taking you prisoner, which always exists.' Edward, though, was obsessed with the desire 'to be found worthy and to share in the risks and struggles of men'.[23] He could not bear to stay safely behind the line while his compatriots were dying in their tens of thousands. Ziegler has recorded that he never stopped trying to get to the front line and never stopped hating it when he was there – he found the shelling terrifying and was ready to say so.[24] After spending his first night in the trenches in July 1915, Edward wrote to his father:

My impressions that night were of constant close proximity to death, repugnance for the stink of the unburied corpses ... and general gloom and apprehension. It was all a real eye opener to me, now I had some slight conception of all that our officers and men have to go thro!! The whole life is horrible and ghastly beyond conception.[25]

Edward was horrified at the ineffectiveness of the Allies' strategy, with its repeated fruitless attacks, achieving at best the occupation of a few trenches.[26] During the Battle of the Somme he wrote that, 'These continuous heavy casualty lists make me sick ... I can't keep the wretched infantry being slaughtered out of my thoughts.'[27] His admiration of the fighting men and a sense of his own inadequacy made him reluctant to wear the war decorations he was given. In 1916 he was awarded the Military Cross, which he felt he had not deserved.[28]

He eventually got himself posted to the staff of the British Expeditionary Force's commander in France. Whenever possible, he moved to the battle zone, and had a narrow escape visiting positions at the front before the Battle of Loos. However, he did not take unnecessary risks, according to General Sir Ian Hamilton: 'He *did* take risks, but they were always in the line of duty. We *did* worry about him . . . but not because of any insubordination on his part.'[29] His most important role in the war was to boost the morale of the soldiers – a job at which he excelled. One soldier later wrote to him a letter of thanks for his encouragement:

Our King, I saw you in the trenches in front of Arras in March or Feb 1917. The [Battalion] did not know you were there, it was your youth that made me recognise you, being 17 myself I wondered at you looking so young & your face & medals flashed a photograph into mind that I had seen of you in uniform & I knew & I worried & pondered, you should not have been there. But it gave me courage to carry on when sometimes all hope had fled.[30]

In 1916 the Prince went on a morale-boosting visit to the Canal Zone in the Middle East, where he met Australians and New Zealanders evacuated from the battle of Gallipoli.

The Aga Khan, the leader of the Ismaili sect of Muslims and a very wealthy and cosmopolitan man, also met Edward during the war. He recalled later that he knew 'the man who has said so poignantly and so truly . . . "I learned about war on a bicycle" – endlessly trundling his heavy Army bicycle along the muddy roads of Flanders, to places like Poperinghe and Montauban and the villages around Ypres.' Edward's spirit, added the Aga Khan, was stamped forever by the slaughter and waste of those years of trench warfare.[31]

During his four years on the Western Front, Edward achieved a 'quite novel popular touch' by rubbing shoulders with thousands of ordinary people in the trenches, observed Lloyd George.[32] An American soldier said that his 'manner was so simple and unassuming – he was simply one soldier among a group of soldiers – that he won the liking and respect of all of us.'[33] Soldiering brought to the Prince of Wales, as to many other fighting men of the ruling classes, contact with men outside their own narrow circles. 'The First World War', he wrote later, 'had made it possible for me to share an unparalleled human experience with all manner of men.'[34] In a letter written from Belgium at the end of the war, he told Freda Dudley Ward that, 'One can't help liking all the men & taking a huge interest in them.'[35] Harold Macmillan, who came from a very wealthy family and also served with the Grenadier Guards, made the same point after the war:

By the daily life, working in close contact with the men in one's platoon or company, we learnt for the first time how to understand, talk with, and feel at home with a whole class of men with whom we could not have come into contact in any other way. Thus we learnt to admire their steadfastness, enjoy their humour, and be touched by their sentiment.[36]

The young Prince of Wales may have been disappointed that he was not allowed actually to go 'over the top' with the other soldiers. But he saw far more of the war and of the servicemen than did his brother Albert, who was a midshipman on the battleship HMS *Collingwood* when war broke out. After just three weeks, Albert was brought home by an attack of appendicitis, to his bitter disappointment. This was the start of three years of almost constant sick leave, caused by a gastric ulcer.[37] To his great relief, he had rejoined the *Collingwood* when it opened fire in the battle of Jutland; and although he was then in the sick bay, he insisted on going to his battle station. But he fell ill again soon afterwards. He spent most of the war working at the Admiralty – a tedious job, which he endured without complaining.[38] This was a humiliating experience for Albert: men who did not fight were generally regarded as cowards, and white feathers were sent to them in the post. Edward understood how badly he felt. He wrote to his mother on 6 December 1918 to suggest that 'Bertie' stay as long as possible in France after the Armistice. 'By remaining with the armies till peace is signed,' he told her, 'he will entirely erase any of the very unfair questions some nasty people asked last year as to what he was doing, you will remember.'[39]

After demobilization, Edward took an active interest in the work of Toc H, an organization that was set up to provide a refuge for veterans of all ranks of men and officers, and the British Legion, which was founded in 1921 to cater for their welfare. His commitment to ex-servicemen was uncompromising. When he was in Belgium in 1923, one of his duties was to visit a hospital for the treatment of English soldiers suffering from facial disfigurement. He was introduced to the patients but, noticing that there were only twenty-seven present out of the twenty-eight known to be in the hospital, he asked to see the absent man. The officer in charge explained that his was such a frightful case – repulsive, even – that the patient had been kept away. But the Prince insisted on seeing him – as far as he was concerned, this man had the highest claim to his sympathy. He was taken to the patient's room, where he went straight up to the man and kissed him.[40] This heartfelt compassion for the casualties of war was captured by newsreel reports. During a visit to North Wales, where he walked down lines of veterans, a Pathe newsreel lingered on his visible grief as he talked to a blind soldier who had lost his sight in battle.[41] 'I've seen both in France during the Great War and at home [how] the interests of your Subjects however humble (Especially Ex Service men) have been *one* of *your* interests', wrote a veteran to the King from his London basement in 1936. 'To me *you* will always be *OUR TEDDY*. You shook my hand at the First British Legion Gathering at the Crystal Palace. What a handshake.'[42]

Edward's concern for ex-servicemen embraced everyone, regardless of their background or nationality. In 1936 he invited to a garden party at Buckingham Palace six thousand Canadian war veterans who – like himself – had shortly before attended the unveiling of the Canadian War Memorial at Vimy Ridge in France to mark the single victory in the Battle of the Somme. The garden party was a remarkable and alien sight to the conservative-minded officials of the royal court. The Deputy Comptroller of Supply at Buckingham Palace was astonished to see the Canadians

strolling round the Palace grounds and passing through the famous Bow Saloon . . . dressed in lounge suits, all wearing their war medals, and many of them with berets on their heads. It was in striking contrast with the usual elegant, morning-coated, top-hatted guests at the normal Palace garden-parties.

When it started to rain hard, the King hurried indoors. A minute or two later he appeared on the balcony of the first floor, bareheaded, and gave a short speech of welcome. Never before, observed the Deputy Comptroller, had a sovereign spoken so informally at a garden party at the Palace. In the royal household, opinion about his behaviour was divided: 'The older ones, naturally, were taken aback by this new example of the changes that were taking place in Royal procedure.' But the younger ones like himself, he said, 'took the view that this was a fine thing . . . for the King to step down for a moment from his exalted isolation and talk almost as man to man to the men who had been under fire with him in the muddy trenches of France and Flanders.'[43]

This affinity with war veterans was something that Edward's father, King George V, did not share. In 1923, he rode in an open carriage with the Prince of Wales and some other members of the royal family to review some 35,000 Silver Badge ex-servicemen in Hyde Park. He was given an enthusiastic reception, 'but there was also another spirit abroad' – the dissatisfaction of ex-servicemen. They were angry – because they had returned home not to the 'Land Fit For Heroes' promised them by Lloyd George's slogan, but to unemployment and poverty. They had decided to tell King George of their bitterness:

As if by a prearranged signal, hitherto concealed banners with slogans were defiantly unfurled among the milling humanity which pressed about the King. In so tense an atmosphere there were possibilities of serious trouble, but fortunately the police were able to extricate the King without incident.

George V failed to understand the feelings of these men. Back at Buckingham Palace, he muttered, ' "Those men were in a funny temper" – and shaking his head, as if to rid himself of an unpleasant memory, he strode indoors.'[44]

But to Edward, both as Prince of Wales and later as King, veteran soldiers and sailors looked faithfully as their royal patron. They begged him to use his influence with the Government to do something for them. In 1927, Edward became an enthusiastic patron of the National Council of Social Service, and went to hundreds of clubs and schemes for the unemployed and visited the poorest homes.[45] The majority of the men waiting for Edward in South Wales and Monmouthshire in

November 1936, at least those who were middle-aged, were ex-servicemen like himself. The local press stressed this link between the King and his subjects: ' "I served in the War with the King", many a be-medalled veteran would say, and then, to leave no shadow of doubt in the mind of the listener – "Was in the trenches with him." '[46] Even an old horse at Cwmavon, said the *South Wales Argus*, had survived the battles of the war. 'His name . . . is either Sergeant or Major . . . and served in Flanders.'[47]

The horror of the war seemed to linger on into the thirties, in the sufferings of the long-term unemployed. In 1934, Harold Macmillan, now a Tory MP, drew a parallel between the despair of the trenches and the despair of unemployment. On learning in the House of Commons that the Government was planning to investigate conditions in the distressed areas of Britain, he remarked with bitter irony, 'I am glad that there has been on this occasion a visit from Whitehall to the Passchendaele of Durham and South Wales.'[48] Ex-servicemen were bitter, too. The representative of the Central Ratepayers Association in Portsmouth explained to the King, 'I served my Country TWICE, during [the] Great War, and got "NOW'T" for it.'[49] One man who in 1934 was sent to a camp for the unemployed, High Lodge in Durham, could hardly believe that

They had us digging trenches. Dig down so far then start further down, in stages as it were. We thought we were learning to dig trenches for war. It was just like a trench on the bloody Somme. We would dig it down one day then the next day another group would come and fill it in. That is all we done for three months. It was murder because all the time you were digging through chalk. Bloody hopeless it was.[50]

When the King returned to London from South Wales in November 1936, he immediately sent a message to the Lords Lieutenant of the regions he had visited, asking them to pass it on to the men who were unemployed. 'I would urge them', he said, 'not to lose heart and to rest assured that their troubles are not forgotten. – Edward R.I.'[51] The people had been immensely encouraged by his visit. 'He came amongst us, he has seen, and will assuredly never rest content until happiness is abundant and useful work has been restored to the submerged tenth of Darkest Wales', observed the *Western Mail & South Wales News*. 'The whole nation', it added, 'has been stirred by the events of the wonderful tour.'[52] The *South Wales Argus* thought the same. Referring to Edward's 'kingly brotherliness', it pointed out that he was ready to go 'among the humblest of his people in order that he might see for himself how the poor lived – in order that he might open the eyes of the nation to evils which need to be redressed.'[53] 'It may not be out of place', wrote John Rowland from the Welsh Board of Health to Sir Kingsley Wood on 20 November,

if I write to tell you that the King's Visit to South Wales has everywhere been a tonic to the people. I have not heard a single discouraging note; on all sides there is a strong hope that something very definite is to be done soon . . . Merthyr is placing her hopes very high.[54]

Beyond Wales, too, there was widespread approval of the royal visit and of the King's words at Dowlais. They 'reverberated round the country like a thunderclap', wrote William Deedes in an article for the *Morning Post*.[55] Most national newspapers were enthusiastic. 'Standing bowler-hatted before the towering cobwebbed chimneys of the once-famed steelworks of Dowlais, South Wales,' reported the *Daily Mirror* in November 1936, 'Britain's monarch spoke four live-wire words':

> Spurring a Government.
> Electrifying a nation of loyal subjects.
> 'Something', he said, 'must be done . . .'[56]

'Never has the magic of personal leadership been better shown', observed the *Daily Mail*, 'than by the King's visit to South Wales.'[57] It drew a sharp contrast between the King's energy and the National Government's inaction. Unlike Government Ministers, it observed, 'the Sovereign examined their plight and drew from them the tale of their trouble . . . the King has called for action . . . The contrast to the way in which national questions are customarily approached can escape nobody.'[58] Everyone knows, enthused the *New Statesman*, 'that . . . he is genuinely and deeply troubled about the misery and poverty which successive Governments have failed to relieve.'[59] The *News Chronicle*, the chief organ of non-conformist opinion, commented that what the King had done was 'in the sole interest of truth and public service . . . The man in the street feels that Whitehall stands condemned.'[60]

The 'man in the street' was certainly encouraged by Edward's visit to Wales. The President and Secretary of the United French Polishers' London Society wrote that his organization admired the King's interest in the Special Areas 'and your Majesty's promise "Something will be done" to relieve them'.[61] The genuine sympathy which he had recently displayed in South Wales, wrote a woman to the King from a village near Manchester, 'is only one of countless actions by which you have forged a bond between yourself and your people.'[62]

But other sections of the population were nervous about Edward's trip to Wales. 'Peers and politicians who resented his "demagogic" interest in labour', commented an American magazine, 'watched his trip nervously.'[63] The statement that 'something must be done' was seen as particularly offensive because it carried an implicit criticism of Government policy and Government practice – and it was reported in this way in much of the national press. Ramsay MacDonald, who was Lord President, expressed his annoyance with the King in his diary. Referring to a meeting on 21 November with Sir George Gillett, the newly appointed Commissioner for the Special Areas, MacDonald recorded that they 'talked Distressed Areas & King's visit to S. Wales which has roused expectations; and the promises he has made will embarrass the Govt. These escapades should be limited. They are an invasion into the field of politics & should be watched constitutionally.' Members of the royal family, he added, were supposed to be above politics.[64]

It was not just the ministers of the National Government who were irritated by Edward's visit to South Wales. Dismay was felt across the whole matrix of the Establishment – that is, the groups of men and women who ruled Britain by reason of their traditional prominence or their wealth. The Establishment represented a very powerful alliance of the Conservative party, the Church of England (which was – and still is – the official or 'established' church) and the Tory press, especially *The Times*, the *Telegraph* and the *Morning Post*. H. G. Wells mocked these groups by describing them as 'the Bishops and the Court people and the Foreign Office and the Old Gentry and Bath and Cheltenham and Blimpland and all that.'[65]

At the centre of the Establishment was 'Society' – the exclusive circle of upper-class men and women who were closely tied to each other by birth, marriage and culture. Society was a tiny fraction of the population, but enormously influential in terms of social and political power. At its apex was the royal family, supported by the senior functionaries of the court.[66] It was understood that either you were 'in' Society, or you were 'out'. If you were 'in', then you shared with other members of Society a horror of anything vulgar – the word 'common' was used to express contempt. If you were 'out', then you simply did not belong. Businessmen were mostly 'out', unless they came in through the door of Conservative politics. Baldwin tried to imagine, said Beaverbrook, 'that he had the mind and habits of a country squire'.[67] But in fact his family had made their money in iron and steel.

Going to public school, then to Oxford or Cambridge, was the standard route to adult life for men of Society. For women it was necessary to be a debutante and to 'come out': some eight thousand women were presented to the monarch each year at the four courts held in Buckingham Palace. Social barriers were starting to break down in the 1930s, but the power structure of British society was overwhelmingly monolithic.

On behalf of the Establishment, the editor of *The Times*, Geoffrey Dawson, was determined to set things straight on the matter of Edward's visit to South Wales. Dawson, in his early sixties, was a severe-looking man with thinning silver hair. A graduate of Eton and Magdalen College, Oxford, he was a Fellow of All Souls and a member of the Beefsteak Club, the Travellers Club and the Athenaeum, exclusive London clubs where he lunched and dined and discussed national affairs with other members of the male elite. In a written account of the period in which Edward went on his tour of the Welsh valleys, he objected that the *Daily Mail* had made a 'monstrous attempt to contrast his Majesty's solicitude for the unemployed in South Wales with the indifference of his Ministers.'[68] He wrote a short leader on the impropriety and danger of this attitude which appeared in *The Times* on 24 November 1936. 'The King's Ministers are His Majesty's advisers,' it insisted, 'and to contrast his personal and representative concern for the well-being of a section of the people with the administrative slips of his advisers is a constitutionally dangerous proceeding and would threaten, if continued, to entangle the Throne in politics.'[69]

But as far as the King was concerned, he had simply responded to the tragic situation he found at Dowlais. 'I was quoted', he explained years later in his memoirs, 'as having said in the midst of some dismal scene of ruined industry, that "something must be done" to repair the ravages of the dreadful inertia that had gripped the region.'[70] But this statement, he added, 'was the minimum humanitarian response that I could have made to what I had seen.'[71] It was motivated not by a political aim, said Edward, but by a simple humanity. This was exactly how the visit was perceived by many of the ordinary people of Britain. 'When . . . King Edward came to Wales and said, "something must be done," he got into trouble for saying that, but he was not wrong. I would have said the same thing myself', observed a man who grew up in the Glamorgan town of Penarth in the 1930s.[72]

The Government could not afford to ignore the King's visit to South Wales. A 'wife and mother' observed in a letter to the *Daily Mirror* that although it was not the King's job to pay any attention to the suffering of the long-term unemployed, 'he had to do it before anything was done by the politicians.'[73] Neville Chamberlain, the Chancellor of the Exchequer, felt obliged to alter a speech he delivered in Leeds on 20 November, a couple of days later, to acknowledge the problem of the Special Areas. The Government was continuously studying the situation in those areas, he insisted, and searching for new ways to help them. But he admitted that in South Wales, in particular, the situation was no better than it was when they had begun to look at the problem. He warned that the Government could not promise any 'spectacular plan which in a trice would solve one of the most obstinate, baffling problems that has ever faced a Government in this country.'[74]

On their own, Edward's democratic leanings might have been ignored. But combined with his massive popularity they were a cause of grave concern to the Government. Stanley Baldwin, the Conservative Prime Minister of the National Government, made it clear to a colleague that he was increasingly perturbed about 'the delicate situation created by the personality of the new King'.[75] Clement Attlee, the leader of the Labour Party, noticed Baldwin's anxiety at a meeting of the Accession Council after the death of George V.[76] Chamberlain had his own doubts about the new King. 'I do hope he "pulls up his socks",' he wrote in some notes, 'and behaves himself now he has such heavy responsibilities, for unless he does he will soon pull down the throne.' It was known, according to Montgomery Hyde, writing in his biography of Chamberlain, that he

drafted a memorandum for Cabinet circulation, urging that the King should 'settle down', wear conventional clothes, work at his 'boxes' and not make remarks in public, which were apt to be reported in the newspapers, about such topics as the slums and unemployment. It is also known that the Prime Minister thought it wise to suppress this memorandum.[77]

Geoffrey Dawson was horrified by the popularity of King Edward. He knew that he would have to take this into serious consideration when thinking about 'the possible value of publicity' in any campaign to force the King's hand on the matter of Mrs Simpson. On 12 November 1936, in the period leading up to Edward's visits to the Home Fleet and South Wales, Dawson noted in his diary that if 'newspaper criticism were to begin before these engagements it might be taken as an attempt to undermine HM's popularity in advance; if immediately after them, as an attempt to minimize his influence. It was a very difficult problem, on which SB [Stanley Baldwin] professed himself quite unable to give advice.'[78]

Many of the leading members of the Government belonged to a different generation from the King. In 1936 Edward was forty-two, whereas Baldwin was sixty-nine and Chamberlain sixty-seven. But it was not simply a matter of years. More importantly, it was a matter of experience: Baldwin's generation had not seen the horrors of the

First World War at first hand. Indeed, this generation would not have been so dominant in Westminster and Whitehall, had it not been for the deaths in battle of so many young men. 'It is only at times you notice it,' wrote the Labour MP Ellen Wilkinson in 1930,

but when you do it comes as a shock to realize that a whole generation has dropped out of the House of Commons. In the seats of the mighty in all parties are the men over sixty. The criticisms come from the under or early forties. And of the intermediaries, the men who should be bridging the generations there are just a scattered few, the survivors of the Great War.[79]

These survivors, all over Britain, were haunted by grief and terrible memories – of violent death, of the continuous and useless carnage at battles like Passchendaele, and of the dreary and terrifying reality of trench life. They had a comradeship and a shared knowledge that nobody else could ever understand.[80]

King Edward VIII shared in this comradeship – by reason of his war service, and by reason of his generation. 'You are *our age, the age* who's [sic] youth sacrificed during the Great War', said one letter to Edward in 1936.[81] 'You mean so much to our generation,' insisted the writer of another letter, 'which shared with you as with no one else the danger and trials of the War, and for whose present problems you show such deep understanding and practical sympathy.'[82] Nor was this appreciation of Edward limited to British war veterans. A French woman who had been an English interpreter during the war wrote from Paris to tell the King that he was 'loved by the World, especially we French people who have not forgotten those days of War.'[83]

The author Vera Brittain shared this sense of belonging to a generation blighted by war. She had been a member of the Voluntary Aid Detachment, nursing in France, and had been so horrified by the slaughter that she became an ardent pacifist. 'I belonged, like Edward VIII,' she said, 'to a generation which was still on the early side of middle age but had already seen almost more history than any generation could bear.'[84] Brittain gave an account of her war experiences in her autobiographical *Testament of Youth* (1933). In *Honourable Estate*, a novel published in 1936, she described the many changes in manners and morals that had taken place since – and because of – the war. Bertrand Russell wrote in 1918 that, 'One sees how our generation is a little mad, because it has allowed itself glimpses of the truth, and the truth is spectral, insane, ghastly.'[85]

The brutality of the war had made many of Edward's generation long for a new kind of society, free of the social injustice that had characterized the pre-war world. 'The dark ages are past and the twentieth century rolls on!' declared one of Edward's subjects.[86] 'Your words and actions since you have been King have made us, and thousands of people like us,' wrote one woman,

realise that you are far closer to the people in your aims and beliefs than any previous Sovereign. We admire your courage and honesty, your pacifism and your sympathy with the people in the Distressed Areas . . . And specially for disliking red carpets & all they stand for. You appear to us to belong to the Spirit of the Age.[87]

This spirit was contrasted with the decay and self-interest of the governing classes. 'England needs a good hoovering', wrote one woman to Edward, emphasizing her point by referring to the vacuum cleaner, which was starting to simplify housework in the homes of the better-off. But 'these politicians and folk of a previous generation', she added, 'refuse to see the grime and dust their antiquated hard brushes cannot cope with . . . We feel that *you* are the hand with the Hoover and hope you will continue – we are with you.'[88]

The hearts of Baldwin and his Government must have sunk when they heard after the King's visit to South Wales that he was making plans to visit *another* Special Area – this time, the North-East. The King 'asked for big maps of Tyneside and the North-East districts', reported the *Daily Mirror*. 'Minister of Labour Brown was phoned for consultation several times,' it added, 'and officials were called to the Palace to help to arrange the programme.'[89] The local press in Wales was delighted: 'The second Special Areas tour, we learn, will probably take place in February. And it may extend to Westmoreland and Cumberland.'[90] Local dignitaries in the North-East region and the Tyne Improvement Commission in Newcastle rushed letters of enthusiasm to the Special Areas headquarters.[91] It may have been Malcolm Stewart, the outgoing Commissioner for the Special Areas, who recommended such a visit to the King, during the royal dinner party at Usk on 17 November. Certainly Stewart had spoken more than once of the desirability of the King visiting the North-East.[92] On 1 December, when Dawson was having lunch at the Travellers, he ran into Tommy Lascelles, a royal courtier. Dawson noted in his private diary that Lascelles 'looked thoroughly worn and told me that he was busily engaged in arranging another Royal tour ... which he felt in his heart would never come off.'[93]

Nobody seemed to know whether the King was *really* making plans for another royal tour, or whether it was just a rumour. 'So far as I have yet been able to ascertain, the story about the King's visit to the North-East in the near future is nothing more than a *Daily Mail* stunt', replied an official at the Special Areas Commission to a letter of enquiry.[94] But even a rumour must have horrified the Government. For although there would be opportunities in the North-East to show economic recovery, such a trip would have to include Jarrow – which had an unemployment rate as high as 80 per cent. In the very month before Edward's visit to South Wales in 1936, protesting jobless steelworkers had walked all the way from Jarrow to London, where they cheered King Edward in the Mall.[95] The march had been organized by the local council, with the support of both Labour and Conservative councillors, and was covered sympathetically by the press and in newsreels. 'They're foot-slogging all the way, 280 miles,' reported the narrator of British Movietone's *Jarrow Crusade*, which was shown in cinemas on 8 October 1936. 'Everyone must sympathize', it added, 'with this orderly demonstration which has such a deserving object. Here's wishing them a happy march and good luck at the end of it!'[96] The next report by British Movietone, *Jarrow Marchers*, told the story of their arrival in London. Ellen Wilkinson, said the soundtrack, was at the marchers' head, 'and marching with them is the dog that has joined the crusade. The demonstration has been most orderly. Their object – a petition to aid their town – a worthy one. So here's the very best of luck to them – every one.'[97] Baldwin refused to meet the Jarrow marchers on their arrival in London. 'This is the way civil strife begins,' he said, 'and civil strife may not end until there is civil war.'[98] But the nation was deeply touched by the marchers' desperate plight.

It was certain that a visit by King Edward to the North-East would be given full attention by the media and the newsreels. Once again, cinema-goers would see Edward walking among the poor and work-less. Once again, he might say that 'Something must be done.' It was not an attractive prospect for Baldwin's Government or for any of the Establishment who were fearful of change.

4

'King to marry Wally'

The growing intimacy of Wallis and Edward was watched with apprehension by the small circle around the King. Concern started to grow
that Edward might want to *marry* Mrs Simpson – and make her his
Queen. This was not a welcome prospect. 'So long as you have a
Queen,' observed Cecil Headlam, the Conservative MP for County
Durham, 'she must be head of Society and no one really wants anyone
in that position unless she is a lady.' Supposing then, he added,

the King had pitched upon some young woman of virgin purity, but with a
cockney accent or something of that kind – it is ridiculous to suggest that she
would have made a suitable Queen . . . if you want a King and a Court, you
must recognize the fact that it implies class distinctions and forms and etiquette
– not social equality.[1]

However, there was little that anyone could do, from a constitutional
point of view, to prevent an unacceptable marriage by the King. For
Britain's monarch was free to marry anyone he liked, except a Roman
Catholic. The Royal Marriages Act of 1772 gave him the power to
prohibit the marriage of any member of the family, no matter what
their age might be – but nobody had the legal right to prohibit his own
marriage. The King was entitled to please himself.

On the very day that King George V died, 20 January 1936, Stanley
Baldwin had summoned Duff Cooper to 10 Downing Street to discuss
Edward's 'relations' with Mrs Simpson. Baldwin told Duff that 'if it
becomes generally known the country won't stand it.' If she were
'what I call a respectable whore', he said, then he wouldn't mind. By

this, observed Duff in his diary, he meant somebody whom the Prince occasionally saw in secret but didn't spend his whole time with. 'I think the Prince's staff are very much against him', added Duff.[2]

On 13 February 1936, just a few weeks after the start of Edward's reign, Ramsay MacDonald went to Buckingham Palace and noticed the courtiers' disapproval of the King. He recorded in his diary that he 'found the folks there not happy. Mrs S[impson]: Belvedere arriving at 3 a.m. & so on.' Lord Wigram, who had been Private Secretary to George V, told MacDonald that Edward 'wants [to] marry & get rid of her husband; in this his mind seems to be made up.'[3]

However, Edward's affair with Mrs Simpson was not the only source of friction between the King and his courtiers. He did get on well with his own staff, such as his cousin Lord Louis Mountbatten, his equerry Charles Lambe, and Ulrick Alexander, who was the Keeper of the Privy Purse and who was devoted to him. But he was treated with suspicion and distrust by the courtiers who were loyal to the styles and values of his father, George V. 'Clearly King G.'s men are not for King E.', observed Cecil Headlam in his diary entry for 18 November 1936, the day on which Edward began his tour of South Wales.[4] In an article entitled 'Palace battle', the intellectual magazine *This Week* observed that those members of the court who in the last reign had occupied positions in which they could influence the throne were bitterly disappointed that this power had come to an end.[5]

Lord Wigram, who initially served the new King as Private Secretary, soon resigned, to be replaced by Major Hardinge. 'Before very long,' wrote Sir Horace Wilson, Chief Industrial Advisor to the Prime Minister, 'we knew from Lord Wigram and others that there was grave doubt' that any hopes for the King's reign would be fulfilled. Before Wigram went, said Sir Horace, he told Baldwin of his fears and made it clear that, in his view, this was a case where it was almost impossible to appeal to reason and judgement.[6] There were regularly used channels of communication between the top levels of the civil service, the royal household and government. These were augmented by the multiple connections knitting Society together – Wigram's wife was Neville Chamberlain's daughter, for example.

Edward had begun to replace some of his father's courtiers, a process that was customary for any new monarch. This did not please the old guard. When Lord Cromer agreed to stay on as Lord Chamberlain, he did so, he said, out of a sense of duty rather than desire – because he knew 'that war was in effect declared against the old gang'.[7] Cosmo Gordon Lang, the Archbishop of Canterbury, who had been a long-standing intimate of George V and a key figure in his court, took the same view. 'There is not only a new reign, but a new *régime*,' he lamented. 'I can only be most thankful for what has been, and for what is to be, hope for the best.'[8]

Charles Lambe was aware of a 'great deal of whispering and secrecy', with 'one courtier always bleating, a centre of discontent. Another – *ancien régime* – outraged, pompous and ineffectual.'[9] Edward was evidently not able or not willing to take control and manage his royal staff. Lambe observed that from the start of Edward's reign, the organization seemed wrong:

The nominal Executive Head was the Lord Chamberlain but inside the Palace there was no Chief of Staff. Consequently the good old atmosphere of competition for the King's Ear prevailed, as it must always have done in history. A really big understanding man could have made the system work by earning not only the loyalty of his own department but of all the many others who, while trying to co-operate, owed him no direct allegiance in a disciplinary sense.[10]

If Edward had managed to take charge, he might have secured the court's backing and support. Even Wigram could not help liking him. He 'confessed' to Hilda Runciman, the wife of the President of the Board of Trade, that the King

was quite irresistible in spite of being very trying and annoying to a sec[retary]: . . . Wigram said he took care to avoid a quarrel . . . just changed the subject, but of course he has to tell him his duty and he only wishes he had had him younger![11]

But in any case, Edward – as Prince of Wales, and then as King – found many aspects of court life absurd. One of these was the 'coming out' of girls during the London season, when Society girls were presented to the monarch personally. Contemporary newsreels show how bored he was by these occasions: at a Palace garden party in July 1936 he was seen to give each girl a hurried nod and then, when it began to rain, he abruptly brought the ceremony to a close.[12] At the State Opening of Parliament on 3 November 1936, he arrived in a Daimler and wore a cocked hat, as Admiral of the Fleet. This angered many members of the court, who expected him to travel in a gilded coach drawn by a team of eight horses and to wear a golden crown.[13] Edward's dress was a further source of annoyance – he preferred comfortable clothes, rejecting the starched shirts and rigid dress conventions favoured by his father. At a formal meeting at the Jockey Club he caused a minor sensation by appearing in a lounge suit and straw hat, when his official hosts had donned morning coats and top hats in his honour.[14] His brother Albert did not approve of these sartorial innovations. In a letter to Lord Londonderry about what decorations to wear at small dances, he said,

I will have a talk about it with my brother this coming week . . . I know you will not repeat this, but he is rather difficult on these matters & has different ideas about them from anyone else. We ought to conform to what he does, really, but this is often difficult knowing that he is in the wrong, or at least out of order with what has been done on a similar occasion previously.[15]

Edward was equally 'out of order' in his attitude to the routine of the royal circuit established by his father, which he largely dropped. He also introduced a new air of informality. The Deputy Comptroller of Supply at Buckingham Palace was surprised to find that from time to time

we had visits from the King. He would suddenly appear in the kitchens, the cellars, and the store rooms, or other 'behind the scenes' parts of the Palace, walking round, alone, or with one equerry, on tours of inspection. It was all very informal, and quite unlike anything we had seen King George V do at the Palace.[16]

In a way, he added, 'it was quite a refreshing change after the rigidly fixed time-table of King George V's day, when you could predict with absolute certainty the movements of the King and Queen several months, indeed, a year ahead.'[17]

Nor did Edward enjoy the standard leisure pursuits of upper-class men, such as hunting and shooting, which had been the favourite pastimes of his father. While out stalking at Balmoral, Edward disappointed everyone by taking nothing more lethal than a cine-camera with which to 'shoot' the stags.[18] 'The fact is,' wrote the *South Wales Argus* approvingly on 19 November 1936,

that His Majesty does not like shooting either stags or birds. In this he is a great contrast to his late father. With George V all shooting was a passion and he had shot not only stags, pheasants and partridges in Great Britain, but all kinds of wild animals all over the world.[19]

Indeed, shooting had occupied George's leisure time for six months of the year (at one pheasant shoot he shot a thousand out of the total bag of four thousand birds).[20] Alexander Hardinge also loved to shoot: his letters to Helen Cecil, when they were engaged, reported on numerous grouse shoots at Balmoral. On one day in the summer of 1922, he reported a 'fine shoot' of 1,335 grouse.[21] In order to procure more daylight for shooting, George V had kept the clocks at Sandringham half an hour fast. Edward and some others, including the Duke of York and Queen Mary,[22] had disliked this eccentric way of doing things, and just hours after his father's death, Edward put the clocks back from 'Sandringham Time' to Greenwich Mean Time. Senior courtiers were dismayed,[23] and Archbishop Lang lamented, 'I wonder what other customs will be put back also!'[24]

But many others approved. It was one of the ways, observed the American journalist John Gunther, in which Edward began his reign on a note 'of sensible modernity' – at once, it was apparent that 'a new freshness, a note of informality and daring, was blowing through royal affairs.'[25] 'The trouble is,' claimed one of his subjects sympathetically, 'that you are a hundred years ahead of your time. All advanced thinkers are with you.'[26]

Edward was a man who 'Prefers a Simple Life', reported the *South Wales Argus* with satisfaction.[27] He liked 'gardening and golf and jigsaw puzzles and dancing to the gramophone and even darts.'[28] In the evening, he did his embroidery – he had learnt from Queen Mary how to do gros point.[29] He frequented nightclubs such as the Kit Kat, the Café de Paris, and especially his favourite, the Embassy Club on Bond Street, where he and Wallis relaxed by dancing and listening to jazz and other modern music. Here they spent evenings with Prince George and his wife Marina, and mixed with musicians, artists and writers, including the novelist Michael Arlen, author of the best-selling *The Green Hat* (the Embassy reserved special tables for both Edward and Arlen). Edward regularly played polo with Sir Philip Sassoon, who shared his interest in social welfare and had built a model working-class housing estate in Folkestone, with a free dental clinic.[30] Despite these relatively simple pleasures, Edward gained the reputation of a playboy. But he was most unlike a typical playboy of the time, such as Aly Khan, the heir to the immense fortune of his father, the Aga Khan. Aly Khan's interests were strictly limited to polo ponies, fast cars and beautiful women.

In the atmosphere of resentment and mistrust that dominated the royal court, it was inevitable that gossip about King Edward VIII would thrive – especially the rumour that he planned to marry Wallis. On 10 October 1936, Alexander Hardinge visited the Duke of York at his house on Piccadilly to warn him that the situation was so grave that it 'might end with the abdication of his elder brother'.[31] This was an odd warning to give, since – as Hardinge himself observed in his diary – there was 'nothing concrete on which any representation could be based.'[32] Hardinge was a man of absolute rectitude – so absolute, indeed, as to be inflexible. For him, there was a correct way and an incorrect way of doing things, and his conception of 'correct' was closely bound up with tradition and with the values and customs of the narrow social circle to which he and his family belonged. Edward and Hardinge were the same age and had been in the same Guards regiment during the war, but Hardinge's loyalties lay elsewhere: he had been King George V's Assistant Private Secretary for sixteen years, and his attitudes reflected those of the previous court. Sir Horace

Wilson had his doubts about the decision to appoint Hardinge as Edward's Private Secretary: 'his feelings seem to have led him to make remarks that were to say the least of it tactless and some of them were said to have been retailed to the King.'[33] Hardinge was not at all a suitable Private Secretary for Edward VIII, who would have benefited from the firm support of a more gentle and humorous man, particularly one who was in tune with modern ideas.

The Prime Minister, Stanley Baldwin, decided to see whether there was anything concrete underneath all the rumours of a possible marriage. On 14 October he sought an interview with the King, hoping to discover some information, one way or the other. But to his disappointment, the King chose not to raise the subject of Mrs Simpson at all. The next day, matters came to a head. Hardinge was telephoned by the Press Association with the news that Wallis Simpson was suing for divorce. The case was set down for trial on 27 October at Ipswich Assizes – 'Of all places!' sneered Sir John Simon, the Home Secretary, when he heard.[34] Until 1920, all actions had been heard before the High Court in London; but then, over the protests of the London lawyers, it was agreed that 'poor persons' and undefended actions could be heard in certain assize towns, which reduced the costs of a divorce. To Simon, therefore, Ipswich was horribly vulgar. But the lists in London were full for a year or more, and Mrs Simpson and the King were anxious to have the matter dealt with before the coronation, which was set for the following June.[35] And Ipswich was away from London and seemed more discreet.

Hardinge immediately contacted the Prime Minister, urging him to see the King and to arrange for the divorce proceedings to be stopped. The danger in which they placed the King, he believed, 'was becoming every day greater . . . it was clear that once Mrs Simpson was in a position to marry the King, grave constitutional – and not only moral – issues might only too easily arise.' He added, 'there was little doubt what the opinion of the people would be, once they were allowed to know the facts.'[36] Given the narrow circle in which the Hardinge family moved, however, it would have been difficult for him to estimate 'the opinion of the people'.

The Prime Minister met for discussions with Hardinge and his wife,

Helen, on 17 October. Remarkably, he was fired up with energy to deal with the crisis. Over the summer and early autumn he had been forced by exhaustion to take three months of rest; and on returning to Westminster, he confessed to a friend that he was 'not yet sure whether he could stand the strain of heavy Parliamentary work.'[37] But now he was somehow revived by this new challenge. He took it upon himself to ask the King for an audience. This time he planned to ask the King directly about Mrs Simpson and the implications of her divorce. Charles Lambe, driving to Sandringham on 18 October, found on his arrival an urgent telephone message from Baldwin for the King. Lambe had no idea why Baldwin was so eager to see Edward, but discovered the reason next day: 'Next morning, after breakfast, Tommy Lascelles [a courtier] said, "Isn't this Ipswich business frightful." That was the first I knew. He then told me that it was on account of the divorce that the PM wanted to see the King.'[38]

The Prime Minister and the King finally met at Fort Belvedere at ten o'clock on the morning of Tuesday 20 October. They repaired to the octagonal drawing room and sat in front of the fire. Baldwin was apparently at his ease, but he betrayed some anxiety when he asked for a whisky and soda. When the butler had brought a tray for him, wrote Edward in his memoir,

Mr Baldwin rose and, picking up the decanter and a glass, looked inquiringly at me, asking, 'Sir, when?'

As gravely as I could, I hoped even severely, I answered, 'No, thank you, Mr Baldwin; I never take a drink before seven o'clock in the evening.'

The Prime Minister seemed to give a slight start, then went ahead and poured his own drink.[39]

They spoke for an hour. Baldwin outlined his concerns about the King's friendship with Wallis and about the stories in the American and Canadian press. If they were to continue, he said, this might endanger the position of the monarchy. He finally moved to the heart of the matter: Wallis's divorce petition. 'Sir, must the case really go on?' asked Baldwin. Edward wrote later that he brushed the question aside. He had no right, he said firmly, to interfere in the affairs of another individual, simply because she was a friend of the King.[40]

Baldwin was consulting a number of people on the royal matter, including Geoffrey Dawson, the editor of *The Times*. 'As for the Government the Prime Minister probably saw a great deal more of me at this time than he did of any other journalist', Dawson admitted, but added in his defence that this 'was due rather to an old friendship and habit of discussion than to the slightest desire to influence me. He never in fact told me any secrets, nor did I ask for them.'[41] Other men with whom the Prime Minister spoke included elder statesmen and civil-service mandarins. On 21 October, Baldwin met 'on this business' with Sir Horace Wilson, who was his economic adviser (later to become Neville Chamberlain's chief confidant during the appeasement period, and Head of the Civil Service in 1939).[42]

On 26 October, the Archbishop of Canterbury, Cosmo Gordon Lang, called on Alexander Hardinge to discuss the royal crisis. So did Geoffrey Dawson. 'My husband was grateful to Mr Dawson for calling,' wrote Mrs Hardinge, 'for it provided him with a rare opportunity to confide in an outsider whose discretion he trusted.'[43] These men inhabited a narrow world, with their own exclusive meeting-places. Dawson, the Archbishop, Lord Halifax and Lord Simon were all Fellows of All Souls College, Oxford. They also met at Hatfield House in Hertfordshire, the seat of the influential Cecil family and home of the current Lord Salisbury. The Hardinges were often at Hatfield, because Helen Hardinge was the daughter of Lord Edward Cecil (and therefore a granddaughter of Lord Salisbury, the Conservative Prime Minister of the Victorian era). Cosmo Lang met with the Prime Minister at Hatfield on 1 November.

The Archbishop viewed the idea of Edward marrying Wallis with horror. How could he crown a king who was married to a woman twice divorced, with both ex-husbands still living? It was bad enough, as he wrote in a note to Buckingham Palace shortly after George V's death, that Edward 'knows little, and, I fear, cares little, about the Church and its affairs'.[44] In a diary he kept in 1936, Archbishop Lang recorded that 'as the months passed . . . the thought of my having to consecrate *him* as King weighed on me as a heavy burden. Indeed, I considered whether I could bring myself to do so.' His only comfort was a presentiment that the decision would be taken out of his hands: 'But I had a *sense* that circumstances might change. I could only pray that they might, either outwardly or in his own soul.'[45] For now, though, he was uncertain how to proceed. A particular difficulty for him was that an evangelistic campaign was being planned for 1937, in association with the coronation. This campaign, 'A Recall to Religion', was going to urge the people of Britain to dedicate themselves to the service of God and their country.[46] The 'recall' was felt to be necessary because of the dwindling membership of the Church of England.

Most citizens of Britain at this time were Christian in background: Church of England, Roman Catholic or Nonconformist. But religious faith was losing its hold. One important reason was the brutality of the Great War, and the sight of bishops and priests blessing guns and tanks. Ecclesiastical anathemas counted for much less, noted the historian John Grigg, than those who pronounced them liked to believe.[47] Many ordinary people were not bothered, for example, that their King did not attend church. 'It is said you are entirely indifferent to the public practice of religion', wrote one of Edward's subjects living near Worcester, who was a Christian. But he added, 'I don't think that matters. What does is that you do many Christian acts. You love your fellow man and therefore love God.'[48] The King 'is a real Christian,' wrote one middle-aged Scottish woman, 'following Christ in deeds not words, helping his Brother Man, visiting the poor, looking after those in lowly walks in life.'[49] Many took a dim view of 'Bishops and old Church Law & Phraseology which no man worries about these days, being too busy trying to keep the wolf from the door.'[50] A contrast was drawn between Christianity and 'Churchianity – which is not true Christianity',[51] and few people had patience with 'muddling ministers and pompous parsons'.[52]

Nonetheless, the Church of England was still a force to be reckoned with, because it was the established church. In Wales, a massive Nonconformist campaign had brought about the disestablishment of the Anglican Church in the principality in 1920. But in England, nothing had changed. The Prime Minister had the ultimate say in the selection of bishops and the appointment of the Archbishop of Canterbury. Parliament was opened with prayers, and the Cup Final was introduced by the mass singing of the hymn 'Abide with Me'. Twenty-six Anglican bishops sat in the House of Lords, and Anglican dignitaries officiated at just about every important state occasion. Against this background, the growing lack of religious faith among ordinary people had little impact on the role of the Church in the life of the nation.

It was reasonable enough, once Wallis's divorce suit was announced, to assume that Edward was thinking of marriage. For, as Hilda Runciman pointed out, 'there seemed no adequate reason for the disadvantage of the divorce scandal unless marriage was intended'.[53] Only once before had Edward wanted to marry. In France in 1917 he had fallen in love with a Red Cross nurse, Rosemary Millicent Leveson-Gower, who was the daughter of the Duke of Sutherland. Although she was charming and beautiful, with very blonde hair and blue eyes, Edward was most struck by her compassion for soldiers suffering from shell-shock. In February 1918, when they were both in England, he asked Lady Rosemary to marry him – and despite some initial hesitation she agreed. But the marriage was forbidden by Edward's father, George V. He felt it would not be suitable because Lady Rosemary's mother was separated from her second husband (her first husband had died), and her brother, the Earl of Rosslyn, had been twice divorced, twice bankrupt, and was a heavy drinker.[54]

In the following year, 1919, Edward heard of Lady Rosemary's engagement to Lord Ednam. He told Freda Dudley Ward that he could not help 'feeling a little sad', because 'she was the only girl I felt I ever could marry & I knew it was '*défendu*' by my family!!' He hoped they would be happy – 'as she's such a darling & I guess he's a very lucky man!!'[55] After this episode he resisted his family's efforts to find him a suitable wife and objected to the constant speculation about whom he was going to marry. While in Paris in 1919, he was horrified to see a claim in the French newspapers that he was engaged to the Queen of Italy's eldest daughter. 'I've asked the Embassy to get at the French press & insist upon an immediate contradiction', he told Mrs Dudley Ward, adding that 'it naturally infuriates me, particularly as the girl has a face like a bottom!! . . .' In any case, he wrote, 'I just can't bear the thought of having to marry.'[56]

But in 1936 he *did* want to marry Wallis. 'Oh! my Wallis I know we'll have Viel Gluck to make us one this year. God bless WE', he wrote to her on New Year's Day.[57] Wallis's letters to her aunt and to Edward suggest that however much she too wanted to be 'one' with him, she was aware that any plans for marriage were so riddled with difficulty as to be almost impossible. 'I am sad because I miss you and being near and yet so far seems most unfair', she wrote to him in early February 1936, adding that 'perhaps both of us will cease to want what is hardest to have and be content with the simple way.'[58] The 'simple way', presumably, was to be a mistress rather than a wife. Decades later, Wallis stated definitively that

I told him I didn't want to be queen. All that formality and responsibility . . . I told him that if he stayed on as king, it wouldn't be the end of us. I could still come and see him and he could still come and see me. We had terrible arguments about it. But he was a mule. He said he didn't want to be king without me that if I left him, he would follow me wherever I went.

She added, 'What could I do? What *could* I do?'[59]

Keeping a mistress was unacceptable to Edward. But it was a practical solution, one which had been shown to work in the numerous affairs conducted over the centuries between kings and mistresses. Mrs Simpson's presence would have been acceptable to the British as his mistress, believed Helen Hardinge, as this would raise no constitutional issue – 'but not as his wife, which would'.[60] Most recently, the affair between Alice Keppel and King Edward VII had demonstrated the viability of such a relationship, provided it was managed with care (it also showed the tolerance of the long-suffering Queen Alexandra). Mrs Keppel had met Edward VII when he was Prince of Wales, in 1898: she was twenty-nine, he was fifty-six. All of Society knew about the affair, and many of the general public too. Mrs Keppel, with her husband and children, accompanied the King to Biarritz for Easter on the royal yacht *Britannia*. Edward VII had other mistresses – the Princesse de Sagan, the Countess of Warwick, Lillie Langtry –

but none of them meant as much to him as Alice Keppel. After Edward VII's death, Alec Hardinge wrote a tribute to her 'wonderful discretion'.[61] She was still a busy member of Society in 1936, by which time her lover's grandson was on the throne.

But Edward did not want a discreet affair – he desired nothing less than a proper marriage. According to Ernest Simpson, the King had told him so early in 1936 – 'that he was in love with his wife, and that he wanted to marry her'. This was an extraordinary piece of news. Ernest told the King that he must be mad to entertain such an idea; that he must realize that she was already married and, even if she were divorced, it would be impossible for him to marry a woman who had been twice divorced. He had a long talk with the King, pointing out the position he held in the state and the traditions of the royal family with regard to family life. The King became very emotional, said Ernest, and eventually broke down.[62]

Winston Churchill understood Edward's wish to marry the woman he loved. Thinking about Edward's life as Prince of Wales and then King, he ventured that 'A life of flittering public pomp without a home and some human comfort in the background would not be endurable to the vast majority of men. One must have something real somewhere. Otherwise far better die.'[63] Edward wanted 'something real' like the marriage enjoyed by his younger brother George, the Duke of Kent, and his wife Marina. In the autumn of 1934, the thirty-two-year-old Prince George had married Princess Marina of Greece and Denmark, to his family's immense relief. 'How much in love Princess Marina is with Prince George', oozed Jean, Lady Hamilton. It was the romance of the year. 'She is the one woman with whom I could be happy to spend the rest of my life', wrote the Duke of Kent. 'We laugh at the same sort of thing. She beats me at most games and doesn't give a damn how fast I drive when I take her out in the car.'[64]

Although George was eight and a half years his junior, wrote Edward in his memoirs, they were more than brothers – they were close friends, too, with similar characters and a shared sense of humour.[65] The Duke of Kent was the most cultured and artistic of all the children of George V: he played the piano and knew a great deal about music and antiques. He had also been very kind to John, the youngest child of the family, who was mentally handicapped and epileptic. John was kept away from the rest of the family and from the world in a cottage in Sandringham, until his early death in 1919. George had visited him every day when he was at Sandringham; when he was not, he regularly sent him postcards.

Despite her royal connections, Marina had had to struggle: at one time she had posed for publicity photographs to promote Pond's Cold Cream, and in Paris she had even travelled by public transport. But nobody seemed to mind – or perhaps they simply didn't know. 'It all sounded so young, gay and fairy tale-ish', enthused Lady Hamilton, from the moment that Marina and her two sisters 'alighted in their pretty light garments at our dull foggy Victoria Station and lit up the platform where stood Queen Mary and Princess Mary in their dowdy clothes.'[66] Of this same meeting at Victoria Station, shortly before the wedding, George reported to Prince Paul of Yugoslavia, his future brother-in-law, that

Everyone is so delighted with her – the crowd especially – because when she arrived at Victoria Station they expected a dowdy princess – such as unfortunately my family are – but when they saw this lovely chic creature – they could hardly believe it and even the men were interested and shouted, 'Don't change – don't let them change you!' Of course she won't be changed – not if I have anything to do with it.[67]

Lady Hamilton suspected that Elizabeth, the Duchess of York, might not like this enthusiasm for Marina. She had heard that Elizabeth's hairdresser 'reports the Duchess as being in a "*très mauvais humeur*". I wonder! She always looks very sweet.'[68] Certainly the sheer beauty of Marina, Duchess of Kent – like the elegance of the pin-thin Wallis – contrasted with the more fussy and pretty appearance of Elizabeth. By 1931, comments her biographer, Penelope Mortimer, the Duchess of York had 'put on a good deal of weight; her face was rounded, her eyes smaller; she was no longer a wistful waif, a Barrie heroine, but a pneumatic mother of two with a roguish twinkle.'[69]

While Wallis was becoming more and more involved with Edward, her marriage to Ernest Simpson was crumbling. This was not helped by

Edward's manifest intoxication, which made Wallis feel sandwiched between him and Ernest. 'I had a long quiet talk with E[rnest] last night,' she wrote to Edward, 'and I felt very eanum at the end. Everything he said was so true.' She appealed to the King:

The evening was difficult as you did stay much too late. Doesn't your love for me reach to the heights of wanting to make things a little easier for me. The lovely things you say to me aren't of much value unless they are backed up by equal actions. I should have come back Sat and I didn't. Then last night you should have left by 8. Then you telephone the second time – which just did finish the evening and made a row.[70]

But Edward could not bear to leave her alone with her husband, wondering if Ernest was seeking any kind of intimacy, physical or emotional. 'I do hate and loathe the present situation', he told Wallis, '. . . and am just going mad at the mere thought (let alone knowing) that you are alone there with Ernest.' He felt keenly possessive of her and willed her to give herself to him: 'God bless WE for ever my Wallis. You know your David will love you and look after you so long as he has breath in this eanum body.'[71]

Ernest, in any case, was in love with another woman – an old school friend of Wallis's from Baltimore, Mary Raffray. His infidelity had come to light through what Wallis would later describe as 'one of those coincidences that are stranger than fiction – a letter meant for Ernest that was inadvertently addressed to me.'[72] Mary and Ernest had spent time together in New York in 1935 and discovered they had serious feelings for each other. In the spring of 1936, Mary came to stay at Bryanston Court, and Wallis became painfully aware that it was not herself that Mary had come to see. Mary and Ernest left London for three days in a hired motor, reported Wallis to her aunt, and 'I then had them followed and of course got the expected report etc. He now says he is in love with her and she has a service flat here. Isn't it all ridiculous? Anyway, we will work it all out *beautifully* I hope.'[73] Wallis could not resist a few sour remarks about her old friend – 'Mary's clothes are rather naked for here . . . I still haven't found out how long Mary will stay. We are absolutely jammed for clothes room as she has an extensive line of undress.'[74]

Ernest and Wallis had been drifting apart for a while. Their kitchen maid thought they couldn't have been happy, because 'they were never living together, only at short intervals. Mr Simpson went away on business to Paris and to other places, and when he returned home Mrs Simpson went away for a time.' She said that the Prince of Wales was the most frequent visitor at Bryanston Court, coming round several evenings each week, and on many occasions not leaving until after midnight – usually when Ernest was away on business. A parlour maid also noted that 'Mr Simpson was often away, sometimes abroad'.[75]

On 4 May 1936, Wallis wrote to her aunt with the news that she was planning to live apart from Ernest – not to seek a divorce, but simply to take a house in the autumn and live alone for a while. She would then be able to spend her time more freely with Edward. She was aware of the risks involved. 'Should HM fall in love with someone else,' she said,

I would cease to be as powerful or have all I have today. Perhaps I have made a few new friends and kept some old ones . . . but I expect nothing. I should be comfortably off and have had a most interesting experience, one that does not fall to everyone's lot and the times are exciting now and countries and politics madly thrilling. I have always had the courage for the new things that life sometimes offers.

She was worried, though, about Edward's plan for them to marry. 'The K on the other hand', she told her aunt, 'has another thing only in his mind. Whether I would allow such a drastic action depends on many things and events and I should never allow him if possible . . . to do anything that would hurt the country and help the socialists.' In any case, she added, 'there is a new life before me whereas I can't go back to the old – nor can I continue as I am.' She was 'quite prepared', she insisted, 'to pay for a mistake.'[76]

Despite this initial show of confidence, Wallis started to feel less secure as the prospect of a divorce from Ernest became more real. On

16 September she wrote to Edward from Paris, where she was confined to bed with a heavy cold, to break off their relationship. She thought it would be a good idea, she said, if she were to return to live with her husband. 'I am sure', she explained, that 'you and I would only create disaster together. I shall always read all about you – believing only half! – and you will know that I want you to be happy.'[77] However, Edward appears to have taken little account of these anxieties, pushing forward instead with his plans for their future together. Wallis, in her turn, made no further mention of any thoughts of returning to Ernest. She finally gave way to the King's pressure and prepared to divorce her husband.

In order to qualify for a divorce hearing at Ipswich, Wallis had to establish her residence there by living within the area of the court's jurisdiction for a month. In October 1936 she went to stay at Beach House in the nearby seaside resort of Felixstowe with her friends George and Kitty Hunter, and a housekeeper. Her chauffeur and a detective checked into a hotel that was next door but one. The detective slept at the hotel during the day and was on guard duty during the night at Beach House. The hotel was besieged by American reporters.[78]

Wallis felt very much alone, and doubts rushed into her head. 'I can't help but feel you will have trouble in the House of Commons etc and may be forced to go', she wrote to Edward. 'I can't put you in that position. Also I'm terrified that this judge here will lose his nerve – and then what? I am sorry to bother you my darling – but I feel like an animal in a trap.' She asked him to think things over and decide what best to do: 'Together I suppose we are strong enough to face this mean world – but separated I feel eanum and scared for you, your safety etc. Also the Hunters say I might easily have a brick thrown at my car. Hold me tight please David.'[79] Edward swept her anxieties aside. 'I know it sounds easy to say dont [sic] worry,' he replied, 'but dont too much please Wallis. I'm doing half the worrying and looking after things this end. Oh! how I long for you here and everybody and everything at The Fort misses you too dreadfully . . . God bless WE my beloved sweetheart.'[80] The King secretly visited Wallis at Beach House, staying overnight. Two valets came too, and were put up for that night at the hotel; they carefully avoided signing the visitors' register.[81]

The night before the divorce hearing, wrote Wallis in her memoirs, she spent in sleepless worry, pacing the floor. She was terrified that what she was about to do would harm the King and ruin any possibility of their spending the rest of their lives together. And she was unable to make any plans of her own for her future. For a woman as independent as Wallis, this must have been a terrifying situation.

The case of *Simpson* v. *Simpson* was heard at Ipswich Assizes on 27 October. Preparations for the hearing had been made at Fort Belvedere, where Edward and Wallis consulted their legal advisors – Walter Monckton, who had been appointed Attorney-General to the Duchy of Cornwall in 1932; George Allen, the King's solicitor; and a brilliant barrister, Norman Birkett, who had been instructed to appear for the petitioner.[82] The hearing itself was no different from any other divorce hearing, apart from the presence of a large number of American journalists. Evidence was furnished of Mr Simpson's misconduct by employees of the Hotel de Paris, at Bray, in Berkshire, who said they had found him in bed with a woman named in the petition as Buttercup Kennedy. (This was probably Mary Raffray, who was known in London by the nickname 'Buttercup' because of some headgear she liked to wear.) The suit was undefended, and the decree nisi was duly awarded; once it was made absolute, in April 1937, Mrs Simpson would be free to marry again. Straight after the hearing, Wallis returned to London. She went to her new home – 16 Cumberland Terrace, a furnished Regency house off Regent's Park – for which she had arranged the lease before the *Nahlin* trip.

The news of Mrs Simpson's divorce was greeted with headlines in America. 'King To Marry Wally', announced the New York *Daily Mirror* on its front page. William Randolph Hearst's *New York Journal* promised in banner headlines an inch and a half deep: 'KING WILL WED WALLY'. The Boston *Record* went five inches deep with headlines announcing, 'KING SETS JUNE FOR WEDDING TO MRS SIMPSON'.

But there was barely any coverage in the British press. According to Deedes, *The Times* carried twelve lines, the *Morning Post* a ten-point paragraph and the *Daily Telegraph* twenty-two lines – 'but on an away page, sandwiched between "Colonel accused in private" and "Boy with a mania for silk stockings".'[83] This restraint was the result of special arrangements made by Lord 'Max' Beaverbrook, the owner of the *Daily Express* and the *Evening Standard*. On 16 October, at Edward's request, he had gone to Buckingham Palace (despite the fact that he was 'cursed with toothache and heavily engaged with his dentist'), where he was asked to suppress advance news of the Simpson divorce and to limit publicity after the event. The reasons Edward gave for this wish were that

Mrs Simpson was ill, unhappy, and distressed by the thought of notoriety. Notoriety would attach to her only because she had been his guest on the *Nahlin* and at Balmoral. As the publicity would be due to her association with himself, he felt it his duty to protect her.

Beaverbrook was satisfied with the request and, with the support of Esmond Harmsworth, who was the heir to Lord Rothermere's *Daily Mail* press empire and the Chairman of the Newspaper Proprietors' Association, he came to a gentleman's agreement with the rest of the British newspapers. It was understood that they would report the divorce case without any sensationalism and with no reference to the King.[84]

This discretion was not apparent in the drawing rooms of the handful of people who knew about the royal crisis. 'Everyone in this circle is convinced that the King will marry her', commented Bruce Lockhart after an evening of gossip. The only doubt, he said, was whether the wedding would be before the coronation or afterwards.[85] Diana Cooper, said Chips Channon, was convinced that Wallis and the King would marry in secret, immediately after the coronation. 'I half hope so,' he wrote in his diary, 'half believe it is fated.'[86] If he married her, argued his wife, Honor, 'he would have to abdicate immediately for if he did not, we would have unrest, a Socialist agitation and a "Yorkist" party.'[87] By a 'Yorkist' party, he meant a party of those wanting Albert, Duke of York, to be king, instead of Edward.

The day after the divorce hearing, the Hardinges had the Yorks to dinner, to bring them up to date.[88] The two families were good friends, and Elizabeth had been the maid of honour at the Hardinges' wedding in 1921. Their friendship underlined the absence of any kind of intimacy between Hardinge and Edward, since it was the King – and not the Duke of York – for whom Hardinge worked. This created a conflict of interest, which is apparent in Helen Hardinge's diary entry for 27 November 1936:

Go out to see the Duchess of York who is an angel as usual. Much cheered by those delicious children [the Princesses Elizabeth and Margaret] who came in from the swimming bath with terrific accounts of their own exploits . . . Alec saw Prince Bertie [the Duke of York] this morning. HM was surprised because his brother had dined with us![89]

Wallis had boldly told Aunt Bessie in May of 1936 that if her relationship with Edward proved to be a mistake, it was one she was willing to pay for. But she may not have expected to start paying for it so quickly, or so painfully, as she did. For it soon became clear that those people who had patronized her as Edward's mistress were not willing to approve of her as his wife. Edith, Lady Londonderry, the granddaughter of the Duke of Sutherland and the wife of the Conservative politician the Marquess of Londonderry, decided to intervene in the affair. As a key member of the highest echelon of Society, she felt she had an obligation to do something about the scandal surrounding the King. She knew all the great political figures of her time and regularly brought these influential people together at Londonderry House. At receptions to mark the opening of Parliament, Edith had stood at the top of the staircase, next to the Prime Minister, to welcome her guests. Now, she appointed herself as the spokeswoman for moral values. On Friday 6 November, at an evening party given by Emerald Cunard at her home on Grosvenor Square, she told Wallis that if the King had any idea of marrying her, he ought to give it up. The English people, she said, would never put up with a queen or king's consort who had been divorced twice and whose previous husbands were both still living.

How Lady Londonderry knew the minds of the English people, she did not reveal. Probably, it was a simple confidence in how things *ought* to be. But her warning appears to have made an impression on Wallis, who next day wrote a letter to Lady Londonderry, saying that she had thought over their conversation the night before. She was conscious, she said, that 'perhaps no one has been really frank with a certain person in telling him how the country feels about his friendship with me . . . I am going to tell him the things you told me.'[90]

Lady Londonderry's intervention was presented to Wallis as genuine concern for Edward and for the nation as a whole. More painful for Wallis was the growing hostility of the royal circle, led by Elizabeth, Duchess of York, who had snubbed her on a particularly miserable evening at Balmoral in the last week of September. At a dinner that was attended by the Yorks, Wallis had stepped forward to greet them, holding out her hand as a gesture of friendship. Edward had evidently asked Wallis to perform the role of hostess. The Duchess was furious. She walked straight past Wallis and said in a loud voice, 'I came to dine with the King.' Throughout the evening, she continued to ignore Wallis, and she and the Duke were the first to leave.[91] But if Wallis's gesture of friendship was a breach of royal etiquette, then it was Edward who was responsible. He wanted Wallis to be treated as if she were his wife, with all the social status that was attached to that position – and it must have been this that offended Elizabeth. Her rudeness cannot be explained by moral outrage at a sexual relationship outside marriage, as she had been perfectly friendly in the past to Thelma Furness.

'Poor Wallis, the cynosure of all eyes,' Chips Channon had sighed, 'she can do no right. All her tact, sweetness and charm – are they enough?'[92] Protective of Wallis, Channon was protective of Edward, too – 'not for loyalty so much as for admiration and affection for Wallis, and in indignation against those who attack her.'[93]

5

'I had declared myself'

In the middle of November 1936 came a new development in the royal crisis in the form of a letter written to the King by Alec Hardinge, his Private Secretary. Edward found the letter waiting for him on Friday 13 November, when he returned from his visit to the Home Fleet at Portland. Written on Palace stationery, it gave an account of some facts 'which I know', said Hardinge, 'to be accurate'. He warned that although the majority of the population of Britain were still ignorant of his relationship with Wallis, the silence of the press would be broken in a matter of days. And judging by letters from British subjects living in foreign countries where the press had been outspoken, he added, 'the effect will be calamitous'.[1]

Years later, Helen Hardinge explained why her husband had decided to give such a warning to the King. She said that Geoffrey Dawson had shown him a very long letter he had received from the United States which deplored the publicity surrounding the King's friendship with Mrs Simpson. The letter had been sent on 15 October by a British man living in the USA who called himself 'Britannicus in Partibus Infidelium'. In the view of Britannicus, the prevailing opinion in America was that the foundations of the British monarchy were under threat and that 'its moral authority, its honour, and its tradition cast into the dustbin'. Nothing, he said, 'would please me more than to hear that Edward VIII had abdicated his rights in favour of the heir presumptive, who I am confident would be prepared to carry on in the sterling tradition established by his father.'[2] In Dawson's view, this letter 'seemed to me to sum up opinion in America so well that it ought to be seen by others' – so he took it to Hardinge.[3]

Dawson asked Hardinge to show this letter to the King. It is surprising that either of these men regarded the Britannicus letter as being 'of historic importance', as Hardinge's wife claimed.[4] For it took a view that was altogether different from most of the American press, which was mostly delighted about Edward's relationship with Wallis.[5] Dawson, as a top newspaperman, must surely have been aware of this. Over the next few weeks, indeed, as American interest in the story grew ever stronger, Edward was sent a number of supportive letters from the USA which were enthusiastic about Edward and Wallis and congratulated them on their love for each other. Their message was more one of good luck than of condemnation. A letter from Wisconsin sent 'best wishes to yourself and Mrs Simpson', adding that Edward was Britain's own Franklin Roosevelt.[6] The President of a brewing company in Pennsylvania sent his congratulations 'on your clean and crystal clear romance'.[7] 'DO know one thing,' wrote a woman in New York City, 'that almost all the women of America are with YOU – and the women of America ARE America.'[8] Some letters of censure also arrived, such as one from a British citizen living in the USA – another 'Britannicus'. If the King 'knew the attitude of the average American toward the average Britisher', he said, then he would not subject them to such embarrassment. 'Their attitude towards us', he explained, 'is really one of envy for our superior culture'.[9]

Having justified the urgency of the matter by reference to mail from America, Hardinge continued his letter to the King by saying that the Prime Minister and senior members of the Government were meeting to decide on action. The resignation of the Government, he warned, was a real possibility. Hardinge said he had reason to know that an alternative government was impossible, which would leave only one course – a dissolution of Parliament and a general election, fought over the issue of Mrs Simpson. The King was urged to send her away immediately:

If Your Majesty will permit me to say so, there is only one step which holds out any prospect of avoiding this dangerous situation, and that is for Mrs Simpson to go abroad without further delay, and I would beg Your Majesty to give this proposal your earnest consideration before the position has become irretrievable. Owing to the changing attitude of the Press, the matter has become one of great urgency.[10]

'What a courageous & forthright role Alex played', wrote Violet Milner, Hardinge's mother-in-law, in her diary some years later. 'It was he who "belled the cat".'[11] But Edward was horrified. He felt betrayed by his Private Secretary, whose post required complete and mutual trust between himself and the king he served. A private secretary was not appointed by ministers and was not responsible to Parliament – he was a royal servant, not a civil servant.[12] It was perfectly reasonable, said Edward later, for his Private Secretary to warn him that a Cabinet crisis was impending as the result of his relations with Mrs Simpson. But it was *not* reasonable for him to be acting on behalf of the Government, which was patently the case. Edward suspected that the only person who could have given Hardinge all his information was the Prime Minister, and this was acknowledged by Hardinge himself, years later, in an article for *The Times*.[13]

Hardinge had shown a draft of his letter to Geoffrey Dawson. Knowing that this action laid him open to the accusation of conspiracy, Hardinge later justified it:

At this moment of anxiety and distress, I desperately needed an outside opinion as to the general wisdom and propriety of my letter, as well as its accuracy; and, as it seemed to me, no one could help me more over this than a man with the discretion, experience, and integrity of Geoffrey Dawson, who was at the same time very much 'in the know'.[14]

But this was disingenuous, to say the least. For Hardinge had been conspiring on the matter of this letter with various senior Ministers and civil service officials for nearly a week. On 7 November, Sir Warren Fisher, Permanent Under-Secretary at the Treasury and Head of the Civil Service, reported to Neville Chamberlain that Hardinge had come to see him that morning, 'very privately', with a suggestion which he thought was rather good. Fisher mentioned to Chamberlain an ultimatum that was under consideration – presumably by himself, Chamberlain, Baldwin and others – which would force the King's hand. But, he said, Hardinge had proposed an intermediate stage, rather than present the ultimatum straightaway.[15] He had drafted a letter to the King, to be signed by Baldwin, which urged Edward to end his association with Mrs Simpson. The letter, which was copied to Chamberlain, warned of a 'very disturbing movement of public opinion' and a revulsion of feeling that might threaten the stability of the nation and of the Empire.[16]

As well as this draft letter, Fisher sent Chamberlain a copy of a letter, again drafted by Hardinge and to be signed by Baldwin, that was more forceful and was framed in such a way as to represent an ultimatum. If the King did not give up Mrs Simpson, it warned, then the Prime Minister and the Government would resign.[17]

Accompanying the two letters was a copy of a memorandum written by Parliamentary Counsel on 5 November which discussed the role of the sovereign's Ministers in giving advice. The ultimate sanction lying behind the tender of advice, explained the memorandum, was the resignation of the Ministers. 'But I assume', added the memorandum's author, 'that on an issue of such gravity they would have secured the concurrence of the leaders of the Opposition in the step which they were proposing to take, in which case the King would have no alternative Ministry on whom he could fall back for support.' The King would therefore be left with no Ministers at all, and 'since no English monarch could hope to govern this country even for a day as a dictator,' unless he had a very substantial body of public opinion behind him, he would be compelled either to accept the advice tendered 'or to abdicate'. If abdication were a possibility, added the memorandum, then 'there is an heir presumptive to the Throne ... whose qualifications for the succession are not in doubt.'[18]

The letter which Hardinge handed to the King on 13 November – signed by himself, not by Baldwin – was a blend of the drafts written by himself and sent by Fisher to Chamberlain on 7 November. It had some of the informality of the first draft letter, but it contained the threat of the second, and was underpinned by the advice and information in the memorandum by Parliamentary Counsel. Clearly, therefore, the writing of Hardinge's letter was not a personal act by Hardinge himself, with some assistance from Dawson, but the outcome of a conspiracy of strategic thinking and planning. On the day that Hardinge presented his letter to the King, Baldwin had held an urgent meeting of senior Cabinet Ministers – Neville Chamberlain; Viscount Halifax, Lord Privy Seal and Leader of the House of Lords; Sir John Simon; Walter Runciman; and Ramsay MacDonald, the Lord President. After the meeting, Baldwin went to see Hardinge.[19] Presumably this was the moment when Hardinge was instructed to give the King a letter signed by himself, but which in effect had been written by a group of men who were all hostile to the King's position.

The conspirators carefully covered their tracks, for it appeared that Hardinge had decided himself to write to the King. Sir Horace Wilson lied about the background to the letter in a later account of the royal crisis: 'This letter was written by Major Hardinge on Friday 13th November. He brought it to the Prime Minister, enquiring whether Mr Baldwin saw any objection to his reference to possible action by Ministers. I was present . . .' Sir Horace went so far as to criticize Hardinge's letter, saying that it 'may very well have made the worst possible impression'.[20] This cover-up was most likely arranged as a safeguard against any allegations that members of the royal household might have cooperated with the Government in dealing with the King. As Fisher had commented in the margin of his letter of 7 November to Chamberlain, 'Of course I assured Hardinge that he has *not* been in the picture.'[21]

Edward was shocked by Hardinge's letter, as well as hurt and angry, but he did not immediately tell Wallis what had happened. Always trying to protect her from worry, he was especially keen not to cause her any concern, as her aunt had arrived recently from Washington and they were enjoying a weekend together at the Fort. Wallis noticed that he was preoccupied and his manner abstracted. 'All the upwelling of joy that he had brought back from the Fleet', she observed, 'was gone . . . But he gave no hint or sign of what was troubling him.' The next day, he showed her the letter. She was stunned, realizing that the Government was preparing for a showdown with Edward. Her first reaction was to declare that she would indeed leave the country, as Hardinge had advocated – but Edward would have none of it. Instead, he told her that he was going to send for Baldwin the next day, to have it out with him. 'I'm going to tell him that if the country won't approve our marrying, I'm ready to go.'[22]

According to Wallis's own account, this was the first time that the possibility of him stepping down from the throne was mentioned between them. She was appalled, imploring him not even to talk of such a thing. But he was adamant that he would never give her up. Later, Wallis reproached herself for not leaving England at this time, 'the fateful moment – the last when any action of mine could have prevented the crisis'. But what kept her from going, she said later, was 'the fundamental inability of a woman to go against the urgent wishes of the man she loves.' Edward was determined that she stay. 'He insisted that he needed me,' wrote Wallis, 'and as a woman in love I was prepared to go through rivers of woe, seas of despair, and oceans of agony for him.'[23] Friends said that Wallis and Edward 'acted like a couple in love who wanted to get married, and were plainly horrified by the momentous events this simple desire had set in motion . . . You couldn't help loving them for it, they were honestly so damn naive.'[24]

But a turning point had been reached. After receiving Hardinge's letter, the King withdrew further and further from court life, where tensions had reached an unbearable level. 'I knew nothing of what passed,' wrote Lambe, his equerry, 'but could not help feeling the anxiety and stress which daily grew over everyone.'[25] In a postscript to his letter, Hardinge had added that he was going after dinner on the day of writing, 13 November, to shoot at High Wycombe; the Post Office, he said, would have his telephone number and 'I am of course entirely at Your Majesty's disposal if there is anything at all that you want.'[26] But Edward did not respond either then, or at any time later, to Hardinge's offer of an open door. He left him in his post in Buckingham Palace, but eschewed any contact with him beyond what was absolutely necessary (such as the enforced proximity to Hardinge on the royal tour of South Wales, which must have been an ordeal). He now turned for advice and support to Walter Monckton, an outstanding lawyer who was not only Attorney-General to the Duchy of Cornwall, but was also a long-standing friend from his student days at Oxford.

Because Edward believed that Hardinge was reporting to Baldwin, he tried to conceal from him Monckton's visits to Buckingham Palace. Although their meetings were held in a room on the ground floor, to which there was direct access along a passage from the Privy Purse entrance, the King told Monckton not to use that entrance – because it would have brought him past the Private Secretaries' rooms. Instead, Monckton used the visitors' entrance on the other side of the Palace. Here he was shown into a lift, taken to the top floor, marched across the Palace, taken down again in another lift and at last shown into the King's room. The return journey was accomplished in the same manner. But the omniscient Hardinge was not fooled – and on one occasion a footman handed Monckton a note from Hardinge, inviting him to join him for a drink on his way out.[27]

If Edward felt he was being watched, he was right. In fact, both he and Wallis – and also Ernest – were being watched in a way, and to a degree, that would have astonished them had they found out. Since 1935 they had been under surveillance by the Special Branch of the Metropolitan Police. One brief report on Edward, when he was Prince of Wales, was made by Canning, the Superintendent in charge of Special Branch, to the Commissioner of the Metropolitan Police, Sir Philip Game, on 25 March 1935.[28] A longer report by Canning was devoted to Ernest Simpson, sketching out his background and his business interests. It described the reserved and quiet Mr Simpson 'as of the "bounder" type. He makes no secret of his wife's association with P.O.W. and seems to enjoy some reflected glory because of this and to make what capital he can out of it.'[29] This contradicts Ernest's own claim, made two years later, that once he became aware that his wife was associating very frequently with the Prince of Wales, he talked to her about it. He warned her that comments in the American press might affect his business and would certainly affect him socially. He told her, he said, 'that she was going too far, but she made evasive answers and said that the matter must take its course.'[30]

The Special Branch report on Ernest Simpson adds that one of the visitors to the Simpsons' flat was Lady Emerald Cunard, who is 'reputed to be a drug addict' and who is 'the mother of the notorious Nancy Cunard who is very partial to coloured men and who created a sensation some few years ago by taking up residence in the negro quarter of New York.' The racist attitudes of Superintendent Canning – and the rumour-driven nature of his reports – are further revealed in the last sentence of the report – 'The Simpsons are regarded in some circles as Jews.'[31]

According to Canning, Mrs Simpson 'is the woman who is now associated with P.O.W. She is reputed to be very attractive and to spend lavishly on dress and entertainment.' Within the last few weeks, it stated, she had visited an antique shop in Kensington 'in company with P.O.W.':

The conversation showed that they were on very affectionate terms and addressed each other as 'Darling'. A number of purchases were made and orders given for the goods to be sent to York House and marked 'Fort Belvedere'. The opinion of the dealer expressed after his distinguished client had left was that the lady seemed to have P.O.W. completely under her thumb.

Although 'she now spends a great deal of time with P.O.W.', added the Superintendent, 'it is said that she has another secret lover who is kept by her. Particulars of the young man concerned could not be ascertained.'[32]

In a further report, dated 25 June 1935, the Superintendent told the Commissioner that he was still unable to produce these particulars, although 'Contact with the Simpsons is still being maintained.' Mrs Simpson was described as 'spending as much time as possible with P.O.W. and keeping her secret lover in the background'. Ernest Simpson was said to be 'bragging to the effect that he expects to get "high honours" before very long. He says that P.O.W. will succeed his father at no distant date. He has mentioned that he expects, at least, to be created a Baron. He is very talkative when in drink.'[33]

The 'secret lover' was finally identified by Superintendent Canning and named in a report to the Commissioner dated 3 July 1935. He was Guy Marcus Trundle, 'a very charming adventurer, very good looking, well bred and an excellent dancer. He is said to boast that every woman falls for him.' Evidently, he had also boasted about his conquest of the woman who was associated with the Prince of Wales: 'He meets Mrs Simpson quite openly at informal social gatherings as a personal friend, but secret meetings are made by appointment when intimate relations take place. Trundle receives money from Mrs Simpson as well as expensive presents.' Trundle had married in 1932 and was a 'motor engineer and salesman . . . said to be employed by the Ford Motor Company'. It appears that this information largely came from Trundle himself – 'Trundle claims to have met P.O.W. through Mrs Simpson.'[34]

It is hard to believe that Wallis Simpson could have found time for 'intimate relations' with Trundle. She found it difficult enough, as she told her aunt, to manage her marriage and the relationship with Edward, and was also caught up in a whirlwind of activities and social occasions which she found exhausting. The reports are so thin as to be suspect – they lack any information about the many eminent guests visiting Bryanston Court. As the head porter noted, 'the Mountbattens and other distinguished visitors came as guests when Mrs Simpson gave parties . . . many titled visitors attended Mrs Simpson's parties.'[35]

Canning, now promoted to Chief Constable in charge of the Criminal Investigation Department, continued to file reports to the Commissioner. One of them, dated 30 June 1936, refers to a speech given by Harry Pollitt, the leader of the Communist Party of Great Britain, at the Leeds Peace Congress in which 'he was said to have brought the house down with his declaration that "if gas masks are to be given out we should demand the same kind of gas mask for our wives as will be given to the Duchess of Kent and Mrs Simpson".' A trip to France by Wallis and an American friend, Mrs Gladys Kemp Scanlon, was also mentioned in the report:

The Special Branch officer at Folkestone had previously received a telephone message direct from Inspector Evans at Buckingham Palace notifying the journey and asking for assistance. On 6th June last Mrs Simpson, accompanied as above, returned to Folkestone from Boulogne, and Inspector Evans was at

Folkestone to meet them. Remarks by railway and shipping officials overheard by the Special Branch officer at Folkestone indicated that the association of Mrs Simpson and the King was well known there.

This report also refers to a dinner given by the King at St James's Palace and lists the guests, who included Mr and Mrs Simpson as well as the Prime Minister and his wife, Lady Diana Cooper and Duff Cooper, Colonel and Mrs Lindbergh, Lady Cunard and Lord Wigram. However, this information had been made freely available in the Court Circular, so was hardly confidential. The final statement of the report refers to a rumour 'that efforts are being made to get Mr Ernest Simpson a post in the diplomatic service. China has been mentioned in this respect.'[36] A handwritten comment on the report, dated a few days after the report was filed, adds, 'There is also the question of when he goes abroad. ?No Special Branch man (unless asked for). ?Any official intimation to the French police.'[37]

According to a further report by Canning, in October 1936, Wallis encouraged photographers to take pictures of her when she was with the King 'because it satisfies her vanity and provides a means of developing certain commercial undertakings in which she and her friends are interested.' There was no doubt, asserted Canning, 'that Mrs Simpson's association with the King is now being discussed and commented upon by the people generally, especially among the working classes.'[38] He listed the magazines and newspapers (mostly American, but also *Cavalcade* in Britain) in which Wallis's name had appeared over the previous five months.[39]

Neither Edward's nor Wallis's memoirs, published many years later, suggest that they were aware at any time of being watched by Special Branch. It is unclear who gave the instructions to Special Branch to watch the Prince of Wales and then the King, why they did so, or to whom the reports might have been passed by the Metropolitan Police. What is certain, though, is that Sir Philip Game met with the Home Secretary, Sir John Simon, on a regular basis, so they would presumably have discussed these reports about the most important person in Britain and the Empire. However, there is no evidence that Canning's reports to Game about Wallis's alleged relationship with Trundle were disseminated to other Ministers, senior government officials or members of the royal household. If they were, they do not appear to have been used to persuade Edward against continuing his relationship with Wallis.

At no time during this period did Edward turn to his brother Albert for comfort or counsel. There had been a substantial change in the relationship between the two brothers since the early post-war years, and as Albert moved into his mid-twenties, he identified more and more strongly with his parents. Shortly after Edward's return in 1922 from a long journey to the Far East, Albert wrote a letter to his mother saying that, 'We must all *help* him to get him back to our way of thinking.'[40] Edward was away from home for many months at a time, on his overseas tours, which may have increased the emotional distance between himself and his family. Albert was abroad far less often, and, once married, he and Elizabeth visited the King and Queen on a regular basis. In July 1923, when Hardinge was with the royal family at Holyrood Palace in Edinburgh, he sent his wife a description of palace routine. While 'we all have our meals by ourselves which is a great relief', he wrote, the King and Queen 'have theirs with Elizabeth and D. of Y. who are staying here.'[41] Elizabeth had quickly gained George V's approval, to the point where they could easily discuss controversial subjects. 'The King during dinner was busy talking to Lady Elizabeth about birth-control!' reported Hardinge in some surprise, adding, 'Of which I gathered that he was much in favour!'[42]

Edward saw far more of Prince George, the Duke of Kent. In the late summer of 1936, George and his wife, Marina, joined Edward and Wallis at Balmoral; other visitors included Lord and Lady Mountbatten, the Duke and Duchess of Marlborough, the Duke and Duchess of Buccleuch, the Duke and Duchess of Sutherland, and the Earl and Countess of Rosebery. Herman and Katherine Rogers, who were now living in the South of France, came too. Cosmo Lang, the Archbishop of Canterbury, who had always been invited by George V to Balmoral in the late summer, was not on the guest list. But the Archbishop still got his holiday in Scotland, because the Duke and Duchess of York asked him to stay at their Highland home at Birkhall, which was on the

Balmoral estate. 'The kind Yorks bade me come to them at Birkhall', he wrote in some notes, and were 'kindness itself'. After tea on the second day, 'The children – Lillibet, Margaret Rose and Margaret Elphinstone [a cousin] – joined us. They sang some action-songs most charmingly. It was strange to think of the destiny which may be awaiting the little Elizabeth, at present second from the throne! She and her lively little sister are certainly most entrancing children.' As he left Birkhall, the Yorks told him that he must come again, so that 'the links with Balmoral may not be wholly broken'.[43] Edward was furious when he learned that his brother had invited Lang. Wallis later told a friend that Edward was upset

not only because the Duke of York had seemingly gone against his wishes but also because he took it as a not-so-subtle declaration of war against his authority. In effect, she explained, the Yorks had chosen to follow the traditions established by [George V] and in doing so appeared to be setting up a rival court to that of the King.[44]

On 15 November, Mr and Mrs Stanley Bruce, the Australian High Commissioner and his wife, lunched with Stanley Baldwin and Baldwin's wife, Lucy. Stanley Bruce, who had been Prime Minister of Australia between 1923 and 1929, was a very conventional man and had a reputation of being anti-Labour. He was most perturbed about the royal crisis and had shared his concerns in a conversation with Queen Mary; he had also written a letter on the matter to the Duke of York.[45] It was the chief topic of conversation during lunch with the Baldwins, according to some notes written by Bruce shortly afterwards. Baldwin believed, said Bruce, that the King's conduct was antagonizing the people and that his popularity was disappearing.[46] If Baldwin thought he was reflecting the views of the general public, this was simply not possible since the public didn't know about Edward's relationship with Wallis. Moreover, the King's popularity had not waned in the slightest – as his visit to South Wales in the next few days would demonstrate. Bruce put it to Baldwin that the 'Prime Minister's job was to do everything possible to break the entanglement and to get Mrs Simpson out of the country, by appeals to the King's patriot-

INDEX

Western Mail & South Wales News 59

Westmoreland 65

Wheatley, Dennis 162, 190

White Lodge, Richmond Park, Surrey 279

White's club, St James's, London 261

Wigram, Lord (Clive) 69, 70, 98, 115, 122–3, 177, 178, 236, 263, 275

Wilkinson, Ellen 20, 64, 66

Williams, Francis 138

Williamson, Hugh Ross 249–50

Wilson, Sir Horace 69, 73–4, 76, 93, 215, 216, 218, 251, 252, 278

Windsor, Duchess of *see* Simpson, (Bessie) Wallis

Windsor, Duke of *see* Edward VIII, King

Windsor Castle, Berkshire 5, 175, 237, 238

Windsor Great Park 219, 253

Wittering Aerodrome 141

Wolmer, Viscount 106

women, and the franchise 103, 235

Wood, Sir Kingsley 5, 14, 59

Woolf, Virginia 40, 136, 137, 169, 172, 188, 238–9, 242

Woollcott, Alexander 50–51, 111

World War I *see* Great War

World War II 196, 278, 279

Wynyard Park, County Durham 4, 166, 189

York, Duchess of *see* Elizabeth, Princess, Duchess of York

York, Duke of *see* Albert, Prince

York, William, Archbishop of 256

York House, London 14, 41, 96

Yorkshire 28

Yorkshire Post 134, 135, 147

Young, G. M. 195

Ypres 54

Yugoslavia 20

Yugoslavia, King of (Peter II) 43

Zetland, Lord 113, 169, 205–6

Ziegler, Philip 50, 53, 196

ism, sense of duty, etc.'[47] Bruce appears to have been a powerful influence on Baldwin. Lady Milner certainly thought so: she went to see Bruce, she wrote in her diary on 2 December, and he gave her 'a really astonishing account' of his conversation and how he had forced Baldwin to 'take action on the great "Question of the Hour".'[48]

It seems likely that Bruce was also a party to Hardinge's letter to the King. On the day he delivered the letter, Hardinge had lunched with Bruce. After this meeting, Bruce made some notes for Baldwin to assist him in his next talk with the King. They carried much the same message as Hardinge's letter – that if the King were to marry Mrs Simpson,

The people of this country and the Dominions would never accept her as Queen, quite possibly the House of Commons would cancel the Civil List, the Throne would be imperilled, the Empire would be endangered, there would be a demand for the King's abdication, the Government would resign and it would be impossible to get an alternative Government . . .[49]

Galvanized by Hardinge's threat that the silence of the press was about to be broken, Edward sought out Max Beaverbrook, owner of the *Daily Express*, the *Sunday Express* and the *Evening Standard*. Beaverbrook was in no way an ardent monarchist, but the King had been pleased with his success in urging the British press to be discreet about Wallis. To his dismay, Edward discovered that Beaverbrook was on his way to America, to seek respite from his chronic asthma in the desert of Arizona and then to visit his home in New Brunswick, Canada. The King sent Beaverbrook a telegram at sea on Monday 16 November, urging him to come straight back to London. Beaverbrook said he would, and he kept his word: he returned after just four hours in New York.[50] Much as Beaverbrook liked to spend the winter free of asthma, he liked even better to be at the centre of the action and the news. Even more importantly, perhaps, he enjoyed the prospect of engaging in battle against his old foe, Stanley Baldwin. It was Beaverbrook's view, as he sailed back to Britain, 'that the King had only to persevere in order to prevail'.[51]

Soon after midday on 16 November, the King telephoned Hardinge at Buckingham Palace, saying that he wanted to see Baldwin, Chamberlain and Halifax that evening. He added that he wanted Duff Cooper, a personal friend who was the Secretary of State for War, and Sir Samuel Hoare, a fellow undergraduate from Oxford days, also to be at the meeting. Certainly their presence might have resulted in a very different discussion from the one that actually took place. But the Prime Minister replied that it would not be right to take selected members of the Cabinet to see him on a matter that had not yet been considered by the Cabinet as a whole. He therefore proposed that it should be a private meeting between the two of them, and said he would come on his own.

Once the meeting had begun, Baldwin said that he and senior Cabinet colleagues were disturbed at the prospect of the King marrying someone whose marriage had been dissolved by divorce. He was not, of course, speaking on behalf of the Cabinet as a whole or in any formal sense, since the Cabinet had not been consulted. The general public, said Baldwin, would never put up with the King's plan for marriage:

You may think that I am an old man dating from the Victorian regime, but I do know public opinion in this country. Since the War there has been a lowering of the public standards and of public morals, but people expect even more of the Monarchy and they won't tolerate what they did tolerate in the early part of the last century.[52]

Baldwin spoke, said Edward years later, like 'the Gallup Poll incarnate'.[53]

Baldwin was undoubtedly right that some people – the forces of the Conservative Establishment, for example, and the gentry – were not likely to tolerate the idea of their King marrying a woman who was twice divorced. But 'the people' was not a homogenous group and included many other important strands, such as the working class, and more liberal members of the middle class, who were grateful to Edward for his democratic concerns. Baldwin did not include these classes, the great majority of the population, in his notion of 'what the people would tolerate and what they would not'. Nor did he ask himself if those people who identified themselves as the post-war generation, and who made clear their appreciation of Edward's modern style, would really object to a queen from a different social background and culture. Even support for the Church of England's position was uncertain – for, as Baldwin was aware, such was the Church's own crisis that the Archbishop of Canterbury was planning a national 'Recall to Religion' in 1937.

Perhaps it is not surprising, in the light of Britain's history of electoral reform, that the Prime Minister should have overlooked whole sections of the population in his appraisal of the views of 'the people'. It had been less than two decades before – in 1918 – that the vote and the right to stand in parliamentary elections were extended to all men over twenty-one. Before then, these rights had been based on property and were limited to male householders, thus excluding large numbers of men. All women were excluded from the franchise until 1919, when women over the age of thirty were finally given the vote; the age limit was not lowered to twenty-one, the same as for men, until 1928. Universal suffrage, therefore, and the idea that every citizen was entitled to a political voice, was still a novel phenomenon in 1936.

It is always possible, in any case, that Baldwin's emphasis on public opinion was not motivated by a simple concern for the feelings of the general public. It may also have been influenced by the Memorandum by Parliamentary Counsel sent by Fisher to Chamberlain on 7 November, which Baldwin most probably saw. 'In all matters of this kind, where there are no precedents to guide,' observed the author of the Memorandum, referring to the King's wish to marry Mrs Simpson,

Ministers have to act as interpreters of public opinion; and if they are satisfied that public opinion generally is strongly behind the advice which they think that they ought to give, I cannot doubt that constitutional principle not only empowers, but requires, them to tender it.[54]

In other words, Baldwin – in an age of universal suffrage – would be backed by Constitutional principle if he was able to claim that he was speaking for public opinion.

At their meeting on 16 November, the King did not argue with Baldwin. Instead, he simply announced that he was going to marry Mrs Simpson. If the Government opposed the marriage, he said, then he was 'prepared to go'.[55] This was a dramatic step: Edward was declaring his intention to abdicate. Baldwin's reaction, recorded Ramsay MacDonald in his diary, was 'ebullient'. He ran into the Prime Minister shortly after the meeting with the King, which had started at 6.30 p.m.:

7.30 met PM ebullient. Put his arm in mine & to my enquiry if he had seen HM he said he had but that he must think over things & would tell me everything to-morrow. Meanwhile the King was determined to marry Mrs S and was prepared to abdicate. Nice kettle of fish!![56]

Hardinge heard the news, possibly from Baldwin himself, and rushed home to tell his wife, Helen.[57] Helen's mother, Lady Milner, discovered what had happened from her friend, Geoffrey Dawson, who 'came to see me in the morning. Couldn't sit down. We neither of us sat down during a long talk.' Writing in French to discourage the prying eyes of servants, she observed in her diary that the Prime Minister had seen the king – that he was a complete idiot – '*Le roi est archifou*'.[58] Word spread rapidly through the Court. In his diary for 18 November, Cecil Headlam commented that Frank Mitchell, an Assistant Private Secretary to the King, had 'darkly hinted that a climax to the Simpson business was inevitable within a short space of time, and he seemed certain that HM would rather abdicate than give her up.'[59]

Baldwin's wife, Lucy, was extremely distressed at the turn of events, summing them up in her diary entry for 16 November as 'Very grave news.'[60] She blamed Wallis for sabotaging Edward's reign. Writing to Edith, Lady Londonderry, she exclaimed, 'It makes one sigh for the so called good old days when one could clap women as well as men in the Tower!!'[61] But there were some who actually welcomed the idea of getting rid of the King – and who regarded his impossible wish to marry Wallis as a godsend. 'I had a talk to both SB and the Archbishop', wrote Lord Linlithgow, the Viceroy of India, in a secret letter sent to Dawson from New Delhi on 17 November. At this talk, which had taken place in London before he had sailed for India, he had told them

that I was sure that one thing alone could steady [Edward], the knowledge that his popularity with the general public was at stake . . . I said to both that I hoped the thing might be kept fairly quiet till after the coronation, but that when once the excitement of that ceremony had subsided, *I felt sure the public would turn on him* . . . I gave it as my opinion that the public interest will best be served by bringing matters to a head as soon as possible. I think you should see SB and push him into calling into counsel: Neville; Halifax; Hailsham; Simon; Sam Hoare; and I suppose that old ass Ramsay Mac, by way of providing SB with support . . . I think, too, that the 'Times' should weigh in with a leader of unmistakable point.[62]

The King joined Queen Mary for dinner 16 November, to tell her of his decision to abdicate from the throne. Punctually at 8.30 p.m., he appeared at Marlborough House in white tie and tailcoat; he found his sister, Princess Mary, there too. The women were appalled. 'The word "duty" ', wrote Edward later,

fell between us. But there could be no question of my shirking my duty. What separated us was not a question of duty but a different concept of kingship. I was, of course, eager to serve my people in all the many ways expected of the King as the head of the State . . . But I would stand on my right to marry on my own terms.[63]

He asked his mother if he might bring Wallis to meet her, so that she would get to know the woman he loved so much that he was willing to renounce the throne for her. He was confident that once his mother knew her even a little, she would understand his decision. But she refused. She also made no attempt to dissuade Edward from the action he contemplated. When they parted, she expressed the hope that he would make a wise decision for his future, adding that she feared his imminent visit to South Wales would be a trying one.

After speaking to his mother and sister, Edward set about taking his brothers Bertie, Harry and George, into his confidence. He saw them one by one. George, his favourite, was the most moved. Bertie said little. This was a momentous development for him, since he was the heir presumptive. Once Edward had given up the throne, then he, Albert, would be King and his wife, Elizabeth, would be Queen. It must have been impossible for him to engage with Edward's news with any kind of equanimity. Instead, after a few days, he wrote a letter in which he said that he longed for his elder brother to be happy, adding that he of all people ought to be able to understand his feelings. He was sure, he added, that whatever Edward decided would be 'in the best interests of the country and the Empire'.[64]

Baldwin's meeting with Edward took place the day before the King departed for South Wales – and the day before a heated debate in the House of Commons on the renewal of the Special Areas Act. There was opposition to the Government from its own side. Sir Robert Horne, a Conservative, spoke at length on conditions in South Wales. He was especially critical of the Government's failure to heed the recommendations of Malcolm Stewart, the former Commissioner for the Special Areas who had just resigned in protest. Horne was supported in this view by about fifty of the younger Conservatives in the House, led by Viscount Wolmer, all of whom threatened to vote for the Opposition unless some better attempt was made to deal with the problem of long-term unemployment. Neville Chamberlain, as Chancellor of the Exchequer, was forced to respond. He promised to bring forward an amending Act 'which should embody such of Mr Stewart's recommendations as the Government found acceptable'.[65]

This was not a favourable time for the forces of Conservatism. In the American general election on 3 November, Roosevelt had led the Democrats to victory once more, winning virtually 61 per cent of the popular vote. He was elected on the strength of the New Deal, set up to alleviate the worst effects of the Depression, and had concluded his presidential campaign with a rousing attack at Madison Square Gardens on the 'organized money' that opposed him.[66] Corporate leaders had denounced him for what they regarded as socialist policies, but the electorate still wanted to keep him as President. Some Americans saw a similarity between the hostility to Roosevelt and King

Edward's developing problems in Britain. On 25 November, a New
Yorker (who was president of an organization called 'Association
Better Citizenship, Inc.', which aimed to dispel ignorance, misunder-
standing, superstition and prejudice) wrote in a letter to the King that

It is with a feeling of great concern I learn of the mental attitude of the
reactionaries in your Court. You are of the same nature as our great President.
If he were in your position he would do as he damn pleased. We, in America,
are putting the reactionaries back on their heels. They are a necessary adjunct,
to any organization or kingdom, but they have to be kept in their place, or the
progress of the world would be stopped ... A Queen of American descent
sitting upon the Throne (with you) would bind England and America indissolu-
bly. All those that love you, and there are many in America, wish you and
Mrs Simpson all the happiness in the world.[67]

Not just Conservatism, but Stanley Baldwin in particular, was
beleaguered in the autumn of 1936. On 12 November, during a debate
on rearmament, he admitted to the House of Commons that he had
misled the country three years earlier on this issue. 'I put before
the whole House my own views with an appalling frankness', he
announced, before explaining that because of the strong pacifist feeling
running through the country in 1933, he had sought – and won –
re-election on an anti-war platform. 'My position as the leader of a
great party', he explained, 'was not altogether a comfortable one. I
asked myself what chance was there ... within the next year or two
of that feeling being so changed that the country would give a mandate
for rearmament?' Supposing that he had gone to the country and
said that Germany was rearming and that Britain must rearm,
he said, 'does anybody think that this pacific democracy would have
rallied to that cry at that moment? I cannot think of anything that
would have made the loss of the election from my point of view more
certain.'[68]

Churchill, not a friend of Baldwin in any case, was not impressed.
'This was indeed appalling frankness', he observed many years later –
'That a Prime Minister should avow that he had not done his duty in
regard to national safety because he was afraid of losing the election

was an incident without parallel in our Parliamentary history.'[69] Leo
Amery, the Imperialist statesman and writer, also took a dim view. It
was a 'most lamentable confession,' he wrote in his diary on
12 November, 'and one which filled the House with dismay. Then SB
sat down almost in dead silence.'[70] The leader in the *Daily Mail* on
23 November drew a contrast – in a paragraph of bold lettering to
emphasize the point – between this speech and the King's concern for
the Special Areas:

Surely those who have recently confessed that they dared not tell the people
the truth three years ago and who have since accomplished so little towards
defence will realise the gulf between their conduct and the King's methods in
Wales.[71]

The outbreak of the Spanish Civil War in July 1936, just four
months before Edward's visit to South Wales in that year, seemed to
divide the people of Britain into two opposing camps – those on the
left and those on the right. On the right were the Conservatives,
aristocrats and businessmen who supported Franco's military uprising
against Spain's legally elected Republican Government. On the left
were many of the working-class and unemployed, as well as middle-
class Marxists and liberals, who supported the popular front of the
Republicans. 'Left and Right', observed the American journalist Janet
Flanner, 'no longer referred to man's hands but to his politics.' This
was a time, she added, when suddenly everybody began being interested in politics – 'President Roosevelt's New Deal, Stalin's Five-
Year Plan, Mussolini's *Mare Nostrum*, Leon Blum's *Front Populaire*,
Hitler's *Lebensraum*, and Franco's Civil War finally began altogether
their full, their delayed, their conflicting implications.'[72] Many people
were terrified, wondering where all this conflict was going to lead. The
Spanish explosion, wrote George Bernard Shaw to Beatrice Webb,
was a 'deliberate refusal to accept the democratic substitution of
the ballot for the bullet.' At present, he said, the Spanish Government was only a muddle. But, he added, 'after the Russian success
against overwhelming odds anything may happen. Well, *après nous,
le déluge*.'[73]

John Buchan, the famous author of the espionage thriller *The Thirty-Nine Steps* and Governor-General of Canada, wrote a letter about the crisis in Europe to Edith Londonderry on 18 September. 'We do not want to be mixed up in this dog-fight of Fascism and Communism', he said, adding that 'I dislike both, though of the two evils I slightly prefer the former, like Sir Percival, who, when he found a lion fighting a snake, helped the lion as "it was the more natural beast of the twain".'[74] King Edward shared this horror of Communism and regarded it as a threat that must be resisted in every way possible. No doubt his feelings were influenced by the murder in 1918 of his Russian relatives, the family of the Tsar Nicholas II, by the Bolsheviks. Like most of the ruling class, he believed that Russia and international Communism was a greater threat to Britain than the growth of Fascism in Italy and Germany. Along with a large section of the Conservative Party, he opposed the idea of sanctions against Italy after Mussolini's invasion of Abyssinia. He believed that it would be foolish to annoy Mussolini on this issue, on the grounds that there was little the British could do, and in any case he believed that the Italians had some grounds for the invasion. He also thought that nothing should be done to drive Mussolini into Hitler's arms.

Britain's best safeguard against war, argued Edward, was to have a strong fighting force, and on issues of rearmament he was at one with Churchill.[75] He also had great hopes for an Anglo-American alliance and expressed the view that the USA and Britain should 'get definitely together . . . the only hope for us and the world was to stand together.'[76] Overwhelmingly, however, he was haunted by the carnage and brutality of the Great War and shared the common view that every possible effort should be made to avoid another conflict.

The political situation in the autumn of 1936 seemed to many to be unstable and explosive. It reflected the more personal situation in which Edward now found himself. By now, he wrote later in his memoirs, he felt that his affairs had 'reached a highly explosive state, and a careless spark from outside might touch off the charge.' Just thirty-one hours after the momentous meeting with his Prime Minister on 16 November, he bade farewell to Wallis and boarded the night train for the journey to South Wales. The King's work still had to go on, even if he was leaving behind in London a personal crisis of unbearable proportions:

As the train clanked and rattled through the night, I lay in my berth reflecting on the turmoil that I knew must by this time have gripped Whitehall. Yet I was at peace with myself. My spiritual struggle was over. I had passed the climax. The public struggle remained, and in many ways it would be more pitiless. But I had declared myself.[77]

6

'The Battle for the Throne'

By the time Edward had returned to London from South Wales, he had changed his mind: he now hoped to stay on the throne *and* to marry Wallis. This, said Baldwin to Archbishop Lang, was because he had seen 'evidence of his popularity' while on his Welsh tour.[1] It did not occur to the Prime Minister that, faced with the desolation of Merthyr and Dowlais, Edward would feel an overwhelming sense of responsibility for the unemployed – that 'something *must* be done'. Seeing the pinched, worn faces of the poor in South Wales may have suggested to the King that he had a moral obligation to stay on the throne and do what he could to help. Such a view was consistent with his stated beliefs. When Alexander Woollcott, an American writer who broadcast on the BBC, was asked in 1935 to explain his own liberal and humanitarian convictions, he drew on a philosophy that had been put to him by Edward. He always remembered, he said, 'a pungent bit of advice, given, oddly enough, by His Royal Highness the Prince of Wales. He suggested to those about him in England that, pending the millennium, each man take hold of a piece of the depression next him and do something about it.'[2]

But Edward's change of mind had in any case been influenced by a new plan, which Baldwin had not anticipated: a morganatic marriage, as an alternative to the stark choice between giving up Wallis and abdication. Inviting Wallis to lunch at Claridges while Edward was in Wales in mid-November, Esmond Harmsworth, chairman of the Newspaper Proprietors Association, had put this idea to her. He explained that it had been thought of by his father, Lord Rothermere, the owner of the *Daily Mail* (and rival to Lord Beaverbrook, who owned the *Evening Standard* and the *Express* Group – between them they controlled most of the British mass-circulation press). By the morganatic arrangement, were she to marry the King she would remain a private citizen, and any children they might have would not be in the line of succession. Although unprecedented in England, this was not an uncommon strategy in the royal courts of Europe for solving a conflict between love and social status. Queen Mary's own paternal grandparents, Alexander, Duke of Württemberg, and Claudine, Countess Rhedey, had had a morganatic marriage. Harmsworth explained to Wallis that a marriage of this kind ought to remove any difficulty, given that Mr Baldwin's stated objection to the marriage was that Edward's wife would have to be Queen. As a morganatic wife, Wallis could style herself after one of Edward's subsidiary titles, and be known as the Duchess of Lancaster, for example, or of Cornwall; she would be 'Her Highness', but not 'Her *Royal* Highness'. She would rank in the social hierarchy below the three royal duchesses and would not be entitled to curtseys.

Wallis was astonished by the idea. At the time, she said later, she was sure of only one thing – that she knew 'less than ever of the marvellous workings of the British political mind'.[3] She told Harmsworth that she felt unable to express an opinion, but he persuaded her to pass the suggestion on to the King. This she did, during the weekend of 21–22 November, when she and her aunt were with Edward at Fort Belvedere. At first he reacted with distaste, but gradually it appeared to him to be a real solution to the dilemma. The plan had the support of Winston Churchill and Beaverbrook. 'Max [Beaverbrook] rang me up to say he had seen the gent,' wrote Churchill, '& told him the Cornwall plan was my idea. The gent was definitely for it. It now turns on what the Cabinet will say. I don't see any other way through.'[4] Churchill called it the 'Cornwall plan' because he assumed that, as the King's morganatic wife, Mrs Simpson would become the Duchess of Cornwall.

Edward returned to London from the Fort at the end of the weekend. He sent for Harmsworth and asked him to put the idea informally to Baldwin. The Prime Minister replied that he was interested, but did not commit himself in any way. In fact, he was unsure how to proceed. According to Geoffrey Dawson, he was 'getting more and more worried, though he told me very little and confined himself, as on Friday, to discussing various possibilities and the popular reaction to them. He was quite clear however that I ought to give up a visit to Yorkshire planned for the week-end . . .'[5] The ball was now in Baldwin's court, which changed the balance of power between him and Edward. From the moment the King proposed a morganatic marriage, argued the historian A. J. P. Taylor, 'he put himself at the Government's mercy. He was now asking them for something, whereas previously they had been asking him.'[6]

On Tuesday 24 November, Baldwin moved into action.[7] He summoned to Downing Street the three men who had the potential to form an alternative government: Clement Attlee, Leader of the Opposition; Sir Archibald Sinclair, Leader of the Liberal Party; and Winston Churchill. He told them that if the King refused to abandon his idea of marriage to Wallis, the Government would resign. Sinclair and Attlee gave their word not to form governments if this were to take place. Attlee told Baldwin that Labour voters would have no objection to the King marrying an American in principle, but would not accept Mrs Simpson or a morganatic marriage. 'Despite the sympathy felt for the King and the affection which his visits to the depressed areas had created,' wrote Attlee later, 'the Party – with the exception of the intelligentsia who can be trusted to take the wrong view on any subject – were in agreement with the views I had expressed.'[8]

Winston Churchill said that 'though his attitude was a little different, he would certainly support the government'.[9] Despite this assurance, there was some suspicion that Churchill would exploit the crisis as an opportunity to challenge Baldwin. If the Government resigned in direct confrontation with the King, worried Lord Zetland, the Secretary for India, would 'Churchill resist the temptation to take up the gauntlet and endeavour to form an alternative ministry?' In such a scenario, he added, 'There would be a grave risk of the country being divided into two camps – for and against the King. This would clearly be fraught with danger of the most formidable kind.'[10] These anxieties were fuelled by a widespread mistrust of Churchill, who was widely regarded at this time, in the words of the historian David Cannadine, as 'a cad', a 'half breed', a 'dictator', a 'rogue elephant', and 'the greatest adventurer in modern political history'.[11] Walter Elliot, the Scottish Conservative MP, was 'full of fears', said the wife of Baldwin's Parliamentary Private Secretary, 'as to what Winston Churchill would do in conjunction with Lord Beaverbrook as to forming a King's party.'[12]

The editor of *The Times*, Geoffrey Dawson, took up his pen. On 24 November he wrote a leader for the newspaper in which he 'took the occasion to introduce one or two passages on the importance of keeping the Crown and its representatives remote from "glaring public scandal" and above "public reproach or ridicule".' The significance 'of this and yesterday's leaders', he noted in his diary, 'was not lost on the American Press or indeed on many people in England.' Dawson also 'happened to meet both Neville Chamberlain and Alec Hardinge lunching with Lady Milner, and saw N[eville] C[hamberlain] again later in the day; but they added little to what I knew already.'[13]

Alec Hardinge knew all about the morganatic plan, even though the King had asked Baldwin not to tell him. 'I apologize for everlastingly bothering you,' wrote Hardinge to the Prime Minister on 22 November, 'but the Queen has told me what the King made you promise not to tell me.' If, under these circumstances, 'you feel that you can speak to to [sic] me about it,' he added, 'I should very much like to see you before you see the King again.' He offered to come round to see him that night.[14]

On 25 November, Thomas Jones, who had worked in Baldwin's private office and was close to him, told a friend about a revealing conversation with the Prime Minister. 'I cannot tell you all that was said between us,' he told his friend, 'but I can tell you the essential fact. The king agreed [before going to South Wales] to go out quietly, and he afterwards told this to his Mother and his brothers. But he has clearly now gone back on that. Mrs S was down at Fort Belvedere over the weekend and has talked him out of it.' Meanwhile, added Jones, 'I am collecting opinion from all over the place. I've seen Bruce of Australia and heard from John Buchan.'[15] Those making plans were still working on the assumption that Edward would give up his throne.[16]

Queen Mary was not at all impressed by the idea of a morganatic marriage (though she herself was the granddaughter of such an arrangement). 'Really!' she was heard to remark, 'this might be Roumania!'[17] On 25 November the Duke of York wrote to Sir Godfrey Thomas, Assistant Private Secretary to the King, to assure him of his complete cooperation in the event of abdication. 'If the worst happens & I have to take over,' he promised, 'you can be assured that I will do my best to clear up the inevitable mess, if the whole fabric does not crumble under the shock and strain of it all.'[18] Some members of the royal court had been thinking for quite a while that it would be better to have Albert on the throne than Edward. Clive Wigram had said 'that if he had the Duke of York he could make him into another King George [V]', noted Mrs Runciman in her diary. 'I suppose there is a great sense of duty there which HM doesn't entirely lack but he has been spoilt.'[19]

There were many reasons for Albert's appeal to the court as a replacement for Edward. He was seen as dependable, just as his father had been, and was like him in many other ways, too. He was a family man and had the same zest for shooting. He also, said Edward, found 'the same abiding contentment in Sandringham and Balmoral. He collected stamps as had my father, and also made a hobby of collecting rare plants . . . there was the same disinterestedness in foreign ideas and the same disinclination for foreign travel.'[20] The patterns of their lives

were much the same, with the steady swing of habit taking them both year after year to the same places at the same time and with the same associates. Strongly rooted each in his own existence, they tended to be withdrawn from the hurly-burly of life that I relished.[21]

Albert was a deeply conservative and conventional man, and he and his wife enjoyed good relations with all the key representatives of the Establishment: Baldwin and the Government ministers, the Archbishop, and the chief courtiers.

Albert had lived in the shadow of Edward's personality and talents for most of his life, but he could adopt a commanding manner when he needed to. In 1922 Helen Hardinge wrote a letter to her husband in which she described an occasion on which

The Duke of Y[ork] had dined with all the gang at Claridges. They all danced afterwards & when he was going away 4 or 5 of them came to see him off. He said a ceremonious goodnight to them & then signing to Elizabeth [Bowes-Lyon, his future wife] said 'Get in', pointing to his car which was waiting. Elizabeth tripped in the royal-auto and they departed together about 1 o'clock in the morning!![22]

Although Albert had worn splints on his legs as a child, he became a proficient horseman and a tennis ace, playing in the doubles of the 1926 Wimbledon championships;[23] he was also 'particularly nimble' when dancing at Balmoral.[24] He suffered from a stammer from childhood, but sought help for this in 1926, with the support of his wife.

One important reason for Albert's favour with the court was the approval of his late father. 'You have always been so sensible and easy to work with and you have always been [so] ready to listen to any advice and to agree with my opinions about people and things', George V had written to Albert in 1923, 'that I feel that we have always got on very well together (very different to dear David).'[25] The idea of the second royal son being more qualified to reign than the first had a precedent in the previous generation, for Edward VII's first son, Prince Albert Victor, known as 'Eddy', had been generally regarded as hopeless by the court. There was widespread relief when he died before his father, thereby making his brother – soon to be George V – the heir presumptive.

Waiting in the last days of November to hear Baldwin's views on the proposed morganatic marriage, Edward consulted Samuel Hoare and Duff Cooper. These were the two men that he had wanted as witnesses to his previous meeting with the Prime Minister – a request that had been refused by Baldwin. Edward mentioned these friends again, and Baldwin agreed that the King could consult them on a private basis. Edward had been careful to observe the formality of this application, Duff later wrote, in the same way that he 'behaved with punctilious constitutional rectitude throughout the crisis'.[26]

Edward first saw Hoare, who was sympathetic but not encouraging. He warned that any attempt to press the marriage plan would meet with a stone wall of opposition from the Cabinet. Duff Cooper took a different, more optimistic, view. He was determined that Edward should stay on the throne but strongly advocated delaying the marriage. He urged Edward to ignore the furore and go ahead with his coronation, staying away from Wallis in the meantime. People would then see, said Duff, that he had done his best to get on without her but found it impossible. He might then, as King, proceed to marry Mrs Simpson. But the King refused even to consider the suggestion of postponement – 'for a reason', said Duff, 'which did him credit. He felt it would be wrong to go through so solemn a religious ceremony as the Coronation without letting his subjects know what it was his intention to do. I could not argue against such scruples, but could only respect them.'[27]

Edward summoned his Prime Minister on 25 November and asked him whether he had considered Harmsworth's proposal. Baldwin replied that he was not yet ready to offer a considered judgement. But if the King wanted a 'horseback opinion', he added, it was his view that Parliament would never agree to pass a Bill allowing a morganatic marriage. He then asked the King if he wished him to examine the proposition *formally*. This, he said, would require putting it before the whole Cabinet and also before the Prime Ministers of the Dominions – Canada, Australia, New Zealand, South Africa and the Irish Free State.[28] The Dominions were formerly British possessions that were now independent states, joined to the mother country by a common bond of allegiance to the Crown.

Edward agreed to Baldwin's proposals. The Prime Minister left quickly; the meeting had been short, and an agreement swiftly reached. But it was yet another turning point in the crisis, even more significant than the Hardinge letter. As the door closed behind Baldwin, it dawned on the King that 'with that simple request I had gone a long way towards sealing my own fate'.[29] For by submitting the issue as a matter for constitutional 'advice', he had put himself and his marriage into the hands of his Ministers. He had now bound himself to submit to whatever he was told – since the 'advice' would, in practice, take the form of an instruction from the Prime Minister to the King. If the Cabinet and the Dominion governments would not support a morganatic marriage, then the King would have no choice but to follow the 'advice'. In other words, Edward had put himself at the Government's mercy. 'The Battle for the Throne has begun', wrote Chips Channon in his diary, when he heard about the meeting.[30]

Baldwin was acting correctly in considering the wishes of the Dominions. The Statute of Westminster of 1931, which followed the Imperial Conference of 1926, had formally recognized and defined the new concept of Dominion status, and declared in its preamble that any change in the royal succession, style or title required the assent of Dominion parliaments (neither Australia nor New Zealand had adopted the Statute by 1936, but they were expected to behave as if they had).[31] Baldwin had a fair idea already of how at least one of the Dominions would respond, since he had discussed the topic at length with Stanley Bruce, the Australian High Commissioner, on 15 November. Bruce had made it clear to Baldwin that the Australian Prime Minister, Joseph A. Lyons, took the same view as himself – that marriage to Wallis was simply unacceptable.

Max Beaverbrook returned to London from his truncated trip to North America on the following day, the 26th, and drove straight to the Fort. He was appalled at the rapid turn of events and strongly urged delay. Baldwin's offer to consult the Cabinet and Dominions would carry great risks for the King, he argued, and should be stopped immediately. But Edward felt unable to do so: he feared that this would involve him 'in a long course of seeming dissimulation for which I had neither the talent nor the appetite.'[32]

Beaverbrook resigned himself to the inevitable. He later attributed Edward's weak strategy – indeed, absence of any viable strategy at all – to his lack of political nous:

His interests were never political. They were social in both senses of the term. They were social in the sense that he liked sports, parties and the company of brisk and lively people. They were also social in the sense that he was deeply interested in conditions of ordinary life and work, and in the expansion of British export trade in the markets of the world.

But now, said Beaverbrook, he was facing 'a grave political problem quite unprepared for the task'. He had shown the same lack of political savoir faire in his dealings with the court. It was not that King Edward was inexperienced, rather that the kind of experience he had gained was of no use to him in dealing with political men. 'He had mixed more freely with the people than any Heir Apparent had ever done before,' wrote Beaverbrook, 'but he had hardly mixed at all with politicians . . . he had friends in coal-mines, but not in the Cabinet.'[33]

Baldwin and Chamberlain were not allowed to forget about these 'friends in coal mines', once Edward's visit to South Wales had taken place. On 26 November, during Oral Answers in the House of Commons, questions were put to Ernest Brown about the usefulness of what was being done in the Special Areas. These questions made implicit references to the King's recent visit to Wales and used the phrase 'something must be done'. 'As this matter has been in the hands of the right hon. Gentleman and his Department for the last 15 months,' asked the Labour MP George Hall, 'is it not time something were done?'[34] Even though it was not permissible to refer directly to the King, for constitutional reasons, the radical Glasgow MP, David Kirkwood, was determined to mention directly the King's tour of Wales. 'Seeing that the right hon. Gentleman was in such close contact with the King,' he asked Brown, reminding the House in this way that Brown had accompanied the King to South Wales, 'did not the King suggest that the means test should be done away with?' The Speaker admonished Kirkwood with the reminder that, 'The hon. Member must not bring in the King's name',[35] but Kirkwood had successfully used the King's visit to draw attention to the Government's failure on unemployment. He had also given weight to the policy of the opposition by associating with it the name of the King.

Despite his left-wing politics, Kirkwood had been a staunch supporter of the King for many years, ever since he had been summoned by Edward, when Prince of Wales, to give an account of his political views. 'I have never talked to any man in my life', he said after the meeting,

who was more eager to know just what the workers were thinking ... We were two British citizens talking about our land and our people. A man's a man for a' that. It was as if we were on a ship in a storm, when class and creed and caste are forgotten.

Kirkwood added that he felt he had 'been in the presence of a man who had a big job to do, and is earnest, and determined to do his job well.'[36]

The King's visit to Wales had led to increased concern outside the House of Commons about the Special Areas. In the week that followed, the *New Statesman* sent some journalists to South Wales to investigate conditions there. 'What is to be done about it?' they asked. '*Something ought* to be done at once ...'[37] 'The people want *something done*', observed John Rowland at the Welsh Board of Health, 'and they think the King is out to help.'[38] The *Seaham Weekly News*, a local paper in the impoverished region of County Durham, made the same point. Referring to the dreadful conditions which were being allowed to continue in South Wales, Durham and other distressed areas, it argued that, 'What is needed is action, immediate and stern, not columns of words, with much promise and little performance.'[39] Fear was expressed, too, that the anger of the unemployed would erupt in serious unrest. Edward himself, as Prince of Wales, had warned the American Ambassador, Robert Bingham, of this risk in 1934. There had to be change in conditions in Britain, he said, and a correction of social injustice among the English people which would relieve poverty and distress – 'that this must come and that it would come either wisely, constructively and conservatively, which would save the country, or it would come violently, which would destroy it ...'[40]

In May 1926, just ten years before the King's visit to Wales in 1936, a General Strike had almost brought the nation to a standstill. It had been sparked by an attempt by coal owners to cut wages and extend working hours in the pits, which was firmly resisted by the miners. The workers of Britain had rallied to the miners' cause, in a national strike that was seen by the Government as a serious threat to stability. 'Constitutional government is being attacked', warned Baldwin, the Prime Minister. The General Strike, he added, 'is a challenge to Parliament, and is the road to anarchy and ruin.'[41] Those who identified themselves with the position of the Government – the ruling classes – rushed to take over the running of essential services. Most of these volunteers had never done any menial work in their lives before, commented the *Illustrated London News*:

Armoured cars escorted convoys of lorries carrying food through the London streets and a battalion of the Grenadier Guards marched into the docks. Young men from Oxford and Cambridge poured into the capital to volunteer as bus drivers, train drivers and special constables.

'We feel that the heart of England must be sound', added the magazine, 'when we read that Mr C. E. Pitman, the Oxford stroke, is driving a train ... the Headmaster of Eton ... and about fifty of his assistant masters have enrolled as special constables ... Lord Chesham is driving a train and the Hon. Lionel Tennyson is a special.'[42]

After only nine days, the General Strike was brought to an end. The miners stayed out until December, with little support apart from nearly a million pounds sent to the Miners' Relief Fund from the trade unions of Russia. The miners were eventually forced back to work by cold and starvation, having to accept both longer hours and lower wages. Baldwin then introduced the Eight Hours Act to lengthen the seven-hour day officially. It was swiftly followed by the 1927 Trades Disputes Act, which made any repetition of a general strike illegal. The disaffection of the people continued to fester, especially after the Depression of 1929. Just after the creation of the National Government in 1931, the men of the Atlantic Fleet at Invergordon refused duty in protest against cuts in the pay of the ratings – some lost more than 10 per cent. The Board of Admiralty responded swiftly to reduce the cuts, but the nation was shocked by this naval mutiny. It was one of the reasons for the suspension of the Gold Standard, and it contributed to the climate of concern that led to the Special Areas Act in 1934. In the Areas themselves, social unrest grew.

Protests against the Government became increasingly common, especially hunger marches from the Special Areas to London. In one of the largest marches, in 1934, there were eighteen main contingents of Scottish, Welsh and English unemployed people. Before reaching London they had slept in 188 towns and marched through many hundreds of other towns and villages.[43] When they finally arrived in the metropolis, conflict broke out: police charged the crowds, and fighting between them and the marchers broke out in and around Hyde Park.[44] This intrusion annoyed Chips Channon. 'I walked to the House of Commons,' he wrote in his diary on 10 November, 'as we had been warned not to bring cars.' The lobbies were full of hunger marchers, he complained,

come to protest against the new unemployment regulations, the so-called Means Test . . . Later, I went out into the lobby and found it full to suffocation with marchers, who were being incited by Communists. Many of them wore red shirts and ties. At the door was a queue singing the Red Flag. It really seemed as if trouble must break out. But it didn't, and about 8.30 I took the last look at these unfortunate people who have been goaded and misguided by their leaders into walking from Lancashire and South Wales.[45]

'These marchers are a public nuisance and a public danger,' warned the *Daily Telegraph* on 29 October 1936.[46] Demonstrations were held locally, too. In February 1935, thousands of people in Merthyr, including women with prams and young children, stormed the office of the Unemployment Assistance Board, breaking windows and destroying records. Next day, the unpopular benefit scales that had been introduced by the Board were suspended.[47] The anger of the poor and unemployed was making itself felt.

Behind the strikes and hunger marches, as well as the growing influence of the Labour Party, the classes of wealth saw the spectre of Communism stalking Europe. 'These Stay in Strikes are a product of Russia,' wrote Lord Wigram to the Viceroy in June 1936, 'and without doubt Russian influences have been at work both in France and Spain.' He added, 'One cannot help admiring Mussolini.'[48] The ruling class feared that 'the Labour Party might at any moment turn red as rapidly as a lobster in a kettle of boiling water', commented the novelist Sir Compton Mackenzie[49] – and that the anger of the unemployed would erupt in revolution.

South Wales was seen as a flashpoint. The *Spectator* warned in September that South Wales was 'ripe with atheism, and ripe for revolution'. It argued that although Communism was making slow headway in South Wales (not more than thirty seats out of many hundreds had been won on Borough and County Councils by the Communist Party), the influence of Communism was growing, fanned by measures of social injustice such as the Means Test.[50] In a leaflet entitled 'The People Can Save South Wales!', a militant socialist stated that

The struggle against the Means Test and the New Regulations can be ten times more effective by challenging the whole policy of the National Government towards South Wales . . . Today *the flag of revolt* needs to be raised to new heights to save the people of South Wales from destruction.[51]

Many of the unemployed in Wales regarded the National Government as a government of capitalists whose interests were directly opposed to those of the working class. The *South Wales Slave Act Special*, published by Lewis Jones for the South Wales National Unemployed Workers Movement, made this point clearly. The Government, it said, 'is supported in Parliament by 196 company directors who hold between them 836 directorates, 33 landowners, 144 high society people, 136 Army, Navy and Air Force officers, and 135 lawyers to put them right when they go wrong . . . SUCH A GOVERNMENT MUST BE BROUGHT DOWN.'[52] In this climate of popular disaffection, the King's visit to Wales in November – drawing attention to the poverty of the unemployed and insisting that something must be done – was most unwelcome to the Government. It was yet one more example of a series of episodes in which he seemed to side with the working class against those in power.

In every way, in his public life and in his private life, King Edward

VIII was a headache for the Establishment. Baldwin decided to throw his energies behind the easier problem: the King's wish for a morganatic marriage to Mrs Simpson. On the morning of Friday 27 November, he summoned a meeting of the Cabinet in his room at the House of Commons. The press was informed that the Cabinet was going to discuss the gravity of events in Spain. But although the conflict there was certainly grave, it was not on the agenda. Instead, for the first time in Cabinet, Baldwin raised the marriage crisis. Armed with press cuttings from American magazines and newspapers, he brought Ministers up to date and told them he believed the King to be passionately in love. He also reported on Edward's proposal of a morganatic marriage, saying that he would not ask Cabinet for a decision that day. It was clear, though, that nearly everybody shared the Prime Minister's opposition to the idea. Only Duff Cooper pleaded on the King's behalf, arguing that he should be crowned as planned in May 1937 – and that only then should the marriage question be brought forward.[53]

Baldwin explained that he would need to consult the Dominion prime ministers, and it was agreed that Chamberlain, Simon, Hoare and Sir Thomas Inskip, as well as himself, would help Malcolm MacDonald, the Secretary of State for Dominion Affairs, to draw up telegrams to send to the Dominions.[54] The discussion was kept secret from Edward, even though, as head of state, he was supposed to receive the papers relating to Cabinet meetings. The following day, he was eagerly awaiting the arrival of the usual red box of official documents, expecting to see the minutes of the meeting. 'But the solitary paper that I found inside, purporting to describe the momentous discussions of that day,' he found to his disappointment, 'was blank except for a perfunctory paragraph relating to the carriage of arms to Spain.'[55]

Telegrams were sent from Baldwin to the prime ministers of Canada, Australia, New Zealand and South Africa at 12.15 p.m. the next day, 28 November. No telegram was sent to the Irish Free State; instead, a message was taken to Dublin personally by Sir Henry Batterbee, the Acting Permanent Under-Secretary of State for Dominion Affairs. The leaders of five overseas nations were thus being informed about a

British problem that was still unknown to most of the people of Britain. Baldwin set out the background to the crisis and presented three choices:

(1) The King's marriage to Mrs Simpson, she to become Queen.
(2) The King's marriage to Mrs Simpson without abdication but on the basis that she should not become Queen, and accompanied by the necessary legislation on this basis.
(3) A voluntary abdication by the King carried out in favour of the Duke of York.[56]

The Dominion prime ministers were advised that at a later stage they would be asked to consult their respective cabinets. In the meantime, said Baldwin, he would appreciate their personal views and their thoughts on how the public in their Dominion might view the matter. To maintain strict secrecy, special arrangements were made to encode and decode the messages by trusted staff. All the telegrams were marked 'Secret and Personal' and bore the special prefix 'A'. In the course of the crisis, 333 telegrams on the subject were despatched from the Dominions Office and 90 were received in reply.[57]

Beaverbrook was appalled when he heard that the King had not even seen the text of the cables to the Dominion prime ministers. 'Sir,' he exclaimed, 'you have put your head on the execution block. All that Mr Baldwin has to do now is to swing the axe.'[58] Certainly there was nothing whatsoever in the telegrams that put the King's case. On the other hand, Baldwin made his own view – that neither of the first two choices were realistic options – very clear. 'I feel convinced', he stated in the telegram,

that neither the Parliament nor the great majority of the public in all parties here should or would accept such a plan [for a morganatic marriage], any more than they would accept the proposal that Mrs Simpson should become Queen. Moreover, I think it very probable that if such an arrangement were agreed now, it would prove to be temporary and that later on pressure would be brought to bear with a view to the King's wife being given her position as Queen.[59]

'The ball had been passed to the Dominions and they were busily returning it', wrote Dawson in his diary on 29 November.[60] But another ball was being tossed around in London. In need of reassurance, Dawson decided to ring Stanley Bruce, the Australian High Commissioner, who was said to be lying ill at his house in London. 'I talked to Mrs. B[ruce], who said that the doctors had forbidden him to see a soul; but a little later she telephoned to say it would do him less harm to have a talk than to worry over what I might have to say.' He went to see Bruce, who was able to confirm that the Australian Prime Minister, Joseph Lyons, was completely behind Baldwin. Dawson was pleased. 'My enforced stay in London', he was relieved to note in his diary, 'may not have been altogether useless after all.'[61]

In the royal household, tensions had reached an unbearable level. The week after the visit to South Wales 'was horrible', said Edward's equerry, Charles Lambe. 'Everyone looked ill and desperate and old and spoke in whispers. Up to then I knew no details.' One evening, Mountbatten explained to him that the King was determined to marry Wallis. 'All that week I had nightmares', he wrote in the notes he was keeping at the time. 'I woke sometimes terrified, sometimes angry, and sometimes just unutterably miserable. There was nobody to speak to except Dickie [Mountbatten]. The subject just wasn't discussed in the Palace and one just had to wait and think.' Because he was 'emotionally exhausted', he went to an afternoon matinee of the film *Romeo & Juliet*, and was 'profoundly moved'.[62]

Meanwhile, Edward's own 'Juliet' was becoming increasingly distressed. The King told her little about what was going on, and she felt that he had become withdrawn, even from her. This left her with the alarming sense of having no control over her own situation or her future. Society appeared to hate her, now that they realized Edward wanted to marry her, not just keep her as his mistress. She and Bessie saw strangers loitering on the pavement outside their house in Regents Park, watching them. Among them may have been an operative or two sent by Special Branch to gather information for Superintendent Canning. Journalists, too, are likely to have lurked outside the house.

Hostile letters were arriving, both signed and anonymous, including one that threatened:

Had you been living 200 years ago means would have been found to rid the country of you, but no one seems to possess the courage required to send you back to the United States. It has fallen to my lot as a patriot to kill you. This is a solemn warning. I will do so.[63]

Wallis felt ready to believe the warnings she had received from Lady Londonderry and others – that the people of Britain would never put up with a marriage between the King and herself. She started to feel a 'mounting menace in the very atmosphere':

It was by now almost impossible for me to get about the streets without strangers turning to stare . . . It was as if some mysterious and silent means of communication was carrying the story of the hidden crisis into ever-widening circles of the British public.[64]

In fact, it was still the case that very few people had even heard of Wallis. But from her isolated position, unable to influence the development of events, the glances of strangers must have seemed as terrible as the bitter condemnation of whole crowds. She was later to declare that she 'did not know England very well, and the English not at all.'[65] In England in the autumn of 1936, she must have felt very much an outsider – a foreigner in a culture she could not understand.

Ill with worry, Wallis made plans to get away. 'Darling Sybil,' she wrote on 30 November to Sybil Colefax, 'I have been put to bed for a week's true isolation policy – I am very tired with – and of it all – and my heart resents the strain so I am to lie quiet.' She was making plans, she said, to leave London:

I am planning quite by myself to go away for a while – I think everybody here would like that – except one person perhaps – but I am constructing a clever means of escape – after awhile my name will be forgotten by the people and only two people will suffer instead of a mass of people who aren't interested anyway in individuals feelings but only the workings of a system. I have decided to risk [?] the result of leaving because it is an uncomfortable feeling to remain stopping in a house when the hostess has tired of me as a guest.

I shall see you before I fold my tent – much love – Wallis.[66]

To Foxy Gwynne, another close woman friend, she sent a similar message. A small trip away, she hoped, would 'give it all time to die down – perhaps returning when that d—d crown has been firmly placed.'[67]

Churchill, Duff Cooper and Beaverbrook, who were liaising with one another in their efforts to keep Edward on the throne, also thought it would be a good idea for Wallis to go away for a time. This would arrest the speed at which the crisis was developing and allow it to settle down – and the King to be crowned. But Edward, who could hardly bear Wallis to be out of his sight, was not willing to let her go. Instead, when he heard on Friday 27 November of a plot to blow up her house, he sent a note telling Wallis and her aunt to come immediately to the Fort, where they would be safe. Once she was installed at the Fort, Wallis began to comprehend the magnitude of the crisis and was utterly dismayed. The telephone rang constantly, the faces of the servants were drawn, and there were 'constant comings and goings, between the Fort and London, of advisers, aides, and courtiers.'[68]

Meanwhile, Baldwin and his Ministers took steps to shift the balance of public opinion in the Government's favour, both at home and in the Empire. They still assumed that Edward would abdicate, even though Edward had now decided against this in favour of a morganatic marriage. They met and decided that 'every effort should be made to synchronize the publication of the Message [announcing abdication] in Parliament and its publication in the Dominions. It would also be desirable, if possible, to avoid a time of publication which would enable the evening newspapers in London to criticize the event in a hostile fashion.' It would be necessary for the Press to be informed in advance in order that 'the morning newspapers might be in a position to guide public opinion' – this would, 'of course, be done in the usual manner and through the usual channels.'[69] H. A. Gwynne, the editor of the *Morning Post*, agreed. It was important, he said, that if and when the Government found it necessary to take the public into its confidence, the Prime Minister 'should assemble all the principal Editors and explain to them the course of events and the line which Ministers felt obliged to take. It was hoped in this way it might be possible to avoid a press cleavage.'[70]

On 2 December, Baldwin was due to see the King for a fourth interview, exactly one week after their last meeting. He prepared the ground for this interview at a Cabinet meeting in the morning, proposing to tell the King that 'the Cabinet were not prepared to introduce the necessary bill to legalise the morganatic marriage.' Everyone agreed to this, with the exception of Duff Cooper, who made another vain plea for delay.[71] Walter Monckton was summoned to 10 Downing Street and told of the Cabinet's decision, which he relayed to the King. Writing about this meeting in his diary, Ramsay MacDonald expressed some anxiety about what would happen when the British people actually found out what was going on. Unlike Baldwin, he was not convinced that all the electorate would support the position of the Cabinet:

I share the PM's views that the country when the issue has been put fairly before it will uphold the Cabinet, but not his optimism that it will be practically unanimous. To underestimate the resources of the King (the PM believes his word that he will abdicate without trouble, whilst I doubt it), Beaverbrook & very likely Churchill, would be a mistake.[72]

MacDonald was the only man in the Cabinet from a working-class background: he had been raised in a cottage in the Scottish Highlands, the son of a single mother who had been a domestic servant. This background may have given him a keener sense than his colleagues of the likely reaction to the royal crisis of people who were outside the circles of the elite.

In the evening, Baldwin went to Fort Belvedere to see the King, and reported that his enquiries into the views of the Dominion prime ministers were not yet complete. He added, however, that the enquiries had gone far enough to indicate that no support would be forthcoming for a morganatic marriage. To support this statement, he produced a strongly worded telegram from Prime Minister Lyons of Australia, who opposed both alternatives to abdication. Baldwin said that he regarded this telegram as a clear indication of the position of the Dominions. For years afterwards he maintained that the 'decisive factor was the uncompromising stand of the Dominion Premiers, and especially of the Prime Minister of Australia.'[73] Baldwin also told Edward at this meeting that General Hertzog of South Africa had expressed opposition to the marriage.

Baldwin's answer to Edward was not entirely honest or straight-forward, however. At 2.40 a.m. on 2 December, the day Baldwin met with Edward, he had received a telegram from Michael Savage, the Labour Prime Minister of New Zealand, backing the plan for a morganatic marriage. It rejected the idea of Wallis becoming Queen, but affirmed that 'The great affection felt in New Zealand for His Majesty and the desire of the people in this country for his happiness inspire the thought that some such arrangement might be possible.' There could be insuperable obstacles, but 'if some solution along these lines were found to be practicable it would no doubt be acceptable to the majority of the people of New Zealand.' Savage concluded by saying that because of the 'enormous popularity of the King with both races in Zealand – Pakeha and Maoris', a decision to abdicate would be received with the deepest regret; but if this were the only course open, the Dominion would be guided by the decision of the Home Government.[74] The Governor-General sent a telegram to London explaining that his Prime Minister's assessment of public opinion was based on the King's popularity among all classes in New Zealand after Edward's tour of 1920, and his belief that Edward's personality was much more inspiring than the Duke of York's.[75]

The Prime Minister of Canada, William Lyon Mackenzie King, was hesitant. It was his personal view that neither Parliament nor public opinion in Canada would accept Mrs Simpson as Queen or as the morganatic wife of the King. On these grounds, he believed that a voluntary abdication would be the 'honourable and right course for the King to pursue'. But he emphasized that such an abdication *must* be voluntary:

Were it believed King's abdication were something imposed by his Ministers (or were such in fact the case) solely because of His Majesty's intended or actual marriage to Mrs Simpson, and not a step voluntarily proposed by His Majesty himself for reasons of State, the whole matter would, I believe, be very differently regarded. Public opinion would be sharply divided.

'Sympathy with the King in his desire as a man to marry the woman of his choice', he added, 'will be widespread, if indeed it will not be universal.'[76] Mackenzie King had already indicated his sympathy for the King, when he had been in London in October and resisted several appeals from members of the court to approach the King about the harm he was doing to the Empire. On 1 December, the High Commissioner sent a message to London: 'I think it my duty to tell you that in my opinion [Mackenzie King] is unduly influenced by what he describes as King's obligations to Mrs Simpson.'[77]

The Irish Free State sent no response at this stage, though the Prime Minister, Eamon de Valera, had made it clear that his own position was one of detachment. He told Sir Harry Batterbee, who had brought him the message from Baldwin, that 'at first blush' he was inclined to favour the option of a morganatic marriage. He pointed out that Edward was undoubtedly popular everywhere including Ireland, and he thought that 'every avenue ought to be explored before he was excluded from the Throne.' It was true, he acknowledged, that divorce was not recognized in Catholic countries, but Edward was a Protestant king of a Protestant country with different divorce laws and different attitudes to divorce. 'Many – especially young people – throughout the Empire would, in these democratic days, be attracted by the idea of a young King ready to give up all for love.'[78]

Sir Harry was surprised by de Valera's reaction, and also by the fact that it was shared by John Whelan Dulanty, the Irish Ambassador to London, and Mr Walshe, another advisor, who were both present for most of the meeting. He tried to persuade them that the United Kingdom public saw things differently from the Irish public and would not tolerate the King marrying a woman 'of the nature of Mrs Simpson'. Caesar's wife, he said, 'must be above suspicion'. Eamon de Valera replied that if that were so, he supposed there was nothing for it but abdication.[79]

Baldwin did not explain to Edward the details of the replies from New Zealand, Canada, and the Irish Free State. But he told him there was little hope, given the opinions of the Dominion leaders, of pressing on with his plan for a morganatic marriage. The King was in a very weak position. Indeed, his position was now far weaker than it had been before the visit to South Wales, for his Government had now been formally consulted and had given 'advice' – which he was bound to accept. In every way, the plan for a morganatic marriage had turned out to be a mistake. It required legislation which the Government refused to introduce. And it had removed Edward's great strength – that constitutionally, he was entitled to marry anyone he liked, except a Roman Catholic.

The King replied to Baldwin's report on the Dominion premiers with a request. He said firmly that he wanted Parliament to be consulted. For even though Baldwin and the National Government had a majority – and the Labour and Liberal leaders had agreed not to oppose the Government on this issue – they by no means spoke for all elected MPs. Representative of the electorate, Parliament was the proper and best channel for a full exploration of the views and reactions of the citizens of Britain.

In his memoirs, Edward later recorded this conversation between himself and the Prime Minister:

'What about Parliament?' I asked.

'The answer would, I am sure, be the same.'

'But Parliament has not been consulted', I persisted. 'The issue has never been presented.'

He answered, unruffled. 'I have caused inquiries to be set afoot in the usual manner. The response has been such as to convince my colleagues and myself that the people would not approve of Your Majesty's marriage with Mrs Simpson.'[80]

Baldwin never explained the nature of these enquiries. By 'the usual manner', he probably meant consultations with Government MPs through the whips and with party managers of the Opposition. This was standard practice: such consultations are designed to give a picture of what is thought by the House of Commons, political associations and the leaders of local communities. Baldwin would be entitled to express confidence in their reliability. But the views of these people are not necessarily the same as the views of the ordinary people, especially in such a socially divided nation as Britain in 1936. Baldwin, his Government – and Edward and Wallis too – had yet to find out what the general public thought about the idea of the King marrying an American woman, twice divorced.

7

'The People want their King'

At 4.30 p.m. on Tuesday, 2 December, news editors in Fleet Street were springing from their chairs and shouting, 'It's begun! Look at this!' They had been waiting for months for the story of Edward and Wallis to break, and now there was a definite sign that it was about to happen. The Press Association tape machine was flashing through the news that the Bishop of Bradford, Dr Blunt, had publicly uttered words of reproof to the King in the course of an address at the Bradford Diocesan Conference.[1] Criticizing the outspoken Bishop of Birmingham for his suggestion that the coronation should be secularized, Blunt had declared that

The benefit of the King's Coronation depends, under God, upon two elements: First, on the faith, prayer, and self-dedication of the King himself, and on that it would be improper for me to say anything except to commend him, and ask you to commend him, to God's grace, which he will so abundantly need, as we all need it – for the King is a man like ourselves – if he is to do his duty faithfully.

He added, piously, 'We hope that he is aware of his need. Some of us wish that he gave more positive signs of his awareness.'[2] The address was reported in the *Yorkshire Post* and picked up quickly by some other provincial papers. The *Birmingham Post* commented that nobody, cleric or layman, had thought fit to address such words of reproof to the King of England for hundreds of years.[3]

Readers were astonished to learn that a bishop of the Church of

England had rebuked the King, and in such a gratuitous way. A man who was the same age as the King and worked in his family's linen business in Belfast described his own reaction in his diary on 1 December: 'A little paragraph appeared in paper tonight,' he wrote, 'recording speech made by Bishop Blunt about the leaving out of the Communion Service from the Coronation Service. He is against the leaving of it out, & said one would wish that the King would give a little more evidence of his regard for religious duties!'[4] From a village in Sussex, a seventy-year-old woman wrote to the Palace on 2 December in indignation at the Bishop. 'Who made *him* a judge & a ruler?! Does *he* follow the teaching of Jesus Christ in dressing up in expensive robes & a mitre?' She was Church of England, she added, but thought that there was 'so much humbug in it' – and that if the bishop came to her neighbourhood, she would 'protest against him, even if I were turned out of the church.'[5] A man in Glasgow made the following rather desperate offer to the King:

If your Majesty desires that the Bishop of Bradford be bayoneted I shall if you will so command be happy to do the needful, even though I am at heart a pacifist. If I should fail, any one of 4 millions of your Scottish subjects will be prepared to do the needful.[6]

The first sentence of a letter from a man in Aberdeen to the Bishop of Bradford (which he copied to the King) was, 'I think you may be fairly described as a toad.'[7]

After such a long period of strained silence by the press on the royal love affair, 'Blunt's mildly reproachful words, given prominence in the *Yorkshire Post*,' commented the journalist Bill Deedes, 'acted as a sort of starting-pistol.'[8] The press started cautiously to publish articles linking Blunt's judgement to the King's love affair. At first, only the provincial newspapers, including the *Manchester Guardian* and the *Birmingham Post*, covered the story. But these articles were 'the advance guard', commented the English journalist Malcolm Muggeridge, 'and soon heavy artillery, cavalry, tanks, pursuit planes, and even poison gas, were brought into action. All other news was discarded, all restraint laid aside.'⁹ The press agreement collapsed completely – 'The fat is in the fire today,' observed Cecil Headlam in his diary on 2 December.¹⁰

By 3 December, the story was well and truly out, throughout Britain and the Empire. 'Now, we are – without a King? With a Queen? What? The Simpson affair is on the surface', wrote Virginia Woolf. 'All London was gay & garrulous – not exactly gay, but excited.'¹¹ Lady Milner, who went to a 'news reel' to glean expressions of opinion, wrote in her diary that the 'streets have been packed all day & newspapers sold as fast as they were printed.'¹² Marie Stopes, the birth control pioneer whose book *Married Love* had caused a storm when it was published in 1918, hastened to offer the King the benefit of her advice. Thousands of his subjects, she wrote in a letter to him, had turned to her on every imaginable problem of marriage. She suggested that a talk with her might be helpful – 'when I could place at your disposal my unique experience and an ingenuity of mind which is entirely devoted to Yourself. I hold myself entirely at Your Majesty's immediate disposal at any time and place in the hope I may be of a little help.'¹³

All the morning papers sold out, and the headlines showed that the lines of battle were clearly drawn. *The Times*, the *Morning Post* and the *Daily Telegraph* were against the King, and the headline of *The Times* warned grimly of a 'Constitutional Crisis'. However, the *Express* and the *Mail* backed the King with enthusiasm, reflecting the opinions of their owners, Beaverbrook and Rothermere. The headline of the *Daily Mail* insisted that, 'The People want their King'. The *Daily Mirror* and the *Daily Sketch* were also strongly for the King, and the leader in the *News Chronicle* advocated a morganatic marriage. The circulation of the first group of newspapers was roughly 80,000, while that of the second group was close to nine million,¹⁴ and it appeared, observed Beaverbrook with satisfaction, that the King had a 'wider and more influential support in the Press than we ever anticipated.'¹⁵

The public queued up for the evening editions, which were illustrated with photographs showing the King and Mrs Simpson together at Ascot, at restaurants, on the yacht *Nahlin* and just about everywhere else. For months now, wrote the journalists Frank Owen and R. J. Thompson, these pictures had been stored in every newspaper office, and now 'the public gasped at them'.[16] 'Spain, Germany, Russia – all are elbowed out', observed Virginia Woolf in her diary. 'The marriage stretches from one end of the paper to another. Pictures of D of York & the Princesses fill every cranny. Mrs Simpson is snapped by lime light at midnight as she gets out of her car. Her luggage is also photographed.'[17] A travelling salesman remarked to a woman who was a book buyer for a department store in Kensington, London, that he would never forget 'when going to business the day the news broke, waiting on Earls Court Station – crowds of people all reading their newspapers & dead silence. It was eerie.'[18] According to the London daily, the *Evening Standard*, the Duke and Duchess of York returned to London from Edinburgh in the early morning, then went to Marlborough House to see Queen Mary. They had many engagements in London but 'All were cancelled.'[19]

The newsreels had a story ready, too. *The Constitutional Crisis*, distributed by Universal, observed that, 'The strain is intense for the King, his ministers, his people and for the lady of his choice.' Photographs of 'the lady', looking sweet-natured and attractive, were shown repeatedly in the newsreel. The King himself was pictured looking handsome and thoughtful. The newsreel commented that the 'modern tendency for greater personal freedom is in sharp contrast with the confines of constitutional latitude.' It ended with *God Save the King*, and offered the opinion that 'One thing is in no doubt: the sympathy of the British people goes out to him that as a man his happiness be achieved and that as a king, long may he reign over us.'[20]

From Stanley Baldwin's point of view, thought Tom Dugdale, his Parliamentary Private Secretary, this was the ideal way for the story to break. 'Now we are in for an upheaval of public opinion,' he said to his wife, Nancy, 'one which could not have been brought about in a more desirable, and a less scandalous way; purely religious, non-political, non-sectarian – just SB's luck!'[21] *The Times* was at pains to present Baldwin's position in favourable terms and to encourage criticism of the King. 'I thank you for your admirable leader in the "Times" this morning', wrote the Archbishop of Canterbury to

Dawson on 3 December. 'I note that the "Daily Mail" has broken lose [sic]', he added, 'and ventilates the impossible compromise [that is, a morganatic marriage]: also *News Chronicle*. I do most earnestly hope that the Government will stand firm. The two essentials of the present situation are swiftness and decisiveness.'[22] At first, Francis Williams, the editor of the pro-Labour *Daily Herald*, took the attitude of, ' "Good luck to the King" and let him marry whoever he pleases.'[23] Soon afterwards, though, the paper argued that the King was bound to abide by the advice of his Ministers.

Much of the press coverage blamed Baldwin for the fact that for so long the people of Britain had been deliberately kept in the dark about the story. 'May I suggest that if we are to believe the teachings of our Church,' asserted a letter published in the *Daily Mirror*, 'the All Highest did not think it beneath His dignity to take unto himself "a commoner" to wife, thereby giving us The Master – The King of Kings.'[24] 'We do not believe', argued the *Evening News*, 'that the British people or the people of the Empire any longer consider it a part of the kingly duty to forgo marriage with the lady of his choice – a privilege enjoyed by the lowliest of his subjects – in the interests of constitutional tradition.' More important than the maintenance of any tradition, it added, was the need to keep on the throne a man 'whose kingly capacity has already stood the test of long and faithful service.'[25] The *Star* agreed:

Why should he [the King] be denied the common happiness of mankind? We see no insuperable reason. The Cabinet may tender him advice in one direction, but there is more than one way in which the interests of the State and of the King can be reconciled. Talk of abdication does not alarm us, but it is folly, a form of disloyalty to the King and the people.

It was up to the statesmen, insisted the *Star*, to find a way of keeping the King on the throne and also to promote his personal happiness. 'There may be better Prime Ministers,' it added, but 'there is no better King.'[26]

A particular disappointment for Baldwin was the view of the *News Chronicle*. Since this newspaper was the traditional voice of Nonconformists, who were generally seen as puritan in their approach to sexual morality, he thought he had reason to expect its support. But it was not forthcoming. There are 'many people in this country who would not desire to see as Queen of England a woman who had previously been married' and also some who would object to 'an American citizen occupying that high rank', observed the *News Chronicle*. 'But,' it added,

if the King, who is of an age to know his own mind, is sufficiently in love to persist in his intention, the public would, we think, wish that he should marry the woman of his choice, but that he should do so in his capacity as Duke of Cornwall. His wife's position would then be that of King's Consort, not that of Queen of England.[27]

Lady Milner, who was pleased to note that the *Morning Post* and the *Telegraph* were 'very good', was far less happy with the evening papers, which 'are rather pro-Simpson – as is the *News Chronicle*'.[28] Politically, thought Beaverbrook, Baldwin was 'in danger of being killed stone dead. There appeared to be a tide now running with immense and gathering force in favour of the King.'[29]

The 'King's crisis [is] now public property', commented Bruce Lockhart, who edited the 'Londoner's Diary' in the *Evening Standard*, in his personal diary on 3 December. But the reaction of the public was not, found Lockhart, what Baldwin had expected. 'For weeks,' he observed, 'MPs have been saying that [the] whole country is seething about [the] King's conduct and Mrs Simpson and that they were being deluged with letters from their constituents. Probably true; but letters came from Mrs Rector and Mrs Town Councillor.' It was now quite clear, he said, 'that ninety per cent of [the] country had never heard of Mrs Simpson. Now there will be – for [the] moment at least – a reaction in favour of [the] King.'[30] In the first days after the news broke, 90 per cent of the letters received by the national newspapers were said to be in favour of the King.[31]

The King himself was sent thousands of letters, most of them offering him support. Letters and telegrams, addressed to Buckingham Palace, Fort Belvedere and St James's Palace, started to arrive daily, from all over the nation and also from abroad. Within the next ten days the King or his personal staff received nearly five thousand letters and telegrams. 'My Dear Wife and myself having just read in the *Daily Sketch* that your postal deliveries are now sent to you by motor van, due to the quantity, the majority possibly from loyal subjects,' wrote one man to the King, 'we also wish to express our loyalty likewise.'[32]

Most of the letters and telegrams were sent by people of the working and middle classes, though not entirely. Some of the letters are written in an uneven hand and with spelling mistakes, suggesting that their authors did not have much formal education. 'I suppose this will never get to you,' said one letter, 'but who ever get it don't give it to the press the writing and spelling is bad but my heart is good.'[33] Many people were determined to write, regardless of the difficulty this might pose or, indeed, of the cost of a stamp which, for an inland letter in 1936, was one and a half (old) pence – no inconsiderable sum for a poor family. According to a report by the British Medical Association in 1936, 'The average [weekly] income per head, exclusive of rent and rates, is shown to range from 4s 9d [four shillings and nine old pence] for the unemployed, to 10s 6d for the employed. This weekly sum has to cover not only food but clothes, heating and lighting.'[34] The decision to spend one and a half pence on postage, therefore, using up money for food and other essentials, would not have been taken lightly.

It is not clear whether Edward saw any of the letters arriving for him, as it was customary for a king's Private Secretary to deal with the mail and only to show him anything of particular importance. The rush of events at this time, in any case, would have allowed few opportunities for Hardinge to attend to the King's correspondence. Some of the letter-writers had little confidence in the likelihood of their messages reaching the King. 'As a one-time Private Secretary to one of your present Ministers,' wrote a man called Claude Davis on 6 December, 'I realize there is small chance of this letter reaching your own eyes.' But the urge to help him in any way in his 'solitary position', he said, 'compels and justifies the effort.'[35] Another letter from London was equally doubtful. 'I suppose this letter may not find its way into your hands? I hope it does, because I wonder if you have any means of knowing how your "common" people think during the present crisis.'[36] Certainly it would have been helpful for the King to read these letters of support, which offered a very different view to that of the Britannicus letter.

Many letters were full of warm enthusiasm for Wallis. 'Please accept one of your loyal subjects' congratulations on your forthcoming marriage with, I am certain, one of the sweetest of ladies', wrote a Denbighshire woman. 'Our own King can not choose wrongly! . . . And long may *you* and your *beloved* lady live. Again, God bless you *both*!'[37] Another woman, living in London's Baker Street, hoped that he would marry 'the lady of your choice, but please don't abdicate, England needs you too. You have the courage to marry, have the courage to carry on. You are doing a marvellous job, don't leave it, England may appreciate it when she wakes up.'[38] From the tearoom at Wittering Aerodrome came the hope that 'you will marry this lady you love & tell them all to go to the deuce. We *don't want anybody else as King*, so please don't abdicate.'[39] 'My mother has a milk round in this village,' wrote a teenage boy (who said he had sent a 'stinker' to the Bishop of Bradford),

& has out of curiosity asked some of the customers their opinion on the crisis & they solidly state that the King should marry whom he likes & that they want him & nobody else as King. These I am sure are the thoughts of 90% of the British nation . . . Long live the King & Queen (to be).[40]

From a poor widow with two sons who had been in the navy and one son who was partially blind came the message, 'You are the People's King and nothing can kill their Love and Faith in You . . . Long life and happiness with the dear Lady You have chosen, "God bless our King".'[41] 'We are all with you', urged a letter giving the New Zealand High Commission on the Strand in London as its address, 'to the last ditch.'[42]

Behind most of the correspondence was a wish to comfort and reassure the King. 'Cheer up!' urged one letter. 'You must and will triumph over your difficulties.'[43] Knowing from the newsreels and the press that Edward liked to visit his subjects in their homes, as he had done on the Penygarn Estate in South Wales, a number of people sent him an invitation to their own home. They hoped to provide him with the peace and quiet he would need to get through this difficult time. 'We're newlyweds and still furnishing bit by bit,' wrote one man,

but if at any time you look for sympathy in the upper ten thousand or million, and find it lacking; remember it awaits you here with an easy chair, tobacco and a fireside whose privacy is our most treasured possession, yet whose welcome to Your Majesty is complete and unconditional.[44]

Many letters were from ex-servicemen and members of the British Legion, who gave their regiments, ranks and, sometimes, their numbers. They were often written in the language and with the imagery of the Great War, especially that of trench warfare: 'We are with you . . . to a man'; 'If Mrs Simpson is good enough for His Majesty we want her. Stick to your guns'; 'Stand on your ground'; 'Stick to your Post'; 'Stand firm'.[45] A telegram from the Caledon Shipyard Workers urged the King, 'Whatever you decide the straight eye at your command.'[46] 'I beseech your Majesty to "Carry on",' wrote another ex-serviceman, 'so its "eyes Right", Hold your heads up. "Steady" – !!!'[47] After a visit to the Kempton races, one man wrote:

the majority of the sporting world are with you body & soul. A message from Wembley reads: – 'All ex-servicemen are furious at what they consider the interference of the Bishops.' Wonder if the Bishop of Bradford will reply to my letter!!! My King – a British-American Alliance would assure world peace. Stand by your guns![48]

Ex-servicemen abroad, too, wrote to encourage the King. From Halifax in Nova Scotia came the message, 'Trust in God and Keep your powder dry.'[49]

Geoffrey H. Wells, a minor author writing under the pseudonym of Geoffrey West who lived in Oxford and was the son of a Cardiff businessman (but no relation of H. G. Wells, although he shared his surname and, indeed, wrote his biography in 1930), was soon fed up with the fever of excitement: 'Oh God it goes on', he wrote in his diary,

> If the King *does* back down, my respect for him will totally vanish (not that I've ever had a lot!): if they want a dummy, not a man, for the job then it really is time to abolish the job. God save us from the long-faced Duke of York – who would, I'm sure, be the best of good boys!

The fact that Wallis was divorced with her two ex-husbands still living did not bother him in the slightest: 'I should have thought if the king didn't mind it was no-one else's business.'[50] The mathematician Alan Turing took the same attitude. 'I should tolerate no interference by bishops,' he told his mother, '& I don't see that the King need either.'[51]

In America, where news about the King had been unfettered for months, the press trumpeted the King's cause. The *New York Post* published an open letter to King Edward from Sinclair Lewis, the author of such novels as the satirical *Babbitt*. Addressed to 'David Windsor', it said, 'We don't know what's happened, but one thing we can tell you – that the whole of America is so excited that you've become a human being instead of just the King of England.' He urged Edward to come to America, where he would 'be received as no guest ever has been'. Americans believed, he added, that

> a man must have his own conscience and his own life. We believe that perhaps the most important thing that has happened in the last hundred years is whether David Windsor shall have his own life or not. We believe that it is perhaps more important to the British Empire that a young man in England named David Windsor should be completely loyal to the girl he loves than to a British mirage.[52]

'Don't you believe Baldwin about the people of this country being against you!' wrote a man in Virginia to the King. 'All the right thinking people here are for you and Mrs Simpson and I wish you great luck and happiness.'[53] A man in Atlanta wrote to say that 'the American People are with you in choosing the Woman of your Choice in Mrs Simpson. I am with you Heart & Soul. God Bless you Both.'[54]

Love and sympathy were sent from the Associated Negro Press, based in Chicago – 'your loyal coloured subjects in the United States of America', it said, were praying for him.[55]

But if Americans generally and the majority of people in Britain seemed to be backing the King, it was also true that Lockhart's Mrs Rectors and Mrs Town Councillors did not. 'My wife has just returned from a Liberal National Women's Committee,' wrote a man from Glasgow, 'and she tells me all her colleagues were boiling over with indignation as, of course, she herself has been since the news came out.'[56] But these feelings were by no means limited to women. 'Bad show!' exclaimed a Sussex farmer in his diary.[57] A retired engineer who had been secretary to the Governor of the United Provinces in India, and was now living in Kensington, London, wrote in his diary that, 'the papers are full of the King's crisis with the Govt. We all hope he will be wise & sacrifice his own feelings towards Mrs Simpson.'[58] A woman working in the book department of Barkers, who was a regular reader of *The Times*, wrote in her diary that

The dominions – India – & the common people are united in the matter considering that Mrs Simpson is an unsuitable person to occupy the English Throne. Newsboys posters & Carmen are very blunt about it, describing the lady as 'The American Whore'. Everyone in cafes & tea shops was agog with the news . . . Tim came home with stories in rather bad taste from the club – It's an appalling state of affairs.[59]

Suddenly it was permissible to enjoy sexual innuendo, even in polite circles. 'There are a good many lewd limericks etc going round in male circles', noted the Sussex farmer. 'We hear the new Cunard liner will be named Mrs Simpson,' he added a few days later, 'because she is slightly faster than the Queen Mary!'[60]

Lockhart thought he saw clear signs that Whitehall *wanted* the King to abdicate. 'Lunched in the City at the Rothschilds – talked of nothing but the King', he wrote. 'Gather that Whitehall wants King to abdicate in any case – altogether too irresponsible.'[61] On the following day, Lockhart 'Lunched with Harold [Nicolson] and Sibyl Colefax at Boulestin's. Harold says bulk of House and of serious people in City and Whitehall want King to go anyway; too irresponsible and now his prestige damaged.'[62] 'Of course there yet may be some way out of the impasse which will save abdication', wrote the Conservative MP, Cecil Headlam, in his diary. 'I confess, however, that I can see no such way – and I feel myself that it would be a pity to find one.' The King, he said,

has shown himself so obstinate and unbalanced in this affair that it would be a mistake in my opinion to let him get away with it – it would only mean some other 'crisis' in the future. He is clearly not the right kind of man to be a constitutional monarch and, unpleasant though all this business is, it may be a blessing in disguise.

'The Yorks', he added, 'should do the job admirably.'[63]

Baldwin sent a telegram on 3 December to the Dominion prime ministers: 'So far as I can tell from my informal conversations with [the King] it is likely that he will decide to abdicate.'[64] However, the Prime Minister was evidently uncertain about this 'likelihood'. Referring to a draft of the Abdication Bill, which was telegraphed at the same time, he asked the Dominions for their cooperation in avoiding public debate. 'We feel,' said Baldwin, 'and we hope that you will agree, that in the circumstances of the case the less legislating, and therefore the less opportunity for public discussion and debate, the better.'[65]

Baldwin started to pressure the King and to bargain with him. When Monckton urged an immediate decree absolute for Mrs Simpson, enabling Edward to marry Wallis immediately if he abdicated, Baldwin suggested to his Cabinet that it might be possible to pass special legislation in order to arrange for it. But Duff Cooper pointed out to Baldwin that as well as being somewhat amoral, this would lay the Government open to the charge of wanting to get rid of the King. It would be said, said Duff, that while they had been unwilling to pass special legislation for a morganatic marriage in order to keep him, they had been willing to introduce legislation which, according to existing law, would legalize adultery simply to expedite his departure. Cooper was so obviously right that the scheme was quickly dropped.[66]

Some people, including journalists, assumed that Blunt's speech was a deliberate attempt to break the news of Edward's wish to marry Wallis. Lady Rhondda told Mr Baldwin that 'in common with most of Fleet Street I believed ... that the public break of the news at the moment when it occurred had probably been arranged for' (she added that she saw no harm in this).[67] Certainly, Baldwin had been encouraged by some key figures to bring the news into the public domain. Just days after Edward's tour of South Wales, Archbishop Lang had told Baldwin that if there was to be any announcement, 'it should be made as soon as possible'. Lang added that if this course were taken, the King

must leave as soon as possible. It would be out of the question that he should remain until the decree is made absolute. It is needless to dwell on this necessity ... Only the pressure of our common anxiety – and hope – can justify this letter. It is written shortly and hurriedly. Forgive it.[68]

In the face of mounting suspicion about Blunt's reasons for mentioning the King in his speech, the Bishop of Bradford became defensive. 'I studiously took care to say nothing with regard to the King's private life,' he insisted, 'because I know nothing at all about it.'[69] But then, wondered some, why mention the King's private life at all? If it was a breach of protocol to mention the monarch in parliamentary debate, then surely, at the very least, it was odd to mention him at a diocesan conference? Blunt explained that it had nothing to do with Mrs Simpson – that when he had prepared his speech, nearly two months before the conference, he had never heard of Mrs Simpson. He acknowledged, though, that by the time he actually gave the speech, he *did* know about her.[70] Certainly it would have been surprising had it not come up as a topic of conversation between himself and Dawson on the weekend of 31 October, when he had gone on church business to Langcliffe, in the West Riding of Yorkshire – for Dawson went there too, to Langcliffe Hall, his country home. 'Then came a hurried week-end visit to Langcliffe', wrote Dawson in his written account of this period, 'for the consecration of our Churchyard extension by the Bishop of Bradford, who was eventually to play so conspicuous, if unintentional, a part in precipitating the crisis on to the public stage.'[71]

Years later, the Bishop of Bradford informed Geoffrey Dawson's biographer that neither on 31 October, nor on any other date, did he exchange a word with Dawson on the royal matter.[72] This would have required tremendous restraint on Dawson's part, however, since by the end of October he was so preoccupied by the crisis that he seemed to be always talking about it – with Chamberlain, with Baldwin, with Violet Milner, with the Archbishop of Canterbury and with Alexander Hardinge.

Dawson said that he had first found out about Blunt's speech on 1 December, when he returned to his office after dinner and found on the table a report of the address. With the report, he added, was a long quotation from the leader to appear in the next day's *Yorkshire Post*. Assuming that the Rothermere and Beaverbrook organs would not explode with the news about Wallis Simpson, and with assurance from Lord Camrose regarding the *Telegraph* and from H. A. Gwynne regarding the *Morning Post*, he 'felt pretty confident now that the whole London Press was safe'. He therefore decided to wait until the next day before taking any action in *The Times*, restricting himself on 2 December to printing the full text of the bishop's address. He also printed 'a prophetic leading article on the wonderful reception' of Albert and Elizabeth, the Duke and Duchess of York, in Edinburgh:[73]

Two of King George's four surviving sons have found their brides in ancient Scottish families to the general satisfaction of the nation; and that loyalty which has always been part of the fiercest pride of Scotland, and which overflows so spontaneously from the Sovereign to all his kind, is combined with a special affection for the Prince in whose posterity another race of Scottish descent may some day be called to the Imperial Throne . . . Nevertheless this visit of the HEIR PRESUMPTIVE to the great fortress that now stands aloft as a symbol of indissoluble union . . . encourages the speculation whether a time may not some day come when these historic 'Honours' may be used again, with the free consent of the Scots, in the crowning of a King of Scotland on the Stone of Destiny.[74]

Beaverbrook later described this report, as well as some earlier statements in *The Times*, as part of a campaign by Geoffrey Dawson against the King, 'almost in secret code'. To anyone who could read the code, he said, the message was clear – that 'The King was causing scandal, that he could count on support from no Party in Parliament, and there was a popular Heir Presumptive waiting in the wings.'[75] John Gunther had also detected this 'secret' code. In an 'otherwise meaningless editorial', he wrote, *The Times* had uttered a curious warning on 30 November, the day before Blunt's speech. 'The Commons', the editorial had declared, 'may well prove itself what the country has often required in similar times . . . a Council of State [to govern] in any crisis, foreign or domestic.'[76] On the next day, 'as if by prearranged signal,' said Gunther, 'the Bishop of Bradford struck against the King.'[77] It was his opinion that there had been some kind of arrangement between Blunt and Dawson.[78]

Edward was doing everything he could to protect Wallis from the press. Robin Barrington-Ward, the assistant editor of *The Times*, promised Walter Monckton that the paper did not intend to publish the 'full life' of Mrs Simpson in the next issue. But this was an implicit threat to publish such an article at a later date. It was said in Fleet Street, commented Beaverbrook later, that the 'full life' would carry photographs of her two former husbands, her mother's boarding house and other illustrations. A promise to refrain from publication for the 'next issue', therefore, said Beaverbrook, 'was regarded as a cat-and-mouse game, and the King was the mouse. Torture.'[79]

Dawson and Baldwin understood the power of the press, both to intimidate Edward and to influence the public. They met together twice on 2 December and agreed that the story of Wallis and Edward needed careful presentation – 'The idea that the King might marry her must now be broached, but *only as unthinkable*.' Later that day, Baldwin phoned Dawson, telling him that the King had asked him to stop any attack on Mrs Simpson in the press. 'In vain,' commented Dawson in his diary, 'SB had explained that the Press in England was free and that he had no control over *The Times* or over any other newspaper.' However, Baldwin asked to see the leader so that he could inform the King of its contents: 'by this time . . . the paper was just going to press; but towards midnight I sent a proof of the leader by messenger to Downing Street and heard no more about it. SB – with Tommy Dugdale and all the other faithful staff who were supporting him – was able at last to go to bed.'[80]

The first few days of December were harrowing for Wallis. She was horrified when the story broke in the press and had no idea of the level of popular support for the King or for herself. Indeed, she would have had far less sense of what the population felt than did Edward, who had met so many of the ordinary people on his numerous visits to the provincial and industrial areas of Britain since 1919. Some of them seemed to realize how isolated she must feel. A woman in Middlesex who was desperate to help the King wrote, 'If only I could go to your lady and tell her just how we feel about it and give her a word of sympathy from the people, and let her know that our hearts are full of sorrow and wishing only for the best for you both.'[81] Many regarded Wallis as a force for good who would share Edward's democratic ideals. A letter that arrived later in the week advocated that he reserve the right to marry until after the coronation – to anyone he liked. In the meantime, it suggested, 'Mrs Simpson might well become known to the public as Your Majesty's friend. On unofficial occasions, such as visiting distressed areas, housing estates, etc., she could be in the party; and she might find ways of coming into touch with people herself through art, music, or child welfare . . .'[82]

By 2 December, Wallis was close to a nervous breakdown. Edward realized with dismay that the situation was becoming intolerable for her and agreed that she should leave the country, quickly. Wallis had only a day to make preparations and had no chance to return to her house at Cumberland Terrace to make arrangements with the servants and organize her affairs. All she could do was send her maid, Mary Burke, to London to pick up a few clothes. Meanwhile, Edward arranged for her to travel with Perry Brownlow, his Lord-in-Waiting, as well as Inspector Evans of Scotland Yard. Educated at Eton and Sandhurst, and a Lieutenant in the Grenadier Guards, Lord Brownlow had succeeded his father as sixth Baron Brownlow in 1927. Now thirty-seven, he was dignified 'to a degree', remarked an item in the press, 'that a stranger might mistake for pomposity . . . a man of the highest integrity.'[83] He and wife Kitty had named their son, born in March 1936, after Edward, who was his godfather. So loyal was Perry's friendship that Edward knew he could trust him completely to look after the woman he loved.

Wallis decided to go to the south of France to the home of Katherine and Herman Rogers, the American friends she had stayed with in Peking. They had insisted that she turn to them for help at any time. 'You are still my one living example of a perfectly wise and complete person', wrote Herman Rogers in October. 'We are with you always . . . Come to us if and when you can . . .'[84] Although he and his wife had lived for many years in New York, they had a second home in Cannes. This was a villa called Lou Viei – a twelfth-century monastery above the city, on a ledge below a hill, making it an ideal refuge. Accommodation was arranged for Wallis and Lord Brownlow on a Channel steamer, which had been booked in the name of Mr and Mrs Harris. It was not possible for Mrs Merryman to come too, because the journey would be difficult and unpredictable. Wallis also had to leave behind Slipper, her cairn terrier, a gift from Edward. 'In the bitter days that followed,' wrote Edward in his memoirs, 'I was to be grateful for his companionship. He followed me around The Fort; he slept by my bed; he was the mute witness of my meetings with the Prime Minister.'[85]

On the evening of 3 December, Brownlow arrived at the Fort to collect Wallis for the journey. He found the King looking 'rather pathetic, tired, overwrought, and evidently dreading Wallis's departure, almost like a small boy being left behind at school for the first time.'[86] His parting words to Wallis were, 'I don't know how it's all going to end. It will be some time before we can be together again. You must wait for me no matter how long it takes. I shall never give you up.'[87] As they departed, the King leant across to Wallis, said Brownlow, 'to get one last touch of her hand – there were tears in his eyes and on his cheeks, and his voice was shaking – "Wherever you reach tonight, no matter what time, telephone me. Bless you, my darling."'[88] They left at 6.00 p.m. and then, Edward later recalled, 'A sense of acute loneliness filled me.'[89] Yet he had every confidence that he would be with her again and that all would turn out well. Wallis, though, was in complete despair, believing that she would never see Edward again.[90]

As soon as they had left, Brownlow urged a change of plan – instead of going to France, he should take Wallis to Belton House, his estate in Lincolnshire. This plot had been secretly hatched by Brownlow with Churchill and Beaverbrook: they thought that at Belton, Wallis would be safely out of the crisis but still close enough to exert an influence and, hopefully, to persuade the King against giving up his throne. If necessary, she would be able to go to London to see him in person. There was also a worry that if Wallis went to France, Edward might miss her so terribly that he would rush after her – which would precipitate him into abdication. Going to Belton would have been a much easier journey for Wallis, and staying with the Brownlows would have given her a period of calm respite, which she sorely needed. Belton is a gracious seventeenth-century house in peaceful surroundings: elegant gardens and acres of parkland, with avenues of oak and ash trees and fields of sheep. Wallis knew Belton House well, because she had stayed there with Edward several times, as the guest of the Brownlow family. But on this occasion she was not willing to go. It would break her agreement with Edward and risk weakening the bond of trust that united them. Belton was firmly refused, and she and Brownlow started their journey to France, driven by the King's chauffeur, Ladbrook.

As they travelled south, Wallis and Brownlow talked almost incessantly, but they had different perspectives on the problem. Brownlow's hopes and instructions were based primarily on *no* marriage; while Wallis was still talking vaguely about the morganatic plan. 'We crossed the Channel, Wallis and I,' Brownlow reported to Diana Vreeland, 'and our first night was in Rouen, where we found rooms in a hotel, just like ordinary tourists on the road.' Here Brownlow telephoned the King, who had been lying awake all night, worrying, to tell him they were safe.[91] Wallis was completely overcome by fear and anxiety, recalled Brownlow later:

'Perry,' Wallis said to me through the door, after we'd been in our separate rooms for what seemed like an eternity, 'will you please leave the door open between your room and mine? I'm so frightened. I'm so nervous.' I did. Then she called to me: 'Perry, will you please sleep in the bed next to me? I cannot be alone.'

He went into her room, fully dressed, and pulled the blanket over himself. But then she started to cry. 'Sounds came out of her', Brownlow told Diana Vreeland, 'that were absolutely without top, bottom . . . that were *primeval*. There was nothing I could do but lie down beside her, hold her hand, and make her feel that she was not alone.'[92] The next morning, they set off on the rest of the two-day drive through France. It was a nightmare journey. Their identity had been discovered, and the registration number of their Buick appeared in the French press. They were pursued by journalists, and Wallis was repeatedly forced to crouch on the floor of the car, concealed by a rug.

After two days and numerous detours to escape the press, they finally arrived at Lou Viei, at two o'clock on the morning of Sunday 6 December. Before they could drive through the gates to be welcomed by Herman and Katherine Rogers, they had to negotiate a crowd of several hundred reporters hovering outside the villa. They were completely exhausted, and Wallis felt utterly hopeless. She was separated by the English Channel and nearly a thousand miles from the man she loved, whom she now believed she would never see again. Her beloved Aunt Bessie was far away, and so was her loyal maid, Mary Burke. She was trapped behind the gates of Lou Viei; any attempt to leave would have been disastrous and possibly dangerous. How different was her predicament from the one imagined by Helen Hardinge, who telephoned her mother, Lady Milner, with the news that, 'Lord Brownlow had been the luckless companion of the flight of Mrs Simpson across France. All done for the cinema! An offer has already come from Hollywood.'[93]

8

'Tell us the facts, Mr Baldwin!'

Before Wallis left, she had urged Edward to make a radio broadcast to the people and put his dilemma to them. If the British people were ever to know what was in his heart and mind, she said, he *must* speak out without delay. She was aware, she said later, of the immense impact on public opinion of President Roosevelt's 'fireside chats', and also of the popular Christmas broadcasts by Edward's father, George V.[1] She wanted him to say he would give her up – 'tell the country tomorrow I am lost to you'.[2] That he adamantly refused to consider, but he seized on the idea of the broadcast. As Prince of Wales, he had made seventy-five radio broadcasts and he understood well the power of speaking to people in their own homes.[3] A woman who hoped that 'nothing on Earth' would stop his marriage told the King that her father, who had recently died, 'loved to hear your speeches on the Wireless also your dear Father's King George.'[4] For as Sir John Reith, the Director-General of the BBC, had observed ten years before, men and women of every social class were now listening to the wireless, even in the most inaccessible regions of the country.[5]

The plan for Edward to speak directly to the people in this way was backed by Winston Churchill, Lord Beaverbrook and the King's solicitor, George Allen. Discussing the idea at Stornoway House, Beaverbrook's home in the St James's district of central London, all three men agreed that the King should make a broadcast and that it would win public support.[6]

A broadcast was also recommended in many of the letters for Edward that arrived each day from the general public. 'A Royal Broadcast . . . a "man to man" radio talk is better than camouflaged newspaper reports', urged one writer, 'May You and the lady of your choice be very happy.'[7] A man in Somerset went to the trouble of writing a draft speech for the King, in case it was of any use.[8] 'Frankly we would all far rather you married any one at all than left us,' said a letter from Kent, 'let alone somebody you love and she makes you happy. Can you speak to us over the wireless . . . What we all want to know is what you are feeling, not what the MPs and the papers tell us.' The letter added,

Though this is only a village it has every kind of opinion in it, but everyone is agreed for once – we would all rather anything happened than that you should go . . . There are thousands of villages like us all over the country. Remember us when you are deciding.[9]

A London caretaker reminded the King of the time when 'you gave me a £1 to help me and asked about work' for her husband. 'Now I want to help you', she wrote. 'My Lady [her employer] is in Broadcasting, and BBC. She says how you should Broadcast on Sunday to the Empire . . . it's only fair you should say what your Lady is really like and just that, to correct the lies . . . I hope you will.'[10] Another 'loyal and devoted subject' in London urged him to

Override all argument and opposition, broadcast to your Empire if necessary, remembering that the critical opinions of ministers and press are not necessarily those of your people.

Incidentally, such an Anglo-American bond would do more for world peace than anything before in history. God bless you Sir, and your gracious Queen to be.[11]

From America, too, came advice to broadcast to the people. 'Congratulations on your reported determination to marry whom you choose, in spite of hell, high water, and Stanley Baldwin', wrote a man from New York, adding,

may I call to your attention the example of our American President. A majority of our newspapers oppose him. But he steps to a microphone, and over their heads he speaks to the people of America. A frank statement of your belief that a king's private life is as much his own affair as a commoner, would end this whole silly business for all time.[12]

A man in Ontario, Canada, suggested that Wallis should broadcast. 'Could she speak to us through a Radio (Wireless) broadcast or in some such way', he asked, 'as she would be our Queen.'[13]

Alone without Wallis and desperately worried about her safety, it was difficult for Edward to concentrate. However, he settled down to the challenge of drafting a speech. He wanted it to be dignified, but to convey the strength of his love for Wallis. After the broadcast, he thought, he would go abroad – to give people time to make up their minds and to allow himself a brief withdrawal from the 'overheated atmosphere'.[14] He arranged for aeroplanes to stand by, ready to take him away after the broadcast.[15] Once he had written a draft, he gave it to Allen to take to Churchill and Beaverbrook, with a request for improvements. They made several suggestions, but suspected that Baldwin would never allow the King to make the broadcast. They strongly recommended that, though the King should read the draft to Baldwin, he should on no account give him a copy.[16]

Edward went to Buckingham Palace for a meeting with Baldwin, asking for permission to speak to the public on the airwaves. The Prime Minister replied that he would call a special Cabinet meeting the following morning to discuss the matter. At the meeting a draft of the broadcast was read to the Cabinet, which meant that somehow or other Baldwin had obtained a copy (in his memoirs, years later, Edward wrote that he could not remember whether he had given Baldwin a copy or not). In fact, a copy of the whole of the broadcast was sent to the Dominions in a telegram on 4 December at 10.30 p.m.[17]

'I could not go on', the draft began, 'bearing the heavy burdens that constantly rest on me as King, unless I could be strengthened in the task by a happy married life; and so I am firmly resolved to marry the woman I love, when she is free to marry me.' Edward referred specifically to Wallis and argued the case for a morganatic marriage – that neither Mrs Simpson nor himself had 'ever sought to insist that she should be Queen. All we desired was that our married happiness should carry with it a proper title and dignity for her, befitting my wife.' He concluded by saying that he would go away, giving the nation time to think, hoping dearly to be able to return. 'I shall always have a deep affection for my Country, for the Empire, and for you all.' Underneath the draft of the speech which was kept with government papers there is a pencilled 'No word about abdication'; this was presumably written by one of Baldwin's advisors.[18]

The Cabinet's answer, when it came the next day, 4 December, was a resounding 'no'.[19] It was unanimously decided, recorded Chamberlain in his diary, that it would be impossible to allow Edward, while he was King, to broadcast or make any public utterance which had not been approved by his Ministers, 'since constitutionally they must be responsible for his words'.[20] Baldwin offered this explanation in a letter to the King, adding that

Apparent exceptions to the rule that the King's public utterances must be such as are approved by his Ministers (such as King George's Christmas message) are not really exceptions at all. In such cases Ministers are willing to give an experienced Monarch who thoroughly understands and has always strictly observed Constitutional limitations, a discretion as to what he would say, and are content to take full responsibility knowing well that the Monarch would say nothing of which His Ministers would not approve.

There was a further principle, Baldwin warned: a broadcast by the King would divide his subjects.[21] With this statement, Baldwin revealed some doubts about his claim that he had public opinion behind him.

At this point Edward could have made an effort to communicate with Sir John Reith, to find some other way of speaking to the nation. In fact, though Edward would not have known this, such an attempt would not have succeeded. For Reith had assured Baldwin of his full backing of the Government's position.[22] Indeed, the Director-General had telephoned Sir Godfrey Thomas twice on 3 December – at 7.00 p.m. and again at midnight – to point out that the BBC could broadcast any official statement, or anything the Prime Minister might find helpful, 'not only at home but also to the Empire, at any hour of day'. He said he would be pleased to be given any official statement direct.[23]

But Edward did not contact Reith or anybody else who could have helped him to broadcast his appeal to the nation. He behaved throughout the crisis honourably and with strict propriety – and simply obeyed orders. One of the reasons for this may have been the strict sense of discipline drummed into him during his years at school. He had been sent away to Naval College: first to Osborne, when he was thirteen, and then to Dartmouth. Boarding school may have provided some respite from Palace routine, but it was a harsh and, at times, merciless environment. It was especially difficult for Prince Edward and for Prince Albert, who followed his elder brother when he was old enough. At first they were picked on by the other boys, and they had to prove that despite their royal status they had no airs and graces. They were not given any privileges: both were treated the same as other cadets, sleeping in dormitories, living in gunrooms, working and playing games with the rest of their 'Terms'.[24]

The historian A. J. P. Taylor has commented that 'duty was the deciding factor' in Edward's behaviour. If 'they' thought that Edward should not marry a divorced woman, he explained, 'it was his duty to accept this ruling, just as the ex-servicemen, whose representative he was supposed to be, had once gone blindly to the slaughter when instructed to do so by their officers.' It was 'Edward's weakness', added Taylor, that he shared this feeling. In his view, Edward 'was not the man to shatter the Establishment, at best only to niggle at it.'[25] The British emphasis on duty, wrote one of Edward's subjects to the King, was too prevalent and also harmful. 'In England,' she said, 'there are many unhappy hearts because duty is put first: we are too strictly duty bound: Follow your heart, marry the lady of your choice, God bless her . . . I am so divinely happy in my marriage, that I feel I must wish you, all happiness & love – .'[26] Edward's weakness was not simply an acceptance of duty, however. It was also an extreme manifestation of chivalry. He was so very chivalrous – to the woman he loved, to the ordinary people and to the Government – as to be quixotic.

This made him incapable of taking on shrewder minds such as Baldwin and Dawson.

Edward did possess a natural intelligence. He took an interest in languages and spoke Spanish and German fluently. He had a remarkable memory, as did his mother, Queen Mary, and 'knows hundreds of facts', observed Nancy Mitford.[27] Cecil Beaton was impressed by the King's mind when he met him in November 1936:

He knows an enormous amount of general knowledge, never forgets names, knows statistics and really has the mind of the average man par excellence. He will be a very popular King and one cannot help respecting him. His quips and sallies were trite and often vulgar . . . but he has no pettiness, no interest in gossip and gossip of personalities.[28]

But Edward was in no way an intellectual: he did not reflect at length on issues or try to develop an understanding of them through reading. Rather, he reacted in a direct and straightforward – and sometimes naive – way to any situation in which he found himself.

While the King was waiting to hear whether he would be allowed to speak to the nation, Baldwin decided to make a public announcement to the House of Commons. He was growing anxious about the attitude of the general public, as a telegram sent to the Dominion prime ministers on Friday, 4 December revealed. 'Situation here has become in many ways much more serious,' he warned. He explained that, the evening before, he had spoken to the King, who had made it clear that he still wanted a morganatic marriage and to stay on the throne. 'A section of the popular press is also canvassing the idea', he reported, and although he felt certain that such a course was not acceptable to the majority of people in the country, 'nevertheless a weekend campaign in favour of it is obviously from every point of view extremely undesirable.' The Cabinet had therefore decided that he should make a statement on the matter to the House of Commons that afternoon, before it adjourned until Monday. In this statement, he told the Dominion prime ministers, he would explain that the Government had no choice but to refuse the King's request. He would also say that it would be unacceptable to the Dominions. 'I feel this is an essential part of the statement', he explained. 'I greatly regret not being able to consult you prior to statement being made but feel that you will understand need for urgent action.'[29]

Through a speech in the House of Commons, which would be aired by the BBC, Baldwin may have hoped to keep control of the media spotlight; if so, he reckoned without the newsreels in the cinema. For while he was giving to the nation the Government's account of the crisis, the newsreels were offering close-ups of the handsome king, with visual reminders of his concern for the unemployed and his trip to South Wales. There were close-up photographs, too, of Wallis Simpson: beautiful and elegant like Gracie Fields, Greta Garbo and Norma Shearer, the most popular women film stars. None of the newsreels denied that there was a crisis going on, but they presented it in terms of a compelling love story – 'the soul-rending drama being fought out in the solitude of Fort Belvedere'. To be placed in the position of 'having to choose between love and a throne', observed British Movietone News, 'is one of life's most tragic dilemmas.'[30] And many people drew a clear distinction between good (Edward and Wallis) and bad (the Church of England and the Government). Letters came to the King from abroad, as well as Britain, comparing the two camps. 'Last night in the Paris Daily Mail of Friday December 4,' said a letter from Trieste, 'a sweet face confronted me, dressed in Quaker simplicity – on the other side, the narrow-eyed, time-serving photo of the Bishop of Bradfield [sic].'[31] 'When the news reels here in New York show your picture,' wrote a woman from New York, 'there is much applause. When they show Stanley Baldwin there are hisses.'[32]

It is unlikely that Baldwin and his colleagues saw the newsreels, as they were so busy and preoccupied. In any case, many men and women of their class generally looked upon the cinema as vulgar and common. Even worse, it was seen to represent the baleful influence of America, as most of the feature films shown in Britain and the Empire were from the USA.[33] 'England has become Americanized', complained Lady Londonderry in her memoir, *Retrospect*, which was published in 1938. 'Now,' she said, 'the young English gentleman, or man about town, more frequently than not tries to appear in his dress and manners as an American tourist.' It would seem, she objected, 'as if there had been a process of levelling down everywhere. A modern young woman's aim, in these days, is to look as much like her pet film star as she can.'[34]

The reaction of cinema-goers in the first week of December 1936 offered a clear indication of the widespread support for Edward from ordinary people. It was then customary for the National Anthem to be played both at the start and at the end of the programme, and the audience was expected to stand in respect for their monarch. 'Dear "Neddy" don't let us down', wrote a woman from Liverpool. 'You should see the way the poor commoners stand to attention at the theatre or pictures when the National Anthem is sung. They all join in Jew, Christian, any denomination. It's an inspiration. Please don't desert us. We all love you so much.' She urged him to 'Stick to your guns like you did in the great War. Take a humble subject's advice. Choose who you like for a wife and be hanged to them but, don't run away. We will all love you better if you stay. I think she is true blue by her photos. You know who!!'[35] A 'poor mother of ten children' living in York said she had 'watched your picture on the screen with tears in my eyes', adding that she and her family 'pray hard for your Love and Happiness with the sweet Lady Mrs Simpson. She I am sure will be your loving & faithful companion in your darkest hour.'[36] 'I have just returned from a cinema where the National Anthem was heartily clapped', wrote a woman from Knightsbridge in London. 'Your people trust you.'[37]

Winston Churchill made a friendly reference to the King at a rearmament meeting in the Albert Hall on the evening of 3 December (this was the first great meeting of the 'Arms and the Covenant' movement, which had been set up by Churchill, Lady Violet Bonham Carter and some others to strengthen the League of Nations and British defence). Churchill's reference to Edward drew a storm of applause. He made his own feelings clear to the audience. In a few minutes, he told them, they were going to sing *God Save the King*:

I shall sing it with more heartfelt fervour than I have ever sung it in my life. I hope and pray that no irrevocable decision will be taken in haste, but that time and public opinion will be allowed to play their part and that a cherished

and unique personality may not be incontinently severed from the people he
loves so well.[38]

Baldwin gave his speech to the House of Commons in the late
afternoon of 4 December, a cold and wintry day.[39] 'The Royal Marriages Act of 1772', he said, 'has no application to the Sovereign
himself. Its only effect is that marriage of any other member of the
Royal Family is null and void unless the Sovereign's consent declared
under The Great Seal is first obtained. This Act therefore has nothing
to do with the present case.' Therefore, he explained, 'The King himself
requires no consent from any other authority to make his marriage
legal.' But whomsoever he married, he added, must become Queen.
'Suggestions have appeared in certain organs of the press yesterday
and again today', he acknowledged, 'that if the King decided to marry,
his wife need not become Queen.' But these ideas were without any
constitutional foundation – 'There is no such thing as what is called
morganatic marriage known to our law.' Consequently, the wife of
the King must enjoy 'all status, rights and privileges which both by
positive law and by custom attaches to that position, and her children
would be in direct line of succession to the Throne.' The only possible
way in which this result could be avoided, Baldwin argued, would be
by legislation dealing with a particular case. However, 'His Majesty's
Government are not prepared to introduce such legislation. Moreover
the matters to be dealt with are of common concern to the Commonwealth as a whole and such a change could not be effected without
the assent of all Dominions. I am satisfied from enquiries I have made
that this assent would not be forthcoming.'[40] Implicit in this account
by Baldwin was the possibility that the King might defy his Ministers
– that he might insist on his right to marry and to remain as King.
By so doing, he would compel the Government to resign. However,
the King had not given anyone the impression that he might choose
to act in this way.

The speech was heard on the wireless that evening. A 'lover of
Church & State' in Weston-super-Mare, Somerset, wrote to Mrs
Baldwin after the broadcast to thank her and her husband for their
stand on the royal crisis:

It is impossible to refrain from expressing profoundest gratitude for the news broadcast by the Premier this evening . . . Both of you understand well, the value & significance of a holy happy wedded life, & of its immense importance to the *spiritual* & human – social stability & destiny of the British Empire . . . Our beloved King George continually preached & practised this great truth. It would break his heart if he knew of the present state of affairs – Dearly beloved as our Sovereign is, we shall *welcome* the transfer of royalty to those who will carry on the traditions set by Queen Victoria & Queen Mary, should the change occur.[41]

But overall, Baldwin had misjudged the feelings of the British public – for there was widespread dissatisfaction with his account of events. That Friday evening, diners rose at restaurants and addressed the tables, proposing a loyal toast to the King which few people refused.[42] 'I am at a banquet of over 1050 people representative of business men of the country', wrote a woman to the King from Grosvenor House on Park Lane. 'The pointedly unusual fervour with which "The King" was toasted and the Anthem sung and the cheers after it,' she added, 'showed the temper of the people – undoubted sympathy for the King . . . Of course Baldwin & Co have their knife into [the King] because he hates humbug and is *honest* and gets down to bed rock – and called in Malcolm Stewart [the Special Areas Commissioner who had just resigned in protest at the government's constraints on his job].'[43] Popular sentiment was displayed wherever the ordinary members of the public collected together. The novelist Dennis Wheatley wrote to the King to say that, 'At a Fleet Street luncheon of a hundred men which I attended on Wednesday the unanimous view expressed was that if only you would rely upon the love, sympathy and understanding of the masses your "will would be done".' The 'decayed portion' of the country, he added, was arrogating to itself an authority it did not possess.[44]

Many of the general public could not understand Baldwin's hostility to Wallis. 'After 6 o'clock news when I heard Mr Baldwin's statement I sighed', wrote a woman in Essex to Edward, 'and said oh dear dear our poor poor King they are not going to allow him to marry.'[45] 'When your lady becomes our queen,' promised a letter from London, 'we will offer to her our love and devotion.'[46] Admiration was expressed 'at the splendid way in which you are being true to the Lady of your choice.'[47] 'Keep your chin up Skipper Ted', urged a Londoner.[48] Apart from gratitude for Edward's concern for the welfare of the poor, there was a view that a title and a noble background were worth nothing in comparison with love and happiness. A woman living in Llandeilo, South Wales, who supported the Conservative Party, wrote a letter to the King saying that she and her husband thought highly of Mrs Simpson. 'A Commoner has a Soul & is worthy in the sight of God,' she said, adding that

It is character that Counts here, & in the Great Beyond, not a Tytle [sic]. The greatest thing in life is love & sympathy, & Your Majesty should be allowed to choose your Queen and help mate in life. Mrs Simpson must be worthy, otherwise she would not appeal to Your Majesty. I fail to see what it has to do with the Cabinet or anyone.[49]

'The Lady of your choice having been in a humbler position one time', commented the wife of a man in the British Legion who had been out of work for six years, meant that she 'will know how to help you in doing what you have for the poor. Not like some who has never known what it is to want a meal, the same as I have . . . My wish is you will make the Lady of your Choice our Queen.'[50] How different was this approach from that of Alice Keppel, who, said Lady Hamilton, was very amusing in a discussion of Mrs Simpson, 'saying it was her want of class that mattered so.'[51]

However, Edward's support was by no means exclusively working class. One person wrote to say that among her acquaintances under fifty years of age, of all political views, there was scarcely one who did not resent the attitude of the Government. 'My friends', she added, 'are of the middle classes.'[52] Some members of the upper classes supported Edward, sending him letters from their clubs in London or from their stately homes in the country. Their servants sent letters, too – the butler to Sir William and Lady Nora FitzHerbert in Derbyshire wrote to say that he was 'willing and ready to die if it will help Your Majesty or will assist in any way.'[53] Concern for Edward was fuelled by a fear, based on recent events in the Soviet Union, that abdication might lead to revolution. The fact that the abdication of Tsar Nicholas II had been closely bound up with the 1917 Russian Revolution and the creation of a Communist state was seen as a grim warning. 'We want you, not the Duke of York,' wrote some British women from Trieste, Italy. 'The Czar resigned, and see what has happened.'[54]

What was becoming very clear was that, as a man in Glasgow pointed out in a letter to the King, 'Mr Baldwin announced that "the country" was against this, before taking any steps, before indeed any could have been taken, to find out the opinion of British electors. If a referendum were taken I think Your Majesty would win, and Mr Baldwin receive the kick in the pants he so richly deserves.'[55]

Friday 4 December had been 'another trying day', wrote Dawson, wearily. The 'Simpson Press had got going by this time, and there was a regular barrage of pleas for delay, for reference to the people, for anything that would keep a popular Sovereign (and, it was not obscurely hinted, get rid of a bad Prime Minister).'[56] There was some outrage at the behaviour of *The Times*. 'The prejudice of "The Times" against Mrs Simpson', in the opinion of a letter-writer from London, 'is as unjustified as it is unrepresentative of public opinion.'[57] In the pages of his paper, Dawson defended the Government's position. Referring to the 'acute constitutional crisis' between the King and his Ministers, he argued that the situation had been misunderstood and that Ministers had not interfered in the private affairs of the Sovereign. It was simply, he said, that they had been asked a question and they had given their answer.[58] The same day, he encountered hostility to the Government among his social peers. 'It was the celebration of Founder's Day at Eton,' he noted, 'and I spent most of the day there.' His neighbours at dinner included John Maynard Keynes, the prominent economist who contested the Treasury view that unemployment was incurable. In his *General Theory of Employment, Interest and Money*, which was published in 1936, Keynes pioneered the idea of full employment. He 'seemed to suggest (as so many of the Liberal intelligentsia did)', said Dawson indignantly, 'that there was some deep laid plot on the part of the Government to get rid of the King.'[59]

Keynes was solidly for Edward VIII.[60] 'I thought today's leader in *The Times* absurd', he told his wife Lydia in a letter written that Friday. 'Won't sympathy gradually increase for the King against the Archbishops oozing humbug? If the Government offered him a morganatic marriage, that would be all right. But apparently – I don't know why – they refuse this.'[61]

Many intellectuals and liberals, among them George Bernard Shaw, shared Keynes's view on the royal crisis. 'On the one side there stands Dr Lang, Archbishop of Canterbury; on the other there stands George Bernard Shaw, Archbishop of Everywhere', said a letter to the King from South London. 'For God's sake,' it urged, 'choose Shaw!'[62] When the writer Vera Brittain was in Dunfermline speaking about her new book, *Honourable Estate*, the Nonconformist minister with whom she was staying increased her sympathy for Edward VIII by his adamant disapproval of the lovers and his undisguised commiseration with Queen Mary – '"I'm sorry for her", he said righteously. "She must feel she has utterly failed as a mother."'[63] H. G. Wells also sided with the King, against the Government. This was very irritating to Robert Bernays, the National Liberal MP for Bristol, especially after a conversation with him at a dinner party. 'I cannot stand Wells for any length of time', he complained in his diary. 'He is such a tremendous theorist and really knows nothing of modern conditions outside his coterie in London. He was talking the greatest nonsense about the King saying that as a whole the public would welcome the marriage.'[64]

The Archbishop of Canterbury, Cosmo Lang, was starting to realize that it was not possible to count on the support of the public. In a diary he kept on 'The King's Matter', he recorded that on the afternoon of 4 December,

I saw the Moderator . . . and Secretary . . . of the Federal Council of Evangelical Free Churches and gave them as much information as I thought it was possible to give. I discussed with them the reactions of public opinion. They believed the mass of the people would support the Government, but acknowledged that *a large proportion, especially of the young to whom the King was a popular hero*, and who knew little of the real circumstances, felt a strong sympathy with him.

Young people, realized Lang in dismay, might say, 'He is doing the honourable thing. He wants to marry the woman he loves. Why shouldn't he?' This might be one bad outcome, he feared, of keeping the story from the public for so long. 'I suppose that those who, like myself, have known the whole business for two years', he thought, 'can scarcely realise the effect of this sudden crisis on minds wholly unprepared for it . . .'[65] Certainly the sudden crisis seemed highly romantic to many of the population. 'Am told today', wrote the critic James Agate in his diary on 4 December, 'that owing to this affair of the King's marriage the big bookshops are completely deserted. I understand this. Why spend seven-and-sixpence on romance when you can get reality for a penny?'[66]

By Saturday 5 December, Britain was utterly gripped by the royal love affair. 'Papers full of the harpy & the King', wrote Lucy Baldwin in her diary that day.[67] The crisis was so terrific, complained Headlam in his diary, that Edith Londonderry 'feels that she and Charley must be in London – so the weekend party at Wynyard [in County Durham] has to be deprived of its host and hostess.'[68] The royal crisis, noted Evelyn Waugh in a tone of some amusement,

has been a great delight to everyone. At Maudie's nursing home they report a pronounced turn for the better in all adult patients. There can seldom have been an event that has caused so much general delight and so little pain. Reading the papers and even listening to announcements that there was no news on the wireless took up most of the week.[69]

A taxi driver in London was reported as saying, 'We drivers ain't doing no business. We just goes out and collects the news and comes back to the shelter and discusses it . . . We says – let Him have her – Why shouldn't 'e be happy.'[70]

Nothing else, observed James Agate, was treated as of any importance, even cricket. 'England collapses on the first day of the Test match,' he observed, 'and Leyland rescues the side with a century. What Test match?' (The test series in Australia had just got under way.) In a reference to the legendary cricketer, Donald Bradman, he added, 'News came this morning that Bradman is out. But what people are asking is whether the King is going to be out.' The immediate effect of the rumpus, he said, was chaotic. 'I am very nearly run into by a man driving a car and reading a special edition of the evening paper at the same time – he has the paper spread over the steering-wheel!'[71]

That Saturday's *Evening Standard* printed an 'extremely witty' article by George Bernard Shaw which easily disposed, said Agate, 'of the objections to the lady on the score that she is an American and a commoner.'[72] In this article, entitled 'The King, the Constitution and the Lady', Shaw set the nation's crisis in a fantasy – in 'the Kingdom of the Half Mad', where the King was not allowed by his Government and Church to marry a woman called Mrs Daisy Bell. Mrs Bell was an American who had been married twice before – 'and was, therefore, likely to make an excellent wife for a King who had never been married at all.' But, explained Shaw, you could never count on anything going off quietly in the Kingdom of the Half Mad, because

The Government, for instance, would let whole districts fall into ruin and destitution without turning a hair, and then declare that the end of the world was at hand because some foreign dictator had said bluntly that there were milestones on the Dover Road.

The King of the Half Mad told the Prime Minister and the Archbishop that he had to consider the views of 495 million subjects, only 11 per cent of whom were Christians. Therefore, he said, it was fine that the Church would not solemnize his marriage – for a civil marriage would enable him to be married legally without offending the religious feelings of a single soul in his Empire. When accused by the Prime Minister of being entirely mad, the King answered that 'To a little London clique some two or three centuries behind the times I no doubt seem so . . . The modern world knows better.' The Archbishop complained that the King's arguments were 'so entirely off the track of English educated thought that they do not really belong to your world and mine.' But the King retorted, 'Would it be too brutal of me to remind you that there are others' who might form a King's party? 'The people are behind me. You may have to resign in any case long before the Coronation.'[73] Shaw's article was widely enjoyed. 'Thanks for sending Shaw's phantasy, which is the most real thing I have seen written about the situation', wrote the Labour politician Sir Charles Philips Trevelyan to his wife, Mary. 'It is saying in telling and literary form', he added, 'what I have been saying in half a dozen letters.'[74]

Charley Londonderry told Headlam that Churchill and Beaverbrook had been called by the King and were 'going to use this opportunity to have another go for SB.' These men, he said, would 'not stop at anything to secure their own ends'. This showed, thought Headlam, 'how little they know of public opinion – the country is not behind HM and the sooner he realizes it the better it will be.'[75] It was certainly true that some of the country were not behind the King, as Headlam claimed. But it was clear that many others were. 'Whatever you may be told,' wrote a Brighton resident to the King on 5 December, 'the Truth is that the People of England – if their voice could be heard – have only one wish, & that is to see you a happy man . . . & to have you & none other'. 'Good luck. Stand firm' urged a civil servant and his wife from Surrey. 'That part of your people which matters is behind you; but is desperately afraid you may not know it. We want a King who is a man and no hypocrite.'[76]

Some people took straw polls. Three-quarters of his friends and acquaintances, reported an Aberdonian, regarded the King's intentions with approval.[77] A disabled ex-serviceman from Cheltenham believed that 90 per cent of Edward's subjects were behind him – 'for the sake of the workers,' he pleaded with the King, 'don't abdicate'.[78] A letter from a jobless man in Lancashire claimed that at least 90 per cent of the unemployed and 'the man in the street' were with the King in his 'gallant fight against the combined forces of cant & humbug & hypocrisy' that were marshalling against him.[79] ' "Vox populi, vox Dei" – *and rub it in*', enjoined a postcard from Northampton to Winston Churchill, who was known to be backing the King.[80]

'God Save the King! Tell Us The Facts, Mr Baldwin!' proclaimed the headlines on the front page of Saturday's *Daily Mirror*. 'The Nation Insists', it continued, 'on Knowing the King's Full Demands and Conditions. The Country will Give You the Verdict!' The newspaper backed the King completely and published letters of support

1. *King Edward VIII's tour of industrial South Wales in November 1936.*
'Everywhere the people looked delighted and hopeful at his visit.
They obviously loved and trusted him.'

2. 'I saw you in the trenches ... it gave me courage to carry on when sometimes all hope had fled.' Edward (centre) on the Italian Front in 1917.

3. On a tour of Canada in 1919: 'The Prince Charming ... who could send a thrill through great crowds.'

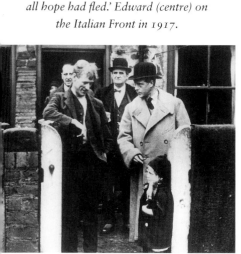

4. Visiting a miner's home in County Durham, 1929. 'He was not only the "People's King", but even more than that ... the People's Friend.'

5. Presenting medals to unemployed men after a football game. 'We shall never forget, how you have worked for us, unemployed, and from the bottom of our hearts we thank you.'

6. *Edward impatiently receiving debutantes at Buckingham Palace in July 1936. 'We admire [you] … for disliking red carpets and all they stand for.'*

7. *Edward with his parents, Queen Mary and King George V, in 1917. 'You are far closer to the people in your aims and beliefs than any previous Sovereign … You appear to us to belong to the Spirit of the Age.'*

8. *'If … I have to take over, you can be assured that I will do my best to clear up the inevitable mess.' Albert, Duke of York, and his wife Elizabeth (the future King George VI and Queen Elizabeth) with their daughter Princess Elizabeth (later Queen Elizabeth II).*

9. *Wallis Simpson on holiday in Europe in 1929 with her Aunt Bessie, 'the wise and gentle woman who had raised her from childhood'.*

10. *'You couldn't miss Wallis Simpson … there was something about her that made you look twice.' Relaxing in Austria, September 1936.*

12. *'No companionship could have appeared more natural.' A celebrated photograph published in America in summer 1936, but kept out of the British press.*

11. *Wallis and Edward in Italy in 1936: 'A couple in love … You couldn't help loving them for it, they were honestly so damn naive.'*

13. *Winston Churchill in conversation with Prince Edward in 1919. 'In this Prince there was discerned qualities of courage, of simplicity, of sympathy, and, above all, of sincerity rare and precious.'*

14. *Cosmo Gordon Lang, the Archbishop of Canterbury.*
'My lord Archbishop, what a scold you are! And when your man is down, how bold you are!'

15. *'There is no such thing as what is called morganatic marriage known to our law.' Stanley Baldwin speaking to a packed House of Commons on 4 December 1936.*

16.

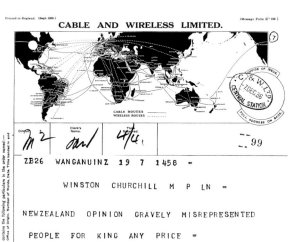

Printed in England. (Sept. 1935.)   (Message Form S/–152.)

CABLE AND WIRELESS LIMITED.

⑦

CABLE ROUTES
WIRELESS ROUTES

OFFICE OF ISSUE
C. & W. LTD
CENTRAL STATION
17 DEC 36
FULL ADDRESS ON BACK

Origin	Clerk's Name.	Time handed in.		
M²	Jan	4/4		⎯ .99

ZB26   WANGANUI NZ   19   7   1458 =

WINSTON   CHURCHILL   M   P   LN =

NEWZEALAND   OPINION   GRAVELY   MISREPRESENTED

PEOPLE   FOR   KING   ANY   PRICE =

BANKS   SON   SIR   REGINALD   BANKS   ✪

THE
CHARTWELL
TRUST

The first line of this Telegram contains the following particulars in the order named :—
Prefix, Letters and Number of Message, Office of Origin, Number of Words, Date, Time handed in and
Official Instructions—if any.

L. & P. (c).

NO ENQUIRY RESPECTING THIS TELEGRAM CAN BE ATTENDED TO WITHOUT PRODUCTION OF THIS COPY.
REPLIES SHOULD BE HANDED IN AT ONE OF THE COMPANY'S OFFICES.

17.

To **His Majesty The King.**   18.

May I appeal to
you, as one of your
subjects,

Please do _not_
Abdicat, as we poorer
Class people will lose
a would be great and
loyal King.

~~an~~ An appeal from
one of your subjects.

19.

12 Sheringham Rd
Holloway N7
Dec 4th

The King
Sir
Marry Mrs Simpson
After all your happiness comes
before anything else. And I
wish you all the happiness in
the world. Good Luck and
God Save our King.
A loyal Subject
Harold H Eastlate

20.

If Mrs Simpson is good
enough for His Majesty
we want her.
Stick to your guns.

*Widespread support for Edward's wish to marry
Wallis Simpson: 'a tide now running with immense
and gathering force in favour of the King'.*

21. *'The agony of not being able to see you after all you have been through.' Wallis in the South of France shortly after the abdication.*

22. *Edward and Wallis on their wedding day, 2 June 1937, at the Château de Candé in France: 'a supremely happy moment'.*

23. *Husband and wife: 'all accounts show them entirely happy and as much in love with each other as ever.'*

from its readers. 'This Crisis Can be Settled', urged the leader. 'No More Talk of The King's Abdication.' The vast majority of the people, it told its readers, 'hate seeing a man bullied when he thinks he is right. They respect the man who will stand up for his rights.'[81] The *Daily Express* strongly criticized the Government's role in the crisis. 'Mr Baldwin and his Government', it objected, 'are making a direct challenge to the King':

The result is that if there was a crisis yesterday there is a worse one today. There is no need for it. This grave issue has not been forced upon us by outside events beyond our control. It is a man-made crisis, and made here at that. But as men have made it they are capable of ending it. This thing can be brought to a close whenever Mr Baldwin and his Government desire – by withdrawing their opposition to the King's intention of marrying.'

The paper insisted, 'We cannot afford to lose the King. We cannot let him give up the Throne.'[82] As Lord Zetland, the Secretary of State for India, warned in a telegram to Lord Linlithgow, the Viceroy, 'Government are being attacked . . . for their refusal to countenance proposal for Morganatic marriage, and they are charged with attempt to rush King into a decision to abdicate.'[83]

In the Beefsteak Club, said Virginia Woolf, 'only Lord Onslow & Clive [Bell] take the democratic view. Harold [Nicolson] is glum as an undertaker, & so are the other nobs. They say Royalty is in Peril. The Empire is divided. In fact never has been such a crisis.'[84] But outside the Beefsteak it was a different story. When Archbishop Lang left 10 Downing Street in the middle of Sunday afternoon, a man ran out from the crowd calling, 'We want King Edward.' Later that evening, while the Cabinet was in session, reported *The Times*, large crowds assembled in Downing Street and in Whitehall. The National Anthem was sung, and a section of the crowd started to chant 'We want the King.'[85] There was a demonstration at Marble Arch by a group of young men and women carrying banners on which they had painted in red and blue lettering, 'After South Wales you can't let him down.'[86] Outside the home of the Duke of York, on Piccadilly, a young woman clambered up the railings and held aloft a newspaper picture of the

King for the crowd to see. Men removed their hats, and there were shouts of 'We want Edward!'[87]

'Whatever Your Majesty decides is right' was the message of a telegram sent from Queen Mary's Hospital for the East End.[88] 'Please, England cannot do without you, as surely you must see by the loyal demonstrations in the towns all over the country', appealed another subject.[89] Similar sentiments were expressed all over the nation. 'The workers of Coventry are with you to a man (and woman)', urged a loyal supporter. 'Good luck! and confound the politicians.'[90] From Leeds came this telegram: 'Baldwin and Bishops utterly wrong. Leeds people support Your Majesty.'[91] From the Midlands a letter assured the King that

HER'S YOURN!
HEIR'S OURN!
    Opinion in the Black Country, in the event of Your Majesty's marriage, could be summed up in the above couplet.
    . . . what the Black Country thinks today, the rest of the Empire will think tomorrow. Keep calm! Don't abdicate![92]

'I have been walking the streets of London with a placard, "Hands off the King. Abdication means Revolution"', wrote a woman to the King. She enclosed a newspaper cutting showing a photograph of herself carrying the placard. 'My impression', she said, 'is that I have all the working classes with me, but I was insulted by some of the upper classes. I did not know that there was so much humbug and hypocrisy amongst the English.' She begged him not to give in. 'However as the Common People are all obviously for you and don't care a damn who you marry,' she said, 'I feel if you stick out for a Morganatic marriage that you will get it. Forgive my writing but I have had a good opportunity of gauging public opinion.'[93]

9

'Cavaliers and Roundheads'

To some who supported Edward VIII, the crisis recalled an earlier king – Charles I, whose conflict with Parliament had led to the English Civil War and to his execution in 1649. 'We have all become King's men or Cabinet men', commented Beaverbrook. 'It is as if the whole country had slipped back into the seventeenth century again.'[1] Now, in the twentieth century, the nicknames for the King's supporters and the Parliamentarians seemed appropriate once more. 'The world is now divided into Cavaliers and Roundheads,' wrote Chips Channon in his diary on 7 December.[2] The evening before, on the Sunday, he had held a dinner party attended by the King's supporters, while the 'Oliver Stanleys had a rival festival of 11 people, all Roundheads and violently anti-King.'[3] Some letters and telegrams sent to the King at this time were sprinkled with antique language, recalling the earlier crisis faced by the monarchy. 'Good luck where 'ere befalls', urged one telegram, while a woman living near Reading assured the King that 'The Lady Mrs Simpson is a pearl of great price among women. One day you will have your heart's desire. I raise my Glass to Both of you in my toast & Say, Gentlemen, *The King*.'[4]

The analogy between Edward and Charles was largely based on the perception of Edward as a tragic royal figure, beleaguered by his parliament. 'You stand for the principle of the people and you will remember', one letter reminded the King, 'that your martyred ancestor King Charles died for His principles.'[5] There was also a degree of similarity between Charles's French wife, Henrietta Maria, and Wallis. For although the chief objection to Henrietta Maria – her Roman Catholicism – did not apply to Wallis, they both came from a foreign country and were perceived as extravagant, cosmopolitan and *unEnglish*, with an undue influence over the King.

Baldwin was the chief Roundhead, Winston Churchill was the chief Cavalier. 'The different interests are queuing up behind Baldwin, or Churchill', noted Virginia Woolf.[6] The Viceroy, Lord Linlithgow, declared in a letter to the Secretary of State for India, Lord Zetland, that 'Winston Churchill is prominent in attack upon Government'.[7] Lady Milner shared this view. She wrote in her diary that 'Churchill, Lloyd George, Beaverbrook & Harmsworth are running a pro-Simpson campaign.'[8] Certainly Churchill remained Edward's staunch supporter throughout the crisis and did everything he could to keep him on the throne. 'I have never repented of this,' he said later, 'indeed, I could do no other.'[9] Walter Citrine, the leader of the trade union movement, gave an account of a conversation with Churchill in which he proclaimed his absolute support for the monarch. 'Very quietly,' wrote Citrine, Churchill remarked,

'I will defend him. I think it is my duty.'

'What?' I said. 'irrespective of what he has done?'

Winston looked grave, and, putting his hands on his breast, he said with emotion, 'He feels it here', at which I looked at Mrs. Churchill's thoughtful face, but said nothing more.[10]

Churchill had a strong attachment to the King that went back to their first meeting, when Edward was proclaimed Prince of Wales in 1911. During the 1920s, Churchill had coached the Prince on writing and giving speeches, and they had discussed public affairs and played polo together. When Edward became King, Churchill sent him a letter expressing his confidence that 'your majesty's name will shine in history as the bravest and best beloved of the sovereigns who have worn the island crown.'[11] Churchill's own mother was American, which may have softened his attitude towards Wallis. He had a private nickname for her in his letters to his wife – 'Cutie'.[12] In any case, Churchill was a romantic, and his own marriage was a love match (a nickname in *Punch* for the devoted Churchills was 'The Birdikins'[13]). But he regarded Wallis as a nuisance because he believed that it would not be possible for Edward to marry her *and* to remain King, at least before the coronation.

He had first become involved in the King's dilemma on 7 July 1936, when he was consulted by Walter Monckton for his views. Monckton had explained that Mrs Simpson was contemplating a divorce and that her husband was more than ready to go along with this as he was involved with someone else. He had assured Churchill that the King had no thought of marrying Mrs Simpson, but could not bear her to be married to another man, as his 'possessive sense' was strong.[14] Churchill was opposed to the idea of a divorce, since this would expose the King to the criticism that he had destroyed the marriage of an innocent man.[15] He also advised against inviting Mrs Simpson to Balmoral on the grounds that the castle was an official residence[16] – that such an invitation would not be appropriate, as Wallis was the King's mistress, not his wife. Not very pleased with this advice, Edward did not turn again to Churchill for several months. But Churchill remained ready to help him, whenever he chose. When a small deputation of elder statesmen, led by Lord Salisbury, met with Baldwin to discuss the King's affairs on 17 November 1936 – the night on which Edward left for his tour of South Wales – Churchill did not attend. He told Salisbury that he could not join because he was confident that Edward would wish to consult him at some point. And if he was known to have joined the deputation, he explained, this might undermine his influence with the King.[17]

Once the news of Edward's love for Wallis had become national news, in the first days of December, Churchill began to confront Baldwin on the actions of the Government. 'Would my right hon. Friend give us an assurance', he asked Baldwin at Question Time in the House of Commons on 3 December, 'that no irrevocable step will be taken before a formal statement has been made to Parliament?'[18] This intervention was welcomed by MPs. 'The House broke into cheers as Mr Churchill asked [his] question', reported the *Evening Standard*.[19] Churchill's request was very reasonable. As the chairman of the Trades Union Congress insisted at this time, 'the Government of the country must be by and through Parliament, and it is this great institution that enables us to govern ourselves with the consent and will of the people. It must be preserved at all costs.'[20] Baldwin replied to Churchill's request that he had nothing to add, but that he would examine the question. He was flustered by Churchill's intervention and not sure how to react. The King was not allowed to speak to the public, and Mrs Simpson was in Cannes – but Churchill was a quantity over which he had far less control.

On the next day, 4 December, at Question Time in the House, Churchill put his request to Baldwin for a second time. This time, Baldwin was 'irritable, as though to complain', observed Malcolm Muggeridge, then a journalist working for the *Evening Standard*, as if 'surely he had enough to bear without that being brought up again.'[21] But Churchill was greeted with cheers. Baldwin was told by the Government's Chief Whip that support for Churchill's views was growing and was shared by at least forty MPs.[22] And evidence of popular support was arriving in the post for Churchill every day: over the next few days, he received nearly five hundred letters and telegrams, nearly all of which praised him for his stand. 'We feel', said one woman, a nonconformist, 'that the genuine public opinion and not the public opinion as interpreted by Mr Baldwin should be heard . . . we are prepared to support you, actively if necessary.'[23] Only Churchill, stated another letter, was willing to speak up for 'we the "gagged" millions of this country'.[24]

'It is hard to believe that this is happening,' wrote one woman, 'in England with a House of Commons.'[25] Another woman said she was writing to Churchill because this was the only means at her disposal of making her feelings known. 'It is a comment on the working of a democratic system that decisions should be given in the name of public opinion when no steps have been taken to test that opinion', she observed.[26] 'Millions will back you, whatever line you take,' wrote another supporter, 'in your fight against hole and corner hustling of the King.' What would happen, he wondered hopefully, 'if the Duke of York were to say that he would not be party to driving his brother out?'[27] From the city of York came gratitude to Churchill for his stand 'against all the selfish "snobbery" and "Hypocrisy" with which he, & Mrs Simpson are *contending with*!! God bless the kind & true hearts of them both – and *yours also*!'[28]

Churchill met with the King at Fort Belvedere on 4 December. Edward had sought permission for this interview the day before, pointing out to Baldwin that Churchill was 'an old friend with whom he could talk freely'.[29] Baldwin had agreed – not knowing, he told Tom Dugdale later, 'the full extent of the Churchill–Harmsworth–Beaverbrook activities'. By giving this permission, he feared afterwards, 'I have made my first blunder.'[30] Chamberlain agreed that Baldwin had made a mistake and sent him a memorandum objecting that, 'This constitutes Mr Churchill one of [the King's] advisers although he is not His Minister. This is utterly unconstitutional. I doubt if such a thing has ever occurred since the time of James II.' He believed that, 'Obviously Churchill will advise him to fight, tell him that public opinion is with him. I must resist this plan in Cabinet.'[31] The Cabinet as a whole was unhappy about it, but could see that the Prime Minister had little choice but to accede to the request.

At the Fort, Churchill stressed the need for delay. This was timely advice: earlier that evening, Baldwin had told Edward that he would like a decision about Mrs Simpson to be reached as soon as possible – during the weekend, or even that very evening.[32] It was clear to Churchill that Edward was feeling very pressured. 'Your Majesty need not have the slightest fear about time', he assured him. 'If you require time there is no force in this country that would or could deny it you.' After all, he pointed out, Baldwin would not be able to resist him. If he did, he said,

you could remind him that he himself took nearly three months rest in order to recover from the strain of the session. Your strain is far more intense and prolonged. Mr Baldwin is a fatherly man and nothing would induce him to treat you harshly in such a matter. Ministers could not possibly resign on such an issue as your request for time.[33]

But if Baldwin persisted in building up the pressure on the King, advised Churchill, then he should retire to Windsor Castle and close both gates. His doctors, he added, should act as sentries.

After this meeting, Churchill went off to London to speak to Max Beaverbrook. He urged the King to work with Beaverbrook: 'He is a tiger to fight. A *devoted* tiger! Very scarce breed . . .'[34] He sent a letter to Baldwin, describing the great strain on the King and urging the Prime Minister to allow Edward more time to reach a decision. 'It would be a most cruel and wrong thing', he insisted, 'to extort a decision from him in his present state.'[35]

Churchill also drafted a statement to the press, explaining why delay was so important. There was no need for haste in any case, he pointed out, since a marriage could not legally take place for another five months, when the decree nisi became absolute. Parliament, he objected, had not been consulted or allowed to express an opinion. He also criticized the Cabinet for securing from the leaders of the Opposition parties, Attlee and Sinclair, a promise not to participate in the formation of a new government were the present one to resign. The effect of this, he said, had been to confront Edward with an ultimatum. He pointed out, too, the disadvantaged position of the King – that he could not communicate with his people except with the permission of his Ministers. 'The wise and eloquent appeal issued in today's Press of the Right Honourable Winston Churchill', wrote a man in Leeds to the King, 'surely voices the sentiments and views of the vast majority of your subjects.'[36]

Now, and throughout the crisis, Churchill did his utmost to plead both with Baldwin and with the public for patience and delay. This was also the position of Duff Cooper and Beaverbrook, and of many members of the public. 'Don't let the snobs rush you, we will clean them up', wrote a sailor in Brighton to the King.[37] 'Do NOT hurry – you will win in the end', wrote a Londoner.[38] As the Minister of Health admitted in a Cabinet meeting, 'what people were saying was, "Give the King time".'[39] Even as far away as Australia, W. M. Hughes in the *Sydney Morning Herald* observed that 'the earnest prayer of every section of the Australian people was that no irrevocable decision should be made without the lapse of a period for quiet reflection.'[40] Earl de la Warr wrote to Baldwin with a personal plea:

like many others, I have had my personal difficulties. In these moments of madness time means so much – and one so often needs much more time than one deserves . . . Again please forgive me for writing – but if I had not once had more time than I deserved I might have made a terrible mistake.[41]

But *The Times* presented the opposite view. There was a 'widespread desire', it claimed at the end of its leading article on 5 December, 'that this profoundly disturbing difficulty should be rapidly settled.'[42]

Churchill had insisted on the need for delay because there was always, as he explained later to Dawson, the possibility that the King might fall out of love with Wallis and change his mind. The problem would then disappear – 'this situation might never arise for a year or two ahead or never arise at all, because many things happen to human beings in a year or two.'[43] But there were some who were not sure that they wanted him to change his mind. In his diary, Chamberlain expressed a hope that the King would renounce his plan to marry Mrs Simpson, as he believed this was what the country wanted; but he also admitted that 'I have felt all through that we should never be safe with this K.'[44] Many others shared his view. 'I had lunch with Geoffrey Dawson on Friday and with Patrick Duff and Geoffrey Fry yesterday', wrote Thomas Jones to Lady Grigg in a letter on 8 December. 'All hope personally', he added,

that H. M. will go. You know as well or better than I do what a 'problem' he has been and is . . . This King has done the popularity side of his job supremely well – he has the memory for persons, a quick if shallow intelligence, and a sense of drama. But he dislikes work and escapes from it and delays and postpones its performance . . .[45]

Lord Wigram, who had been a key figure in the court of King George V, thought that the King should abdicate because he was mentally ill. Geoffrey Dawson heard from one source that Wigram had confirmed

what I had heard from another trustworthy source – that H. M. is mentally ill, and that his obsession is due not to mere obstinacy but to a deranged mind. More than once in the past he's shown symptoms of persecution-mania. This, even apart from the present matter, would lead almost inevitably to recurring quarrels with his ministers if he remained on the throne.

Edward was likened to yet another of the previous monarchs of Britain – 'It's an odd and tragic throw-back to George III.'[46] Lord Wigram was so concerned that he called on the Lord Chancellor and told him, 'I did not think the King was normal, and this view was shared by my colleagues at Buckingham Palace. He might any day develop into a George III.' It was 'imperative', added Wigram, 'to pass the Regency Bill as soon as possible, so that if necessary he could be certified.'[47] Clearly, King Edward could not count on much in the way of support from the members of his royal household who identified with the court of George V, and who now seemed ready to pack him off to a mental asylum.

In fact, Edward showed every sign of being a well-balanced and sensible man. He had not flinched when, the previous July, a man had thrown an object which looked like a bomb in front of his horse while he was riding down Constitution Hill in London. He simply reined in his horse, before proceeding slowly and unflustered on his way.[48] It later emerged that the object was a loaded revolver, wielded by one George McMahon, who was unbalanced mentally and suspected of being a Nazi sympathizer. Edward was under severe nervous strain in late November and early December, but even then he appears to have coped with the rush of events remarkably well (although he smoked a great deal). Baldwin said so himself on 6 December, when he discussed with his Cabinet the letter from Churchill, pressing for delay on the grounds of Edward's impaired health. He said he had 'never known the King more cool, clear-minded, understanding every point and arguing the different issues better. No man could have done this better.'[49]

It is odd that Edward did *not* show any 'symptoms of persecution-mania'. Certainly he knew that some key figures wanted him to give up the crown. Baldwin had even said so, to his face, during the discussion with Edward in which he told the King he would not be allowed to broadcast to the nation. In this exchange, which was reported to the Cabinet on 4 December,

His Majesty then said, 'You want me to go, don't you?' The Prime Minister agreed. He recalled that the King had told him that he wanted to go with dignity, in the best possible manner for Mrs Simpson and himself and his successor, without dividing the country . . .'[50]

It seemed to many that a division of the country, between the Cavaliers and Roundheads, might in fact be imminent. 'Clearly if the Gov. were to put pressure on HM they must be sure of everyone,' wrote Hilda Runciman in her diary. 'If the Gov. resign because HM wont [sic] take their advice cd. any one else form a Gov.?'[51] Obviously some members of the general public thought Edward could. 'Marry whom you please, call on Winston Churchill, form government,' came a telegram from the chairwoman of the Barnet Urban District Council.[52] 'Dismiss the Cabinet,' urged one letter-writer. 'They are not worth a pennyworth of You. Ask Mr Churchill to form a Govt and all will be well.'[53]

There was a broad spectrum of support for the King: from Conservatives who feared that he was being pressed unreasonably, to left-wingers such as Harry Pollitt, Secretary of the Communist Party of Great Britain, who admired his principles. 'The spectacle of the National Government laying down a code of morals and behaviour for the King', said Pollitt, 'is indeed a sight . . . there is no crisis in all this business for the working class. Let the King marry whom he likes. That is his personal business.'[54] The Communist politician Walter Newbold wrote a letter of support to Churchill on 6 December – 'Count me all in once more with yourself in the line you are taking in respect of the King.' The sooner 'the old gang' were debunked, he added, the better.[55]

One problematic source of support for the King was Sir Oswald Mosley, the leader of the British Union of Fascists (BUF). At a large meeting on Friday 4 December held in London's East End, Mosley asserted the King's right to marry whom he wished. The next day, the BUF published a special four-page newspaper entitled *Crisis*: the two inside pages covered Sir Oswald's speech and the meeting, while the front page showed the King against a background of the derelict pits of South Wales.[56] Mosley believed that the line of division between those who supported the King and those who did not was 'broadly the line dividing the younger from the older generation'. However, the organizer of the BUF's northern campaign, who received reports on scores of meetings, came to a different conclusion. It was his view that the middle class, particularly the lower middle class, abhorred the marriage, while the working class was solidly for the King.[57] Anthony Heap was a Londoner who admired Fascism and belonged to the BUF. He wrote in his diary that he did not share Mosley's enthusiasm for the King. 'The Cabinet *rightly* opposes the scandalous match,' he opined,

for it would not only make the King appear cheap and contemptuous in the eyes of the whole country but depress our trade and lower the country's prestige enormously as far as the rest of the world is concerned. In fact he's made a complete utter fool of himself.

If Edward had a grain of sense, he added, he would have kept Mrs Simpson as his mistress 'without all this fuss (in which case no one would have known anything about it and not cared two hoots if they did).'[58]

An organization called Social Credit Reformers, which regarded itself as a worldwide movement, with a base at the London Social Credit Club in Westminster, and believed that the Establishment was controlled by the banks and international financiers, was adamantly behind the King. They hoped he would assume the role of popular champion against vested interests.[59] They launched an Empire-wide campaign in which similarly worded telegrams – 'Present humble duty and standing for your Majesty's freedom of choice fervently desire you retain crown'[60] – were sent to the King from Australia, New Zealand, Canada and South Africa, as well as different parts of Britain.[61] On one such telegram from Sydney, someone at the Palace pencilled the following comment: 'The Social Creditors all over the Empire have evidently been given the word to support HM.'[62] A mass meeting of support was held in London's Hyde Park.

Lady Houston, the eccentric right-wing editor of the *Saturday Review*, believed that Baldwin was acting on instructions from Moscow. Her journal, with its covers of red, white and blue, emblazoned with the Union Jack, pressed her support for the King. 'The dislike of certain persons for divorce', it said, 'is fully recognized and respected and understood.' But did this mean, it asked, that the entire Empire should give up 'a splendid and hard-working King? For the King is being asked to pay the price of abdication for his desire to lead a happy married life. We have to ask, "What would be the price, *for his people*, of the King's abdication?"'[63] The *Catholic Times*, to many people's surprise, declared that the whole business was a ramp against the King and that financiers were using a moral issue to force an artificial crisis. 'We are for the King', declared the paper. 'We are against the financial and political powers which are forcing King Edward from the throne.' The *Tablet*, another Catholic newspaper, said that if the King were to renounce Mrs Simpson, 'he is entitled to expect in return more recognition than is now extended to his right to an initiative in the government of the country'. Referring to this suggestion, the Anglican *Church Times* commented that 'Here is one more striking example of the growing Roman Catholic opposition to democracy'.[64]

But these were scattered demonstrations of loyalty. All they had in common was a desire to back the King – not a wish to cooperate to form any kind of King's Party. There was no centre, apart from the small group of men who stayed with the King in the stronghold of Fort Belvedere. 'It so happens', wrote Major Ulick Alexander, Edward's Keeper of the Privy Purse, three decades later, 'that I am the only survivor of the small staff of three that resided at Fort Belvedere during the last 10 days of the crisis.' Major Alexander was a man of high ability, great courage in the war (during which his health had been impaired by the heavy fighting of 1914) and complete loyalty to King Edward. The other two, explained Alexander, were Monckton and George Allen, the King's solicitor:

I was, of course, not present at the private discussions between the Prime Minister and the King which were always held at Fort Belvedere during this period, but what was said was always discussed afterwards by the King with the three of us, and I found it, and I know at least one of my colleagues also found it, extremely difficult to decide on what line Mr Baldwin was proceeding.[65]

Moreover, Churchill never had any intention of leading a popular movement of any sort. 'There was no party of King's friends', claimed the journalists Owen and Thompson. 'There was only a party of King's enemies. They held the superior power in the press, the parliament and the pulpit, a mighty "3-P. Alliance".'[66] Rumours of a King's Party were fed by the emotions of the moment, which often had little to do with the King himself. Since Lord Londonderry was bitterly angry at Baldwin for removing him from the position of Secretary of State for Air, it was feared that he might throw his weight behind Churchill. A friend of the Londonderrys expressed the hope that 'Charley would not do anything foolish.' He need not have worried, wrote the biographer of the Londonderry family, since Londonderry 'felt as everybody else did . . .'[67]

But if Edward *himself* had wanted a King's Party, could he have organized one? Many people felt that Baldwin had treated him unfairly. A Sheffield churchwoman who was married to a surgeon objected to the 'bullying dictatorial hectoring by Baldwin and his friends' and said that most people would welcome Mrs Simpson as their queen. 'At a big dinner-party and at a luncheon party during the last few days we all stood and drank to the King and Mrs Simpson.'[68] There was widespread sympathy for Edward's love of Wallis. 'Here is a fellow of my own age, evidently going to give up a throne. The Kingship of the greatest Empire the world has ever known', observed the draper in Belfast who had been shocked by Bishop Blunt's comment on Edward's religious behaviour. As a homosexual who risked imprisonment simply because of his sexual choice, the draper felt keenly and bitterly aware of the need to experience love in an open way. 'Supposing', he wrote in his diary,

I met a boy I loved, and of whose love I was assured, I would give up all – even the promise of Eternal Life wouldn't tempt me so I suppose that the King is in that position – so I cannot blame him if he gives up this throne – I only hope the woman will appreciate what it all means.[69]

But more than anything, Edward was admired and appreciated for his concern for ordinary people. This was seen to make everything else irrelevant – especially the status of his beloved, marital or otherwise. A man in the poverty-stricken region of Sunderland, who said he had been in and out of prison all his life and had just been released, urged him to marry Mrs Simpson: 'She is worth fighting for. I am only one of millions of working trod downed class [sic] who wish you every happiness with this Lady.'[70] From 'A Loyal Cottage. England' came the message 'I am only of the "poor" class, but working with that class I can say with honest truth that the people are with you to the ends of the earth if needs be. Please fight the Cabinet for your rights. – Parliament, I am certain, will stand by you.'[71]

At this very moment, while Edward was suffering the agony of his dilemma, the problem of the unemployed was receiving attention in the House of Commons. The Liberal MP Megan Lloyd George, who was the younger daughter of David Lloyd George and a fierce fighter for the underdog, challenged the Government: if they really weren't going to do anything for the distressed areas, they should say so – 'because I think that to raise the hopes of these people once again, or to trifle with them in any way, would be quite unpardonable.' She pleaded with the Government

not to delay any policy which they may have in mind, but to bring it forward. I would like to see it brought forward before Christmas, and I feel that most Members of the House would gladly sit for the longer time that might be needed, because postponement to the New Year really means that these people will have to go through another winter without any relief at all.[72]

Megan Lloyd George's warning was the same as the one that had emerged from the King's visit to Wales just weeks before – that *something must be done.*

It was not just the poor and the working class who remained loyal to the King. A prominent member of the Norfolk gentry sent a telegram to Edward on 7 December pointing out that 'England has had two Prince Consorts neither was crowned. Why not a princess consort a duchess consort or simply consort. Even an archbishop's wife does not share title. Plenty of precedents for altering the succession. Don't be bounced.'[73] A group of upper-class young women, who described themselves as 'sub debutantes' and were studying in Paris, sent a telegram of 'love and support'.[74] Above all, Edward had the support of many of his generation. 'Particularly those from 50 downwards ... We all pray that if you are forced to abdicate, you will allow us to support your Majesty as Ruler, perhaps Dictator, of a nation', urged a journalist in London.[75]

There were grounds, believed Edward, to assume that if he so wished he would be able to convert his popularity into something more forceful – to topple Baldwin and to protect his position as monarch. 'Had I made a move', he wrote in his memoirs, years later,

to encourage the growth of this movement, it might have grown. If I had made an appeal to the public I might have persuaded a majority, and a large majority at that. I shall go further and say that had I remained passive while my friends acted the result might well have been the same. For there is no want of evidence that a multitude of the plain people stood waiting to be rallied to my side.[76]

It is not known whether or not Edward read the thousands of letters and telegrams of support that were sent during these days of crisis, though it is unlikely. But had he seen them he would have been in no doubt that many 'plain people' supported his wish to marry Wallis and to stay on the throne. As well as letters and telegrams, there came petitions – from streets, households, shops and organizations all over the country.

One of the ideas frequently put forward in this correspondence was for a plebiscite – a direct vote by the whole of the electorate, on the specific issue of Edward's wish to marry Wallis. This proposal was sent from overseas, as well as from within Britain. '*Vox Populi, Vox Dei* – the Voice of the People is the Voice of God', urged a telegram to the King from Finland. It added, 'Please arrange plebiscite.'[77] 'I am certain of this, if a plebiscite is practical and were taken,' said one letter, then '99 out of every 100 voting from among all the British Nations would see that the marriage is honourable, just as you think so – and would gladly agree – that the lady be Your Queen.'[78] One woman urged the King to 'take a vote of the *people* – The nation wants *you*, no one else, the nation needs *you*, & the nation (the people) is with you, & you have their full sympathy & love.'[79] Some thought that a plebiscite should be held for all the people in the Empire. The sovereign power in the country, said one man, lay not in the Cabinet but in the whole of the Empire – 'Might I respectfully suggest that the question of your marriage should be referred direct to the people . . . A direct ballot of the people should be taken. The ballot could be of the peoples of the whole Empire. Australia has already the referendum and in its case it would be almost routine.'[80]

Many of Edward's subjects advocated governmental change, through a general election that would jettison the Prime Minister. Baldwin's effort to prevent the King marrying Wallis, and possibly bouncing him into abdication, was seen by some to be consistent with his poor record on foreign relations. 'I think that millions of people besides myself', one man wrote to Churchill, 'must in their inmost minds have been saying for a long time past "Will no one ever rid us of this man?"' There were some in the Cabinet, he added,

whom individually I approve very highly, including Mr Duff Cooper . . . but the actual deeds of Mr Baldwin's government in relation to foreign affairs frequently cause me to writhe and groan in impotent anger. Soon, I image, we shall be buying off the hostility of the truculent dictators of Europe by the barter of our possessions . . .[81]

Many people wanted an alternative to the present Government. A letter signed 'Public opinion' urged, 'Call the Cabinet's bluff & let there be an Election if necessary. *You'll win!* The Church have enough to say NOW – as regards unemployment etc they have nothing to say! . . . You offended by being frank after *Your visit to Wales*!'[82] 'Your Majesty has only to force a General Election to gain your point,' said another letter, 'as the people are with you in every way. We do not want the *Duke of York* or any other substitute.'[83] From Nottingham came the suggestion that 'a People's Party with yourself at its head would be acceptable to all.'[84]

'The Country is rising on your behalf. All that we need is Time', wrote a Londoner. 'Do not permit Yourself to be hurried into an irrevocable act. With a few days' delay it will become evident that a Government can be formed to carry out the will both of Your Majesty and of the Country.'[85] The election should be fought, said one letter, on the right of the King to choose his own wife – 'the slogan would be "We want Edward VIII. Not Baldwin."'[86] A man in Brighton asked, 'Should Your Majesty's Government resign, why not a Royal dictatorship? I am ready to fight the issue at an Election on your behalf and instructions.'[87] Some people believed that a King's Party would be able to eliminate the problem of long-term unemployment. 'Undoubtedly there is a strong group most anxious to secure the King's abdication,' said one man. 'Things he said on his visit to South Wales were a tacit rebuke to the Government, and I thought a conflict would come some day.' A new government, he added, 'would represent a new People's Party which would have to be rapidly organised, especially in the distressed areas, and amongst intellectuals who are sick of party politics.' The country should be run, he said, by those who had already demonstrated their ability to deal with social problems – 'Why not put in Malcolm Stewart and a dozen others who are anxious to get on with the job to actually do it without more talk?'[88]

A railwayman from London assured the King that if it came to a choice between him and Parliament, 'the bulk of the people of this country would support yourself ... The present Prime Minister is, from his own lips, a trickster, the church stands for nearly all that is opposed to real Christianity.'[89] Winston Churchill was regarded by some as the best man to organize such an election campaign. A woman working at Elstree Studios, who said she was speaking for friends and associates in the film industry, asked him to act on their behalf. 'I know very little about Parliamentary procedure,' she said,

but isn't it possible for you to approach the King offering to form a Cabinet which will treat the situation on these lines, and put the whole matter to the country? Apart from the domestic crisis, your Freedom and Peace programme would surely win you support from large numbers of Conservatives and Socialists all over the country, who are by now heartily sick of Baldwin and his methods of misgovernment ...[90]

Some of the King's supporters wanted to take up arms for him. A man in Hove told Edward that he had spoken to some people about Edward – 'I said you were the PEOPLE'S KING. That the crowd loved you; that you were democratic; that forms and ceremonies were nothing; that LOVE rules the world, or SHOULD rule. Good luck! good health! And God bless you. *I'll die for you if necessary.*'[91] 'Every ex-service man,' wrote another supporter, 'is behind you, and will obey your orders in Liverpool. We want you to lead, take charge of everything, regarding you, and our Empire. Remember Sire there are 2,000,000 of men willing to die for the first gentleman in the world (Yourself).'[92] And from Durham, a former Lieutenant of the Durham Light Infantry asked the King never to forget 'that there are thousands of men in this country today, who had the honour to serve with you in France, & who will uphold, with *their lives* if necessary, Your Majesty's desires as opposed to convention, as they welcomed your flaunting of convention in the war years.'[93]

Not only were the ex-servicemen behind the King, thought some, but active servicemen too. A composer assured the King that

You Sire have got the Navy and the Army behind you – and the masses – it's the masses that matter. Come out and show yourself to your people. We WONT LET YOU DOWN. We want YOU – YOU – and always YOU . . . What you[r] private life is doesn't matter a damn to us – but come out in the open – you'll find we'll go to Hell cheerfully – if you ask us to . . . Come out into the open and let us see you.[94]

Many of the public pressed the King to show himself, to generate support. 'And come up & show yourself to the people who remember the distressed areas', encouraged one man. 'Come to London.'[95] 'Why not shew on the Balcony at Buckingham when the Crowd shouts "He's a Jolly Good Fellow"?' asked another.[96]

Sunday 6 December was cold, with a biting wind. Baldwin told a meeting of senior Ministers in the morning that 'This matter must be finished before Christmas.' Chamberlain argued that to wait even that long (less than three weeks) was unacceptable, as the Christmas trade was being damaged.[97] This was true. 'Those of us who were authors of recent novels', wrote Vera Brittain in her autobiographical story, *Testament of Experience*, 'soon realised that national tension had killed the Christmas market in the fortnight when book sales normally reach their peak.' One of the biggest British booksellers, she added, which sold an average of a thousand books a day, found itself reduced to fifty a day during this period. Her novel *Honourable Estate*, which had come out earlier that year, joined 'the many minor victims' of this period.[98] Noting that there were '374 less customers in today!', a saleswoman in a London department store regretted a 'desperate day's trade partly the weather partly the King.'[99]

There was a growing sense of urgency and crisis, felt by everyone. Coming past the Palace at night, wrote Virginia Woolf, 'there were crowds waiting in the cold – it is very cold – cant [sic] write – with eyes fixed on the windows. Two or 3 lights were burning in upper windows.'[100] A vicar in Kensington, London, reported that 'At Evensong tonight, after prayers [had] been said for the King, this Congregation in a poor quarter of the Royal Borough spontaneously broke out into the National Anthem with a fervour seldom heard.'[101]

For a brief moment, Edward was tempted to appeal to his subjects. On a 'night of soul-searching', he wrote later in his memoirs, he paced his bedroom floor, weighing the alternatives. Wallis had also paced the floor sleeplessly when faced with her own critical decision, on the traumatic night before her divorce suit was presented at Ipswich Assizes. Eventually, Edward reached the decision 'which had been implicit throughout the course of my action – to put out of mind all thought of challenging the Prime Minister.' Otherwise, he could see, he would leave 'the scars of a civil war'. The price of his marriage under such circumstances, he believed, would be to strike a terrible blow at the social unity of the nation and to the Empire. He would still be King, but not by the free and common consent of all. If he made a stand, it would divide the country.[102]

It is arguable that Edward *could* have imitated in some way the model of dictatorship that was now much in evidence on Continental Europe. Many people in Britain, especially those who despaired of their 1936 Government, were looking to the King for strong leadership as a bulwark against the risk of revolution. 'I believe that first-class leadership will be needed in the near future', wrote a man from Kent, 'if this country . . . is to steer a course between the Scylla of stagnation and the Charybdis of disastrous social conflict. Like many others, I have been looking to you to play your part in that leadership.'[103] Edward not only had a star quality that gave him widespread popularity, but he could draw on the loyalty of many thousands of ex-servicemen all over the country. This kind of support had been crucial to the power bases established by Mussolini and Hitler, who received massive backing from veterans of the 1914–18 war; like ex-servicemen in Britain, they were angry at the lack of employment and the poverty that followed their return home.

Nor would it have been difficult for Edward to make contact with Hitler – either through the many members of the Establishment who supported the Nazi regime, or through Joachim von Ribbentrop, the German ambassador to Britain. Ribbentrop was frequently seen in the best houses of Society, including the glittering receptions that were held at Londonderry House. The Londonderrys were just a few of the many members of the ruling class at the time – including Geoffrey Dawson, Mrs Greville, and a number of politicians in the National Government – who advocated what they called a 'rapprochement' with Hitler's Germany. In 1938, Lady Londonderry complained in her memoir, *Retrospect*, that 'The more positive "isms" are taboo, like Nazi-ism or Fascism, because they imply doing something.'[104] She and Lord Londonderry visited Germany in the winter of 1936, calling on Hitler and Goebbels and attending the Winter Olympics in Munich. In the same week that Edward was visiting the poor of South Wales, Ribbentrop was a guest at Wynyard, the Londonderrys' seat in County Durham; earlier that year, he had stayed at Mount Stewart, the family estate in Northern Ireland.[105] It would not have been difficult for Edward to get in touch with Ribbentrop if he had wanted to seek support and help from Germany. And there is every indication that Ribbentrop (and Hitler) would have been delighted.

But even without any backing from Germany or Italy, the King of Britain could have sought absolute rule, as a kind of benevolent despot. Such a unilateral dictatorship might have been welcomed by numbers of those who were fearful of the threat to Britain of Fascism. Many

THE PEOPLE'S KING

people believed, along with a woman writing to the King from Belfast, that 'The members of your government . . . have so far shown themselves very helpless in their attempts to preserve peace.'[106] The popular novelist Dennis Wheatley sent a message to the King saying that

Britain is the last barrier which stands for justice freedom and tolerance against a state of things the horror of which even my imagination as a storyteller to thirty nations is insufficient to conjure up. A strong and determined prince is our only hope in averting tragedy from a hundred million lives. No one but yourself can fill that role.[107]

The King was needed as an influence on the future of the world, wrote a man speaking as 'one man to another', because of his honesty, truth and straightforwardness. 'At this momentous point in the history of mankind,' he added, 'humanity needs you.'[108] There were 'a number of persons', said another, 'who feel that if our Constitution were brought up to date and you – *you only* – were invested with the powers of a Dictator, our country would become a happier and more progressive place.'[109]

But dictatorship, of any sort whatsoever, was not the path that Edward wished to tread. He was a firm believer in democracy and the sacrosanct role of the elected government. Once he had decided not to appeal to the people, he kept well away from central London, in the seclusion of Fort Belvedere at Windsor, twenty-five miles away. He was aware that his appearance among the crowds might fan the flames of popular support and he scrupulously wished to avoid this. This was noticed and appreciated. 'It is to the credit of the King', wrote Archbishop Lang in his diary, 'that in these hectic days and hours he has cancelled all his engagements and refused to come to London, so as to avoid all demonstrations and do as little as he could to divide the country.'[110]

10

'Don't abdicate!'

Far away in Cannes, Wallis was fighting hard to dissuade Edward from giving up his throne. 'I am so anxious for you not to abdicate', she wrote from Lou Viei on Sunday 6 December. She was afraid that it would put her 'in the wrong light to the entire world because they will say that I could have prevented it.' 'If you will just give Baldwin my plan', she urged him. 'If he turns it down then you have yours and the world could know a second compromise was turned down.' Wallis wanted Edward to say to Baldwin, 'I stand back of everything I have said but I do not wish to create a situation within the country so I therefore will not press this issue at the moment but reopen it in the autumn.' She added, 'No one but Baldwin and the dominions want you to go and as the Aga Khan telephoned they haven't given you a fighting [chance]. The people in the press are clamouring for a word from you . . . Think my sweetheart isn't it better in the long run not to be hasty or selfish but back up your people and make an 8 month sacrifice for them.' In this way, she believed, no one would be able to say he had 'shirked and ran away when the people were rallying to your aid'.

Wallis pointed out that Baldwin had already misrepresented his case in Parliament, by repeating over and over that she must be Queen. The people needed to know, she said, of the morganatic idea: 'Don't be silenced and leave under cloud I beseech you and in abdication no matter in what form unless you can let the public know that the Cabinet has virtually kicked you out . . . I must have any action of yours understood by the world but hidden by B[aldwin] we would have no happiness and I think the world would turn against me. When now we have their sympathy.' She tried to comfort him: 'I'm holding you tighter than ever.'[1]

But while Wallis's encouragement and love were good for the King's morale, they were ineffective as a means of intervening in the struggle between Edward and the Establishment. Nearly a thousand miles from Britain and Fort Belvedere, she had little influence on his decisions. Matters might have been different had Wallis taken the advice of Brownlow, Churchill and Beaverbrook, and gone to Belton House. 'I shall always believe', said the novelist Marie Belloc Lowndes, 'that had Mrs Simpson stayed in England instead of going to France, it is probable that Edward VIII would never have abdicated. It is a very different thing to advise a man over the telephone to do this or that, and to beg him to do what you wish to be done when you are actually with him.'[2]

Ernest Simpson made his own attempt to prevent abdication. On 7 December he telephoned 10 Downing Street, saying he was at the Prime Minister's disposal, if Baldwin thought he could be of any use.[3] He believed he would be able to assist on what he called the 'psychological aspect of the matter' – he knew the mind of his wife, he said, as well as anyone. He was convinced she was not so much in love with the King as the King was with her, and he thought that if his wife was approached by someone in authority she might be persuaded to see reason. However, Mr Simpson does not appear to have understood the psychology of his wife quite as well as he thought. As he himself acknowledged, he had twice threatened to leave her, hoping that such a threat would bring her to reason and persuade her to give up Edward; but neither of these threats had any effect. Moreover, the idea that Wallis would submit to somebody simply because they were 'in authority' is odd, given her spirited character – it is more likely to have been true of Ernest himself, who was more biddable and liked to conform. But in any case, Ernest's offer to Baldwin was not taken up.[4]

Monday 7 December saw an attempt in the House of Commons to support the King. Colonel Josiah Wedgwood, a Labour MP who was himself divorced, put down a motion of loyalty to Edward, asking the Prime Minister to give the House an early opportunity to discuss it. But the moment was short-lived, for Wedgwood was met with a flat refusal from Baldwin. Then, in reply to a question by Attlee, Baldwin announced that he had something to add to the statement he had made the previous Friday. The House was delighted. It had been breathlessly awaiting a new development in the crisis, and now at last something was starting to happen. 'From the beginning of questions,' reported *The Times*, 'there was hardly a vacant seat, and both the side galleries contained an unbroken rank of anxious members.' The Peers' Gallery was filled as soon as the doors were opened, and the peers were standing four and five deep in the narrow gangway between the door and the benches.[5]

Eager interest was by no means limited to Westminster – the whole nation was hungry for news. 'An ordinary day and still no news as to what decision the King will make', wailed a middle-aged classics master at a boarding school for boys – 'Though we got through Evening Chapel in record time so as to be able to hear the First News on the wireless!'[6] While some people were simply curious, many others were desperate to find out what was happening to their beloved King – and were still fervently hoping that he would remain their monarch. A Bristol woman, writing 'on behalf of some of the girls at work', begged him not to abdicate. 'Your Majesty is very popular here in Bristol,' she told Edward,

and we all know how well you have carried out your duties . . . In the factory where we work everyone supports you, and in Bristol itself we can assure you that 90% of the population are on your side. You have only to read the papers to see how much everyone wants you to stay, and further evidence of this is shown at Cinemas, Concerts etc when the National Anthem is played – the people want and need you.[7]

Baldwin told the House that with the exception of the question of a morganatic marriage, the Government had given the King no advice. He added that 'these matters were not raised first by the Government but by His Majesty himself in conversation with me some weeks ago when he first informed me of his intention to marry Mrs Simpson whenever she should be free.' This was not accurate, since it was he – and not the King – who had first raised the subject, in his interview with Edward on 20 October; indeed, he had specifically asked for that audience in order to express his concerns about Mrs Simpson's plan to sue for a divorce, which he had heard about from Alec Hardinge.

Baldwin concluded his speech to the House by saying that it was now up to His Majesty to make a decision. He then proceeded to answer questions about the crisis. At this point, Churchill entered the House. (He had come directly from the Anglo-French Luncheon Club, where Lady Milner had been furious because 'Churchill – who was in the chair – embarrassed us by proposing the King's health in a set speech. He was checked from saying more by the Chairman of the Club.'[8]) He wasn't aware that the Prime Minister had been speaking on the crisis. He therefore rose, for the third time in four days, to demand that 'no irrevocable step will be taken before the House had received a full statement.' He asked Baldwin to bear in mind

that these issues are not merely personal to the present occupant of the Throne, but that they affect the entire Constitution? . . . May I say that the right hon. Gentleman has spoken of rumours? If he were able to give an assurance that the House would have the constitutional issue laid before it, then this anxiety would not persist.

He also pleaded with Baldwin for delay.[9]

But on this third occasion there were cries from all sides of 'No!' and 'Sit down!' Lucy Baldwin, who had gone to the House to hear her husband's speech, recorded in her diary that 'The House wouldn't hear Winston & shouted him down.' Churchill was staggered at how the tide of opinion had turned over the weekend, reported *The Times*. Then, 'with a complete absence of felicity,' added the newspaper, 'he launched into a speech, giving, apparently, the arguments for a fuller statement and some form of the consultation of Parliament.' He was reminded by the Speaker to confine his remarks to a question; and earned further reproof for the way in which he put his question.[10] Baldwin replied that the Government was not prepared to introduce legislation to allow a morganatic marriage, and that the Dominions agreed. At this point (although it was not recorded in *Hansard*), Churchill shouted at Baldwin across the floor of the House, 'You won't be satisfied until you've broken him, will you?'[11] He then stormed out.

The tide had turned in the House – Baldwin had won. Years later, G. M. Young, his biographer, said to him, 'I believe you were the only man on Friday who knew what the House of Commons would be thinking on Monday.' With a smile that was 'half shy and half triumphant', Baldwin replied, 'I have always believed in the week-end. But how they do it I don't know. I suppose they talk to the stationmaster.'[12]

When members of the public who were supporting Churchill read about his defeat in the House, they were bitterly disappointed and urged him not to give up. 'You have my sympathy in your experience in the House yesterday,' said one man, 'but may I respectfully beg of you to stick it out. People I meet are already sick of the press ballyhoo & much less hostile to the King & to Mrs Simpson. In another week they will all be back on the side of the King.'[13] Another letter took a more vigorous approach – 'We regret that this singularly foolish and sheeplike House of Commons should have treated you to an exhibition of trivial, schoolboyish bad manners yesterday. You should spank them.'[14]

The hostility of the House arose most likely from the widespread talk of a King's Party and the suspicion that Churchill might be playing an intriguer's part. The weekend had been dominated by speculations about Churchill and his possible ambitions. Besides, a proliferation of unsavoury rumours, especially in Labour circles, was leading many to believe that Mrs Simpson might come to have an undesirable influence on Britain's foreign policy – for it was said that she was a friend of Ribbentrop, Hitler's ambassador.[15] In fact, though, according to Wallis's memoirs, she had met Ribbentrop only twice, both times at Emerald Cunard's house. The first occasion was a large luncheon, which was also attended by Winston Churchill, and the second was a supper party later the same week. At the luncheon, wrote Wallis, Churchill kept silent, while Ribbentrop held forth on 'the great things' Hitler was doing for the unmarried mothers of Germany. Once Ribbentrop had gone, she heard Churchill telling Lady Cunard, 'Emerald, I hope we never have to hear that broken gramophone record again.'[16]

Philip Ziegler, Edward's official biographer, has concluded that the idea that Wallis was a paid agent of the Nazi Government 'can safely be dismissed'.[17] But the story about Wallis and Ribbentrop helped to check any tendency on the part of left-wing sympathizers in the House to support the royal marriage. It could easily have been squashed by the many right-wingers who actually were friends of Ribbentrop; however, they left the story to grow.

No doubt, Ribbentrop had *hoped* to develop a bond of some sort with Wallis. Like many others, he would have seen her as a passport to the King, with whom Hitler was eager to forge some kind of alliance. But, noted Ziegler, a 'real conversation with the King ... never materialized ... something unforeseen always intervened', to Ribbentrop's regret.[18] Edward himself wanted good Anglo-German relations, but that was not the same thing as support for Hitler.

The image of Mrs Simpson as a kind of foreign agent combined in a lethal mix with the claim that Edward had no regard for government papers and left them scattered around the Fort. 'I have heard rumours', wrote the publisher Francis Meynell in his abdication journal, 'that when the King used to go down to Fort Belvedere he took down all sorts of most confidential national papers to which at any time she [Mrs Simpson] might have had access & had she been so minded communicated their contents to any power. It was said at one time she was very friendly with [Leopold von] Hoesch – an Hungarian statesman [and the German ambassador before Ribbentrop].' These sorts of things, added Meynell, 'were bound to be said but other incidents of which I heard made one view her with much suspicion on this point.'[19] Alan Turing, who was later to work as the key codebreaker at Bletchley Park in World War II, had at first sided with Edward. He wrote to his mother that now he was 'rather divided on my opinion of the whole matter. At first I was wholly in favour of him retaining the throne and marrying Mrs Simpson, and if this were the only issue it would still be my opinion. However I have heard stories recently which seem to alter it rather.' Revealing a budding interest in issues of state security, he commented that, 'It appears that the King was extremely lax about state documents leaving them about and letting Mrs Simpson and friends see them. There had been distressing leakages. Also one or two other things of same character, but this is the one I mind about most.' Nonetheless, he added, he admired Edward 'for his attitude'.[20]

The author Gerald Bullett sent Churchill a letter in which he argued that the pressure being put on the King was ridiculous. Along with many others, he said, he believed that 'the Government's hostility to His Majesty's proposed marriage does not represent popular sentiment, and the sacrifice of the King's personal happiness on a point of punctilio would be both an outrage and a calamity.'[21] According to the official account, he added, the King had asked his Ministers whether they were prepared to introduce a bill into Parliament making it possible for him to contract a private marriage – and the King's Ministers had answered in the negative. In that case, said Bullet, the matter was closed and there was no longer any need to expect an answer from the King:

He has asked a question, and the question has been answered. Surely it is open to him now to say that the subject is closed and that he has no remarks to offer. By taking up that attitude, an attitude which would appear to be constitutionally impeccable, he will put an end to the public clamour, while at the same time reserving his own liberty of action.

'If you approve of this suggestion,' concluded Bullett in his letter, 'and if it has not already been put forward, could you not find means for communicating it to His Majesty?'[22]

But a feeling of inevitability was starting to develop – that Edward was going to *have* to go. And he was going to have to go soon. 'I agree with Churchill in pleading for time – though I see that *that* probably won't be given as there's to be an announcement on Monday', wrote Janet Trevelyan to her husband, the historian George M. Trevelyan. 'Yes, on the whole I do think there was no alternative for poor old Baldwin but to say that a marriage was impossible. But perhaps they'll have a secret marriage one of these days, if she's too "nice" to go on without!' Garvin in the *Observer*, she added, 'is really very eloquent this morning. He writes with his very heart's blood about the ineluctable choice between throne and love, and indeed it *is* very moving.'[23] Perhaps it was especially moving because Edward and Wallis were in their forties, not in the first flush of youth that generates a romantic optimism. 'If you're really in love (and at 40 odd you should know) then marry Mrs Simpson', observed one letter to the King.[24]

It was unfortunate for Churchill – as several people pointed out in letters to him – that David Lloyd George was not in London to give his support. He might have been a useful ally in the House of Commons, on the day that Churchill was censured by the Speaker and shouted down from all sides. But the former Liberal Prime Minister was far away, in Jamaica, where he had gone in November for a rest. His secretary speculated that 'Lloyd George and Churchill working together for the King would have been a far more formidable proposition, and there were many on Baldwin's side who were relieved that Lloyd George was out of the way.'[25] In fact, as soon as the crisis had begun, Churchill sent a message to Lloyd George, urging him to return to London. Frances Stevenson, who was with him in Jamaica (as his mistress, though she later married him after his first wife died), wrote, with obvious partiality, 'I fully believe that the crisis was purposely engineered while LG was out of the country; and I believe that had LG been in England, he and he alone could have persuaded the King where his duty lay. Baldwin knew what an influence LG had always exerted on the young Prince.'[26] She and Lloyd George bought tickets for the next ship home.

On 3 December, Lloyd George sent a cable to his son and daughter saying that,

If Baldwin forbids King to choose his own wife, regard it as impertinence. Nation chooses Queen. King alone can choose own wife. Ought to have same right to select his partner in life as humblest of his citizens. If had not decided to marry the lady not a word would have been said by any of the Scribes and Pharasees [sic].

He was nauseated, he added,

by burst of humbug and hypocrisy of which Baldwin is fitting exponent and Attlee an apt confederate. Had King not exposed callous neglect by Government of distress and poverty and bad housing conditions in realm convinced they would not have shown such alacrity to 'down him'. Hope you are not going to join the Pharasses [sic] who are hunting the King for his crown.[27]

Lloyd George did not think much of Mrs Simpson. 'The woman Simpson is not worth the price the poor infatuated King was prepared to pay', he wrote in a later letter to his daughter Megan. 'There are not in her any of the elements that can possibly constitute a tuppeny romance.' But this did not mean he opposed the marriage: 'All the same,' he added, 'if he wishes to marry her it could have been arranged quietly after the coronation . . . If the King wants to marry his American friend – why not?' In Lloyd George's opinion, Baldwin was determined to get rid of Edward. 'I cannot help thinking the Govt. would not have dealt so brusquely with him', he said, 'had it not been for his popular sympathies. The Tories never really cared for the little man. Labour have as usual played a cowardly part. Everybody here very sad about it.' In the view of Frances Stevenson, it was specifically the King's visit to Wales that had prompted the breaking of the story in the press. When she and Lloyd George had left Britain, she observed, there had been no hint of the crisis. But soon after, 'the new and as yet uncrowned King made his historic visit to the South Wales distressed areas, and the whole situation quickly changed. By December 4th the story of the king's proposed marriage had broken.'[28]

Baldwin's supporters were triumphant at Churchill's defeat. Blanche Dugdale, a niece of Balfour had who been prominent in League of Nations Union affairs, believed that Churchill's career was destroyed. 'I think he is done for', she commented with satisfaction. 'In three minutes his hopes of return to power and influence are shattered. But God is once more behind his servant Stanley Baldwin.'[29] Violet Bonham Carter, a Liberal politician, took the same view, despite a deep personal and political loyalty to Churchill. 'Thank Heaven the forces of decency have routed Beaverbrook, Rothermere, Tom Mosley & Lady Astor,' she wrote in a letter to Dawson, 'but that *Winston* shld. have played this game – just as he seemed to be qualifying to play a really useful part – is tragic & to me quite inexplicable. *Whatever* happens – quite irreparable damage has been done to something we thought invulnerable.'[30] The fall in Churchill's prestige, according to Harold Macmillan, was 'catastrophic'.[31]

Churchill found that he had even alienated his allies, including the loyal Robert Boothby, another Conservative politician. 'There were several moments', Churchill later wrote,

when I seemed to be entirely alone against a wrathful House of Commons. I am not, when in action, unduly affected by hostile currents of feeling; but it was on more than one occasion almost physically impossible to make myself heard . . . I was myself so smitten in public opinion that it was the almost universal view that my political life was at least ended.[32]

The degree of hostility his actions had provoked astonished Churchill – after all, he was only asking for a delay. 'I have never pleaded for anything except the King's unhurried judgement', he pointed out in a letter to Geoffrey Dawson. 'Where I differ has been in the alternative with which he is now unhappily presented.'[33] But this hostility was perhaps inevitable, given the fears of a threat to democracy which had been triggered by the rumours of Churchill raising a King's Party – or that the King might ignore the advice of his Government. 'It is a little difficult for an American', wrote John Gunther,

to realize with what power Constitutionalism is entrenched in England, and with what horror the possibility of a King's party was greeted by a great majority of the House of Commons. Parliament is supreme over the King. Charles I paid with his head for defying it . . . very few indeed would have been willing to envisage a royal dictatorship.[34]

The Liberal MP Robert Bernays believed that opinion had now swung round completely in favour of the Government, and against the King, as a result of Churchill's interventions.[35] That may well have been so in the House of Commons, but among much of the general public support remained strong. Letters and telegrams of support were still arriving for the King and many of them urged him to resist Baldwin. A woman writing from Dorset begged him not to let his opponents 'trick' him. Apart from being the King of England, she said, 'you are absolutely King of *all* hearts. For the life of me I cannot understand all this Hubbub of the constitution.' Although she had to 'grow, dig and sell potatoes', she was 'sure by the Photographs in the Papers of Mrs Simpson she would shake hands with me, honestly dear Sire if I were in the position I would shake hands & kiss you both . . . do not let your opponents trick you.'[36] But the King keeping the throne *and* Wallis was looking increasingly unlikely. A letter with eighty-three signatures of support had been sent to the editor of the *Star* but, to the authors' disappointment, it had not been published.[37] Many of the letters now arriving for the King were marked by a spirit of resignation, and their chief concern was to wish the King happiness with Wallis. 'We bow to the will of OUR FATHER IN HEAVEN' wrote a woman from South London to 'Beloved Courageous King Edward', adding as a postscript, 'All eyes on Deck.'[38]

On 4 December, the Dominions had been told that the King had been made aware of the necessity for a very swift decision. 'A section of the popular press', said Baldwin, was canvassing the idea of a morganatic marriage: 'I feel sure that such a course is not acceptable to the overwhelming majority of people in this country; nevertheless a weekend campaign in favour of it is obviously from every point of view extremely undesirable.'[39] Evidently Baldwin feared that he might lose control of public opinion over the coming weekend. He invited the Dominions to communicate their views directly to the King.

The Australian Prime Minister sent the King a telegram on the night of 5 December stating that his Government preferred abdication to marriage of any kind to Mrs Simpson. The South African and Canadian Cabinets cabled similar messages over the next few days. The Governor-General of New Zealand sent Baldwin a telegram to say that Michael Savage had hoped for some solution that would allow the King to marry Mrs Simpson and to stay on the throne, but had regretfully accepted the British Government's conclusion that this was impossible. The Irish Government tendered no formal advice at this stage, but let it be understood that it did not object to the action being taken by the British Government.[40]

The Australian Cabinet backed their Prime Minister, Lyons, but many of the people of Australia felt they had not been properly informed about what was going on and had been given no chance to influence Australia's official position. The London editor of Smiths Newspapers sent a telegram to Godfrey Thomas, the King's Assistant Private Secretary, to report that cables from Australia revealed a thirst for some real knowledge – and that Australians believed they had heard everybody's views but the King's.[41] The Executive of the Constitutional Association of New South Wales cabled Baldwin with the message, 'Strongly urge full delay. Public opinion in Australia seriously divided.' The message was copied in a telegram to Churchill.[42]

According to the *Sydney Morning Herald* on Tuesday 8 December, 'The King's name was cheered in theatres, cinemas and restaurants in all of the capital cities.' The next day, the paper reported that some of the commercial radio stations, mostly but not entirely Labour-controlled, had rallied behind the King. One broadcast said: 'It is certain that in this battle between autocracy and democracy, the King is on the side of democracy . . . Baldwin, who is a diehard Conservative, is certainly not speaking for the mass of the people . . . Mrs Simpson will make the finest Queen England has known.' The Lyons Government responded by warning all broadcasting stations in Australia that they must refrain from inflaming Australian public opinion on the issue, and in Sydney and Melbourne groups wanting to hold meetings in support of the King were barred from using town halls.[43]

The Australian Parliament was recalled by wireless message. On Tuesday 8 December, John Curtin, the leader of the Labour Opposition, put on record his firm refusal to back Lyons. He questioned the Premier's right to tell Baldwin that the whole of the Australian Government was behind him and stated that 'The Opposition will leave the King unfettered in choosing his wife. It will not agree that his selection in that matter should be impaired by any influence of any sort or description.' The Australian Labour Party, he added, 'hopes that the present King will remain upon the throne of England. It desires to remain, as it will remain, loyal to King Edward VIII.'[44] On Wednesday, when Curtin attempted to move a resolution of 'loyalty and allegiance' to the King, the Government stifled the debate.[45] It was reported that MPs received a flood of telegrams in support of the King.[46] Harold Holt, a young member of the United Australia Party, summed up the feelings of many Australians about Edward – 'he understood us, and we looked to him to lop off from the tree of tradition the dead branches which threatened to interfere with its healthy growth within the British Empire.' Had the King chosen 'to select any woman, to whom he was legally entitled to be married, as Queen,' he said, 'I, for one, would not have hesitated in my loyalty to him.'[47]

Nor was there unqualified support for Baldwin among the people of Canada. 'There is no unanimous point of view,' admitted Dawson, 'as a certain element holds the Monarch's private life to be his own affair and thinks he should be allowed to marry the woman of his choice.' Although Dawson claimed that 'the great preponderance of opinion throughout Canada is seriously disquieted',[48] this was not the whole story. On the one hand, the Establishment newspapers echoed the attitudes of *The Times*. Toronto's *Globe and Mail*, for example, declared that, 'We in Canada can only pray that [Edward] ... will find duty more appealing than personal inclinations.'[49] But other newspapers, such as the *Montreal Gazette* and the *Ottawa Citizen*, made clear their support for the King. According to the *Citizen*, it was probable that, with more time to reflect, the forces of British democracy would align themselves strongly behind the King.[50] The editor of the *Canadian Post* reported to the King that he had interviewed many Canadians, and 'all are with you and [the] lady of your choice.'[51] A telegram sent from New York to Edward on 7 December reported that the Canadian Parliament was divided: that in a late poll of fifteen hundred people from all walks of life, three-quarters were in favour of Edward retaining the throne.[52]

'Full support and sympathy' were sent from the Dominion Federation League to Abolish Poverty, based in Ottawa.[53] 'I am now expressing the sentiments of all the Returned men of this vast Dominion', wrote a man in Vancouver to Edward's Private Secretary, 'when I state

Leabharlanna Fhine Gall

that we, I fear, regard our dear friend more as our Pal than our King and I want to tell him in the hour of this his great trial that no matter what happens now or in the future will always so regard him.'[54] 'Ride-em-cowboy, we know you'll win,' urged a letter from Toronto. 'We like your girl – she's OK with us. We're all cheering for you. Don't abdicate! We want you as our King! . . . these are Canadian sentiments.'[55] 'I would like to see Winston Churchill and you head a British Cabinet', telegraphed a man from Ontario. 'You might astound the world!'[56]

'Mr King – Canada's Prime Minister,' wrote Wallis to Edward some time later, 'has seen it his duty to get up in whatever they have in Canada [she meant their House of Commons] and announce that he told "Mr Baldwin that the people of Canada would not approve King Edward VIII's marriage to Mrs Simpson whether she became Queen or not".' But how, she wondered, 'can Prime Ministers speak for the people when they have never even asked them?'[57] It did seem that, as in Britain, there were sections of the population in the Dominions – the ruling class, the Conservative press, and the clergy – which supported Baldwin's position. But there were also large sections of the working class and the liberal middle classes – as in Britain – which supported the King but were never asked for their opinion. 'Canberra, Ottawa, Wellington, Cape Town – everywhere the story was the same', wrote Edward later in his memoirs. 'There had been no attempt to assess public opinion, which to the small degree that it had been sounded at all appeared to be divided.'[58]

The British Government did what it could to influence public opinion in the Empire. This was a considerable challenge given the vast extent of British rule in the world at this time. There was a flurry of telegrams, all in secret cipher, between London and the British colonies of central and southern Africa. 'It is possible that constitutional difficulties raised by proposed marriage of His Majesty the King may result in his deciding to abdicate', explained Sir William Clark, the British High Commissioner in Pretoria, in a telegram to the resident commissioners elsewhere in Africa. He asked, 'Will you consider and inform me in what manner announcement should be made to natives in event of abdication taking place.'[59]

In the event, reactions from the British colonies of Africa, at least, were reassuring to the Government. A telegram from the Resident Commissioner in Basutoland informed Sir William that the abdication of the King 'would be understood by natives here as marriages of ruling chiefs are similarly restricted.' He added that it 'would not I think affect loyalty to the Throne'.[60] The Resident Commissioner in Mbabane, Swaziland, told the High Commissioner that he was confident about the Swazi people's views on the crisis. He was about to meet with the Swazi National Council at the Lobamba Kraal, 'principally to get the Chiefs and people to do more in the campaign against locusts', and he was sure that 'the Swazis would understand, in the case of the Paramount Chief's principal wife, the one expected to bear an heir to the Chieftainship, the objection which there is to the proposed marriage; she would have to be a spinster of noble birth.'[61]

India was a different matter. Her reaction to the crisis was regarded as critical, and there was considerable anxiety in London about Indian sympathy for the King. While some newspapers, including the *Star of India* and *Amrita Bazar*, a leading nationalist daily in Calcutta, followed the line of the London *Times*, many others had been giving their support to the King ever since the story had broken. The *Statesman* urged: 'let us give our sympathies to our King and turn from evil-minded ones who would have us believe that in his normal desire to marry the lady of his choice he has in any way demeaned himself or forfeited his claim to our loyalty and devotion.'[62] The 'issue has resolved itself into . . . abandonment of the marriage or abdication neither of which can be contemplated with equanimity', observed *Hindu* on 4 December. On the same day, the *Bombay Sentinel* declared that the 'King will win . . . the British public [is] behind the King in his battle with the Baldwin Government.' On 5 December, *Hindu* pointed out that under the existing system in Britain, permitting divorce and remarriage, it would be a matter of simple logic to allow the King to have his way, since there was apparently no obstacle against marriage to the lady in question, either as a commoner or as an American.[63]

Lord Linlithgow, the Viceroy, admitted in a telegram to Lord Zetland, the Secretary of State for India, that although 'responsible

and informed Indian-owned press generally supports line taken by
Prime Minister' it was also the case that smaller papers 'tend to
ignore or to misunderstand importance of constitutional aspect and
to concentrate on human side. *Bombay Chronicle* and *Sentinel* take
line that class distinctions are out of date. There is general sympathy
in press of all shades for King's dilemma.' He had found that Muslims
in particular were likely to support the King: 'A letter I have received
from a Muslim of some position in Delhi urges that if King cannot
marry as he pleases, prestige of Throne will be detrimentally affected,
and one or two Muslim press comments stress absence of class distinctions under Islam.' To these 'straws', he said, 'I attach little significance
. . . sentimental considerations (coupled with support lent by Indian
customs and traditions to view that King should marry where he likes)
bulk fairly large in securing sympathy for His Majesty.'[64]

Efforts were made to shore up support for Baldwin in India. At a
meeting of Ministers on 8 December, 'Emphasis was laid on the great
importance of securing the widest possible publicity in India to the fact
that the King's abdication was entirely voluntary and had been suggested by himself'[65] – even though the abdication had yet to happen.
Zetland cabled Linlithgow with some information on Edward's weak-
nesses, suggesting that it 'may be useful for guidance in publicity'.[66] The
Viceroy asked his governors to report on the reaction of the individual
provinces. The Governor of Bengal sent a telegram informing him that,

Among Europeans many inclined to feel on information published that more
delicate handling at home and in dominions might have extricated King
from an impossible situation. Feeling is virtually unanimous that Simpson
impossible as Queen, but some vacillate on possibility of morganatic marriage.

The Governor perceived a difference between Hindu and Muslim
opinion: that Muslims would take a more sympathetic view of the
King's dilemma.[67] The Governor of Madras reported that 'European
opinion' was shocked and disappointed by the King and did not think
he should marry Mrs Simpson. However, there appeared to be 'no
noticeable Indian reaction'.[68] It was the Governor of Punjab's view
that, 'Generally speaking, only a few educated Indians understand the

constitutional issues involved. To the masses the King is King and the idea that he should be subject to the advice of Ministers is foreign to their conception of Kingship.'[69] The Governor of Assam told Linlithgow that Europeans were firmly against Edward, but that the Indians of Assam were less judgemental. 'They view matters more domestically', he reported, and think that 'a King is a King and may choose a very unworthy woman to be his wife without doing lasting injury to his position.'[70]

The Governor of the Central Provinces informed Linlithgow that local reaction was 'guarded and while sympathizing with King's difficulties recognise that he must follow wishes of people.'[71] An Indian citizen living in London took a different view. 'As one who knows both England and India well,' he wrote to the King, 'I would like to be able to assure Your Majesty that there is no truth in the traditionalists' cry that public opinion both in England and in India has been shocked by your intention to marry the lady of your heart.' He appealed to him not to give up: 'Do not abdicate; do not compromise; do not worry. Be true to yourself and your love. India will applaud such a stand out of her better instincts. And, let England have a ballot on this question.'[72]

The editor of the *Oriental Post* in London said that he was 'one of those Indians' who had had great faith in British democracy. 'But I must confess,' he added, 'it is now shaking.' He pointed out that India was solidly behind the King. 'India has not been consulted,' he observed, 'but we 350 millions will out vote the rest of the 100 millions of the dominions etc, if the issue [comes] before us.'[73] A similar message came from the editor of the *Daily Milap* and the *Daily Hindimilap*, who telegraphed from Lahore to urge the King to dissolve the British and Dominion Parliaments and the Indian legislatures and to make his proposed marriage the sole issue for a referendum. He was sure that the people would vindicate the King 'as against conservative advice of your present ministers. Indian subjects constitute largest percentage have right make their say. Trust Your Majesty will give your people a chance to give their views.'[74]

Edward had delighted many people during his visit to India in the early 1920s. He had offended numbers of the British living there, but

THE PEOPLE'S KING

had won over many Indians. 'Again and again,' observed the Director of Public Information at the time, 'I heard the remark: "If only all you Europeans were like him!" '[75] In an atmosphere of great tension and suspicion of British motives, he had evaded his minders to walk among the people. At Poona, for example, he horrified officials by walking around the stands after laying a foundation stone, so that people could see him – 'They rose to their feet and cheered themselves hoarse.'[76] It was perhaps memories of this day that prompted a number of telegrams to be sent from Poona in December 1936 to encourage the King. From other parts of India, too, came 'divine blessings'[77] and opposition to 'unconstitutional coerced abdication'[78]– from Calcutta, Patiala State, Bombay, Mydrim and Rawalpindi.

As Prince of Wales, Edward had visited not only India but numerous other countries overseas, both within the Empire and outside it. His evident wish to meet the ordinary people of these countries, and his genuine friendliness towards them, had been met with appreciation and gratitude. Now, as Edward's love for Wallis and his wish to marry her became world news, spread by the newsreels and the press, these ordinary people felt great sympathy. Numerous telegrams of support arrived from nations all over the world. 'Barbados supports you. Our King can do no wrong', insisted a telegram from the Caribbean island. 'The People are with the King', declared a banner headline above news of the British crisis in the *Times of Ceylon*.[79]

'Our cock won't fight'

On Saturday 5 December, Winston Churchill sent a letter of cheer to the King:

News from all fronts! No pistol to be held at the King's head. No doubt that this request for time will be granted. Therefore no final decision or Bill till after Christmas – probably February or March . . . Good advances on all parts giving prospects of gaining good positions and assembling large forces behind them.[1]

But it was too late. The King had already decided to give up his throne. 'Tell the Prime Minister', he told his adviser, Walter Monckton, on the morning of 5 December, 'that when he comes to see me this afternoon, I shall formally tell him that I have decided to abdicate.'[2] Monckton duly passed the King's message on to Baldwin. Later, Sir John Simon, the Home Secretary, went to Stornoway House to give Beaverbrook the news. Several MPs were also told of the King's intention, as well as some of the newspaper editors. Very soon, word in the constituencies was circulating that the struggle between King and Prime Minister was over, with victory, as Beaverbrook put it, 'perching on the banners of Baldwin'.[3]

The information had not yet reached Churchill, however, who continued to search for a solution to the King's dilemma. On Sunday 6 December he was at Chartwell, his home in Kent, discussing the problem with his friends, Archibald Sinclair and Robert Boothby. They decided that the best way of avoiding abdication would be a public statement by the King that he would agree to accept the

Cabinet's advice on the possibility of his marriage to Mrs Simpson. That way, since her divorce would not be made absolute until April, the question would be safely avoided for four months. The plan was put to the King on Monday morning. But he turned it down, on the grounds that it would not be honourable to play for time when 'his fundamental resolve' was unchanged, and unchangeable.[4] As Beaverbrook had told Churchill on Saturday morning on a visit to his Westminster flat, the King seemed to have given up the battle: 'I said "Our cock won't fight", and . . . that any further struggles to save him would do no good.'[5]

When on 5 December Monckton had returned from his visit to Baldwin, he told the King that the Prime Minister wanted to see him once more, to satisfy himself that he had exhausted all possible solutions. On Tuesday 8 December Baldwin came to the Fort for this final talk – and to his horror, Edward noticed that he had brought a suitcase with him. This meant that he was planning to stay the night. 'The PM went down to wrestle with the soul of the young man, being prepared to stay all night if it was any use', noted the publisher Francis Meynell.[6] But as Edward wrote in his memoirs, he had already had quite enough of Baldwin – 'His part in my life was over, and I did not propose to have him on my hands that night, snapping his fingers, storing up little homely touches for his report to Parliament.' The King made it clear to Baldwin that he was welcome to stay for dinner, but not for the night. They had a last fruitless talk, followed by an evening meal with other guests. 'We were nine', recalled Edward – 'Mr Baldwin on my right, Sir Edward Peacock on my left; my brothers, Bertie and George, Tommy Dugdale, Walter Monckton, George Allen, and Ulick Alexander.'[7] It was a dinner, wrote Bertie in his own chronicle of events, that he was never likely to forget:

While the rest of us . . . were very sad (we knew the final decision [Edward] had made) my brother was the life & soul of the party, telling the PM things I am sure he had never heard before about unemployed centres etc. (referring to his visit in S. Wales). I whispered to W[alter] M[onckton] 'and this is the man we are going to lose.' One couldn't, nobody could, believe it.[8]

Edward made sure that the royal crisis was never mentioned, not even once.[9]

But it was at the forefront of everyone's mind. After the dinner, as Baldwin and Tom Dugdale drove back to London, the Prime Minister commented, 'This is making history. This is what I like.'[10] Everything seemed settled: Edward was going to abdicate, and Albert would be the new king. 'I had a letter this evening from la chère petite Duchesse,' Lady Milner recorded in her diary on 8 December, referring to the Duchess of York. The 'dear little Duchess', she wrote, had told her 'in a way that was most touching, that she and her husband were looking forward to be of service to "this dear country". This may and probably does mean all is decided. I hope so.'[11]

Then suddenly, there was a setback. From her refuge in Cannes, Wallis had made an intervention in the royal crisis that threatened to dash all of Lady Milner's hopes for Edward's abdication. On Monday 7 December, she had issued a statement to the press declaring that she was willing to renounce the King. She had realized – with horror – that Edward was moving inexorably towards abdication. It was now up to her, said Lord Brownlow, to pull him back from this final act.[12] 'Ever since that awful last day at the Fort,' she wrote in her memoirs, 'much the same idea had been taking shape in my mind: I must wrench myself entirely out of David's life. Since he would not give me up, I would have to give him up and in a way that would leave him no choice but to accept this decision.' She felt there was no alternative. 'Apart from the moral considerations affecting his kingly position,' she said, 'my own self-respect was at stake . . . If I left undone anything within my power to prevent his abdicating, I knew I could never again look into the mirror of my conscience.'[13]

With Brownlow's help, she prepared a statement for the press:

Mrs Simpson throughout the last few weeks has invariably wished to avoid any action or proposal which would hurt or damage His Majesty or the Throne.

Today her attitude is unchanged, and she is willing, if such action would solve the problem, to withdraw from a situation that has been rendered both unhappy and untenable.[14]

On the afternoon of 7 December she telephoned the Fort and read the statement to Edward over a crackly line. At first, he was unbelieving, then hurt and angry – but he agreed to let her go ahead, when she told him that Perry Brownlow and Herman Rogers had approved the statement. He added, though, that it would make no difference. The abdication documents, he told her, were being drawn up and the Cabinet was meeting that very moment to act upon them. 'Of course you can do whatever you wish', he added. 'You can go wherever you want – to China, Labrador, or the South Seas. But wherever you go, I will follow you.'[15]

In despair, and ready to try anything that had the slightest chance, Wallis resolved to follow the plan through. Brownlow gave her statement to the thirty or so correspondents waiting for news at the Hotel Majestic in Cannes. 'That night, for the first time since leaving the Fort five days before,' said Wallis, 'I slept soundly.'[16] Tom Driberg, a columnist (and later MP), was in a Soho nightclub when news of Wallis's statement came through on the wireless. 'I was in Frisco's one night', he later recalled, 'when news came through of a public statement by Mrs Simpson starting with the words: "The situation is unhappy and untenable . . ."' In response, he said, 'We pounced on these words, which seemed to fit a West Indian rhythm then favoured by us, and composed a whole calypso around them.' Later, he regretted this reaction as callous: 'So little did we care about the sufferings of that unfortunate woman.'[17]

Brownlow was heartened by the positive reaction to Wallis's statement from the reporters, who believed that it would end the crisis. 'For some extraordinary reason,' wrote Dawson sourly in his diary, 'this statement . . . was hailed next morning by the *Daily Express* and placarded all over London as the "End of the Crisis".'[18] Neville Chamberlain, the Chancellor, recommended warning journalists that 'it would perhaps be unfair to the public and all concerned if they did not at the same time point out the other possibility, i.e. abdication.' It was the duty of the press, he insisted, to keep before the public the two alternatives.[19]

Dawson was convinced that Wallis's offer was insincere. 'It meant, of course, exactly nothing, and was no doubt dictated from London

by King Edward's constant solicitude for Mrs S.' He wrote the beginning of a leader pointing out that 'the situation was quite unchanged'
and left others to finish it, then 'looked in once more on Alec
Hardinge.'[20] In fact, his response to Wallis's intervention went well
beyond writing a leader. Immediately under the news of Mrs Simpson's
statement of her offer to withdraw, *The Times* printed – as a social item
– the news that Thelma Furness had arrived the day before at Southampton on the liner *Queen Mary* from New York. Lady Furness, herself
a divorced woman, had been Edward's lover when he was Prince of
Wales before he fell in love with Mrs Simpson. This little item in the
paper therefore reminded the reader of the King's history of affairs with
married women. As the official history of *The Times* later observed, the
newspaper's influence on the abdication was 'not undeserving of
mention'. Dawson, it observed, conducted matters with 'supreme skill
and vigour!'[21] His biographer has commented that Dawson's role was
perhaps only second in importance to that of Baldwin.[22]

Some members of the public were as cynical as Dawson about
Wallis's motives. ' "End of the crisis", blithely announces the *Express*
today' was the diary comment of a salesman working for the London
department store, Peter Robinson. 'This on the strength of Mrs S's
offer to withdraw from the match. Offer is the operative word which
is in effect anything but a solution to the difficulty. It merely amounts
to challenging the King: "Desert me now if you dare" . . . End of crisis
be damned. It's hardly begun yet.'[23] A saleswoman at Barkers, another
department store in the capital, made similar comments in her own
diary: 'Mrs Simpson gave a message to the effect that she was "willing
to withdraw if it will help the situation" – that is not good enough',
she wrote on 8 December. 'The British Public can see through that –
she should withdraw instead of putting the onus on the King – it isn't
as though she were a British subject.'[24]

But the fact that Wallis was ready to give Edward up showed that
she was not, as had been claimed, cold and calculating. 'Mrs Simpson's
recent gesture', wrote a working man in Cumberland to the King,
'shows a splendid trait in her character.'[25] One woman felt a strong
sense of female solidarity with Wallis. 'I feel that I must', she wrote to
Edward,

send you the expression of my pride in one who has offered to give up all her chances of happiness because of her great affection. A man has his work, apart from his private life, & he cannot quite realise what the renunciation may mean to a woman . . . this wonderful love will be for you a guiding star, & an inspiration ever present in hours of difficulty & depression.[26]

Another woman, an unemployed dancer, begged Edward not to accept Wallis's generous offer. 'They are trying to make you a slave, a slave to tradition, to power, to money,' she implored him, 'but your people won't WISH this sacrifice . . . Don't let them beat you, and please don't fail her. Remember, that although she has offered to stand aside, she is praying as only a woman can, "Please God give him back to me".' She added, 'I'm praying the same prayer on my own account. We are satisfied with your choice. She's very beautiful, but more than that, there's sweet sympathy and understanding in her eyes . . . Read the *Daily Mirror* and the loyal letters . . . There's 8 of us here think the same.'[27] 'All the members of this family', wrote a mother, 'send you their heartfelt devotion and sympathy, and beg you not to accept the lady's resignation. Stand firm! The people are behind you!'[28]

Letters of support and sympathy were still arriving daily for the King – from families, sometimes signed by every member; from whole streets, cafes or shops; and from individuals. 'Stand your corner, marry the woman of your choice', urged a Sheffield ex-serviceman on 8 December. 'The Country will support you, it is unable to express itself, it has no means to do so . . . I am a wartime Coldstreamer No. 20905. I would take up arms for you if necessary and for making your choice the Queen.'[29] Every wish for his happiness and success was sent from a woman who had worked as a voluntary social worker at the Mobberley Child Welfare Centre in Cheshire for forty years.[30] How proud the people of Scotland would be, said another letter, if their King were to marry the Queen of his choice in Crathie parish church or in St Giles Cathedral.[31] Cinema-goers were still showing their support for the King. 'Only last night at a Cinema,' wrote one woman, it was so wonderful to see and hear the applause you received when your picture was shown on the screen, and words to the effect that the whole nation goes out to you in sympathy during this crisis, and when we all stood to attention, quite a lump came to my throat, and I prayed so hard that we would not lose you.[32]

There was a growing realization, however, that the King might actually abdicate. One 'poor working woman' said that 'if it was left to me I say marry her and be happy', but that it was not for the poor to decide. She therefore pleaded with the King to give Wallis up: 'I know it's a lot to ask you to do, but we all love you so and how could you or Mrs Simpson live happy when you know what it will do for England for many Poor will be thrown out of work.'[33] A Londoner offered a solution. Edward should accede to the throne, he suggested, and a few months afterwards Mrs Simpson should become Lady-in-Waiting to Queen Mary or the Duchess of York. Then, 'following the desire of we The People she be later created a Duchess.' The letter-writer was sure that 'so good, clever and kind a woman would soon by her work endear her self even to those who feel she is somewhat a stranger at present.'[34]

'Only time I was frightened. I thought [the King] might change his mind,' said Baldwin on 8 December, the day after Wallis's press statement was released.[35] Like many others in government and court circles, he had assumed her to be a cunning schemer who would have no interest in keeping the King on the throne if she were not herself going to be Queen. In his mind, her status as a divorcee, and an American one at that, put her into a category of women who were 'loose'– 'fast' and untrustworthy. Many of his circle shared this view. 'More anxiety & more news about Mrs S', wrote Lucy Baldwin in her diary on 8 December – 'a thoroughly bad lot.'[36] She was 'believed to be the kind of person', claimed Ramsay MacDonald in his diary earlier that year, 'who would sell secrets'.[37] Sir Horace Wilson sneeringly concluded that Wallis was 'selfish, self-seeking, hard, calculating, ambitious, scheming, dangerous.'[38]

The royal crisis was regarded as smutty and unsavoury, even though it was actually all about love. 'I felt I must work off the dirt of this horrible crisis', wrote Lady Milner. 'So I went to a Turkish Bath this morning.'[39] None of these people could bring themselves to see Mrs Simpson as an individual who genuinely loved Edward and wanted the best possible outcome for him – even if it meant giving him up. But, as Lord Brownlow wrote on 9 December, 'Mrs Simpson tells me she was and is perfectly willing to instruct me to withdraw her petition for divorce and indeed willing to do anything to prevent the King from abdicating. I am satisfied beyond any doubt that is Mrs Simpson's genuine and honest desire.'[40]

Wallis's generous and unselfish offer of renunciation made her seem less predictable. Baldwin was not sure how to deal with it – or, indeed, with her. He knew, though, that her press statement might influence the opinion of the wavering Dominions and he promptly sent a telegram to the leader of each one, stating that he had 'every reason for doubting bona fides of Mrs Simpson's statement. Believe it to be no more than attempt to swing public opinion in her favour and thereby give her less reason to be uneasy as to her personal safety.'[41]

Baldwin also summoned Wallis's solicitor, Theodore Goddard, to Downing Street, where he showed him a copy of Mrs Simpson's press statement and asked him to go to the South of France to ascertain the real nature of her intentions.[42] Goddard agreed. He had been planning to visit Mrs Simpson in any case. There was some worry – felt keenly by Sir Horace Wilson in particular – that Wallis might be planning to return to London, and Walter Monckton had suggested that Goddard, as her solicitor, should visit her and persuade her to stay away. At about the same time, Goddard had learned of a very real threat to her divorce, because of an impending intervention in the suit. It convinced him that he had an obligation to see his client and discuss the options with her. However, he went against the wishes of the King, who had first approved the visit but then changed his mind.[43] No doubt the news of an intervention in Wallis's divorce, which he was told about, had made Edward uneasy.

Goddard left on Tuesday morning, 8 December, in a small government plane; he was forced to land at Marseilles and went on to Cannes by car. He went to see Wallis the next morning, and found her in a state of distress. She had spoken on the telephone the day before with the King and with George Allen, who had told her about the threat to the divorce. He asked her whether it was wise to continue with the divorce proceedings. If she were to abandon the divorce, he said, 'all possibility of the King's marriage would fall to the ground and the crisis would thus be resolved.' He added, however, that the process would take several weeks, and any reinstatement of her petition in the future would be complicated and 'possibly somewhat untidy'. Not knowing what to do, Wallis turned to Lord Brownlow, who was highly doubtful that such an action could be achieved in time to affect any decision by the King. If the King *did* abdicate, he pointed out, such a step might be disastrous. Edward's motivation all along had been marriage – so that 'for you to scrap your divorce will produce a hopeless anticlimax and an all-round tragedy.'[44] Lord Brownlow was in any case livid with rage that Goddard had brought with him a personal physician – because of his weak heart – who was being described by British reporters as a gynaecologist. He had also brought with him a law clerk, who was reported to be an anaesthetist. Given the powerfully negative views on pregnancy outside marriage in the 1930s, these reports would be very damaging to the good names of Wallis and the King. Brownlow squashed the rumours as quickly as he could.

Wallis was not sure how best to react to Goddard's suggestion. She told him that she was quite prepared to give the King up, but that she believed he would follow her, wherever she went. They made a telephone call together to Edward, who pointed out that any further discussions with Goddard were now irrelevant. He explained that he had already told the Cabinet of his decision to abdicate – 'For me,' wrote Edward later in his memoirs, 'it was all over.'[45] Goddard returned to England that night. There was no plane, so he took a train to Paris, where he was met the next morning, Thursday 10 December, by a secretary from the British Embassy who had been sent by Downing Street to discover the outcome of the interview with Mrs Simpson. He was under instructions to phone back with his findings, as the Prime Minister was going to address the House of Commons that afternoon and wanted the information before he spoke. When Goddard finally arrived at Downing Street, he was met by Sir Horace Wilson, who had already received the report sent from Paris. 'I could not help but gather from my conversation with him', wrote Goddard years later, 'that he already knew all about it and seemed to know something of our conversations with the King.'[46] In other words, he suspected that the telephone line between Wallis and Edward had been bugged.

After Goddard's departure, Wallis and Brownlow decided that she should leave Europe immediately in a final effort to keep Edward on the throne. She would send a statement to the press telling them of her complete withdrawal from the situation and her imminent departure for a distant country. On Wednesday 9 December she telephoned Edward with this news, expecting to bury her love for him 'for ever'. But for once, he cut her short. 'I can't seem to make you understand my position', he said. 'It's all over. The Instrument of Abdication is already prepared . . . The Cabinet has met twice today, and I have given them my final word. I will be gone from England within forty-eight hours.'[47] Wallis was stunned by the finality of Edward's statement. But his mind was irrevocably made up, as he told the Cabinet, when it sent a message asking him to reconsider his decision. 'They would have been in a nasty position if he had changed his mind!', wrote Nancy Dugdale in her diary.[48]

On the evening of 9 December, there was a pall of fog over London. Bertie went to see Queen Mary, and when he had told her of Edward's final decision, he recorded in his chronicle of events, he 'broke down and sobbed like a child'. The Queen described this interview in her own diary. 'The whole affair has lasted since 16 November,' she wrote sadly, referring to the day when Edward first told her of his plan to abdicate, 'and is very painful. It is a terrible blow to us all and particularly to poor Bertie.'[49]

At ten o'clock on the morning of 10 December 1936, just one week after the general public had first read in the papers about the royal love affair, the King executed the Instrument of Abdication. It was the end of a reign of 326 days:

I, Edward VIII, of Great Britain, Ireland, and the British Dominions bey-ond the Seas, King, Emperor of India do hereby declare My irrevocable determination to renounce the Throne for Myself and for My descendants, and My desire that effect should be given to the Instrument of Abdication immediately.[50]

The signing of the Instrument was witnessed by Edward's three living brothers – their Royal Highnesses the Duke of York, the Duke of Gloucester and the Duke of Kent – and made Albert, the eldest of these three, the new King. Queen Mary drove out to Royal Lodge, in Windsor Great Park, where Edward met her and gave a full account of what had happened since they had last met, nearly a week ago. Now that it was all over, recalled Edward, 'her heart went out to her hard-pressed son, prompting her to say with tenderness: "And to me, the worst thing is that you won't be able to see her for so long."'[51]

Baldwin's wife, Lucy, also felt sorry for Edward. 'The King had decided to go', she wrote in her diary. 'Poor dear man but it is for the best.'[52] There was a general feeling of relief among the social elite – 'I don't fancy there will be any King's party or any old revival of the red rose v. the white rose', wrote Francis Meynell to his wife.[53] 'There will be no more of the orgies there used to be when Mrs Simpson did the "*danse du ventre* [belly dancing]",' observed Nancy Dugdale, 'and other un-English performances of unsavoury nature.'[54]

Meanwhile, the general public waited anxiously for news. 'Everybody had been strained all day as it was known that King must come to a decision', reads a London solicitor's diary entry for 10 December.[55] 'All the morning papers prepared us for the news that Mr Baldwin was to give the House this afternoon,' noted a schoolmaster who had been closely following events. 'When I went to spend my free afternoon in T[unbridge] Wells,' he added, 'I knew I should probably come back with Edward VIII no longer King of England. And so it was.'[56] Vera Brittain, changing trains at Edinburgh, saw news-vendors running up and down Princes Street in the centre of the city selling special editions, and on large placards she saw the words 'Abdication fears growing'.[57]

The news was officially broken by Baldwin in the House of Commons at 3.35 on the afternoon of 10 December – 'the most momentous statement of the crisis', observed *The King Abdicates*, a Pathe Gazette newsreel. Earlier, Edward had sent Baldwin a pencilled note asking him to refer in his speech to Wallis's efforts to avoid abdication – 'Mrs Simpson – Has consistantly [sic] attempted to withdraw and even yesterday made a final attempt to dissuade the King from the course he has resolved to take.' Horace Wilson added a sneering comment to this note: 'I asked the PM whether he had any intention of mentioning Mrs Simpson. (If he had, I was quite willing to draft appropriate passages!) The PM said he would make no reference. To make a favourable one would clearly be to go counter to public opinion.'[58]

There was an excited atmosphere in the House during the wait for Baldwin's speech. *The Times* observed that:

Every seat was filled. Members squatted on the steps of the gangways, stood in a serried crowd behind the Bar, and thronged the side galleries three deep. There was even a small overflow upon the steps of the Speaker's Chair. The Peers' Gallery was filled to overflowing, though all the more prominent peers preferred to attend the proceedings in their own House. In the Distinguished Strangers' Gallery was a representative assembly of diplomats, including the French and Belgian Ambassadors; and no member of the public fortunate enough to obtain a ticket had failed to use it.[59]

First, the Prime Minister read to the House a message from the King, declaring his intention to abdicate. 'I shall always remember the . . . wild stampede at the first sentence of the King's statement that he had renounced the throne irrevocably', said Robert Bernays in his diary. He observed 'a tremendous sense in everyone that we were on a great stage and the world was taking account of how we were comporting ourselves.'[60]

Then Baldwin gave a speech. 'He spoke for just under an hour, quietly, slowly, simply,' recorded Nancy Dugdale, who was watching from the Gallery, 'with an acute sense of the world listening to every word he said.'[61] It was an 'amazing performance', according to Bernays.[62] The Prime Minister gave an account of the events that had led up to the final moment of abdication. He paid tribute to the King's determination to 'go with dignity', his abhorrence of the idea of a King's Party and his decision to stay in Windsor, away from the cheering crowds of London. However, the account was very much from his own and the Government's point of view. He did not mention the King's wish to broadcast to the nation, which had been forbidden by the Cabinet. Nor did he respond to the King's request that he explain how hard 'the other person most intimately concerned' had tried to dissuade him from his decision to abdicate.[63]

Baldwin's delivery of his speech was shambling but possibly all the more effective because of this. He referred, said Bernays, to 'little pieces of paper with ideas on them contributed obviously by his colleagues. When he came in with the dispatch box he found that he had lost his key. He desperately searched in his pockets for it and then found it under Neville Chamberlain's legs.' When he then tried to sort the mass of papers, he upset them and had to retrieve them from the floor. At this point, Hoare 'put his papers on top of Baldwin's notes with the result that they were upset again and had to be retrieved from the floor once more.'[64] This fumbling was somehow consistent with his national image: as an Englishman, 'a household figure, almost a family friend', someone who liked to smoke inexpensive pipes.[65]

When it was over, Baldwin felt that the speech had gone well. 'Stan got back to dinner tired but content,' wrote his wife in her diary.[66] But not everyone shared Bernays's opinion that Baldwin's speech was an 'amazing performance'. The Prime Minister, 'who has a natural gift for the counterfeit, surpassed himself' was the acid judgement of Aneurin Bevan. 'He spoke as a pilot who had guided the ship of State safely to harbour through stormy seas, past jagged rocks, and in the teeth of the buffeting winds. The winds, indeed, were boudoir hysteria, the rocks threatened to wreck only his own career, and the official Opposition had not blown even a zephyr across his path.' Bevan was disappointed that the Labour leaders had allowed the problem to be presented as one of Parliament versus King, since Parliament had not been allowed to discuss the matter. Bevan took the view that the constitutional theories of most of his Labour colleagues were mistaken. The real point, he said, was not whether a constitutional monarch must accept the advice of his Cabinet – but whether the Cabinet had given the right advice.[67]

After Baldwin's speech, Winston Churchill rose to address the House. He said that he unreservedly accepted the Prime Minister's explanation that the King had taken his decision freely, voluntarily and spontaneously, in his own time and in his own way. 'What has been done or left undone belongs to history', he added. He defended the efforts he had made to keep Edward on the throne and said he would have been ashamed 'if in my independent and unofficial position I had not cast about for every lawful means to keep him on the throne of his fathers.' He also praised Edward for his honourable behaviour throughout the crisis:

I venture to say that no Sovereign has ever conformed more strictly or more faithfully to the letter and spirit of the Constitution than his present Majesty. In fact, he has voluntarily made a sacrifice for the peace and strength of his Realm which goes far beyond the bounds required by the law and the Constitution.

He reminded his listeners of Edward's place in the hearts of the poor:

Although our hopes today lie withered, still I would assert that his personality will not go down uncherished to future ages – (hear, hear) – that it will be particularly remembered in the homes of his poorer subjects – (Cheers) – and that they will ever wish from the bottom of their hearts for his private peace and happiness and for the happiness of those who are dear to him.[68]

'The streets crowded . . . Baldwin has managed the whole thing admirably,' wrote Cecil Headlam in his diary on 10 December.[69] A proud Mrs Baldwin agreed. The episode was a sad one, she said, but at least

in this case one's Duty was writ so large and clear that the only thing for a man to do was to brace himself for an unpleasant time and go ahead with it. I am indeed happy and thankful that Stanley was the chosen medium to do the work for the throne and Empire and that God should have inspired him to carry it out as he did.'[70]

The abdication was nothing less than a triumph for Baldwin. He had returned to Westminster after the summer a weary and fragile man.

But his 'deft and skilful handling of the Abdication issue', observed Churchill tartly, 'raised him in a fortnight from the depths to the pinnacle.'[71] Baldwin 'had a genius', he added, 'for waiting upon events and an imperturbability under adverse criticism. He was singularly adroit in letting events work for him, and capable of seizing the ripe moment when it came.'[72] He had been refreshed and revived by the royal crisis and now appeared to have rescued the country from disaster. 'The crisis has ended with the end which I had always predicted', observed Lockhart – 'Baldwin is right up again.'[73]

Over the next week or so, Baldwin received about a thousand telegrams and letters from people all over Britain, of every social class. Some were angry, but most of them expressed their gratitude to him for guiding the nation safely through the royal crisis. Many sympathized with the Prime Minister for his sorrow at the abdication, which he had described with eloquent regret in the House of Commons, and thanked him for doing his best to keep Edward on the throne. Members of the Liverpool Disabled Ex-Service Men's Protection Association wrote to Baldwin to offer their sympathy to him on the abdication. 'Our minds wander back to the days of the Great War,' they said sadly, 'when he stood on the battlefields of France and Flanders a mere boy to welcome the troops as they landed to play their part in that great struggle. Nobody feels his abdication more than we ex servicemen.'[74] A girl living in Ottawa sent Baldwin a poem of love for Edward and congratulated the Prime Minister on his statesmanship over the last couple of weeks. 'As you yourself know, Mr Baldwin,' she said, 'he was not only the "People's King", but more even than that, he was the people's friend. He has bid us goodbye, and we should like also, apart from our Government and Press, to bid him farewell and voice our appreciation and understanding.' She asked him to pass the poem on to Edward.[75] 'Didn't I tell you', wrote a poor widow, in shaky writing, that 'the old 'uns were better than the youngsters. Well – you have been just splendid . . . I hope you will all stand solidly by and keep the King in his difficulties. I just loved King Edward. He will live to regret his act.'[76]

Other letters took a robust attitude on the issue of 'proper values'. A letter from Pennsylvania congratulated Baldwin

on your recent triumph in upholding the cause of righteousness and morality
. . . That you have forced his hand, and compelled him to either retire or give
up a woman of questionable past, deserves nothing but praise from every
upright citizen of whatever nationality! More power to you! You have shown
us that truth and lofty character still exist, in this time of lax morals and
cursed disrespect for the finer and nobler things of life.[77]

Edith Londonderry assured Baldwin that 'No one besides yourself
could have managed the little man in the extraordinary way you have.'
It was an issue, she added, 'on which not only the crown but the whole
Empire trembled . . . I was saying to Charley last night that this was
the 4th Sovereign you had served – and that now my refrain would,
be – "That kings may come and kings may go – but 'Stan' goes on
for ever".'[78]

The President of the British Legion, Sir Frederick Maurice, told
Baldwin that at the National Executive Council of the British Legion
there was 'a unanimous & even startling expression of bitter disappointment at the conduct of his late Majesty', as well as admiration
of Baldwin.[79] This was consistent with information obtained by Walter
Runciman, who had been informed that the men of the Legion would
not stand for Mrs Simpson as Queen. His informant had 'made
enquiries from all parts of the country – & the Legion is of course
everywhere & there was no division of opinion.'[80] But these enquiries
were probably confined to the top brass of the Legion, both in London
and in the provinces: it would not have been seen as appropriate to
consult the lower ranks of the Legion on such a 'delicate' affair.
Moreover, as with the telegrams that were sent to the Dominions, it
would have been difficult to frame the question in a neutral way.

Away from the National Executive Council and on the ground, it
was a different story. Many of the ordinary members of the British
Legion – the poor and the unemployed – unswervingly supported the
King. The President of the Spring Hill Branch of the British Legion in
Birmingham wrote to Edward to express regret and sympathy:

I am instructed by my Branch to write expressing our deepest sympathy to
you in your great ordeal . . . many of us have spoken to you, and you have

taken our hand, words fail us to show our regret, we know what you have done for Ex-servicemen, Empire and Country, and in our hearts there will always be a joyous remembrance of you. May God Bless you, is our sincere wish.[81]

A message of sympathy and admiration came from the Secretary of the Penrhiwceiber British Legion and United Services Club and Institute, which Edward had visited during his visit to South Wales in November. 'You have all the people's sympathy in this district,' he said,

Parliament can do nothing and the Church are not worth worrying over. If they had only done their duty by the people as you have done it there would not be so many empty places of Worship. So I can only express myself by saying be the Man you were during the War. You went then, into places where the Bishops & politicians would not go such as 'Ducks Bill', Levantie [Lavente], Passchendaele & Pilkin.[82]

The spirit of these letters echoed others that had been arriving all week from rank-and-file members of the Legion. 'Those who feel their obligations to you', stated a letter from Birmingham, signed 'Legion', 'apologise for the voice of the newspapers and the snobs and other self-centred bodies, we hope you will stand firm and marry who you wish and increase the regard of.'[83] From the Honorary Secretary of the British Legion and United Service Fund in Gateshead came every wish for his future happiness: 'I am writing this from my sick bed & if we in the British Legion in Gateshead can be of any help to you in encouraging your future happiness [we] will be glad to do so.'[84] A member of the Bakewell Branch of the British Legion, who 'had a few kindly words from you, while out in Italy attached in the 140 Field Ambulance, 41st Division', sent loyal support 'upon your pluck'. 'No man understands another man's love', he said,

& I give you credit of being a man, you always have been straightforward & honest over everything you have undertook, & it is most essential you should be on marriage . . . we know quite enough of you to know you are an honest hard working man with a heart that yearns to help all classes & conditions & why should you be deprived of your comforts. Kick your back into them & you will come out top.[85]

Vera Brittain heard the announcement of the King's decision to abdicate in the crowded restaurant of a department store. 'After a silence broken only by the opening and shutting of lift gates,' she recalled later, the expected words of the King, read by Baldwin, came over the radio: 'After long and anxious consideration I have determined to renounce the throne to which I succeeded on the death of my father, and I am now communicating this, my final and irrevocable decision . . . I have accordingly this morning executed an Instrument of Abdication.'[86] Baldwin's speech was then heard verbatim. 'A splendid speech by Mr Baldwin in parliament, explaining all the details, was broadcast from the H of C tonight,' wrote a doctor in Bristol in his diary that night. He added, 'He has acted finely throughout.'[87] 'History was made today', wrote the Londoner who belonged to the British Union of Fascists. 'This was, I think, the most thrilling and exciting news I've ever experienced.' He despaired that the King had 'failed in his duty to his people for the sake of a commonplace cow like Mrs Simpson.' Baldwin's speech, he thought, 'was magnificent. He'll go down in history as the saviour of his country on more than one occasion. A truly great man.'[88] 'What a pity', thought the wife of a Sutton Coldfield dairyman farmer, that 'the man could not find an English Rosebud for a bride? I cannot help but think he is making a mistake – for himself – his mother and as example to his Country . . .'[89] One angry letter to the King did not mince words: 'Dear Ted. I think you are a bugger. Bill.'[90]

But many poor people were not judgemental, just sad. 'With tears in my eyes and my heart heavy with sorrow,' wrote one man, 'I must write these lines to the Truest Sportsman and Greatest King that Britain has ever known.'[91] They were bitterly disappointed to see Edward go – 'The workers, and unemployed have lost their greatest friend, the one man, and a King, who had their interests at heart.'[92] Three 'Loyal Subjects' expressed their 'unspeakable sorrow for a most gallant gentleman' and made 'a toast to your return your majesty with your future bride.' A tenant of a pig farm on a Duchy property in Cornwall sent his deepest sympathies and all happiness, 'which you fully deserve'.[93] 'May God bless you,' wrote an ex-serviceman, who had been in the tunnelling corps and the London Irish Rifles, 'and send you love, joy, happiness and prosperity always'. Though 'powerless to help you', said the author of a letter from Somerset, 'I will storm heaven with my prayers for your happiness . . . *Don't leave us.*'[94]

'My mother, father, and I waited for the news,' wrote a family to the King from Trelewis in South Wales on 10 December, 'but when it did come through on the wireless, it gave us a terrible shock, it was like as if a bomb had dropped, and we are only three out of millions I am sure.' They found it difficult to accept the meaning of the news, saying that 'we sincerely hope that you will still reign as our King.'[95] To the very end, and even afterwards, many of the general public had still not given up hope that abdication could and would be averted. Referring to the King's time in the war and his visit to South Wales just a few weeks before, a man in Kent begged him not to leave the throne:

You have had personal experience of war, have mixed intimately with the fighting men on the field of battle. You have rubbed shoulders with all sorts of men on the race course, in the slums, in factories, and in the 'distressed areas'. You know by personal observation everything there is to be known about your subjects first hand that is more than half the rulers of the country do know. They cannot hoodwink and humbug you, you want things *done* not talked about . . .[96]

'Go to the people,' urged another letter, 'address them over the air, a vote taken and they will show their loyalty to you.' A woman signing herself 'a loyal rose' counselled delay. 'Do not be hurried into signing anything you may later regret', she begged him. 'Wait until after your coronation. Please do not abdicate. Your people want you. A year soon passes. Then do as your heart tells you.'[97] The Church, said another, 'has discredited itself in the part it has taken. In spite of all its power and preachings, it cannot draw men into it, because it stands for hypocrisy. But if ever you came back to us and lifted a finger, you draw all *men* unto you.'[98]

Many of the ordinary people, as well as Bevan and Lloyd George, blamed Baldwin and the Government for the abdication. George Bernard Shaw took a different view: 'The royal family settled the affair among themselves.'[99] Now Edward had gone, believed the courtier Tommy Lascelles, the future of the monarchy was secure. Not only would the more reliable Duke and Duchess of York replace Edward, but 'We now have two young Princesses, who will take his place as the Pets of the world, and on one of whom, certainly, great issues will hang.'[100]

Edward had been suspected by the court of being hostile to the idea of the monarchy. It was certainly true that at times his open mind led him to offer opinions that would have been judged as dangerous by the royal household. In 1920, while on a tour to New Zealand, he complained to Freda Dudley Ward that

The more I think of it, all the more certain I am that really (though not on the surface yet awhile with Britishers) the day for Kings & Princes is past, monarchies are out-of-date though I know it's a rotten thing for me to say & sounds Bolshevik!!

'But this railway strike,' he explained, 'which might become a general strike which completely upsets a so-called 'Royal tour' (how I loathe that — expression) makes me do a lot of hard thinking angel & I really do feel rather helpless & bolshie tonight!!'[101] The tour of New Zealand was exhausting, as were his other overseas tours. What upset him was not the monarchy as an institution, but the more wretched aspects of his job as 'Empire salesman'.

It was said, Edward wrote in his memoirs, 'that I never wanted to be King at all.' It was always possible, he admitted, that if it had been his choice to make, he might not have selected the throne as his career. 'But not to wish to be King was something else.' For once his father had died, he *was* the King. 'And what was more,' he added, 'I wanted to be a successful King, though a King in a modern way.'[102] He had no wish to go down in history as 'Edward the Reformer', preferring to see himself as 'Edward the Innovator'. Lloyd George regarded Edward's approach as a breath of fresh air in the arid and sterile atmosphere of the court, and he much admired his 'plucky defiance of protocol-worshipping court officials'.[103] Especially because of his time in the trenches, he believed, Edward was 'capable of bringing a new democratic touch to the throne, as one emancipated from the stifling grip of the Court.'[104]

'I had no notion,' insisted Edward, 'of tinkering with the fundamental rules of Monarchy.'[105] His solemn respect for its traditions was apparent. For example, at the opening of Parliament on 3 November 1936, his equerry Charles Lambe admired the dignified bearing of the King as he and his entourage entered the House of Lords: 'The candelabra were dull pin-points & the stained glass glowed with colour despite the full outside day. As the King entered, all the lights rose to full brilliance & once again I nearly swooned – such good theatre! He took ample time and did all with great dignity and authority. My only regret', added Lambe, loyally, was that 'more people could not have been there to be impressed as I was.'[106]

Edward may not have seen himself as any kind of threat to the institution of the monarchy. It is easy, however, to understand why he was seen in this way by other members of the Royal Family and by senior courtiers – and the court was able to be ruthless when it felt that its interests were under threat. After the Russian Revolution of 1917, the family of the Tsar Nicholas II, King George V's first cousin, had sought refuge in Britain. But although the Government agreed to provide asylum, King George V refused to have them in the country. His Private Secretary, Lord Stamfordham, wrote to the Foreign Secretary to say that the King was aware of public hostility to the idea of the Tsar and Tsarina coming to Britain, and that this would 'undoubtedly compromise the position of the King and Queen'. The Government concurred, and the Tsar did not come to Britain. He was shot with his entire family by the Red Guards.[107]

*

On 11 December, Parliament passed the Act of Abdication, and Prince Albert, Duke of York, acceded to the throne (although he was not proclaimed King until 12 December). He took the title George VI, rather than Albert I, in order to highlight his similarity to his father. The Tories now have 'just the sort of King which suits them', said Lloyd George contemptuously. 'He will not pry into any inconvenient questions: he will always sign on the dotted line without asking any questions; and he will always do exactly what he is told.'[108] From New York came a letter to the former King, claiming that 'The Duke of York has no personality and I doubt if he could be anything but a puppet.'[109] Even Tom Dugdale had been 'depressed by the dullness of the Duke of York' when he met him at Fort Belvedere, but Baldwin had told him that he was 'very like King George V when a young man. George V was most uninspired and dull, only by perseverance, reliability, example to his people, and a sense of duty did he gain for himself the much loved position he held when he died.'[110]

Albert was not a naturally likeable man, thought Sir Stanley Hewett, the physician who had attended King George V in his dying days. He told the courtier John Aird that he thought 'the Duke of York was the worst of the four sons & had a mean character.' Aird, however, replied that 'I should have put him just as being steady & reliable, even if dull.'[111] There was concern, though, that it would be difficult for him to fill Edward's shoes. Thomas Barnes, the Treasury Solicitor, had wondered whether it would not be a better idea for Queen Mary to become Queen Regent, at least for a while. This would avoid an immediate succession of the Duke of York – 'for a substantial part of the country might still favour the present King and regard his brother as a sort of interloper . . .'[112]

Some of the British public were delighted with their new King, George VI. 'If he errs,' noted a man working at the Peter Robinson department store in London, 'it is only the right side of quietness & reserve.' The 'only possible snag', he added, 'is his wife who (now Queen Elizabeth) has shown an unfortunate tendency in the past to play to the gallery on similar lines to Edward.'[113] But for many others, as the Treasury Solicitor had feared, it was 'a dark day'. 'I shall always

regard King Edward as my King', said one.[114] A young man of nineteen in Kent wrote in a letter to Edward that he would 'always think
of you when Royalty is spoken about or the National Anthem is
sung.'[115] 'I shall always look upon your photo which I have over my
bed, each night, [and pray] that God will take care of you and future
wife', wrote 'a most heartbroken citizen'. She added, 'You will notice
I still call you His Majesty that I shall always do as long as you are
living.' As an 'ordinary, humble married man,' wrote a Londoner,
'let me say that . . . your bravery will be most richly rewarded. You,
Sir, will always be, to us, the King.'[116] An ex-Coldstream Guard
felt certain that 'many hundreds and perhaps millions will never
acknowledge your Brother the Duke of York as King and it will cause
disruption in this beloved land of ours and perhaps I hope and pray
not Revolution.'[117]

'Your brother The Duke of York is no king for England', wrote a
girl who signed herself 'Miss Wales', 'for he is a snob for the aristocrats.
You are for the poor & needy. Please reconsider your answer.'[118] One
correspondent did not accept the idea of Albert's children becoming
the future heirs to the throne. 'While you live I will never acknowledge
another as King, – for any other would be (to me) a Usurper & not
really King, – & if you have children . . . they will be the true Princes
&/or Princesses & legal & true heirs to the Throne, in the mind of
thousands.'[119] An old Lancer in Norfolk, who had progressed through
every rank up to a commission, said he would go through hell to serve
the King. 'Daily whilst I live,' he promised, 'I will be saluting your
photo in Welsh Guards uniform which stands in my modest home,
and my toast will always be, "My King across the Sea!" And I will
also add the words, "scatter his enemies, and make them fall." '[120]
Letters were sent to Winston Churchill, too, expressing regret at the
loss of Edward and at the accession of Albert. 'I have tried time and
again to pay homage to our new King George VI,' wrote one man
from Staffordshire, 'but believe me, I break down, perhaps you will
think I am silly shedding tears at 30 years of age. But I cannot forget,
Our Edward King & friend.'[121]

Walter Monckton went to see the Duke of York in his house on

Piccadilly to tell him that Edward would do everything he could to help and to make things easy for him.[122] Even so, the challenge for King George VI, of taking over the throne from someone who was adored by so many of the people of Britain and the Empire, must have seemed formidable indeed.

12

'God bless you both'

On the morning of Friday 11 December, Britain woke up to fog, followed by an icy drizzle of rain. 'All the world is waiting for King Edward to broadcast at 10 p.m. tonight, when as a private citizen he will give his farewell message to the country', noted the Kent schoolteacher in Kent in his diary.[1] Finally, Edward would have his chance to speak to the people of Britain. A week before he had requested permission to tell his subjects about his love for Wallis and to ask them to support his marriage. Now, he wanted simply to say farewell. Some members of the Government looked coldly on the idea of a broadcast, and Queen Mary tried to dissuade Edward. But he was determined to speak. 'I did not propose', he wrote in his memoirs, 'to leave my country like a fugitive in the night.'[2]

Edward had made hurried plans to leave Britain that night for Austria. At midday he was joined for lunch at Fort Belvedere by Churchill, who wanted to see him for one last time and help him to complete his speech. When Churchill left, he was overcome by grief. 'Winston got into my car with tears flowing,' said his chauffeur, 'and silently we drove home to Chartwell.'[3] Edward recalled later that,

As I saw Mr Churchill off, there were tears in his eyes. I can still see him standing at the door; hat in one hand, stick in the other. Something must have stirred in his mind; tapping out the solemn measure with his walking-stick, he began to recite, as if to himself:

> He nothing common did or mean
> Upon that memorable scene.

His resonant voice, thought Edward, 'seemed to give an especial poignancy to those lines from the ode by Andrew Marvell, on the beheading of Charles I.'[4]

While Edward had been sharing a last meal with Churchill, the dining room of the Ritz, one of London's most luxurious hotels, was packed. 'All London' was lunching there, including Alice Keppel, according to the American journalist, Janet Flanner.[5] How different was this world from a workmen's café in Teddington, Middlesex. 'I have a small café', wrote its proprietor to the King, '. . . and would like you to know that all the men who come in daily are all definitely loyal to you. All they seem to care about is your happiness.'[6] At the Ritz, Mrs Keppel apparently made the remark, 'Things were done better in my day!'[7] But this was an opinion with which many people disagreed. 'Where your ancestors would be satisfied with their "favourites" (to put it politely),' wrote one woman approvingly to the King, 'you will not be satisfied without a *wife*.'[8] In a letter to her friend Bernard Berenson, the art critic, Sybil Colefax reported a conversation she had overheard between two Labour MPs and a trade union secretary, in which one man said that it was 'the disgoosting [sic] hypocrisy of England' that did not approve of the marriage plan, since Edward would have had no difficulty 'had he been content to keep her round the corner' (and the other men added, 'He's been a great Prince & King to us. We must honour his memory in pushing on the job he was at').[9] The Catholic newspaper the *Tablet* regretted that Edward's beloved was divorced. But it had nothing but praise for his resolute commitment to the path of marriage:

No one suggests that had King Edward been content, as so many kings have been, to live out of wedlock, he would have been asked to give up the Throne. It is because he was not willing to follow those common dishonourable precedents that the crisis has arisen, and it is an irony that he is in effect abdicating because of his high sense of propriety, at once too high and not high enough.[10]

The fact that Edward wanted to *marry* Wallis, rather than simply keep her as his mistress, was taken up with interest by the English-speaking Japanese press. 'Even those who most deplore the abdication', commented the *Japan Times*,

must recognize that if the King has committed an error it has been through excessive honesty and generosity. There have been cases before in which Kings have had private friends. But they have remained 'behind the screen'; they have not been seen at Court; they have been concubines but not wives.

Edward's behaviour towards Wallis was seen as reflecting an increase in the independence and freedom of women – 'This royal tragedy is, in its way, the most striking evidence the world has yet seen that the equality of woman is recognized, even in the highest places.' The article concluded that 'His Majesty has evidently refused to adopt a course which he considered would be unkind and, indeed, dishonourable to the lady whom he had chosen.'[11] References were made to the Representation of the People (Equal Franchise) Act of 1928 in Britain, by which women had obtained the vote on an equal basis with men. In the *Japan Advertiser*, a suffragist called Mrs Shigeri Kaneko said she believed that the women of the world should be moved by the King's choice. 'Cannot the womanhood of the world feel greatly moved?' she asked her readers. 'The choice was between love and kingdom', she said, 'and the King took love. From the standpoint of a woman, nothing could be more joyous. That the younger generation in Britain should strongly support the King's action is very natural.'[12]

Not only Edward and Churchill, but also the new King – George VI – and his advisers were making preparations for Edward's farewell broadcast. Sir John Reith, the Director-General of the BBC, had been planning to introduce Edward on air as 'Mr Edward Windsor'. The new royal administration was aghast: this meant that Edward would then have the right, like every other British citizen, to play a role in political life and stand for election to the House of Commons – a real possibility, they thought, given Edward's popularity with the public. In fact, it was not possible for him to be plain Mr Windsor because he was the son of a duke – and that gave him the right to sit in the House of Lords.

But for Edward to have any kind of role in political life would be highly embarrassing and was unacceptable to the court. In a memorandum annexed to his record of the abdication crisis, George VI set down a summary of a meeting held on the morning of Friday 11 December in which a solution was found. The meeting took the form of an interview with the Lord Chancellor's representative, Sir Claud Schuster, and was also attended by Lord Wigram. 'Now as to his name', said the King, 'I suggest H. R. H. D. of [Windsor]:

He cannot be Mr. E. W. as he was born the son of a Duke. That makes him Ld. E. W. anyhow. If he ever comes back to this country, he can stand & be elected to the H. of C. Would you like that? S [that is, Schuster] replied No.

As D. of W. he can sit & vote in the H. of L. Would you like that? S. replied No. Well if he becomes a Royal Duke he cannot speak or vote in the H. of L. & he is not being deprived of his rank in the Navy, Army or R. Air Force.[13]

In this way, by giving Edward a royal style, the new King made sure that Edward would never at any time be able to take part in British politics. In political terms, the former King had been neutered.

George VI had good reason to worry. The letters and telegrams being sent to his brother at this time show that many people were banking on the ex-king's return to public life through politics. They appealed to him to set up a new political party. One Londoner told him, 'the country would stand unitedly behind you, as America has stood unitedly behind President Roosevelt's New Deals, and would insist upon your being made Prime Minister.'[14] From a schoolgirl in Denbigh came the message that everyone at her school was for Edward, and that even if he did abdicate, 'I don't care. You'll still be our King.'[15] Another letter expressed the hope that 'you will return – perhaps not as king – but as the mainstay & hope of the working men of this nation.' It went on, 'you are our leader. Return to public life, don't waste your life; it can mean so much, to us you have the younger generation behind you if you try to give happiness to the miserable.'[16] A family in Middlesex firmly believed that it would not be long before Edward was back, working for the poor: 'we are convinced that your Majesty's action is NOT in accord with the Nation's wish, and we hope that in the not far distant future you will be back again with us to lead us out of the distress and despair into which we seem doomed to be plunged.' They added their sympathy for 'your good Lady', for the ordeal she had been through.[17]

'We may admire your brothers', wrote a woman to Edward, 'but we don't love them.' In particular, she added in a postscript, 'I hate the thought of having a "Queen Elizabeth" – she would never be such a good monarch as her namesake! They never are.'[18] A woman writing at three in the morning on 10 December told Edward that, 'If only you could just wander around London and hear all that is being said – how sad and regretful we all are. If only you could have seen that large, silent, listless crowd that stood outside Buckingham Palace tonight.'[19] The widow of a Coldstreamer killed in September 1916 wanted Edward to continue as King but also to find happiness in his private life to make up for the arduous tasks he had 'so faithfully' performed for his subjects.[20] For one Middlesex woman, 'The bottom dropped out of the whole world' when she heard that he was going to abdicate. She never saw a film of him without having 'a silent weep. It was sheer joy for me to join in with "God Save the King".' In the future, she said, whenever she sang the National Anthem 'it will be of you I am thinking for in my heart there never could be another King. I am only poor, but I would willingly go without food for a year if this could have been avoided, we all loved you so much sir.'[21]

The farewell broadcast was made from Windsor Castle. Reith introduced the new Duke of Windsor to his listening audience as 'His Royal Highness Prince Edward'.[22] 'At long last,' the Duke began, 'I am able to say a few words of my own. I have never wanted to withhold anything, but until now it has been not constitutionally possible for me to speak.' He explained that he had never forgotten the country or the Empire, which for twenty-five years he had tried hard to serve. But it had become impossible 'to carry out the heavy burden of responsibility and to discharge my duties as King as I would wish to do without the help and support of the woman I love.' He said that the decision was his alone and that it had been made less difficult by the knowledge that his brother, 'with his long training in the public affairs of this country and with his fine qualities', would be taking over the role. He added, too, that 'The Ministers of the Crown, and in particular Mr Baldwin, the Prime Minister, have always treated me with full consideration. There has never been any constitutional difference between me and them and between me and Parliament.' He concluded,

I now quit altogether public affairs, and I lay down my burden. It may be some time before I return to my native land, but I shall always follow the fortunes of the British race and Empire with profound interest, and if at any time in the future I can be found of service to His Majesty in a private station I shall not fail.

And now we all have a new King.

I wish Him, and you, His people, happiness and prosperity with all my heart.

God bless you all.

God Save The King.[23]

After the speech, the National Anthem was played.[24] 'King Edward VIII broadcast his farewell message to us at 10 p.m. from Windsor Castle', a woman in Somerset recorded in her diary that night. 'Very Patriotic end to his short reign.'[25]

Not everybody was able to hear the speech. A married couple from Cheshire told the King they did not have a radio. 'We shall be unable to listen in to your Broadcast tonight,' they explained, 'being Unemployed we haven't been able to buy one. We have a family and they must be fed.' But they hoped, they said, that 'when you return to us, and your country, to have the pleasure of hearing you and your future wife. I have a snap I took of you at Wembley some years ago, which I will prize more than ever ... we shall never forget, how you have worked for us, unemployed, and from the bottom of our hearts we thank you.'[26] But everyone who could, listened in. An ex-serviceman in Liverpool, who was the same age as Edward, listened in 'on the wireless at a friend's house to you tonight – having no wireless of my own.'[27]

The freezing weather had developed into hail by the evening. 'There was complete emptiness', wrote Virginia Woolf in her diary. 'All the life had been withdrawn to listen, to judge ... All the omnibuses were empty.'[28] On the night of the broadcast, recalled the writer Ronald Tree, 'we were dining at Blenheim. The radio was turned on and we listened to the King's last words before leaving the country. The men looked grim. Many of the women wept.'[29] Churchill, listening to the speech at Chartwell, was in tears.[30] Days later, he wrote to tell Edward that 'the broadcast was successful, and all over the world people were deeply moved; millions wept. The Government were grateful. They certainly ought to be.'[31]

James Agate, who had been concerned about Baldwin's behaviour throughout the crisis, said he was reassured by Edward's generous words about the Prime Minister. 'The ceremony, for such it was,' he said, 'was moving. Baldwin came out of it very well. It entirely cleared my mind of any possible doubts as to the way in which this thing ought to be looked at.'[32] For the draper in Belfast, though, it was 'a great strain' to listen to Edward. 'He spoke so heart to heart-fashion', he observed. 'It must have been a terrific ordeal for him – his voice was greatly changed from the last time I heard him speak – now it is hoarse – aged – like his father's.'[33] 'How profoundly touched my mother & I were at your wonderful message', wrote one woman. 'We know by all the people we have spoken to that England wished you to stay & marry Mrs Simpson . . . we thank you for all you have tried to do for your country.'[34] One correspondent told Edward that,

Although you only spoke for seven minutes over the wireless the other night I hope I will never hear such another speech because the tears were running down my face. You said in your speech 'God bless you all' and I echoed 'God bless you' . . . I read in the paper the other day that by abdicating you had given up your home in England. While I am alive you are never without a home and if I can ever help you I will be proud to do so.[35]

'Thank you', said another message, 'for broadcasting to us all.'[36] 'I sat alone in my car', said one man, heartbroken, 'and switched on the wireless to listen to your broadcast.'[37]

It was a good speech, thought Lady Milner – 'but how lacking in control must a man be who does what he has done! And *talks* about it!'[38] Helen Hardinge noticed that in St James's Palace they were calling the speech 'very vulgar'.[39] Ramsay MacDonald was equally unimpressed and glad to see the end of Edward's reign. It was 'touching and pathetic and yet not appealing' he observed after the broadcast, adding that 'I perhaps am prejudiced by the immediate harm he has done, and when the future opens up I shall see, as indeed I believe, that it was all for the good. Still, one does not respect so much as be thankful for the tools of Providence.'[40] By 'tools of Providence', MacDonald presumably meant Wallis Simpson.

Some of Edward's critics in the earlier days of the crisis were stirred by the words and tone of his speech. The 'final parting', said a London solicitor, 'was very restrained and dignified and sent one to bed feeling very sad.'[41] The bookseller at Barkers found it 'most moving & sad' and hoped that 'he will not live to regret the irrevocable step he has taken & that the woman of his choice will bring him the happiness that he hopes for. Many people doubt it particularly men – they think he is a young fool – not so very young either at 43. The men say that those very strong feelings do not last.'[42] Even the young Fascist who had been hostile to Edward was grudgingly impressed. 'It sounded pretty awful,' he commented. 'Still, it did convey a certain amount of pathos.'[43]

The broadcast was relayed overseas. Wallis heard the speech in the South of France. 'Everyone in Lou Viei, including the domestic staff,' she wrote in her memoirs, 'gathered around the radio in the sitting-room. David's voice came out of the loudspeaker calmly, movingly.' She was overcome. 'I was lying on the sofa with my hands over my eyes, trying to hide my tears. After he finished, the others quietly went away and left me alone. I lay there a long time before I could control myself enough to walk through the house and go upstairs to my room.'[44] The speech had marked a watershed in Edward's life – but it was a turning point for Wallis, too. It told the whole world about his love for her and his utter, uncompromising devotion. 'Edward . . . may now go down to History as the greatest Lover ever known; and yet every word of his will have a greater power and meaning from now on', observed a spiritualist living in Bradford. She set down in her diary the thoughts that were going through so many people's minds at the time: 'Truth is stranger than fiction. A Beautiful Woman Who Shook an Empire.'[45]

The speech also made Wallis feel that she had failed the man she loved, because she was the cause of his abdication from the throne. She had tried to prevent this final step, but in vain. She wrote to Sybil Colefax of the terrible struggle of the last couple of weeks – 'I still can't write about it all because I am afraid of not conveying the true facts as brain is so very tired from the struggle of the past two weeks – the screaming of a thousand plans to London, the pleading to lead him not force him.' She knew him so well, she told Sybil, that she 'wanted them to take my advice. But no, driving on they went headed for this Tragedy. If only they had said, let's drop the idea now and in the autumn we'll discuss it again. And Sybil darling in the autumn I would have been so very far away. I had already escaped.' The little faith she had tried to cling on to, she added, 'has been taken from me when I saw England turn on a man that couldn't defend himself and had never been anything but straight with his country.'[46] After Edward's broadcast, she 'drained the dregs of the cup of my failure and defeat.'[47] She ached with longing for Edward, who had given up so much to marry her. 'The agony of not being able to see you after all you have been through,' she wrote to him, 'is pathetic . . . Your broadcast was very good my angel and it is all going to be so very lovely . . . I hope you will never regret this sacrifice and that your brother will prove to the world that we still have a position and that you will be given some jobs to do.' With this last sentence, she revealed her anxiety about Edward's future. 'I love you David,' she ended the letter, 'and am holding so tight.'[48]

Lloyd George heard the speech from Jamaica. 'Just heard the King on the BBC', he wrote. 'A fine farewell, courageous, sincere, simple, dignified. He is [a] great little man & he has been hounded from the throne by that arch humbug Baldwin.'[49] An agricultural engineer in Palestine wrote to Edward that he had followed 'during the last years the activities of Your Majesty with great admiration and sincere sympathy, especially Your Majesty's care for the working and unemployed people.' He was sure, he said, 'that the greatest part of the Jewish population of Palestine is feeling the same.'[50]

For New Yorkers, said Margaret Case Harriman, who wrote for the *New Yorker*, the speech was heard on 'a rainy late afternoon with crowds pushing into radio shops, hotel lobbies, and bars, or standing on street corners in the rain, their unabashed tears falling on their wet raincoats as they listened to that infinitely sad yet determined English voice.'[51] One New Yorker wrote to Edward to say that he had heard the broadcast at five o'clock that afternoon. Long afterwards, he said, he sat still, 'too deeply touched to move'. Earlier he had felt that Edward was letting the country down – but 'I never heard or read of a man ever paying so great a price for pure love of a woman.'[52] John Gunther wrote to Margot Asquith from Connecticut:

We simply remain thunderstruck. Most of this week we've been glued to the radio, listening to it all, and each day it got worse. I thought Edward's talk yesterday was one of the finest things I've ever heard; Frances burst into tears and I felt the whole thing to be almost intolerable.[53]

Gunther was shocked to learn that Edward's speech was not sold in Britain on a gramophone record.[54] This was odd because it was quite common at this time for important speeches to be recorded by His Master's Voice, or another gramophone company, and sold to the public. It was another story in America, where the speech was boot-legged. Within a few hours, Macy's, New York's largest department store, put a record of the speech on sale at one dollar.[55]

Walking along Whitehall the other day, wrote Virginia Woolf, 'I thought what a Kingdom! England! And to put it down the sink . . . Not a very rational feeling. Still it is what the Nation feels.'[56] In her view, 'the Nation' was outraged by Edward's abdication – but it is unlikely that many of the Bloomsbury set had much idea of what ordinary people in Britain felt. Nor did Nancy Dugdale, who believed that Edward 'had fallen so precipitously in the esteem of the public, as a shooting star falls through the heavens to end in oblivion.' He will leave many sorrowing hearts, she added, 'for his popularity was of a very personal and touching nature, especially among the poorer classes, owing to his having moved so much in the ranks of his people. Everyone felt they had been personally let down, a demoralizing national feeling.'[57] But Mrs Dugdale knew few, if any, of these 'poorer classes', and she certainly did not know 'everyone'. This tendency of members of the Establishment to equate their *own* feelings with those of 'the nation', 'the public' or 'the people of Britain' characterizes the whole of the abdication crisis. When Susie Buchan, the wife of the Governor-General of Canada, encountered continuing support for Edward on a visit to Britain, she simply explained it away as 'a good deal of sentimentality'.[58]

In reality, ordinary people thought very differently. 'We were with him on the Western Front and will always deem him our leader', read a telegram from London.[59] The Mayor of Llanidloes in Wales sent his thanks 'for the special interest you have shown at all times in the welfare of the people of the Principality. As Welsh men and women we pray for your happiness – so richly deserved.'[60] Hundreds of telegrams arrived offering the King gratitude, love and admiration. 'Remembering all your Majesty's kindness, Dockland begs to wish all happiness and God speed!' said one.[61] 'From one sportsman to a greater one. Good luck. God speed' said another.[62]

For John Buchan, the royal crisis was a question not so much of morals as of manners. 'A certain dignity', he wrote to Edith Londonderry, 'is demanded from the Throne, and I hope that has been now restored.'[63] Lockhart's 'Mrs Town Councillors' and 'Mrs Rectors' generally agreed, and a farmer in Sussex observed in his diary that Edward was a 'frightful ass to get himself in the position he did'.[64] But many did not agree. A teacher at a London County Council school told the King that he would tell his pupils, with pride, of the dignity with which Edward had conducted himself through the whole of the crisis.[65] From the Savile Club in London came the message that 'We have just drunk the health of His Majesty and broke the glass. For he is England's Admiral till [the] setting of his sun.'[66] Lord Robert Baden-Powell, the founder and leader of the Boy Scouts, sent a telegram recalling Edward's hard work for the scouting movement when he was Prince of Wales: 'Boy Scouts offer most grateful thanks for His Majesty's many kindnesses which they will ever remember and offer heartfelt good wishes.'[67]

There was admiration for Edward's courage – but there was also bitter disappointment and a sense of lost hope, especially among minority groups. Marcus Garvey, the President of the General Universal Negro Improvement Association, sent a telegram in which he asked the King to

Please accept from the Negro race deepest sympathy . . . We were looking to you for much but we fully appreciate your noble Christian stand which will do so much to raise the Empire to the position it has lost by the world being able to say through your noble act that an Englishman's word is his bond. History will record you as the noblest character of the twentieth century. May God bless and keep you is the prayer of the Negro race.[68]

All the gypsies, said Queen Viola, the Queen of the Gypsies, joined her in congratulations 'to you, one of the best. To us gipsies you remain our King. The same applies to your future wife. We tender her all happiness in her great trial. God bless you both.'[69]

This was the greatest love story of the decade, and the world was watching. Telegrams poured in from every continent and region: Asia, Europe, Africa, the Middle East, and North and South America. Nearly all of them congratulated the King and offered their best wishes for his future happiness. From a civil servant in India came the judgement that 'The Empire has blundered',[70] which contrasted sharply with the Viceroy's claim that the 'general reactions of press and public could not be more satisfactory'.[71] In Ceylon, a resolution passed on 12 December by the Urban District Council of Kurunegala appreciated 'the high principles which led His Majesty to make that momentous decision', but at the same time expressed 'its deepest regret' at the abdication and sent 'best wishes for His Majesty's future'.[72] Similar sentiments were expressed by the Trinidad Citizens' League. They acknowledged

our deep gratitude for the great services rendered by him as Prince of Wales and as King Emperor . . . we shall always pray that long life and happiness may be in store for him and for the Lady of his choice and our love and affection for him has not been in any way lessened.[73]

Many citizens of the Irish Free State had followed the royal crisis. 'The heart of Ireland is with you now', said one letter. 'You are without a shadow of doubt the most loved one.' It described an instance when 'a poor bare-footed – ragged little girl – went to a small shop – where a wireless is installed and said – "Please my muthor [sic] wants to know the last news about the King?"!'[74] Eamon de Valera, the President, was also sympathetic to the King. On 5 December, Baldwin had sent him a telegram announcing the likelihood of Edward's imminent abdication. This sudden news gave de Valera 'serious cause for anxiety' and he cabled back:

Legislation in our Parliament would be necessary in order to regularize the situation about to be created. Such legislation at the present moment would cause grave difficulties. Is there no alternative to immediate abdication? Surely delay at least is advisable even if no ultimate solution in sight.[75]

De Valera sent a telegram to the King, too, stressing that abdication could not take place without the authority of the Irish Free State – the matter of succession to the throne required the assent of *all* the Dominions, according to the Statute of Westminster.[76] In other words, Edward would continue to be King in Ireland until his abdication was accepted.

It was a worrying situation for the British Government, which feared that de Valera would exploit Britain's dilemma to his own advantage. This is exactly what happened. The President summoned a special session of the Dail on 11 and 12 December, which proceeded to pass legislation that effectively excluded the new King from any position in which he might influence the internal affairs of the Irish Free State, retaining for him only certain functions in external affairs.[77] This move had been planned for the future anyway, but it was now rushed into action – and since Britain was so preoccupied with its own crisis, it was not resisted.

Dawson and *The Times* – the 'Thunderer', as it was known – were widely regarded as instrumental in the drama that had led to the abdication. In a letter written on 12 December, Winston Churchill referred to 'the sledge-hammer blows *The Times* dealt the late King'.[78] Many others expressed heartfelt thanks to Dawson for his role in the affair. The Duke of Buccleuch conveyed his 'Respect and gratitude to you and the "Times" in these days of National misery, and God speed your task of re-establishing the Monarchy.'[79] Hardinge assured Dawson that the one thing that had kept him going was 'the kindness and encouragement of those whose opinions were worth having'. In the end, he said, 'the Empire has, I believe, really profited by this demonstration of unity and common ideals.' Although the work of starting a second new reign was heavy, he added, 'it is like a haven of rest at B.P. [Buckingham Palace] after the bedlam of the last few months.'[80] The courtier Tommy Lascelles told Dawson that, 'merely as a tax-payer, how profoundly grateful I have been to the *Times* every morning lately. In all this sad business, the only cause for real rejoicing is the utter defeat of the Powers of Evil.'[81]

Sybil Colefax took a larger view. 'For the people it's a great loss', she wrote to Berenson. 'He was truly democratic – and they knew it . . . Well it's over but matters more than you think.'[82] Geoffrey Wells, who thought that Baldwin was 'the Dirty Dog of the whole business', was disgusted. He went to the cinema in Oxford on the afternoon of 11 December and wrote in his diary that 'Afterwards they put on such a flood of slosh about The New King & in particular his blasted wife that I got up & walked out. Applause for Baldwin, for Edward, for George VI, applause and hisses for Mrs S.' He came out of it all, he said, 'in a mood of deep disgust for the sheer hypocrisy of the British press & public, the sheer unqualified immorality, which makes a heroine of a woman like Queen Mary, who marries to order, & a bloody adulteress of Mrs Simpson, of whom it knows nothing. After Queen Mary, I could have done with a little Mrs S!' In the evening he listened to Edward's speech and found it 'the wholly dignified moving utterance of a self-possessed, confident man. Listening, one felt him to be the one real man in the affair. I'd like to know what Baldwin & the rest thought as they listened!'[83]

Once the reality of the abdication had sunk in – that King Edward VIII of England had really vacated the throne – there was time for some reflection. Churchill believed that the Government and *The*

Times had behaved unfairly. In a letter to Lord Salisbury, he pointed out that

the pressure which the Government put upon the King and the Press campaign directed against him with so much brutality by the Times, together with the personal strain to which he was inevitably subject, might well have led to his abdication any day last week. In fact the Deeds were all drawn up and in my view the Government expected to announce the abdication on Monday [7 December].

He added, 'What has impressed me most during this crisis has been the King's virtues of courage, manliness and honour; and of his loyalty to his Ministers and respect for the Constitution.'[84] Churchill felt immensely sympathetic towards the King. 'Poor little lamb,' he said to a friend, 'he was treated worse than any air mechanic, and he took it lying down.'[85]

Many were grateful to Churchill for his willingness to speak out on behalf of the King. 'As one of the dumb masses who have not been permitted to express their views on the momentous decision which has been taken & decided by the High Noises over our heads,' wrote a correspondent, 'perhaps you will permit myself & my family to express our gratitude to you that one man was found who was willing to speak a word on behalf of His Majesty King Edward VIII. We do so gratefully & sincerely.' When the 'so-called representatives of the working classes combine with their opponents to dethrone the People's King,' added the letter, 'one can better understand the sentiments of the man who said, "The more I see of dogs the less I care for men." Right or Wrong, he was our King.'[86]

'I have been horror-struck,' wrote Lord Hamilton of Dalzell to Churchill, 'as I am sure you have been – by the readiness with which the word "Abdication" has come to men's lips in the recent crisis. It is a word that can only be spoken, without treason, by one man.'[87] Duff Cooper regretted the loss to the nation of King Edward. 'I was sad at his going', he recorded in his memoirs. 'I felt that we were losing a personality of value to the State . . . He had many qualities that fitted him for his great position'.[88] Prince George, the Duke of Kent, who was devoted to Edward, was devastated. Some of the younger generation in the royal household wondered at the depth of animosity towards the former King. The Earl of Harewood, Edward's nephew, commented that 'it was hard for the younger amongst us not to stand in amazement at the moral contradiction between the elevation of a code of duty on the one hand, and on the other the denial of central Christian virtues – forgiveness, understanding, family tenderness.'[89]

'All through Mrs Simpson', judged a Sussex farmer.[90] But was it? Some people believed that Edward's love for Wallis was not the reason, but an excuse for the abdication – that she was a godsend to those who wanted to see him go. 'I am sorry that Edward VIII has been bounced into abdicating', wrote Alan Turing to his mother. 'I believe the government wanted to get rid of him', he wrote,

and found Mrs Simpson a good opportunity. Whether they were wise to try to get rid of him is another matter. I respect Edward for his courage . . . I don't see how you can say that Edward was guilty of wasting his ministers' time and wits at a critical moment. It was Baldwin who opened the subject.[91]

Geoffrey Wells noted in his diary that a close friend, with whom he agreed, was 'quite sure that the Govt was anxious to get rid of the King because of his determination to be, as King, an individual. Mrs S the excuse.' Wells added that it was 'a kind of ultimate disillusion – the final proof of the utter rottenness of all present political parties.'[92]

In particular, argued some, it was Edward's visit to South Wales that had set the abdication wheels in motion. 'As an Englishman, a Manchester man, turned fifty years of age,' observed a letter to Edward,

I see in this no Constitutional Crisis – and I view the matter as a political red herring, drawn by the present hotch-potch-two-years-behind-the-times government, a herring intended to distract public attention from their inability or desire to implement the assurances you recently made to the South Wales Black Areas that 'Something must be done' to better the lot of their workless.

'Baldwin and his satellites have no plans and apparently no interest for this problem,' he added, 'and their present move is to camouflage their gross and flagrant inactivity.'[93] The Australian newspaper the *Labor Daily*, which was based in Sydney and represented a key strand of Labour opinion, had maintained right from the start that 'the present crisis has been very carefully arranged in an effort to secure a showdown prior to the Coronation.' This, it claimed, was because of Edward's democratic tendencies and his sympathy for the poor.[94]

Vera Brittain was equally cynical about the role of the Government:

The essence of the whole drama, as I saw it in common with many other British citizens sickened by sanctimonious hypocrisy, lay less in the King's attitude to his ministers, which was strictly correct, than in the attitude of the ministers to the problem. Mrs Simpson, we believed, had merely been made a convenient excuse for removing a monarch whose informality, dislike of ancient tradition, and determination to see things for himself had affronted the 'old gang' from the beginning.[95]

Lloyd George agreed with this view. Thoroughly disgusted by the news of the abdication, he had written from Jamaica to his son Gwilym, telling him how angry he was:

The Tories seem to have once more triumphed; they have got rid of a King who was making himself obnoxious by calling attention to conditions which it was to their interest to cover up. Baldwin has succeeded by methods which time and again take in the gullible British public. He has taken the high line in order to achieve the lowest of aims. I have never seen such a blend of hypocrisy and humbug. But once again it has triumphed, and a really democratic King has been driven from his Throne by the Tories with the help of the Labour Party.[96]

'And when the truth of these days is allowed to be known,' wrote the novelist Hugh Ross Williamson in *Time and Tide* on 19 December 1936, 'it will be found that Edward VIII's promise to the derelict areas and the forgotten men: "I will see that something is done" is the essential clue to the events of the last three weeks.' From that moment, he added, 'the King's doom [was] sealed.'[97]

There was resentment among many ordinary people that they had never had a chance to say what they wanted. 'There is a vast body of the English Public inarticulate', wrote one correspondent to the King, 'who are utterly opposed to any talk of Your Majesty's abdication' – but who were unable to have any influence on the outcome of the crisis.[98] 'The People', said another, 'never had a chance' to prevent the abdication.[99] 'At every dinner & social occasion I go to I will always use and ask for a toast to our beloved Duke of Windsor', wrote an Edinburgh man to Churchill. 'I wish Sir you and all our ministers', he added, 'had been amongst the working class, during the Crisis & had heard what they had to say. I might say . . . 99 per cent were & still are for the Ex King.'[100] 'The British people and the London Parliament', observed George Bernard Shaw, 'were not consulted, and are wholly blameless in the matter.'[101]

Tom Harrisson, a young man who had recently returned from an anthropological expedition to the New Hebrides and settled in the Lancashire cotton town of Bolton, was appalled by the way ordinary people had been sidelined and by how little information had been made available. As a direct response, the following month he and some colleagues set up an organization called Mass-Observation to collect and publish information about the public. Only in this way, maintained the new organization, could democracy mean what it says: to allow rule by the people, appraised of the facts. In other words, they aimed to bridge the gap between the rulers and the ruled.[102] The first full-scale book produced by Mass-Observation was *May the Twelfth*, an account of the coronation of George VI in 1937, which revealed that numbers of people resented the new King and longed for Edward. In one village in Somerset, for example, most of the inhabitants thought Edward ought to be King and refused to have the cost of coronation celebrations put on the rates.[103] In Nottingham, a hairdresser reported that she listened to the wireless from half past ten to half past four: 'And you should have seen my mother – she sat in front of it all day – and all through the service while he was being crowned and that, the tears were pouring down her face and she kept moaning, "Oh, it ought to be Edward – it – it – it ought to be Edward." '[104]

There were suspicions in America that the British Government had been motivated by hostility to Edward's sympathy for the poor. 'I hear . . . that in [the] USA rumour has distorted the significance of the visit to South Wales', noted Baldwin's friend Thomas Jones, with some anxiety. 'It is being said that SB sacrificed the King to the demands of the Die-Hards who were enraged at the publicly expressed sympathies of our democratic King.'[105] John Gunther told Margot Asquith that Americans 'completely fail to understand one thing, why Baldwin has not come in for more criticism for what was certainly his extremely undemocratic behaviour, i.e. he decided that a morganatic marriage was impossible and got the whole thing fixed up, fait accompli, before letting the country know a word. Should there have been all that censorship?'[106] The *Milwaukee Journal* accused Baldwin of sabotaging Edward's 'promise to see that something would be done about a decaying region in a rich empire'.[107]

The *Voice*, a newspaper in Hobart, Tasmania, bitterly regretted the loss of 'undoubtedly the most democratic King the world has ever known, "The Poor Man's King".' The editor, Mr Dwyer-Gray, who was Treasurer of the Tasmanian Government, argued that Edward had been forcibly removed – 'The *Voice* will not be silenced. This was as foul a plot as ever disgraced mankind. "Finance" did not want a radical King . . .' The 'Poor Man's King', it added, was given an ultimatum, precipitating a crisis where there was no need for hurry at all. 'Misrepresentations of Dominion opinion were used in London and misrepresentations of London opinion were used in the Dominions.'[108] The knuckles of Mr Dwyer-Gray were severely rapped. When he attended an official dinner to honour Lord Hartington, who was visiting Tasmania, Hartington 'spoke very plainly to him, and said that he was shocked to see such articles from the pen of a Minister of the Crown, and a Roman Catholic one at that.' Lord Hartington sent a copy of the offending article to Sir Harry Batterbee,[109] who forwarded it to Sir Horace Wilson with the comment, 'You may be interested to see the enclosed – pretty disgusting!'[110]

'This is sedition – putting a monarch off his Throne without consulting Parliament', accused Jack Beasley, the Labour MP for New South Wales.[111] H. V. Evatt, a distinguished lawyer and a Justice of the Federal Supreme Court of Australia, who later became leader of the parliamentary Labour Party, wrote to Churchill to express his gratitude that there was 'at least one man in the Parliament at Westminster who in a time of unexampled crisis, served his late Monarch so loyally and so well.' He regretted that no means had existed 'for ascertaining the guidance and extent of the "public opinion" (in the Dominions or England)': 'What a Whip triumph! That a Parliament with no Shadow of relevant popular mandate should effectuate such a charge! And what a triumph for Dictatorship! That a Government should carry through such an affair before any reference to Parliament was made!' All this, he observed, had passed into history. But would not history, he wondered, contrast the two men – 'the politician who by innuendo, by the over emphasis on personal friendship, and by downright misrepresentation, gave the Iago touch to the crisis and the man, the monarch, who was too great for the Parliament and too noble for the individuals who purported to speak for the Dominions.'[112]

Sir Horace Wilson felt some anxieties, too. He wondered whether 'the historian of the future' might not criticize the Government for not starting soon enough to induce the King to change his mind. Baldwin told him not to worry, because the King had been determined to marry Mrs Simpson anyway.[113]

*

While the act of abdication continued to resonate in the lives of millions of people all over the world, Edward's own life underwent a swift and dramatic change. In just a few hours after his farewell broadcast, he would be sailing away from Britain. He did what he could for his staff. Bruce Lockhart heard a story that the King,

on eve of departure for France, sent for Crisp, his valet. 'We're going abroad, Crisp. What about the luggage?' Crisp hesitated. He was married, didn't want to go. King saw at once. 'Never mind, I'll get you a job here.' Rings up his brother. 'Bertie, what about my valet – he's best authority on medals and decorations in the world.' King went without valet. Crisp now with King George VI.[114]

The Windsor family shared a final meal with Edward at Royal Lodge, in Windsor Great Park, after listening to the broadcast. The diners were Edward himself, Queen Mary, Albert, Harry, George, and his uncle and aunt, the Earl and Alice, Countess of Athlone, of whom Edward was very fond. The new Queen Elizabeth was not there. 'That last family dinner was too awful', she said years later to a friend. 'Thank goodness I had flu and couldn't go.'[115] Perry Brownlow, who had been summoned to Windsor from Cannes, witnessed the farewells. He told Diana Vreeland that Edward went up to his mother, Queen Mary, 'and kissed her on both hands and then on both cheeks. She was as cold as ice. She just looked at him.'[116] Lady Iris Mountbatten observed in her unpublished memoirs that Queen Mary 'actually seemed unchanged by the great loss of her eldest son. I could see no outward sign that she had been tormented by heartbreak.' This brought home, she added, 'a sense that I have always had, that my family was not motivated by love or human emotions.'[117] Queen Mary's life, observed Janet Flanner, 'has been one of inhuman self-control.'[118]

Edward then said goodbye to Prince Henry, Duke of Gloucester, and to Prince George, Duke of Kent, both of whom broke down in tears. He finally approached the new King, reported Lord Brownlow, 'who completely broke down. "Buck up, Bertie!" the Duke said. "God save the King!" And with that, he turned, walked away, and that was it.'[119] That evening he left England, as a private citizen. He was bound for Austria, to be the guest of the Baron and Baroness Eugene de Rothschild at Enzesfeld Castle, near Vienna. At two o'clock in the morning of 12 December 1936, wrote Edward in his memoir,

HMS *Fury* slid silently and unescorted out of Portsmouth Harbour. Watching the shore of England recede, I was swept by many emotions. If it had been hard to give up the Throne, it had been even harder to give up my country . . . The drawbridges were going up behind me.[120]

13

'Rat Week'

Once Edward had gone, the nation was able to settle down again to life as it had been lived under King George V. That week's British Movietone newsreel, *Amen: The End of a Tragic Chapter in British Imperial History*, reminded viewers of the highlights of King Edward VIII's short reign, especially his trip to South Wales the month before.[1] But there was a sense of anticlimax, and many people felt jaded. 'Another day in bed – very bad headache', wrote a Sutton Coldfield headmistress in her diary, '& I think the reason has been the fearful happenings of this week – it has seemed one shock on top of another. The affairs of the Royal Family. The abdication of King Edward. The sorrow & sympathy for him. The rejoicings for the New King & Queen etc etc.'[2] Geoffrey Dawson's wife, Cecilia, developed a bad cold with a high temperature, confining her to her bed for days, while Geoffrey himself slept for ten to eleven hours 'without opening an eye'.[3] Nothing, said the Liberal MP Robert Bernays, 'seems to have happened since the King's abdication and nothing seems likely to happen again. The nation has sunk back into a sort of coma. Parliament was quite lifeless the last fortnight and the newspapers are empty of everything except the test matches.'[4]

On Saturday 12 December, George VI was proclaimed King of Britain and its Dominions and Emperor of India. 'Fiji islands was supposed to be the first place – 5.15 a.m.,' noted the saleswoman in the book department at Barkers. 'At Singapore it was proclaimed in 4 languages.'[5] Many of London's streets were closed for the proclamation, and it was bitterly cold. Lucy Baldwin, feeling sorry for Edward, wrote sadly in her diary, 'The new King George VI was sworn in by the Privy Council today. – I decided to go out, I just hadn't the heart for it. – Evening had a telegram of thanks for my letter from King Edward now his HRH the Duke of Windsor.'[6] Some people were angry at the turn of events, including Lloyd George, who turned down an invitation by the Governor of Jamaica to attend the proclamation ceremony in Kingston.[7] 'Are we downhearted?' asked Lady Houston on the cover of the *Saturday Review*. 'YES' was given as the answer, in huge bold type, followed by this poem:

> Goodbye – Goodbye
> We cry with a sigh
> Driven away
> By a law that's a lie
> Great King and True Lover
> For you we would die.[8]

'Got home', muttered Geoffrey Wells, 'just before the Proclamation at Carfax', in the centre of Oxford. '"All this bunkum", as one bus driver, held up by it, said.'[9]

Two days after the abdication, Queen Elizabeth wrote to the Archbishop of Canterbury in her new role as the wife of the Sovereign. 'I can hardly now believe that he [George VI] has been called to the tremendous task,' she said, 'and (I am now writing to you quite intimately) the curious thing is that we are not afraid. I feel that God has enabled us to face the situation calmly . . . When we spoke together at Birkhall only three months ago,' she added, 'how little did I think that such drama & unhappiness was in store for our dear country . . . We were so unhappy about the loss of a dear brother because one can only feel that Exile from this country is death indeed.' She felt that Edward had been ruined by Mrs Simpson and believed that he had lost the love of the people: 'We were miserable, as you know, over his change of heart and character during the last few years and it is alarming how little in touch he was with ordinary human feelings – Alas he has lost the "common touch" . . . We pray most sincerely that we shall not fail our country,' she ended the letter, 'and I sign myself for the first time & with great affection Elizabeth R.'[10]

On Sunday 13 December, the day after the proclamation, the Archbishop of Canterbury, Cosmo Gordon Lang, spoke to the nation on the radio. In a speech entitled 'The Pity of It,' he criticized the former King Edward VIII for having 'sought his happiness in a manner inconsistent with the Christian principles of marriage, and within a social circle whose standard and way of life are alien to all the best instincts and traditions of his people.' Sternly, he warned, 'Let those who belong to this circle know that today they stand rebuked by the judgement of the nation which had loved King Edward.' The Archbishop of York then spoke in a similar vein, though less strongly. Baldwin, Reith, Lord Salisbury and Queen Mary wrote to Archbishop Lang to congratulate him on his speech.[11] Baldwin's letter, written in his own hand, warmly praised the speech 'as the voice of Christian England'.[12]

The Times, predictably, ran an approving article – 'Social Circle Rebuked'. Many agreed. 'The Archbishop's address over the wireless last night was magnificent', enthused one woman: 'each word so well chosen – each phrase so beautifully dovetailed in to convey an exact meaning. He spoke of all King Edward had been to us in the past – of the new King George & his stability of character – He said King Edward had unwise friends – Oh the Pity of it – the pity of it.'[13] A Bristol doctor thought that the broadcast address by the Archbishop was 'splendid'. Earlier that day, at the cathedral, he had heard 'a good sermon from the Bishop on the crisis', and even the singing was 'better than usual'.[14] George Trevelyan was delighted with Lang's message. 'I'm glad the Archb[isho]p said what he did about "the King's friends"', he wrote in a letter, adding that

It wanted saying. I was very glad to find that the feeling of decency about not taking away other people's wives was so general and so strong in the country, after 40 years of writing down marriage by half the principal literary folks, Wells, Shaw, Bertie Russell and all the 'modern' chatter about it.[15]

But there was also widespread disgust at Lang's speech. A contrast was drawn between his vengeful and unforgiving tone and the direct simplicity of the Duke of Windsor's broadcast. At a Foyle's literary luncheon in London on 15 December, the playwright and actor John Drinkwater strongly expressed his criticism of the Archbishop. 'My ancestors came from Canterbury,' he said, 'but thank God they were only publicans!'[16] Lang's speech produced a wave of anti-clerical feeling – not only in the weekly reviews, but even in Establishment papers such as the *Daily Telegraph*. John Gunther observed that after a tale of 'perfect propriety by everyone', these archbishops had added 'a vulgar note when it was all over'.[17] Lang was sent a torrent of critical or abusive letters from outraged individuals – about two hundred and fifty in the first couple of days.[18] The author Gerald Bullett wrote a scathing quatrain on the broadcast. Playing on Lang's title, 'Cantuar' (which is the standard abbreviation of *Cantuariensis*, the Latin word for the Archbishopric of Canterbury), his verse quickly became popular on both sides of the Atlantic:

> My Lord Archbishop, what a scold you are!
>   And when your man is down, how bold you are!
> In Christian Charity how scant you are!
>   How Lang Oh Lord, how full of Cantuar![19]

Lord Brownlow, regarding himself as one of Edward's closest friends, immediately sent an indignant letter to the Archbishop.[20] He received some letters of sympathy for his position from the public. 'We strongly condemn Primate's address as uncharitable and unchristian and causing gross insinuations', cabled a well-wisher to Lord Brownlow on 17 December.[21] Walter Monckton said he had not much enjoyed 'the comments which have reached me attributing the Archbishop's rebuke to myself.'[22]

Cecil Headlam was appalled, even though he shared much of Lang's antipathy to Edward. 'We did not think it a very happy effort; it was pontifical and unctuous and snobbish', he wrote in his diary after the broadcast, adding:

Disliking Edward VIII (as one knows he did), he did not refrain from rubbing it in. I fancy that a good many people will disapprove of this: once a man is down, it never does any good to kick him and people may well ask (unfairly perhaps) why if the Archbishop felt so strongly about the King and his entourage he did not speak out long ago.[23]

Some of those who had been eager for the abdication were suddenly made mindful by the Archbishop's unkind words of the terrible dilemma that Edward had faced: 'Prayed for "Edward up to now our King",' wrote a retired engineer in his diary.[24] Alan Turing condemned the hypocrisy of the Archbishop. 'I consider his behaviour disgraceful', he told his mother. 'He waited until Edward was safely out of the way and then unloaded a whole lot of quite uncalled-for abuse. He didn't dare to do it whilst Edward was King. Further he had no objections to the King having Mrs Simpson as a mistress, but marry her, that wouldn't do at all.'[25] Edward himself had been aware of Lang's lack of visibility during the period of crisis. 'He stood aside', recalled Edward later, 'until the fateful fabric had been woven and the crisis was over. Yet from beginning to end I had a disquieting feeling that he was invisibly and noiselessly about.'[26]

Bruce Lockhart spent most of the morning of 14 December writing a paragraph for the *Evening Standard* attacking the Archbishop of Canterbury. He had been astonished that Lang had not only rebuked the ex-King, but also called on the nation to rebuke Edward's friends. Many of those friends were people from the 'best' families, observed Lockhart:

The people who were closest to him during his reign were: Duff and Diana Cooper, Duke and Duchess of Sutherland, Lord and Lady Brownlow, Euan and Barbara Wallace, Mr and Mrs Fitzgerald, Lord Dudley, Duke and Duchess of Marlborough. Not heavy-weights, but certainly no more deserving of Archbishop's rebuke than ninety per cent of the population![27]

'There has been a perfect storm of anger', wrote Churchill to the Duke of Windsor, 'raised against [Lang] for his unchivalrous reference to the late reign. Even those who were very hostile to your standpoint turned round and salved their feelings by censuring the Archbishop. All the newspapers were inundated with letters of protest.'[28] Lloyd

George's former chief of staff and political adviser said that the King was 'now the victim of the malice of gossips, the hypocritical righteousness of the Bishops, and even, I am afraid, of the Non-Conformist conscience at its most nauseating sanctimoniousness.' This, he said, 'is a great score for the Church, for Morality and for organized Puritanism; and the whole business makes me want to vomit.'[29]

Baldwin received letters about the Archbishop's words. One 'ordinary honest working man' believed that the Archbishop had every right to speak his mind on 'the truth about that section of society gamblers who have caused this most terrible loss to us & "roped in" our beloved King.'[30] A woman in Devon, who kept a little shop selling papers and books, said that she heard in her customers' conversations 'all people's views expressed & since your last triumph tis [sic] wonderful to hear so many changed opinions now expressed – No one but "Stanley Baldwin" could have done such marvellous tasks . . . God bless you always.'[31]

But a woman in Leeds sent a furious letter to Baldwin, holding him responsible for slander. She was '*horrified*', she said, by the Archbishop's speech. 'You said you were [Edward's] friend in the House of Commons', she reminded him, then issued this reprimand:

Well! I ask you to prove that friendship to its limits. What is friendship worth if it cannot defend one who cannot – may not – or will not – speak for himself? Since the heartbreak of December 10th the people of England seem to have gone mad . . . Since the Archbishop of Canterbury's broadcast last Sunday – I have not met one man, woman or child who has not made some terrible accusation against Edward VIIIth . . . Has not the nation had its 'pound of flesh'?

She quoted to Baldwin some of the ugly comments about Edward that her teenage daughter had brought home from school, and implored: 'Mr Baldwin, *I beg of you most humbly and earnestly to please do something*! Please repudiate publicly the people who utter these vile slanders . . . I am so incensed at this evil thing in our midst, that I will leave no stone unturned to get this matter righted, but I have sufficient confidence in you and your sense of Justice.'[32]

A number of people sent letters to Churchill, complaining about the Archbishop. One man was worried that Edward might believe that the people had turned against him. He suggested that 'some form of testimonial might be arranged through you to Prince Edward, to show him what the Country really thinks of him, and not what the Archbishop of cant and the Prime Minister of humbugs think.'[33] 'I am writing to you,' said one woman, 'because you were with our dearly loved Duke of Windsor, only a few hours before he bade us farewell! . . . our hearts are still heavy with sorrow, that he is not in the land of his birth, the country he loved.' She bitterly resented the Archbishop's speech and – not realizing that Queen Mary had actually written to congratulate him on his words – asked, 'What must have been the feelings of our dear Queen Mother, and all the Royal Family? In more humble ranks, too, certain reflections on any section of the community, especially by radio, make it seem unsportsmanlike! The victim or victims cannot reply! Moreover, the Church should be above this.'[34]

It was all part of 'buttering up the new King at the expense of the old one', thought Geoffrey Wells. 'It's dreadful – not one honest voice.' Usually an enthusiastic cinema-goer, his last visit had made him miserable. 'The News *all* King – awful stuff', he complained in his diary. 'Played God Save the King, and all stood up, but *after* what had gone before I could have been kicked from one side of the hall to the other more bearably than standing in that solemn crowd. So I sat tight.' Wells believed that Edward had behaved 'like a man':

I can respect a King who acted, however dictatorially, as a King, even tho' I opposed him to the death: but I could *not* respect those (Baldwin etc) who set up a King and then demand that he behave like a dummy.[35]

Meanwhile, Society behaved as if there had been a royal death. The new King's family cancelled all invitations, as did many London hostesses. At a party for Sir Thomas Beecham, organized by Emerald Cunard, most women wore black[36] (although according to one report,

'Lady Mountbatten looked almost startlingly gay in a dress of aquamarine blue, paillettes matching her aquamarine necklace and a wrap of bright blue ostrich feathers'[37]). Back in London after a brief visit to Edward in Austria, Perry Brownlow was horrified to find himself ostracized. He telephoned Diana Vreeland late one night and asked her to come and see him and his wife, Kitty. Since his return two weeks before, he told Diana and her husband, Reed, everyone had been turning their back on him – 'This is my life: today I walk into White's and every man leaves the bar.' He was shocked to be snubbed in this way by his fellow members of White's, the grandest of gentlemen's clubs in London, in St James's. 'I walk down Seymour Street, where Kitty and I have lived all these years', he told them, 'and if I see a friend he crosses to the other side of the street. Nobody – but *nobody* – speaks to me in London. It's as if people really believed I was a party to the abdication – to a conspiracy!!'[38] 'I stayed there two days with him,' he sighed. 'Now I'm back in London, and this is my reward – I am completely, *totally* alone.'[39] Brownlow soon received yet another punishment for his loyalty to Edward – dismissal from his position of Lord-in-Waiting. He was summarily replaced by the Marquess of Dufferin and Ava, but was not even told officially – he knew only because he read about it for himself in the Court Circular.

Lord Brownlow 'came to see Stan', wrote Lucy Baldwin in her diary on 18 December, adding that he was 'Very harried & very worried at the odium he has earned by looking after Mrs Simpson for King Edward.'[40] He also wrote to Lord Cromer, who was Lord Chamberlain, objecting in the strongest terms:

I am afraid that, when I came back last week, I did not realise the depth of personal feeling against myself in certain circles: perhaps you should have told me more frankly, or maybe I should have understood your hint in the 'formula of resignation' shown to me . . . My resignation from His Majesty's household was both obvious and desirable, but it is perhaps the method of bringing it about, in such a premature and unhappy manner, that has hurt and humiliated me more than I have ever known before.[41]

But Brownlow's loyal efforts on Edward's behalf were appreciated in some quarters. 'I, as one of the poor,' wrote a Towcester woman, 'wish to thank you for your brave deed in standing by the Duke of Winsor [sic] and Mrs Simpson, we have only praise for your good deed.'[42] Wallis herself was grateful beyond measure. 'I can never make you realize my gratitude and appreciation for everything you did for me', she wrote from Cannes on 18 December – 'to go into it only brings tears so you will understand won't you?'[43] Feeling hated by so many people in England, Wallis found great comfort in Brownlow's staunch support. 'There is nothing I can begin to say about Perry's friendship for us', she wrote to Edward. 'It has been absolutely marvellous in every way. Do tell him. I can't because I begin to cry, I have never seen anything like it.'[44]

Others were made to suffer for their friendship with Edward and Wallis. 'The other day in my presence', Queen Mary wrote to Prince Paul, the regent of Yugoslavia,

Bertie told George he wished him and Marina never to see Lady Cunard again and George said he would not do so. I fear she has done David a great deal of harm as there is no doubt that she was great friends with Mrs Simpson at one time and gave parties for her. Under the circumstances I feel none of us, in fact people in society, should meet her.

She was sure that

you will agree one should not meet her again after what has happened and I am hoping that George and Marina will no longer see certain people who alas were friends of Mrs S and Lady Cunard's and also David's . . . As you may imagine I feel very strongly on the matter but several people have mentioned to me what harm she has done.[45]

George and Marina were picked out for this special attention because of the close friendship between George and Edward and because the Kents had often been in the company of Edward and Wallis at Fort Belvedere.

Everyone in Society understood that a purge was underway. 'Are we all on the "Black List"?' wondered Chips Channon. 'Are the Sutherlands, the Marlboroughs, the Stanleys?'[46] Queen Elizabeth thanked Lady Londonderry for her 'thoughtfulness' in inquiring whether or not certain people should be invited to a party. She told her that 'Lady Cunard is really the only one that we do not want to meet just now. The bitter months of last autumn & winter are still so fresh in our minds.' Her presence, she added, 'would inevitably bring so many sad thoughts, that we would prefer not to meet her . . . There is nobody else on your little list, except possibly poor Mrs Corrigan [an American hostess], who one could take any exception to, and I do appreciate your tact & kindness in writing.'[47]

Whereas Brownlow was punished, Hardinge flourished under the new royal regime. 'For your ear only,' he wrote to Dawson, 'I am staying on as P.S. [Private Secretary] to our new King – to which, when I am rested, I am immensely looking forward.'[48] Soon afterwards, at the beginning of 1937, Hardinge became one of the youngest Knights of the Bath on the Civil List. Wigram was rewarded, too. 'I am glad to see Clive Wigram is to be *Permanent* Lord in Waiting, a new post, that he may be always about the King', noted George Trevelyan. 'He was G V's prop and staff, but E had no use for him.'[49] Almost from the start it appeared that Louis Mountbatten, Edward's cousin, 'was going to cross the chasm safely from one reign to the next.' He was appointed Personal Naval Aide-de-Camp to the new King and was made a Knight Grand Cross of the Royal Victorian Order.[50] Charles Lambe, who became the sole attendant on the Duke of Windsor in January 1937, later returned to work in the Royal Household for George VI, at the King's special request. Joey Legh, who went with Edward into exile after his abdication broadcast, came back to England when the new King asked him to be his Master of the Household. Edward's second Assistant Private Secretary, Sir Godfrey Thomas, was transferred to the service of Harry, the Duke of Gloucester, as his Private Secretary.

Osbert Sitwell wrote a nasty poem, 'Rat Week', which claimed that as soon as the King had abdicated, all his friends – and Wallis's, too – deserted them. Sitwell adored Elizabeth, the new Queen. He had been a regular visitor at the Yorks' home on 145 Piccadilly and they shared

many close friends, including Mrs Greville. Sitwell, who saw himself
as an aesthete of the highest refinement, despised Edward, regarding
him as a Philistine with no proper taste or appreciation of art. He
shuddered at Edward's love for an American from Baltimore and he
dismissed his interest in the life of working-class families as irrelevant
and even unpleasant. Sitwell had already used poetry to savage his
enemies, who ranged from Churchill and Beaverbrook to Aldous
Huxley, D. H. Lawrence and his two prize foes, Noel Coward and
Wyndham Lewis.[51] Now he attacked the former King and his beloved,
by disparaging their friends:

> Where are the friends of yesterday
>   That fawned on Him,
> That flattered Her;
>   Where are the friends of yesterday,
> Submitting to His every whim,
>   Offering praise of Her as myrrh
> To Him?[52]

'Rat Week' was accurate in so far as some people had indeed
behaved very badly towards old friends. 'Ratting', it seemed, was de
rigueur.[53] But Sitwell's poem was riddled with untruths. Despite Wallis's
bad press – 'No one has been more victimized by gossip and scandal',
said Churchill[54] – her close friends did not desert her. It was true that
the English 'set' on the Riviera generally shunned Wallis, but she and
Sybil Colefax – a genuine friend – spent Christmas Day together, two
weeks after the abdication, at Villa Mauresque, the home of the writer
Somerset Maugham. In March 1937, Maugham wrote to a friend that
in the early part of the previous winter,

We saw a certain amount of Mrs Simpson and as you know she came to stay
here. I had known her years ago before she became a figure of world-wide
importance and the strange thing about her is that she has not altered at all.
She has always been very loyal to her old friends and that I think is one of the
qualities that has done her most harm.

He added, 'I think she had a very difficult role to play and I doubt whether any woman could have played it successfully.'[55] Daisy Fellowes was another old friend who was delighted to see Wallis in the South of France. And Wallis's old friends from Peking, Herman and Katherine Rogers, who looked after her at Lou Viei, remained loyal and loving even though their lives were thrown into disarray by the drama of Wallis's sudden arrival and her long stay, with an army of journalists continually camped outside their gates.

Nor was Edward rejected by his genuine friends. Duff Cooper, writing his memoirs in the fifties, fondly recalled Edward's 'sympathy with suffering, courage and sincerity'.[56] Lord Brownlow, who had lost and suffered so much through his loyalty to Edward, remained defiant for the rest of his life. At Belton House, his country estate in Lincolnshire, photographs of Edward and Wallis covered the desks and tables – and many of them have stayed there ever since.

Winston Churchill suffered from feelings of almost fatalistic depression, according to his daughter Mary.[57] He was at an extremely low point in his political fortunes and was resented by the new King and Queen – for his loyalty to Edward, and for his energetic opposition to the policy of appeasement to Nazi Germany. He continued to look out for Edward's interests, and reported in a letter to his wife, Clementine, that 'HMG [Her Majesty's Government] are preparing a dossier about the D of W's finances, debts & spendings on acct of Cutie [Wallis] wh[ich] I fear they mean to use to his detriment when the Civil List is considered.' Churchill's letter ended with a postscript: '"*Odi quem laeseris*" (Hate whom you have injured) as the Romans used to say—.'[58] Clementine Churchill had not shared her husband's support for Edward as King, but she did share his revulsion at the way people suddenly turned their backs on their former sovereign. She made her feelings known at a dinner held by Chips Channon for a couple called the Granards which was attended by the Churchills and some other friends. Channon was in any case concerned that his guests were 'a little too Edward VIII for the Granards' – that it was 'a thoroughly "Cavalier" collection'. When, predictably, Lord Granard attacked the former King, Mrs Churchill 'turned on him and asked crushingly, "If you feel that way, why did you invite Mrs Simpson to your house and put her on your right?" "[59] (By putting Wallis on his right, he had been treating her as the female guest of honour and therefore, by implication, as Edward's wife.)

Cinema-goers in America made their feelings known. At the Embassy Theater in Times Square in New York City, reported *Time* magazine, the newsreel reports on the abdication were watched noisily:

Prince Edward (cheers); Mrs Simpson (cheers); her first husband Commander Spencer, USN (boos); her second and present husband Mr Simpson (cheers and boos); new King George and Queen Elizabeth (boos); Prime Minister Baldwin (prolonged catcalls and boos); King Edward and Mrs Simpson bathing in Mediterranean (cheers).[60]

Well-meant offers of help were sent to Edward from the USA. 'Why in screaming thunder don't you marry Wally and come to Hobbs New Mexico. A welcome awaits you', urged one telegram.[61] Another, from Mississippi, promised him 'true Southern hospitality and plantation life'.[62] In Canada, people quickly forgot about the crisis of Edward's abdication, which worried Sir Francis Floud, the British High Commissioner in Ottawa. Although this might simply have been because 'it takes a great deal to disturb the self-centredness of the Canadian', he wrote to the Secretary of State for Dominion Affairs in London on 22 December, there was an obvious danger that respect for the Crown in Canada was deteriorating.[63]

Edward had arrived at Enzesfeld Castle in Austria on Monday 14 December, the day after the Archbishop's speech. He now had to endure a period of suffering that was even more terrible than the last few weeks. He could not see the woman he loved, for whom he had given up a throne, because their lawyers had advised them not to be together at any time until the decree nisi was made absolute. Not until then, in five months time, would they finally be able to marry. Even this was not certain. On the one hand, the affidavit that had been served just days before the abdication, alleging collusion in the Simpsons' divorce, had now been withdrawn as a result of Edward's farewell speech to the nation. The man who had submitted it did not 'feel justified,' he wrote to Goddard, 'in view of the Broadcast at 10 o'clock on Friday evening last to which I listened, in pursuing the matter further.'[64] But on the other hand, a further affidavit had followed, and the King's Proctor was bound to launch an investigation.[65]

When Perry Brownlow went to see Edward at Enzesfeld, 'a footman took him though this cold, lonely castle to a room. He went into the room and there he saw the Duke – who looked just like a little schoolboy sound asleep, with sun coming across his blond hair. His bed was surrounded by chairs . . . and on each chair was a picture of his beloved Wallis.' His love, said Lord Brownlow, 'was an obsession. No greater love has ever existed.'[66]

For Wallis at Lou Viei, this further trial of waiting and worry was unbearable. 'Darling,' she wrote to Edward, 'I want to leave here I want to see you touch you I want to run my own house I want to be married and to you.'[67] Her heart, she said, was 'so full of love for you and the agony of not being able to see you after all you have been through is pathetic. At the moment we have the whole world against us and our love . . . I love you David and I am holding so tight.'[68] In fact, the 'whole world' was *not* against them and their love – but it was impossible for her to know this. She hated the notoriety that had attached itself to her name and learned with horror that Madame Tussaud's had put up a waxwork of her. She asked Walter Monckton to investigate, and he reported back: 'The figure of Mrs S is in the Grand Hall. It stands alone in an alcove draped with black velvet cushions. She is represented in a standing position wearing a red evening dress. There is nothing remarkable about the figure.' She was placed between a group on one side which included Voltaire, Marie Antoinette, Joan of Arc and Louis XIV, and a group on the other side with Allenby, French, Haig, Kitchener, Roberts and Wellington.[69]

To her friend Sybil Colefax, Wallis sent letters expressing her hurt and distress at Edward's treatment. 'I am more than discouraged', she wrote, 'by the propaganda allowed in England against the Duke . . . when the records of his speech were not allowed in England.' Surely, she added, 'it is an organized campaign and not very creditable considering it is against one man who has shown nothing but loyalty to his country.' Every night, she said, 'in spite of bishops I pray to god not to let me become bitter.' The strain had been dreadful and seemed to be reflected in the storms shaking the house: 'The weather is not quieting – every day a wild wind rushing up the valley shrieking, screaming until I think I shall go mad.'[70] She thanked Sybil for sticking by her. 'As you know,' she told her, 'your friendship makes me very happy.'[71]

Telephone calls between Austria and Cannes were frequently interrupted by line failure, and in any case it was difficult for Wallis and Edward to hear each other. In her loneliness, Wallis felt vulnerable and feared he might not love her any more. 'I look a hundred and weigh 110 [pounds],' she wrote in despair, 'you won't love me when you see the wreck England has made me.'[72] Her love for Edward never wavered, but her confidence did, and at moments she even became jealous of Edward's hostess, Kitty, the Baroness Eugene de Rothschild. At first, Wallis had felt warmly towards her. Before Edward's arrival, she wrote to her, asking, 'Dear Kitty – be kind to him. He is honest and good and really worthy of affection. They simply haven't understood.'[73] But shortly after Edward had settled down at Enzesfeld Castle, she began to suffer pangs of insecurity. 'I long for you and love you,' she told him, 'but become eanum suspicious of "all of you". It is odd the hostess remaining on. Must be that fatal charm!'[74] Her jealousy was fed by the rumours that circulated about each of them. 'I have a letter from a woman in Paris,' she wrote in misery to Edward saying that Kitty

has arrived full of new rumours, additional gossip, etc. I can only pray to God that in your loneliness you haven't flirted with her (I suspect that) or told everything about yourself – finances, family matters or hurt feelings over your brothers [sic] treatment of you because Paris will be full of that and once on the telephone she hinted to me that London wasn't treating you well . . . I know my sweet you have a way of telling too much to strangers and heaven knows the Rothschilds were that when you arrived.[75]

Edward replied with understanding and devotion. 'I know WE will so hold tight', he assured her. He knew she would trust him, and was certain that she would never take any notice of anything or rotten gossip that any foul woman or women may try to spread. I hate them all darling and despise them all so. So you do so too and never never believe a word of it because it never never would or will be true.[76]

One great comfort to Wallis was the arrival of both her Aunt Bessie and Wallis's maid, Mary Burke, who left London together on 18 December for Cannes, bringing Wallis's clothes. Bessie stayed at the Carlton Hotel to be near her niece. The day before her departure, she sent Edward a letter telling him 'how constantly I have held you in my thoughts since you left, and, Sir, with what affectionate regard you will always remain there.'[77] Edward replied with equally loving affection, happy that she would soon be with Wallis.[78]

An endless stream of mail arrived for the Duke, including telegrams of good wishes from individual branches of the British Legion.[79] Edward was joined at the castle by his equerry, Charles Lambe, who handled much of the mail: 'letters, letters, letters – lovingly, honestly and dishonestly – the whole world profoundly moved or disturbed.' But Edward was in reasonable spirits, judged Lambe, all things considered. 'He has been surprisingly settled and well in mind and body', he told a friend, and 'there is no looking back and apparently still not even a shadow of a question as to the rightness of his decision. He regards these few months till April as a period of "mourning" or penance and his whole being exists only for that not so distant date.'[80]

The Archbishop of Canterbury, Cosmo Gordon Lang, wrote in his diary, 'My heart aches for the Duke of Windsor . . . I cannot bear to think of the kind of life into which he has passed.'[81] John Buchan, too, was unable to comprehend Edward's love for Wallis. On 15 December, he wrote to Edith Londonderry from Canada to say that he was 'desperately sorry for the late King. I detested the raffish set in which he moved, though I could not help liking him greatly as a human being.' He added that he could not 'get him out of my head, *for I do not see what possible happiness there is in store for him.*' Although Edward had made clear in his broadcast the depth of his devotion and his need for Wallis, Buchan still found it impossible to believe that Edward could or would be happy with her.[82] Robert Bernays, too, believed that Edward was doomed to misery. 'I was terribly moved by his broadcast address,' he wrote in his diary, 'not because I had any sympathy for him but at the stark tragedy of his failure. It was like seeing a man of great promise committing suicide before one's eyes.'[83]

But the priorities of the Duke were different, and he was looking forward to great happiness. He telephoned Norman Birkett, who had acted as counsel for Wallis in the divorce case, to thank him for his work in obtaining the decree nisi. 'I spoke to the Duke of Windsor in Austria last night', Birkett wrote to his cousin. 'It was strange to hear the voice that spoke to millions the other night just speaking to me. He was amusing about the Archbishops! I must tell you all about it sometime, but of course it is all *very private* . . .'[84] Marrying Wallis and continuing as King would have been the most desirable outcome for Edward. But if it came to a choice between the two, he had no doubts – he chose the woman he loved over the crown. To many, this was the right thing to do – it was not a false act or a symptom of some pathology. Indeed, he had been encouraged to follow this path by many of his subjects, when the story broke at the beginning of December – 'Stick to your Gal: & as an ex Guardsman don't desert.'[85]

'I think you are so noble and a real man to stand by your Lady Love,' a girl in Cardiff had written to Edward. 'My daddy deserted my Mummie & I and we are so sad – I had to leave my nice school and friends . . . Your Lady Love must be proud of you.'[86] An ex-serviceman sent his own congratulations: 'I too like countless other thousands went through those awe inspiring years of the War with you . . . your brave Abdication comes right home to me.'[87] 'I hate the thought of you leaving us,' wrote another veteran of the war. 'I fought with you in France & I know how you feel. Your heart has brought you a loved one & you have every right to her'.[88] In one letter was a small packet containing one of a pair of four-leaf clovers. These clovers, explained the man who sent the letter, had been sent to him when he was at Gallipoli in 1915, where the Allies had suffered a terrible and brutal defeat with over two hundred thousand casualties. He had survived, thanks to the clovers, and had carried them with him ever since. Now he hoped the King would accept one of the clovers 'for luck'.[89]

Cosmo Gordon Lang counted his blessings in the new regime of George VI. 'What a relief it was, after the strained and wilful ways of the late King,' he wrote in his diary, 'to be in this atmosphere of intimate friendship, and instead of looking forward to the Coronation as a sort of nightmare, to realise that . . . I was now sure that to the solemn words of the Coronation there would be a sincere response.' At Christmas the new King wrote to him, he said, 'most kindly'. He observed that it would be difficult to see in his handwriting and especially his signature, 'George R I,' any difference from that of his father. '*Prosit omen!*', he declared with satisfaction.[90]

For the two lovers, waiting to marry and commit the rest of their lives to each other, the prospect of Christmas in 1936 was not a happy one. 'It's pathetic,' wrote Edward to Wallis, 'but we'll just have to write this Christmas off and make up for it by so many lovely happy ones in the future.' He added,

I will go to church in Vienna on Friday for eleven o'clock service and pray so hard that God goes on blessing WE for the rest of our lives. He has been very good to WE and is watching over US I know . . . I love you love you Wallis more and more and more and am holding so tight.[91]

Nor was it a happy prospect for many British citizens. 'I am actually blubbing now,' wrote a woman from Dorset, 'and trying hard to prevent the tears from spoiling this paper. The most useful present for everyone this Christmas will be handkerchiefs. England will indeed be called a "Wet Country", floods are not in it!!'[92] 'When glasses are raised to the King at Christmas,' wrote a Quaker, 'many will be to the King across the sea.'[93] From a woman in North Wales came a letter of thanks to Edward for all the love and tenderness he had shown to his people. Her nine-year-old daughter Elaine sent a cross, painted with Balmain's Luminous Paint, so that it would shine out all night. On the front of this cross, which must have been a treasure in a poor house-hold, was written, 'Remembrance Christmas 1936' – and on the back, 'Love and Kisses from Elaine x x x God Bless You.'[94]

Edward's concern for the poor and his recent visit to South Wales were not forgotten. 'Three weeks ago we stood for two hours to catch a glimpse of Your Majesty as you passed through Blaina,' wrote a woman from Abertillery in Wales. 'It is now a most cherished memory,' she added – 'that glimpse of you. We shall now go on with the Social Service work instigated at your request – we will be faithful to the vision which Your Majesty was granted of "depressed areas" becoming transformed through fellowship arising out of voluntary service.' She was writing her letter, she added, in tears.[95]

'It has been a terrible time here,' wrote Winston Churchill to David Lloyd George on Christmas Day, 'and I am profoundly grieved at what has happened. I believe the Abdication to have been altogether premature and probably quite unnecessary.'[96] Lloyd George sent Christmas wishes to Edward. His cable from Jamaica bore greetings from

an old Minister of the Crown who holds you in as high esteem as ever and regards you with deeper loyal affection, deplores the shabby and stupid treatment accorded to you, resents the mean and unchivalrous attacks upon you and regrets the loss sustained by the British Empire of a monarch who sympathized with the lowliest of his subjects.

He received the following reply on Christmas Day:

Very touched by your kind telegram and good wishes, which I heartily reciprocate. *Cymru am byth* [Wales for ever]. Edward.'[97]

14

'We have had such happiness'

Wallis Simpson finally obtained her decree absolute on 3 May 1937. A comprehensive investigation had been carried out by the King's Proctor into the divorce suit of *Simpson* v. *Simpson*, most of it during February 1937. The Simpsons' servants,[1] sailors on board the *Rosaura* and the *Nahlin*, the proprietor of a hotel in Felixstowe, and Ernest Simpson himself were all interviewed.[2] Simpson insisted that 'there was no arrangement between himself and the King or his wife with regard to the divorce proceedings.'[3] While the investigation was going on, Walter Monckton worried about its outcome. 'As you know,' he wrote to Sir Horace Wilson,

I dined with the Prime Minister last week and yesterday I saw the King. I am very anxious that an impression should not get abroad that the powers that be would be glad if the decree were not made absolute. I do not suppose that Mr Baldwin wishes the decree not to be made absolute and I know the King hopes all will go smoothly.

He added that he was 'less certain of some of the others. Personally I feel that if there was a hitch we might well be in for a tragedy before the coronation – certainly for something extremely unpleasant.'[4] In the event, he need not have worried. The King's Proctor took the view that the Simpsons' divorce suit was probably an arranged one, but his enquiries had produced no evidence to support his suspicions.[5]

Throughout this period, regular secret reports were being sent to the Commissioner of the Metropolitan Police from the Scotland Yard detectives who were guarding the Duke of Windsor and Mrs Simpson. Reports by Inspector Evans, staying at Cannes with Mrs Simpson, gave accounts of shopping trips and dinners, and also of the telephone conversations – sometimes almost word for word – between herself and Edward.[6] The Commissioner heard the humdrum details of Edward's routine at Enzesfeld Castle from Inspector Storrier: rounds of golf, skiing, visits to Vienna, and plans to visit Paris to consult his dentist.[7] On 28 April Storrier told the Commissioner that 'HRH is in good health and spends his time writing, telephoning, golfing, visiting towns in the vicinity and mountaineering, although I think interest in the latter is now on the wane.' He also mentioned a plan by the Duke to visit Wallis. The Duke was 'somewhat nervously excited', said Storrier, 'at the prospect of such a move which, so far, is being secretly arranged for Monday, 3rd May [the day Wallis's decree nisi was made absolute]. This is, of course, to Tours, to join Mrs Simpson, an action which I know, Sir, is not viewed in a favourable light by those in authority in the matter in London.' Storrier reported that 'the Press, as usual, are not far behind' and promised to find out more.[8]

The Home Secretary, Sir John Simon, was briefed by Sir Philip Game, Commissioner of the Metropolitan Police, on the reports filed by Inspectors Evans and Storrier. Sir John sought further information about the Duke from Piers Legh, a former courtier of Edward's who had stayed with him for a while in Austria. In a conversation with Legh, Sir John 'observed that nothing was so certain to do injury both to the Duke and to the lady as any suspicion on the part of the British Public that they were attempting a "come back".' Colonel Legh's own view was that 'the lady should never expect to come back to this country at all'.[9]

A month after her divorce had been made absolute, on 3 June, Wallis Warfield married Edward, Duke of Windsor at the Château de Candé in France. It was a warm and sunny day. Wallis's wedding ring had been fashioned from an ounce of Welsh gold, a present from one of Edward's former subjects, and the couple were 'delighted to think that the gold comes from Wales'.[10] The wedding ceremony was 'a supremely happy moment', wrote the Duchess in her memoirs.

Her aunt, who had returned to America in February, came back to Europe for the wedding and helped Wallis to dress in the outfit of blue silk crepe that had been designed for the occasion by Mainbocher. The guests included George Allen, Walter Monckton, Winston Churchill's son Randolph, the Baron and Baroness de Rothschild, and the First Secretary to the British Embassy in Paris. Herman Rogers gave Wallis away, and 'Fruity' Metcalfe, an old friend of Edward's, was his best man.

Edward had wanted his favourite brother, George, to be best man – but, to his and Wallis's huge disappointment, not a single member of the royal family came to the wedding. If any of them were to attend, Sir John Simon had warned the King, 'this would be regarded, and represented, as accepting the future Duchess *for all purposes* into the Royal circle . . . If, for example, it is desired to *dis*courage return to this country, absence from the wedding could be indicative of a desire to maintain a certain aloofness.'[11] The King dispatched a letter to this effect to the Duke on 11 April 1937. 'His Majesty has firmly told him', reported Wigram to Sir John, 'that no brother nor sister can attend the wedding, nor will His Majesty allow one of his chaplains to officiate.'[12] Edward had taken it for granted that a royal chaplain would be officiating. When he learnt that this had been forbidden, he sought another Anglican clergyman who would be willing to perform the wedding service. Each one who was approached refused, but eventually the Reverend J. A. Jardine, a priest from Darlington, offered himself for the role, and Edward gratefully accepted.

Royal courtiers and friends were also discouraged from accepting an invitation. Even Lord Brownlow, after much hesitation, stayed away. He had been firmly advised by a Lincolnshire MP that if he and his wife were to go, his position as Lord Lieutenant would become untenable and he would be forced by 'public opinion' to give it up.[13] The Bishop of Lincoln had added his weight, predicting that 'the Lincolnshire side of your life would become very difficult' if he went.[14] Winston Churchill believed that the Brownlows should attend, saying that 'friendship stood on a higher plane than any other consideration'.[15] But Brownlow chose not to defy the warnings from

Lincolnshire: presumably, he and his family had suffered enough by now. He did, however, condemn the debarring of the Duke's family and friends from the wedding as 'short-sighted, foolish, uncharitable, and cruel'.[16]

Just before the wedding, King George VI sent his brother a wounding wedding gift. He informed Edward in a letter that the title of HRH – 'Her Royal Highness' – could not be extended to his wife. She would be simply 'Duchess of Windsor'. Wallis was not allowed, therefore, to take her place within the royal family. Thus, in the end, Edward *did* have a morganatic marriage – even though Baldwin had insisted to Edward, while he was King, that no such thing existed in England. It was a bitter and painful blow, not least because the Duke of Windsor knew perfectly well that his wife was legally entitled to the status of HRH, just as Elizabeth, Duchess of York had become Her Royal Highness on marrying Albert in 1923.[17] This was also the consensus of law officers at the highest level. They pointed out that 'the wife of an abdicated King who had been allowed himself after abdication to use the title would normally be also entitled.'[18]

Sir John Simon knew this too. Unless appropriate action were taken, he argued at a meeting of the Cabinet, the woman whom the Duke of Windsor proposed to marry would by the mere fact of her marriage enjoy the title of Her Royal Highness. 'Something,' he added, 'must be done'.[19] Evidently, the phrase used by Edward in South Wales in November 1936, which was now world-famous, had crept into the consciousness of the Home Secretary.

Queen Elizabeth and King George were adamant that Wallis should be deprived of the title. 'You are aware how strongly the King and Queen desire this situation to be established,' wrote Sir John in a memorandum to Neville Chamberlain, who was now Prime Minister. 'I believe Queen Mary also has strong views that it should, if possible, be done.'[20] Accordingly, letters patent were issued declaring that the King wished his brother personally to enjoy the title of Royal Highness, but that it was not extended to his wife or possible children.[21] Lord Jowitt, who was to become Lord Chancellor in 1945, argued in 1937 and later that the letters patent proceeded upon a misapprehension of the law. There had been no need for new letters patent to create the

Duke HRH, he said, and the Duchess was entitled to an equivalent rank because she was his wife.[22] Depriving Wallis of the title caused festering pain to Edward and Wallis for the rest of their lives – not so much because it took away her rightful style, as because it symbolized the refusal of Edward's brother and sister-in-law to accept his wife into their family.

The story of Edward's abdication for the woman he loved was the most celebrated love story of the decade. But the wedding was not covered in the newsreels because the British companies came to an agreement to keep the story from cinema screens. It was simply too risky to break the unofficial taboo against anything relating to Wallis and Edward. Gone was the chance to pack every cinema in the country, for days on end,[23] and the people of Britain were not allowed to witness the happiness of the man they had adored as King. On the wedding day, a Londoner decorated the balcony of his Piccadilly flat with flowers and a banner which read 'Long life and happiness to the Duke and Duchess'. He was asked by the agents of the property to take the banner down, and when he refused the police were brought in.[24]

Ernest Simpson's love affair with Mary Kirk Raffray also led to a wedding. She divorced her husband, and in the autumn of 1937 she and Ernest were married. Two years later they had a son, and they stayed together until parted by death.[25]

After visiting the Windsors in the South of France in January 1938, Winston Churchill wrote that, 'The Ws are very pathetic, but also very happy. She made an excellent impression on me, and it looks as if it would be a most happy marriage . . .'[26] He visited them again a year later and observed that, 'all accounts show them entirely happy and as much in love with each other as ever.'[27] He had hoped they would return as soon as possible to live in Britain. 'The only thing now to do', he had written to Robert Boothby on 11 December 1936, 'is to make it easy for him to live in this country quietly as a private gentleman as soon as possible and to that we must bend our efforts.' The more firmly the new King was established, he added, 'the more easy it will be for the old one to come back to his house.'[28]

But the Windsors never returned to live in Britain. They spent the rest of their lives in exile in France, apart from the years of the Second World War, when the Duke was Governor of the Bahamas. Edward made repeated requests for useful employment at home and for his wife to be received by his family, but all were turned down. He was reminded of an alleged agreement to stay away – but, wrote George Allen, 'the Duke of Windsor is quite certain that he never volunteered that he would not return to England without the King's consent.'[29] He was also told that he would get an allowance from the King only on condition that he did not come back to the country. 'I regard such a proposal as both unfair and intolerable', objected the Duke in a letter to Chamberlain on 22 December 1937, 'as it would be tantamount to my accepting payment for remaining in exile.' Edward was horrified by the thought of staying away from the country he loved. 'The treatment which has been meted out to my wife and myself since last December, both by the Royal Family and by the Government,' he told Chamberlain, 'has caused us acute pain.' He warned the Prime Minister that these injustices would anger the people of Britain and might re-ignite 'the very emotions which I was fortunate enough to be able to suppress a year ago'.[30]

The view was held by some of the circle around the royal family that, as Sir Horace Wilson had argued in a letter to Chamberlain in December 1936, Mrs Simpson intended

not only to come back here but (aided by what she expects to be a generous provision from public funds) to set up a 'Court' of her own and – there can be little doubt – do her best to make things uncomfortable for the new occupant of the Throne. It must not be assumed that she has abandoned hope of becoming Queen of England.[31]

King George VI became increasingly worried at the prospect of any return by Edward, even a visit. 'The more I think about his coming here on a visit,' he wrote to Chamberlain, 'the less I like the idea, especially as some sections of the Press are behaving so stupidly about it.'[32] King George and Queen Elizabeth were determined to keep the Duke and Duchess of Windsor out of Britain. 'I think you know', wrote George to Chamberlain on 14 December 1938, 'that neither the Queen nor

Queen Mary have any desire to meet the Duchess of Windsor, and therefore any visit made for the purpose of introducing her to members of the Royal Family obviously becomes impossible . . .'[33]

Many of Edward's supporters when he was King remained loyal to him as Duke of Windsor. In the USA, a society was formed called 'Friends of the Duke of Windsor in America'. 'He is a great democratic force for good,' said its president, 'but England won't use him. Our plan is to create an important international position for him so that he can serve humanity in the way he wants.'[34] A society to defend the Duke's interests was set up in Britain, too, under the name of the Octavians (which was investigated by the police[35]). The Duke's story, believed the Octavians, was a 'sad chapter in the nation's history'.[36] Harry Becker, who had been MP for Richmond in the early 1920s and who identified with the 'lost generation' of men like himself – and Edward – who had survived the war, suggested a yearly pilgrimage to White Lodge in Richmond Park, where Edward had been born, to roast an ox in honour of his service to the country.[37]

When Britain declared war on Germany in 1939, the Windsors returned to London from France so that Edward could offer his services – 'in any capacity' – to King George VI. But according to Leslie Hore-Belisha, an old Oxford friend who was now Secretary of State for War, the King was very disturbed by Edward's return. All his ancestors, complained George to Belisha, had succeeded to the throne after their predecessors died. 'Mine', he said in dismay, 'is not only alive, but very much so.' He thought it better for the Duke to proceed to Paris at once.[38] The Windsors had little choice but to follow this advice.

After the war, Edward renewed his efforts to come home, but he could make no headway against the intransigence of the King and Queen. The message was still the same in 1949, as George VI explained in a personal letter to Clement Attlee, the Prime Minister: 'I feel sure you will tell him [the Duke] that you will not encourage him to think that any alteration can be made at this time . . .'[39] Some of the British elite in Paris, led by the British Ambassador, Sir Oliver Harvey, shunned Edward and Wallis. Churchill heard of this in 1952, and was appalled. As Prime Minister, he sent a brisk minute to his Foreign Secretary, Anthony Eden. At social entertainments, he wrote firmly,

'I do not consider that the Duke and Duchess of Windsor should be given a second-class status. They are residents in Paris at the present time and should have that equality shown them which should be given to persons of distinction in the French capital.' He strongly objected to the Ambassador's 'insulting form of relegating him and the Duchess on social occasions to a position inferior to that of the unofficial notabilities of French society.'[40]

In 1964, eleven years after the coronation of Elizabeth II and twenty-eight years after the abdication, an investigation into opinions about the royal family was carried out by Mass-Observation. It found that the Duke of Windsor was the seventh most popular royal person. Among the over-sixty-fives, who would have remembered the abdication crisis more clearly, he was the fifth favourite.[41] The report stated that:

A little ahead of the Queen Mother as someone who has done most for the country (but coming after the Queen, Prince Philip and George VI), coming next to her, and bracketed with Princess Marina as a favourite royal person, and still very occasionally mentioned as a member of royalty who might take a more prominent part in public affairs, is the Duke of Windsor.[42]

'Outstandingly,' continued the report, 'he is felt to have understood ordinary working-class people and to have demonstrated that a King is also a human being.' People interviewed in the survey had given their opinions of Edward:

He was more of a *public* man; more of an ordinary man.
He visited slums and met the *poorest* people in their homes.
He made himself one of his people and had no high ideas.
He did a lot for the miners and used to go out and see things for himself.
He had a good time but he used to visit everyone, even the out-of-work.
He exposed the poverty of unemployment.[43]

There were still misgivings about the treatment meted out to the Duke by his country. In 1971, the Conservative Prime Minister, Edward Heath, observed in a letter to his Private Secretary that, 'Some of us have long been worried about various aspects of the Duke of Windsor's position, especially in the evening of his life.'[44] The following year, a Hertfordshire woman wrote to the Leader of the House of Commons, saying she had 'been made sad recently by the photographs of the Duke of Windsor looking so frail.' Drawing on the phrase that had been so closely associated with him after his visit to South Wales in November 1936, she pleaded,

Please, please cannot *something be done* to bring him back here to live the rest of his life amongst his own people in the land he loves. Also, after all these years surely the Duchess deserves to be given the full title of HRH, as the wife of a royal duke.[45]

A similar message came from a woman in Lincolnshire. 'It has been most unjust', she objected, 'that he has been kept in a foreign land so long and we, as others, feel strongly about this.'[46]

'Some day – some day – the world will know the whole truth', Wallis had told Adela St Johns, a well-known journalist, in December 1940. She explained that she had not wanted Edward to abdicate, but had not been able to influence him against his own conviction of what was right. She dearly hoped, she said, that when the world knew the truth, it would understand and love Edward 'for his great courage, as I do ... We have had such happiness – do you think, perhaps, that there are people in the world who cannot bear to see great happiness?'[47]

*

It took their deaths for Edward and Wallis to return permanently to England. They lie next to each other in the royal mausoleum at Frogmore.

When Edward died in Paris on 28 May 1972, the bell of St Paul's Cathedral in London was tolled for one hour, beginning at noon. His body was flown back to England and lay in state for three days in St George's Chapel, Windsor. Nearly sixty thousand people came to Windsor to pay their respects, many from afar.[48] At the wish of Queen Elizabeth II, there was a period of court mourning, and flags were flown at half mast from the day of Edward's death until his funeral. Elizabeth invited the Duchess of Windsor to stay with her at Buckingham Palace.[49]

Wallis died in Paris on 24 April 1986, after fourteen lonely years without Edward. And with her, observed the Mayor of Paris, Jacques Chirac, died 'the last symbol of a great love story which set the world dreaming'.[50]

References

Preface

1. John Grigg, 'Edward VIII', in *Political Lives*, p. 344
2. George Eliot, *Middlemarch*. London, Penguin, 1994, p. 896 [1st edn Edinburgh, Blackwood, 1871–2]
3. Godfrey Thomas to Miss Milsom, 18 June 1945, RA, PS/GVI/ABD, Box 5
4. John Copeland to King Edward VIII, 11 December 1936, RA, PS/GVI/ABD, Box 8
5. Gwladys M. Alexander-Williams to King Edward VIII, 4 December 1936, RA, PS/GVI/ABD, Box 5
6. A. Davies to King Edward VIII, 5 December 1936, RA, RS/GVI/ABD Box 1
7. S. Underwood to King Edward VIII, n.d. [December 1936], RA, PS/GVI/ABD, Box 4
8. Note to Mrs Churchill, 19 December 1936, Churchill Papers, CHAR 2/597-A

I

'Something must be done'

1. *The King Visits South Wales*, Pathe Gazette newsreel, November 1936
2. W. F. Deedes, *Dear Bill*, p. 40. 'There is some discrepancy,' writes Nick Smart in his edited volume of *The Diaries and Letters of Robert Bernays*, 'in accounts of whether the King had said "something will/ought to be/must be done", though the last version is probably the best remembered of what he said about unemployment at Blaenavon on 19 November 1936' (p. 278, note 57). Blaenavon was visited the day after the visit to Dowlais, but whatever Edward's exact words on that occasion, throughout the tour of South Wales he reiterated that something needed to be done for the unemployed.

3. Duke of Windsor, *A King's Story*, p. 337
4. *Hansard*, 10 December 1936
5. Duke of Windsor, *A King's Story*, p. 338
6. 'Vote National' leaflet, 1935, listed in Conservative Party Archive catalogue, Vol. 8
7. Alexander Hardinge, Memorandum, 7 October 1936, copy held at Merthyr Tydfil Public Library
8. Thomas Jones, *A Diary with Letters*, p. 332
9. John Williams, Mayor of Merthyr Tydfil and others to *Daily Mail*, 19 November 1930
10. Lady Williams, 'How they live in the distressed areas', *Evening Standard*, 21 July 1936
11. Alfred Shaughnessy, *Sarah*, pp. 149–50
12. Kath Nash, *Town on the Usk*, p. 35
13. Quoted in Michael Foot, *Aneurin Bevan*, p. 239
14. Oliver Warner, *Admiral of the Fleet*, p. 69
15. *Western Mail & South Wales News*, 20 November 1936
16. *South Wales Argus*, 19 November 1936
17. *The King Visits South Wales*, Pathe Gazette newsreel, November 1936
18. H. Powys Greenwood, 'Can South Wales be saved? – 1. First impressions', *Spectator*, 13 November 1936, p. 843
19. W. F. Deedes, *Dear Bill*, p. 40
20. Oliver Warner, *Admiral of the Fleet*, p. 68
21. George M. L. Davies, 'Employment in the Rhondda Valleys', in Felix Greene (ed.), *Time to Spare*, p. 123
22. *South Wales Argus*, 19 November 1936
23. *Merthyr Express*, 21 November 1936
24. W. T. Angell, *Some Observations and Notes* (pamphlet, 1946), p. 13
25. Hywel Francis and Dai Smith, *The Fed*, p. 248
26. Dame Janet Campbell *et al.*, *High Maternal Mortality in Certain Areas*
27. Rhondda Urban District Council, *Report of the Medical Officer of Health for 1934*, p. 13
28. Pilgrim Trust, *Men Without Work*, pp. 140–41
29. *South Wales Argus*, 19 November 1936
30. Hardinge to Chegwidden, 9 October 1936, copy held at Merthyr Tydfil Public Library
31. *Merthyr Express*, 21 November 1936
32. Mollie Pryce-Jones to King Edward VIII, 5 December 1936, RA, PS/GVI/ABD, Box 3
33. Letter to the *Spectator*, 27 November 1936

34. 'One full & loyal heart from Wales' to King Edward VIII, 1 December 1936, RA, PS/GVI/ABD, Box 4
35. *Let Paul Robeson Sing!*, pp. 35–9
36. Duke of Windsor in conversation with James Pope-Hennessy, late 1950s, quoted in Christopher Warwick, *Abdication*, p. 155
37. Quoted in John Grigg, *Lloyd George: The People's Champion*, p. 305
38. Mary Dixon to King Edward VIII, 3 December 1936, RA, PS/GVI/ABD, Box 4
39. J. Evans to King Edward VIII, 8 December 1936, RA, PS/GVI/ABD, Box 1
40. Agnes Sergeant to King Edward VIII, n.d. [December 1936], RA, PS/GVI/ABD, Box 4
41. Sarah Bradford, *George VI*, pp. 104–7
42. Duke of Windsor, *A Family Album*, p. 23
43. Alexander Hardinge to Helen Hardinge, 9 January 1925, Hardinge Papers, U2117, C 1/231
44. Lady Airlie, *Thatched With Gold*, pp. 112–13
45. *South Wales Argus*, 19 November 1936, p. 1
46. Oliver Warner, *Admiral of the Fleet*, p. 69
47. *Ibid.*, pp. 65–7
48. J. A. Chegwidden to A. N. Rucker, 29 October 1936, PRO, MH 58/309
49. (Third) Report of the Commissioner for the Special Areas (England and Wales), 1936, Cmd 5303
50. *The King Visits South Wales*, Pathe Gazette newsreel, November 1936
51. *South Wales Argus*, 19 November 1936, p. 1
52. 'Foreign comment', *Literary Digest*, 28 November 1936
53. Programme of 'Visit of H. M. The King to South Wales', PRO, MH 58/309
54. *Western Mail & South Wales News*, 20 November 1936
55. Philip Ziegler, *King Edward VIII*, p. 182
56. Duke of Windsor, *A King's Story*, p. 249
57. *South Wales Argus*, 19 November 1936
58. J. A. Chegwidden to A. N. Rucker, 29 October 1936, PRO, MH 58/309; emphasis added
59. Hardinge to Chegwidden, 9 October 1936, copy held at Merthyr Tydfil Public Library
60. *South Wales Argus*, 19 November 1936
61. *New Statesman and Nation*, 21 November 1936, p. 798
62. 'WR's trip to Clyde with HM', diary entry for 6 March 1936, Hilda Runciman Papers, WR Add 10, 21 May 1935 to 20 March 1936
63. *South Wales Argus*, 19 November 1936

64. Philip Guedalla, *The Hundredth Year*, p. 258
65. Oliver Warner, *Admiral of the Fleet*, p. 68
66. *Ibid.*
67. Quoted in Michael Foot, *Aneurin Bevan*, p. 239
68. F. J. Riley to King Edward VIII, 8 December 1936, RA, PS/GVI/ABD, Box 6
69. *Western Mail & South Wales News*, 20 November 1936
70. *Ibid.*
71. *Ibid.*
72. *Ibid.*

2

'My own beloved Wallis'

1. Diary entry for 19 November 1936, *Chips: The Diaries of Sir Henry Channon*, p. 82
2. Edward to Wallis, n.d. [autumn 1935], in Michael Bloch (ed.), *Wallis & Edward Letters*, p. 140
3. Quoted in Martin Gilbert, *Winston S. Churchill*, Vol. 5, p. 810
4. Quoted in Philip Ziegler, *King Edward VIII*, p. 276
5. Oliver Warner, *Admiral of the Fleet*, pp. 65–6
6. W. F. Deedes, *Dear Bill*, p. 42
7. H. A. Gwynne to Stanley Baldwin, 12 November 1936, PRO, PREM 1/446
8. Madame M. Dey and Miss Lillian Cohen to King Edward VIII, 4 December 1936, RA, PS/GVI/ABD, Box 4
9. Alan Turing to his mother, 22 November [1936], Alan Turing Papers, AMT/K/1/46
10. W. F. Deedes, *Dear Bill*, p. 41
11. Diana Mosley, *The Duchess of Windsor*, p. 17
12. Duchess of Windsor, *The Heart Has Its Reasons*, p. 65
13. *Los Angeles Times*, 22 November 1936
14. Duke of Windsor, *A King's Story*, p. 364
15. Duchess of Windsor, *The Heart Has Its Reasons*, pp. 87–8
16. *Ibid.*, p. 144
17. *Ibid.*, p. 143
18. Wallis Simpson to Mrs Merryman, 17 May 1933, in Michael Bloch (ed.), *Wallis & Edward Letters*, p. 69
19. Duchess of Windsor, *The Heart Has Its Reasons*, p. 193
20. Duke of Windsor, *A King's Story*, p. 255

21. Margaret Case Harriman, 'The King and the girl from Baltimore', p. 373
22. 'Report of interviews with late servants of Mrs Simpson', for the King's Proctor, n.d. [first quarter of 1937], PRO, TS 22/1/2
23. *Ibid.*
24. Duke of Windsor, *A King's Story*, p. 256
25. Duchess of Windsor, *The Heart Has Its Reasons*, p. 197
26. 'Reports of interviews with stewards employed on the S. Y. *Rosaura* and with the Captain and stewards employed on the S. Y. *Nahlin*', for the King's Proctor, n.d. [first quarter of 1937], PRO, TS 22/1/2
27. Hugo Vickers, *The Private World of the Duke and Duchess of Windsor*, frontispiece
28. Edward, Prince of Wales to Wallis Simpson, n.d. [spring 1935], in Michael Bloch (ed.), *Wallis & Edward Letters*, pp. 116–17
29. Lord Birkenhead, *Walter Monckton*, pp. 125–6
30. Quoted in Martin Gilbert, *Winston S. Churchill*, Vol. 5, p. 810
31. Quoted in Philip Ziegler, *King Edward VIII*, p. 227
32. Duchess of Windsor, *The Heart Has Its Reasons*, p. 202
33. Diana Vreeland, *D. V.*, p. 70
34. Duchess of Windsor, *The Heart Has Its Reasons*, p. 201
35. Duke of Windsor, *A King's Story*, pp. 255–6
36. 'Report of interviews with late servants of Mrs Simpson', for the King's Proctor, n.d. [first quarter of 1937], PRO, TS 22/1/2
37. Diana Mosley, *The Duchess of Windsor*, p. 77
38. John Gunther, *Inside Europe*, p. 252
39. Lord Beaverbrook, *The Abdication of King Edward VIII*, pp. 34–5
40. Duke of Windsor, *A King's Story*, p. 256
41. Wallis Simpson to Mrs Merryman [8 March 1936], in Michael Bloch (ed.), *Wallis & Edward Letters*, p. 167
42. Quoted in Duke of Windsor, *A King's Story*, p. 285
43. Wallis Simpson to Mrs Merryman, 4 February 1936, in Michael Bloch (ed.), *Wallis & Edward Letters*, p. 50
44. Wallis Simpson to Mrs Merryman, 22 [February 1934], in Michael Bloch (ed.), *Wallis & Edward Letters*, p. 90
45. Winston Churchill to Clementine Churchill, 20 September 1913, in Mary Soames (ed.), *Speaking for Themselves*, p. 76
46. Rupert Godfrey, in Duke of Windsor, *Letters from a Prince*, p. xvii
47. Quoted in Diana Mosley, *The Duchess of Windsor*, p. 63
48. Edward Prince of Wales to Wallis Simpson, n.d. [1935], in Michael Bloch (ed.), *Wallis & Edward Letters*, p. 145
49. Duke of Windsor, *A King's Story*, p. 256

50. Duchess of Windsor, *The Heart Has Its Reasons*, pp. 110–11

51. Prince of Wales to Viceroy, 28 December 1921, quoted in Chandrika Kaul, *Reporting the Raj*, Chapter 9

52. Duchess of Windsor, *The Heart Has Its Reasons*, p. 119

53. John Gunther, *Inside Europe*, p. 252

54. Quoted in Montgomery Hyde, article on Lady Londonderry and Mrs Simpson, *Harpers and Queen*, July 1980

55. Entry for 20 January 1937, in Susan Lowndes (ed.), *Diaries and Letters of Marie Belloc Lowndes*, p. 141

56. *Chips: The Diaries of Sir Henry Channon*, pp. 80–81

57. Diana Mosley, *The Duchess of Windsor*, p. 96

58. Quoted in Dale McConathy, 'Mainbocher', p. 155

59. Diary entry by Duff Cooper for January 1936, published in *The Times*, T2, 4 February 2003

60. *Ibid.*

61. Wallis Simpson to Mrs Merryman, 16 March 1936, in Michael Bloch (ed.), *Wallis & Edward Letters*, p. 169

62. 'Report of interviews with late servants of Mrs Simpson', for the King's Proctor, n.d. [first quarter of 1937], PRO, TS 22/1/2

63. *Ibid.*

64. *Ibid.*

65. Diana Vreeland, *D.V.*, p. 68

66. Quoted in Michael Bloch (ed.), *Wallis & Edward Letters*, p. 14

67. Wallis Simpson to Mrs Merryman, 9 January 1935, in Michael Bloch (ed.), *Wallis & Edward Letters*, p. 145

68. Wallis Simpson to Mrs Merryman, 16 March 1936, *Ibid.*, p. 168

69. Postscript by Edward in Wallis Simpson to Edward, Prince of Wales, 8 June 1936, *Ibid.*, p. 122

70. Wallis Simpson to Mrs Merryman, 22 May 1934, *Ibid.*, p. 94

71. Janet Flanner, *An American in Paris*, p. 17

72. *Ibid.*, p. 29

73. Diary entry for 15 January by Jean, Lady Hamilton, quoted in Celia Lee, *Jean, Lady Hamilton*, p. 258

74. Margaret Case Harriman, 'The King and the Girl from Baltimore', p. 373

75. *Ibid.*, p. 371

76. Wallis Simpson to Mrs Merryman, 9 January 1936, in Michael Bloch (ed.), *Wallis & Edward Letters*, p. 147

77. Wallis Simpson to Edward, Prince of Wales, n.d. [August 1935], *Ibid.*, p. 131

78. Wallis Simpson to Mrs Merryman, 13 August 1936, *Ibid.*, p. 188

79. Edward, Prince of Wales to Wallis Simpson, n.d. [18 January 1936], *Ibid.*, p. 148

80. Wallis Simpson to Edward VIII, n.d. [early February 1936], *Ibid.*, p. 156

81. *Chips: The Diaries of Sir Henry Channon*, pp. 82–3

82. Wallis Simpson to Lady Oxford, 18 February [1936], Margot Asquith Papers, MS Eng d 3276

83. Entry for 25 November 1936, in Geoffrey Dawson, 'Diary relating to the abdication of Edward VIII, September–December 1936, typescript, with a related letter from Robin Barrington-Ward to Cecilia Dawson, 28 May 1946', n.d., but produced shortly after the event [hereafter referred to as 'Abdication Diary'], Dawson Papers, MS Dawson 55

84. Entry for 31 January 1936, *The Diaries of Sir Robert Bruce Lockhart*, p. 346

85. Lord Birkenhead, *Walter Monckton*, pp. 125–6

86. Edward, Prince of Wales, to Mrs Freda Dudley Ward, 14 July 1918, *Letters from a Prince*, p. 70

87. Edward, Prince of Wales, to Mrs Freda Dudley Ward, 7 and 9 June 1919, *Letters from a Prince*, pp. 183–5

88. Edward, Prince of Wales, to Mrs Freda Dudley Ward, 22 May 1920, *Letters from a Prince*, p. 373

89. Edward, Prince of Wales, to Mrs Freda Dudley Ward, 24 May 1920, *Letters from a Prince*, pp. 378–81

90. Sophia Watson, *Marina*, p. 88

91. Steven Runciman to the Duchess of Kent, quoted in Sophia Watson, *Marina*, p. 87

92. *The Diaries of Sir Robert Bruce Lockhart*, p. 215

93. Sophia Watson, *Marina*, pp. 88–9

94. Entry for 10 December 1936, *The Diaries of Sir Robert Bruce Lockhart*, p. 361

95. Diary entry, 27 November 1936, *The Diary of Virginia Woolf*, pp. 37–8

96. Geoffrey Dawson, private diary, 2 November 1936, MS Dawson 40

97. Quoted in Celia Lee, *Jean, Lady Hamilton*, p. 254

98. Dugdale diary, 1937, p. 4, Nancy Dugdale Papers

99. Duchess of Windsor, *The Heart Has Its Reasons*, pp. 143–4

100. Quoted in James Crathorne, *Cliveden*, p. 169

101. Nigel Nicolson (ed.), *Harold Nicolson*, pp. 261–2

102. Quoted in James Crathorne, *Cliveden*, p. 140

103. Duke of Windsor, *A King's Story*, pp. 257–8

104. 'Reports of interviews with stewards employed on the S. Y. *Rosaura* and with the Captain and stewards employed on the S. Y. *Nahlin*', for the King's Proctor, n.d. [first quarter of 1937], PRO, TS 22/1/2

105. Quoted in Philip Ziegler, *Diana Cooper*, pp. 177–8
106. Quoted in Philip Ziegler, *King Edward VIII*, p. 285
107. An Austrian living in London to King Edward VIII's Private Secretary, 6 December [1936], RA, PS/GVI/ABD, Boxes 1–6
108. Oliver Warner, *Admiral of the Fleet*, p. 64
109. Quoted in Ross McKibbin, *Classes and Cultures*, pp. 26–7
110. *Ibid.*
111. Sybil Colefax to Thornton Wilder, n.d., quoted in Kirsty McLeod, *A Passion for Friendship*, p. 145
112. Mark Amory, *Lord Berners*, p. 160
113. Entry for 31 January 1936, *The Diaries of Sir Robert Bruce Lockhart*, p. 346
114. Introduction by John Pearson to Osbert Sitwell, *Rat Week*, pp. 10–11
115. Brian Masters, *Great Hostesses*, p. 106
116. *Ibid.*, pp. 100–101
117. Diary entry for 6 July 1936, quoted in Celia Lee, *Jean, Lady Hamilton*, p. 259
118. Diary entry for 20 January 1936, *Ibid.*, p. 258
119. *Chips: The Diaries of Sir Henry Channon*, pp. 80–81
120. Wallis Simpson to Mrs Merryman, 15 June 1935, in Michael Bloch (ed.), *Wallis & Edward Letters*, p. 125
121. Wallis Simpson to Mrs Merryman, 16 July 1935, *Ibid.*, p. 127
122. Wallis Simpson to Mrs Merryman, 8 June 1935, *Ibid.*, p. 121
123. Wallis Simpson to Mrs Merryman, 18 November 1935, *Ibid.*, p. 143
124. Wallis Simpson to Mrs Merryman, 8 June 1935, *Ibid.*, p. 121

3

'The Spirit of the Age'

1. *The King Visits South Wales*, Pathe Gazette newsreel, November 1936
2. Luke McKernan, *Topical Budget*, p. 119
3. Notebook of John Simon, n.d., John Simon Papers, MS Simon 9
4. Charles Chaplin, *My Autobiography*, p. 357
5. Emmeline Davy to King Edward VIII, 12 December 1936, RA, PS/GVI/ABD, Box 8
6. M. B. Taylor to King Edward VIII, n.d. [December 1936], RA, PS/GVI/ABD, Box 4
7. 'A mother' to King Edward VIII, 10 December 1936, RA, PS/GVI/ABD, Box 8

8. Telegram to King Edward VIII, 11 December 1936, RA, PS/GVI/ABD, Box 10

9. Philip Ziegler, *King Edward VIII*, pp. 112-13

10. J. Evans to King Edward VIII, 8 December 1936, RA, PS/GVI/ABD, Box 1

11. Ernest Emanuel Harman to King Edward VIII, 6 December 1936, RA, PS/GVI/ABD, Box 3

12. Louis T. Harlan to King Edward VIII, 1 December 1936, RA, PS/GVI/ABD, Box 5

13. Robert W. Bingham to Roosevelt, 23 April 1934, in Edgar B. Nixon (ed.), *Franklin D. Roosevelt and Foreign Affairs*, p. 79

14. Samuel Hopkins Adams, *Alexander Woollcott*, p. 307

15. John Grigg, 'Edward VIH', p. 344

16. Kenneth Edwards in the *Saturday Review*, quoted in Compton Mackenzie, *The Windsor Tapestry*, p. 447

17. Viscount Templewood, *Nine Troubled Years*, pp. 218-9

18. *Ibid.*

19. Miss G. H. Howarth to King Edward VIII, n.d. [December 1936], RA, PS/GVI/ABD, Box 8

20. Diana Mosley, *The Duchess of Windsor*, pp. 38-9, 70-73

21. Prince Albert to Prince Edward, 16 May 1920, quoted from the Royal Archives by Philip Ziegler, *King Edward VIII*, p. 99

22. The President of Magdalen College, *The Times*, 18 November 1914

23. Duke of Windsor, *A King's Story*, p. 415

24. Philip Ziegler, *King Edward VIII*, pp. 58, 76

25. Quoted in *Ibid.*, pp. 60-61

26. *Ibid.*, pp. 66-7

27. Quoted in *Ibid.*, p. 75

28. *Ibid.*, p. 67

29. Quoted in *Ibid.*, p. 58

30. A. Clayton to King Edward VIII, n.d. [December 1936], RA, PS/GVI/ABD, Box 6

31. *The Memoirs of Aga Khan*, p. 245

32. J. Graham Jones, 'Lloyd George and the abdication of Edward VIII', p. 91

33. Walter B. Beals, Judge at the Supreme Court, State of Washington, Olympia, to Colonel Wedgwood, 13 September 1937, Dep Monckton Trustees 15, fol. 268

34. Duke of Windsor, *A King's Story*, p. 280

35. Edward, Prince of Wales to Freda Dudley Ward, 22 December 1918, *Letters from a Prince*, p. 147

36. Harold Macmillan, *Winds of Change*, p. 100

37. Geordie Greig, *Louis and the Prince*, pp. 87–90

38. Philip Ziegler, *King Edward VIII*, p. 64

39. Quoted in Sarah Bradford, *King George VI*, p. 61

40. Sir Almeric Fitzroy, *Memoirs*, Vol. II, pp. 802–3

41. *The Prince of Wales in North Wales*, Pathe Gazette newsreel, n.d.

42. William Coates to King Edward VIII, 11 December 1936, RA, PS/GVI/ABD, Box 9

43. F. J. Corbitt, *Fit For a King*, pp. 202–4

44. John W. Wheeler-Bennett, *King George VI*, pp. 160–61

45. Margaret Brasnett, *Voluntary Social Action*, p. 76

46. *South Wales Argus*, 19 November 1936

47. *Ibid.*

48. *Hansard*, 20 November 1934

49. Letter from Portsmouth to King Edward VIII, 5 December 1936, RA, PS/GVI/ABD, Boxes 1–6

50. Quoted in Dave Colledge, *Labour Camps*, p. 19

51. *South Wales Argus*, 19 November 1936

52. *Western Mail & South Wales News*, 20 November 1936

53. *South Wales Argus*, 19 November 1936

54. John Rowland to Kingsley Wood, 20 November, PRO, MH 58/309

55. W. F. Deedes, *Dear Bill*, p. 40

56. *Daily Mirror*, 28 November 1936

57. *Daily Mail*, 23 November 1936

58. *Ibid.*

59. *New Statesman and Nation*, 5 December 1936, p. 880

60. Quoted in Compton Mackenzie, *The Windsor Tapestry*, p. 453

61. E. E. Chapman and H. Lavers to King Edward VIII, 7 December 1936, RA, PS/GVI/ABD, Box 1

62. Elsie M. Hayward to King Edward VIII, 5 December 1936, RA, PS/GVI/ABD, Box 3

63. 'Foreign Comment', *Literary Digest*, 28 November 1936

64. Diary of Ramsay MacDonald, 21 November 1936, PRO, PRO 30/69, 1753

65. Quoted in Philip Guedalla, *The Hundredth Year*, p. 276

66. Ross McKibbin, *Classes and Cultures*, p. 3

67. Lord Beaverbrook, *The Abdication of King Edward VIII*, p. 97

68. Entry for 23 November 1936, Geoffrey Dawson, Abdication Diary, Dawson Papers, MS Dawson 55

69. *The Times*, 24 November 1936

70. Duke of Windsor, *A King's Story*, p. 338

71. *Ibid.*

72. Interview with Mr John Lawrence of Penarth, 1986, in *The Experience of the Depression in Wales*, p. 42(b)

73. A 'wife and mother' to the *Daily Mirror*, 5 December 1936

74. *Western Mail & South Wales News*, 20 November 1936

75. According to J. C. C. Davidson: see Robert Rhodes James, *Memoirs of a Conservative*, p. 410

76. Clement Attlee, *As It Happened*, p. 85

77. H. Montgomery Hyde, *Neville Chamberlain*, pp. 83–4

78. Entry for 12 November 1936, Geoffrey Dawson, Abdication Diary, Dawson Papers, MS Dawson 55

79. Ellen Wilkinson, *Peeps at Politicians*, p. 99

80. Harold Macmillan, *Winds of Change*, pp. 92, 101

81. Mrs F. Howe & family to King Edward VIII, 5 December 1936, RA, PS/GVI/ABD, Box 3

82. Anonymous to King Edward VIII, 6 December [1936], RA, PS/GVI/ABD, Boxes 1–6

83. Yvonne Arthur to King Edward VIII, 6 December 1936, RA, PS/GVI/ABD, Box 1

84. Vera Brittain, *Testament of Experience*, p. 162

85. C. H. Rolph, *Kingsley*, p. 252

86. Walter Welsh to King Edward VIII, 3 December 1936, RA, PS/GVI/ABD, Box 4

87. K. (Mrs Philip) Hendy to King Edward VIII, 7 December 1936, RA, PS/GVI/ABD, Box 1

88. Mrs Greta Tench to King Edward VIII, 3 December 1936, RA, PS/GVI/ABD, Box 4

89. *Daily Mirror*, 28 November 1936

90. *Western Mail & South Wales News*, 20 November, 1936

91. A. Blacklock to F. N. Tribe, 27 November [1936], PRO, LAB 23/146

92. F. N. Tribe to T. S. Chegwidden, 2 December 1936, PRO, LAB 23/146

93. Geoffrey Dawson, Private diary, 1 December 1936, MS Dawson 40

94. F. N. Tribe to A. Blacklock, 30 November 1936, PRO, LAB 23/146

95. John Grigg, 'Edward VIII', p. 337

96. *Jarrow Crusade*, British Movietone newsreel, 8 October 1936

97. *Jarrow Marchers*, British Movietone newsreel, 2 November 1936

98. Quoted in W. F. Deedes, *Dear Bill*, pp. 39–40

4

'King to marry Wally'

1. Diary entry, 4 December 1936, *Parliament and Politics . . . The Headlam Diaries*, pp. 100–101

2. Diary of Duff Cooper, January 1936, published in *The Times*, T2, 4 February 2003

3. Ramsay MacDonald diary, 13 February 1936, PRO, PRO 30/69, 1753

4. Diary entry, 18 November 1936, *Parliament and Politics . . . The Headlam Diaries*, p. 98

5. *This Week*, 11 November 1936

6. 'Notes by Sir Horace Wilson, at 10 Downing Street', n.d. [late December 1936 or early 1937], CAB 127/157

7. Quoted in Philip Ziegler, *Edward VIII*, p. 258

8. Quoted in J. G. Lockhart, *Cosmo Gordon Lang*, p. 395

9. Oliver Warner, *Admiral of the Fleet*, p. 60

10. *Ibid.*

11. Diary entry for 2 March 1936, Hilda Runciman Papers, WR Add 10, 21 May 1935 to 20 March 1936

12. Christopher Hibbert, *Edward: The Uncrowned King*, p. 16

13. Piers Brendon and Philip Whitehead, *The Windsors*, pp. 78–9

14. Dina Wells Hood, *Working for the Windsors*, p. 14

15. [Prince] Albert to Londonderry, 18 November 1920, PRONI, D3099/3/13/3

16. F. J. Corbitt, *Fit For a King*, p. 199

17. *Ibid.*, p. 204

18. *Ibid.*, p. 206

19. *South Wales Argus*, 19 November 1936

20. Duke of Windsor, *A Family Album*, pp. 8, 60

21. Alexander Hardinge to Helen Cecil, 23 August 1922, Hardinge Papers, U2117, C1/161

22. Philip Ziegler, *King Edward VIII*, p. 242

23. Helen Hardinge, *Loyal to Three Kings*, p. 59

24. Quoted from his notes in J. G. Lockhart, *Cosmo Gordon Lang*, p. 392

25. John Gunther, *Inside Europe*, p. 250

26. William Abbs, Principal of the Abbs School of Sight Training, to King Edward VIII, 6 December [1936], RA, PS/GVI/ABD, Box 3

27. *South Wales Argus*, 19 November, 1936

28. Compton Mackenzie, *The Windsor Tapestry*, p. 207

29. Diana Mosley, *The Duchess of Windsor*, p. 74

30. Stanley Jackson, *The Sassoons*, p. 194

31. Helen Hardinge, *Loyal to Three Kings*, p. 116

32. *Ibid.*, p. 117

33. 'Notes by Sir Horace Wilson, at 10 Downing Street', n.d. [late December 1936 or early 1937], CAB 127/157

34. Notebook by John Simon, n.d., John Simon Papers, MS 9

35. H. Montgomery Hyde, *Norman Birkett*, p. 455

36. Lord Hardinge of Penshurst, 'Before the Abdication', *The Times*, 29 November 1955

37. *News Review*, 5 November 1936

38. Oliver Warner, *Admiral of the Fleet*, pp. 62-3

39. Duke of Windsor, *A King's Story*, p. 317

40. *Ibid.*, pp. 317-8

41. Prefatory section in Geoffrey Dawson, Abdication Diary, Dawson Papers, MS Dawson 55

42. Helen Hardinge, *Loyal to Three Kings*, p. 116

43. *Ibid.*, p. 124

44. J. G. Lockhart, *Cosmo Gordon Lang*, p. 395

45. *Ibid.*, pp. 398-9

46. *Ibid.*, p. 398

47. John Grigg, 'Edward VIII', p. 340

48. F. Crowsley to King Edward VIII, 3 December 1936, RA, PS/GVI/ABD, Box 4

49. Miss Denham Young to G. S. Edlin, 3 December 1936 [attached to letter to King Edward VIII from Edlin, 4 December 1936], RA, PS/GVI/ABD, Box 4

50. B. Abbott to King Edward VIII, 4 December 1936, RA, PS/GVI/ABD, Box 3

51. Oswald Gregson to King Edward VIII, 5 December 1936, RA, PS/GVI/ABD, Box 3

52. E. B. Walker to King Edward, n.d. [December 1936], RA, PS/GVI/ABD, Box 3

53. Diary entry for 11 November 1936, Hilda Runciman Papers, WR Add 10, 21 March 1936 to 26 January 1937

54. Michael Thornton, *Royal Feud*, pp. 44-7

55. Edward, Prince of Wales to Freda Dudley Ward, 19 February 1919, *Letters from a Prince*, p. 173

56. *Ibid.*

57. Edward, Prince of Wales to Wallis Simpson, 1 January 1936, in Michael Bloch (ed.) *Wallis & Edward Letters*, p. 145

58. Wallis Simpson to Edward, Prince of Wales, n.d. [early February 1936], in Michael Bloch (ed.), *Wallis & Edward Letters*, p. 156

59. Ralph G. Martin, *The Woman He Loved*, p. 12

60. Helen Hardinge, *Loyal to Three Kings*, p. 142

61. Quoted in J. Bryan III and Charles J. V. Murphy, *The Windsor Story*, p. 144

62. 'Note of interview with Mr Simpson', by the King's Proctor, 24 February 1937, PRO, TS 22/1/2

63. Quoted in Martin Gilbert, *Winston S. Churchill*, p. 810

64. Quoted in Christopher Warwick, *George and Marina*, p. 55

65. Duke of Windsor, *A King's Story*, p. 82

66. Quoted in Celia Lee, *Jean, Lady Hamilton*, p. 305

67. Quoted in Christopher Warwick, *George and Marina*, p. 75

68. Quoted in Celia Lee, *Jean, Lady Hamilton*, p. 305

69. Penelope Mortimer, *Queen Elizabeth*, p. 112

70. Wallis Simpson to Edward, Prince of Wales, Tuesday [spring 1935], in Michael Bloch (ed.), *Wallis & Edward Letters*, pp. 118–19

71. Edward, Prince of Wales to Wallis Simpson, n.d. [autumn 1935], *Ibid.*, p. 139

72. Duchess of Windsor, *The Heart Has Its Reasons*, p. 223

73. Wallis Simpson to Mrs Merryman, 11 May 1936, in Michael Bloch (ed.), *Wallis & Edward Letters*, p. 177

74. Wallis Simpson to Mrs Merryman, 1 January 1936, *Ibid.*, p. 170

75. 'Report of interviews with late servants of Mrs Simpson', for the King's Proctor, n.d. [first quarter of 1937], PRO, TS 22/1/2

76. Wallis Simpson to Mrs Merryman, 4 May 1936, in Michael Bloch (ed.), *Wallis & Edward Letters*, p. 176

77. Edward VIII to Wallis Simpson, n.d. [16 September 1936], *Ibid.*, pp. 193–4

78. 'Report of enquiries at Felixstowe', for the King's Proctor, n.d. [early 1937], PRO, TS 22/1/2

79. Wallis Simpson to Edward VIII, n.d. [14 October 1936], in Michael Bloch (ed.), *Wallis & Edward Letters*, p. 200

80. Edward VIII to Wallis Simpson, n.d. [24 October 1936], *Ibid.*, p. 203

81. 'Report of enquiries at Felixstowe', for the King's Proctor, n.d. [early 1937], PRO, TS 22/1/2

82. H. Montgomery Hyde, *Norman Birkett*, p. 454

83. Quoted in W. F. Deedes, *Dear Bill*, p. 42

84. Lord Beaverbrook, *The Abdication of King Edward VIII*, pp. 30–33

85. Entry for 29 October 1936, *The Diaries of Sir Robert Bruce Lockhart*, pp. 356–7

86. *Chips: The Diaries of Sir Henry Channon*, pp. 80–81

87. Entry for 7 November 1936, *Ibid.*, p. 76
88. Greg King, *The Duchess of Windsor*, pp. 197–8
89. Quoted in Helen Hardinge, *Loyal to Three Kings*, p. 149
90. Wallis Simpson to Lady Londonderry, 7 November 1936, PRONI, D3099/3/2/604B/5
91. Michael Thornton, *Royal Feud*, pp. 112–14
92. Diary entry for 7 November 1936, *Chips: The Diaries of Sir Henry Channon*, p. 77
93. Diary entry for 7 July 1936, *Ibid.*, p. 69

5

'I had declared myself'

1. Hardinge's letter is reproduced in full in Helen Hardinge, *Loyal to Three Kings*, p. 133
2. The letter from Britannicus is dated 15 October 1936 and signed 'G W Johnson of East Orange, New Jersey'. The full nine pages of the letter (or a copy thereof) are held in the Dawson Papers, MS Dawson 79
3. Diary entry 26 October, Geoffrey Dawson, Abdication Diary, Dawson Papers, MS Dawson 55
4. Helen Hardinge, *Loyal to Three Kings*, p. 120
5. Philip Ziegler, *King Edward VIII*, p. 296
6. From Wisconsin to King Edward VIII, 3 December 1936, RA, PS/GVI/ABD, Boxes 1–6
7. From Pennsylvania to King Edward VIII, 2 December 1936, RA, PS/GVI/ABD, Boxes 1–6
8. From New York to King Edward VIII, 2 December 1936, RA, PS/GVI/ABD, Boxes 1–6
9. P. V. Burkman to King Edward VIII, 1 December 1936, RA, PS/GVI/ABD, Box 5
10. Quoted in Helen Hardinge, *Loyal to Three Kings*, p. 133
11. Violet Milner, diary entry for 1 August 1950, Violet Milner Papers, VM 5
12. James Coole, 'The Private Secretary', in Lord Altrincham and others, *Is the Monarchy Perfect?*, p. 14
13. Lord Hardinge of Penshurst, 'Before the abdication', *The Times*, 29 November 1955
14. *Ibid.*
15. Warren Fisher to Neville Chamberlain, 7 November 1936, PRO, PREM 1/463

16. Enclosure I, 'Mr Baldwin with his humble duty to Your Majesty', with Warren Fisher to Neville Chamberlain, 7 November 1936, PRO, PREM 1/463

17. Enclosure II, 'When Your Majesty was pleased to receive me on October 20th', with Warren Fisher to Neville Chamberlain, 7 November 1936, PRO, PREM 1/463

18. Enclosure III, 'Secret. Copy of Memorandum by Parliamentary Counsel', 5 November 1936, with Warren Fisher to Neville Chamberlain, 7 November 1936, PRO, PREM 1/463

19. Lord Hardinge of Penshurst, 'Before the abdication', The Times, 29 November 1955

20. 'Notes by Sir Horace Wilson, at 10 Downing Street', n.d. [late December 1936 or early 1937], CAB 127/157

21. Warren Fisher to Neville Chamberlain, 7 November 1936, PRO, PREM 1/463

22. Duchess of Windsor, The Heart Has Its Reasons, pp. 243–5

23. Ibid., pp. 246–7

24. Margaret Case Harriman, 'The King and the girl from Baltimore', p. 378

25. Oliver Warner, Admiral of the Fleet, pp. 62–3

26. Helen Hardinge, Loyal to Three Kings, p. 133

27. Lord Birkenhead, Walter Monckton, p. 125

28. Report by A. Canning, 25 March 1935, PRO, MEPO 10/35

29. Report by A. Canning, 'Ernest Simpson', n.d. [1935], PRO, MEPO 10/35

30. 'Note of interview with Mr Simpson', by the King's Proctor, 24 February 1937, PRO, TS 22/1/2

31. Report by A. Canning, 'Ernest Simpson', n.d. [1935], PRO, MEPO 10/35

32. Ibid.

33. Report by A. Canning, 25 June 1935, PRO, MEPO 10/35

34. Report by A. Canning, 3 July 1935, PRO, MEPO 10/35

35. 'Report of interviews with late servants of Mrs Simpson', for the King's Proctor, n.d. [first quarter of 1937], PRO, TS 22/1/2

36. Report by A. Canning, 30 June 1936, PRO, MEPO 10/35

37. Manuscript note, 1 July 1937, added to Report by A. Canning, 30 June 1936, PRO, MEPO 10/35

38. Report by A. Canning, 23 October 1936, PRO, MEPO 10/35

39. 'Particulars of press extracts in which the name of Mrs Simpson appears from 6th June to 24th October, 1936', Report by A. Canning, n.d. [26 October 1936], PRO, MEPO 10/35

40. Duke of York to Queen Mary, 4 October 1922, quoted from the Royal Archives by Philip Ziegler, *King Edward VIII*, p. 171

41. Alec Hardinge to Helen Hardinge, 10 July 1923 , Hardinge Papers, U2117, C 1/189

42. Alec Hardinge to Helen Hardinge, 24 January 1925, Hardinge Papers, U2117, C 1/245

43. J. G. Lockhart, *Cosmo Gordon Lang*, p. 397

44. Greg King, *The Duchess of Windsor*, p. 171

45. Helen Hardinge, *Loyal to Three Kings*, p. 137

46. Quoted in Cecil Edwards, *Bruce of Melbourne*, p. 252

47. *Ibid.*, p. 253

48. Violet Milner, diary entry for 2 December 1936, Violet Milner Papers, VM 5

49. Helen Hardinge, *Loyal to Three Kings*, p. 137

50. Lord Beaverbrook, *The Abdication of King Edward VIII*, pp. 36–8

51. *Ibid.*, p. 46

52. Cabinet minutes, 27 November 1936, PRO, CAB 23/86 Vol. LIII, 69(36)

53. Duke of Windsor, *A King's Story*, p. 331

54. Enclosure III, 'Secret. Copy of Memorandum by Parliamentary Counsel', 5 November 1936, with Warren Fisher to Neville Chamberlain, 7 November 1936, PRO, PREM 1/463

55. The Duke of Windsor, *A King's Story*, p. 332

56. Ramsay MacDonald diary, 16 November 1936, PRO, PRO 30/69, 1753

57. Helen Hardinge, *Loyal to Three Kings*, p. 139

58. Violet Milner, diary entry for 19 November 1936, Violet Milner Papers, VM 5

59. Diary entry, 18 November 1936, *Parliament and Politics . . . The Headlam Diaries*, pp. 98–9

60. Lucy Baldwin diary entry, 16 November 1936, Lucy Baldwin Papers

61. Lucy Baldwin to Edith Londonderry, 23 November 1936, PRONI, D3099/3/15/8

62. Linlithgow to Dawson, 17 November 1936, Dawson Papers, MS Dawson 79, fol. 14

63. Duke of Windsor, *A King's Story*, p. 334

64. *Ibid.*, p. 335

65. *Hansard*, 16 November 1936

66. Quoted in Thomas H. Eliot, *Recollections of the New Deal*, p. 91

67. Alpheus Geer to King Edward VIII, 25 November 1936, RA, PS/GVI/ABD, Box 4

68. Quoted in Winston Churchill, *The Second World War*, Vol. 1, p. 170

69. Winston Churchill, *The Second World War*, Vol. 1, pp. 170–71
70. Leo Amery, diary entry for 12 November 1936, *The Empire at Bay*, p. 430
71. Leader, *Daily Mail*, 23 November 1936
72. Janet Flanner, *An American in Paris*, pp. 11–12
73. Bernard Shaw to Beatrice Webb, 4 September 1936, in Dan H. Laurence (ed.), *Bernard Shaw*, pp. 441–2
74. John Buchan to Edith Londonderry, 18 September 1936, PRONI, D3099/3/16/55
75. Duke of Windsor, *A King's Story*, p. 277
76. Quoted in Philip Ziegler, *King Edward VIII*, p. 272
77. Duke of Windsor, *A King's Story*, p. 336

6

'The Battle for the Throne'

1. Quoted in Philip Ziegler, *King Edward VIII*, p. 302
2. Quoted in Samuel Hopkins Adams, *Alexander Woollcott*, p. 272
3. Duchess of Windsor, *The Heart Has Its Reasons*, p. 249
4. Winston Churchill to Clementine Churchill, 27 November 1936, in Mary Soames (ed.), *Speaking for Themselves*, pp. 418–19
5. Entry for 23 November 1936, Geoffrey Dawson, Abdication Diary, Dawson Papers, MS Dawson 55
6. A. J. P. Taylor, *Beaverbrook*, p. 10
7. Enclosure III, 'Secret. Copy of Memorandum by Parliamentary Counsel', 5 November 1936, with Warren Fisher to Neville Chamberlain, 7 November 1936, PRO, PREM 1/463
8. Clement Attlee, *As It Happened*, p. 86
9. Robin Birkenhead, *Churchill 1924–1940*, p. 75
10. Zetland to Linlithgow, 27 November 1936, Linlithgow Papers, MSS Eur/F/125.139
11. David Cannadine, *In Churchill's Shadow*, p. 66
12. Nancy Dugdale diary, p. 16, Nancy Dugdale Papers
13. Entry for 24 November 1936, Geoffrey Dawson, Abdication Diary. Dawson Papers, MS Dawson 55
14. Alexander Hardinge to Stanley Baldwin, 22 November 1936, PRO, PREM 1/448
15. Thomas Jones, *A Diary with Letters*, p. 288
16. For example, Sir Maurice George to Sir John Simon, 24 November 1936, PRO, CAB 21/4100/2

17. James Pope-Hennessy, *Queen Mary*, p. 577
18. Quoted in John W. Wheeler-Bennett, *King George VI*, p. 283
19. Hilda Runciman diary, 2 March 1936, Hilda Runciman Papers, WR Add 10, 21 May 1935 to 20 March 1936
20. Duke of Windsor, *The Crown and the People*, p. 42
21. Duke of Windsor, *A King's Story*, p. 258
22. Helen Hardinge to Alec Hardinge, 27 June 1922, Hardinge Papers, U2117, C 2/188
23. Kirsty McLeod, *Battle Royal*, p. 23
24. Helen Hardinge, *Loyal to Three Kings*, p. 41
25. George V to Prince Albert, 26 April 1923, quoted from the Royal Archives by Philip Ziegler, *King Edward VIII*, p. 171
26. Duff Cooper, *Old Men Forget*, p. 201
27. *Ibid.*
28. The Duke of Windsor, *A King's Story*, p. 343
29. *Ibid.*
30. Diary entry for 28 November 1936, *Chips: The Diaries of Sir Henry Channon*, p. 86
31. Nicholas Mansergh, *Survey of British Commonwealth Affairs*, p. 41
32. Duke of Windsor, *A King's Story*, p. 345
33. Lord Beaverbrook, *The Abdication of King Edward VIII*, p. 56
34. *Hansard*, 26 November 1936; emphasis added
35. *Ibid.*
36. David Kirkwood, *My Life of Revolt*, pp. 259–60
37. *New Statesman and Nation*, 5 December 1936, p. 885
38. John Rowland, Welsh Board of Health, to Sir Kingsley Wood, 21 October 1936, PRO, MH 58/309; emphasis added
39. *Seaham Weekly News*, 20 November 1936
40. Quoted in Philip Ziegler, *Edward VIII*, p. 215
41. BBC Broadcast, 6 May 1926, quoted in G. M. Young, *Stanley Baldwin*, p. 117
42. Stella Margetson, *The Long Party*, pp. 51–2
43. Wal Hannington, *Never on Our Knees*, p. 258
44. *Ibid.*, p. 263
45. Diary entry for 10 November 1936, *Chips: The Diaries of Sir Henry Channon*, p. 78
46. Editorial, *Daily Telegraph*, 29 October 1936
47. John A. Owen and Carolyn Jacob, *The Unconquerable Spirit*, p. 21
48. Lord Wigram to Linlithgow, 5 June 1936, Linlithgow Papers, MSS Eur/ F/125.1

49. Compton Mackenzie, *The Windsor Tapestry*, p. 203
50. M. Watcyn-Williams, 'Communism in South Wales', *Spectator*, 18 September 1936, pp. 451–2
51. Idris Cox, *The People Can Save South Wales!*, p. 5; emphasis added
52. *South Wales Slave Act Special*, January 1935, front page, Merthyr Tydfil documents; capitals in original
53. Martin S. Gilbert, *Winston S. Churchill*, Vol. 5, p. 813
54. Cabinet minutes, 27 November 1936, PRO, CAB 23/86 Vol. LIII, 69(36)
55. Duke of Windsor, *A King's Story*, p. 346
56. Telegram 'from Prime Minister [of Britain] for Prime Minister [of the Dominions]', 28 November 1936, PRO, DO 121/32
57. 'The abdication of His Majesty King Edward VIII, Correspondence with the Dominions, Part 1', PRO, DO 114/81
58. Duke of Windsor, *A King's Story*, p. 347
59. Telegram 'from Prime Minister [of Britain] for Prime Minister [of the Dominions]', 28 November 1936, PRO, DO 121/32
60. Entry for 29 November 1936, Geoffrey Dawson, Abdication Diary, Dawson Papers, MS Dawson 55
61. *Ibid.*
62. Oliver Warner, *Admiral of the Fleet*, p. 69
63. Quoted from *Time* magazine in the *Daily Mirror*, 5 December 1936
64. Duchess of Windsor, *The Heart Has Its Reasons*, p. 251
65. Quoted in Philip Ziegler, *King Edward VIII*, pp. 276–7
66. Wallis Simpson to Sibyl Colefax, n.d. [30 November 1936], Sibyl Colefax Papers, MS Eng c 3272, fols 11–12
67. Wallis Simpson to 'Foxy' Gwynne, n.d. [30 November 1936], in Michael Bloch (ed.), *Wallis & Edward Letters*, pp. 213–14
68. Duchess of Windsor, *The Heart Has Its Reasons*, p. 252
69. Report of meeting of Ministers, 2 December 1936, PRO, CAB 127/156
70. 'Notes by Sir Horace Wilson, at 10 Downing Street', n.d. [late December 1936 or early 1937], CAB 127/157
71. Cabinet minutes, 2 December 1936, PRO, CAB 23/86 Vol. LIII, 69(36)
72. Ramsay MacDonald, diary entry for 2 December 1936, Ramsay MacDonald Papers, PRO, PRO 30/69, 1753
73. Statement by Lord Baldwin in 1947 to J. G. Lockhart, quoted in *Cosmo Gordon Lang*, p. 404
74. Telegram 'for Prime Minister [of Britain] from Prime Minister [of New Zealand]', 2 December 1936, PRO, DO 121/35
75. Governor-General of New Zealand to the Dominions Office, 2 December 1936, PRO, CAB 21/4100/2

76. Telegram 'from Prime Minister [of Canada] to Prime Minister [of Britain]', 30 November 1936, PRO, DO 121/33

77. Sir Francis Floud to Dominions Office, 1 December 1936, PRO, CAB 21/4100/2

78. Record of an interview between Mr de Valera and Sir Harry Batterbee at Dublin, 29 November 1936, PRO, CAB 127/156

79. *Ibid.*

80. Duke of Windsor, *A King's Story*, pp. 354–5

7

'The People want their King'

1. Frank Owen and R. J. Thompson, *His Was the Kingdom*, pp. 49–50

2. 'The coronation service. A bishop's reply to Dr Barnes', *The Times*, 2 December 1936

3. Frank Owen and R. J. Thompson, *His Was the Kingdom*, p. 50

4. Diary of David Strain, 1 December 1936, PRONI, D2585/3/16

5. Lydia Bruce Siebenhaar to 'Sir', 2 December 1936, RA, PS/GVI/ABD, Box 4

6. James Wilson to King Edward VIII, 3 December [1936], RA, PS/GVI/ABD, Box 4

7. Charles Nelson Stewart to the Bishop of Bradford, 3 December 1936, RA, PS/GVI/ABD, Box 4

8. W. F. Deedes, *Dear Bill*, pp. 41–2

9. Malcolm Muggeridge, *The Thirties*, p. 283

10. Diary entry, 2 December 1936, *Parliament and Politics . . . The Headlam Diaries*, p. 100

11. Diary entry, 7 December 1936, *The Diary of Virginia Woolf*, pp. 39–40

12. Diary of Violet Milner, 3 December 1936, Violet Milner Papers, VM 5

13. Marie C. Stopes to King Edward VIII, 3 December 1936, RA, PS/GVI/ABD, Box 3

14. British Science Service, Fleet Street, to King Edward VIII, RA, PS/GVI/ABD, Box 5

15. Lord Beaverbrook, *The Abdication of King Edward VIII*, p. 78

16. Frank Owen and R. J. Thompson, *His Was the Kingdom*, p. 61

17. Diary entry, 7 December 1936, *The Diary of Virginia Woolf*, p. 39

18. Diary of Florence Turtle, 8 July 1936

19. *Evening Standard*, 3 December 1936

20. *The Constitutional Crisis*, Universal Talking News newsreel, December 1936

21. Diary of Nancy Dugdale, p. 5, Nancy Dugdale Papers

22. Cosmo Lang to Geoffrey Dawson, 3 December 1936, Dawson Papers, MS Dawson 79, fol. 25

23. Francis Williams, *Nothing So Strange*, p. 141

24. Quoted in Kingsley Martin, *The Magic of Monarchy*, p. 66

25. *Evening News*, 3 December 1936

26. *Star*, 3 December 1936

27. *News Chronicle*, 3 December 1936

28. Diary of Violet Milner, 3 December 1936, Violet Milner Papers, VM 5

29. Lord Beaverbrook, *The Abdication of King Edward VIII*, p. 72

30. Entry for 4 December 1936, *The Diaries of Sir Robert Bruce Lockhart*, p. 360

31. Sir Charles Petrie, *The Modern British Monarchy*, p. 176

32. F. J. Riley to King Edward VIII, 8 December 1936, RA, PS/GVI/ABD, Box 6

33. S. Underwood to King Edward VIII, n.d. [December 1936], RA, PS/GVI/ABD, Box 4

34. 'Memo from Lady Williams with regard to advisory leaflets', 1936, National Birthday Trust Fund Papers, F2/5/2(4)

35. Claude Davis to King Edward VIII, 6 December 1936, RA, PS/GVI/ABD, Boxes 1–6

36. Letter from London to King Edward VIII, 6 December 1936, RA, PS/GVI/ABD, Boxes 1–6

37. Grace Walker to King Edward VIII, 3 December 1936, RA, PS/GVI/ABD, Box 4

38. Miss M. Naylor to King Edward VIII, 3 October 1936 [but most likely 3 December 1936], RA, PS/GVI/ABD, Box 4

39. Eve Horne to King Edward VIII, 4 December 1936, RA, PS/GVI/ABD, Box 4

40. Dougal Duncan to King Edward VIII, 7 December 1936, RA, PS/GVI/ABD, Box 6

41. Mrs E. Bartlett to King Edward VIII, n.d. [December 1936], RA, PS/GVI/ABD, Box 3

42. G. S. Edlin to King Edward VIII, 4 November 1936 [but most likely 4 December 1936], RA, PS/GVI/ABD, Box 4

43. Clara Rohnn to King Edward VIII, 4 December 1936, RA, PS/GVI/ABD, Box 4

44. Alan W. Elphick to King Edward VIII, 3 December 1936, RA, PS/GVI/ABD, Box 4

45. These letters are in RA, PS/GVI/ABD, Boxes 1–9

46. Telegram from Caledon Shipyard Workers to King Edward VIII, 4 December 1936, RA, PS/GVI/ABD, Box 10

47. John Watson to King Edward VIII, 9 December 1936, RA, PS/GVI/ABD, Box 6

48. David Dale to King Edward VIII, 4 December 1936, RA, PS/GVI/ABD, Box 3

49. E. H. to King Edward VIII, 7 December 1936, RA, PS/GVI/ABD, Box 4

50. Diary of Geoffrey H. Wells, 3 December 1936

51. Alan Turing to his mother, 3 December [1936], Alan Turing Papers, AMT/K/1/48

52. 'Opinion in the Dominions', *The Times*, 4 December 1936

53. From Newport, Virginia to King Edward VIII, n.d [December 1936], RA, PS/GVI/ABD Boxes 1–6

54. Frank B. Hubin to King Edward VIII, n.d. [December 1936], RA, PS/GVI/ABD, Box 7

55. Rudolph Durbar to King Edward VIII, 8 December 1936, RA, PS/GVI/ABD, Box 1

56. V. Hardie to Sir John Simon, 9 December 1936, PRO, HO 144/21070

57. Diary of John George Harmer, 3 December 1936, Acc. 6220/Box 9

58. Diary of Herbert M. Willmott, 3 December 1936

59. Diary of Florence Turtle, 3 December 1936

60. Diary of John George Harmer, 7 and 11 December 1936, F/Wlm/16

61. Entry for 4 December 1936, *The Diaries of Sir Robert Bruce Lockhart*, p. 360

62. *Ibid.*

63. Diary entry, 6 December 1936, *Parliament and Politics . . . The Headlam Diaries*, pp. 101–2

64. Prime Minister of Britain to the Prime Ministers of the Dominions, 3 December 1936, PRO, CAB 21/4100/2

65. *Ibid.*

66. Cabinet minutes for 6 December, PRO, CAB 23/86, Vol. LIII

67. Lady Rhondda to Stanley Baldwin, 31 December 1936, PRO, PREM 1/459

68. Cosmo Gordon Lang to Stanley Baldwin, 25 November 1936, PRO, PREM 1/448

69. Quoted in *A Diary of the Last Days of the Reign of King Edward VIII*, p. 4

70. O. B. Stokes, Editor-in-Chief, *Yorkshire Observer* and *Telegraph and Argus*, Bradford, in letter to Editor, *The Times*, 9 May 1956

71. Entry for 31 October 1936, Geoffrey Dawson, Abdication Diary, Dawson Papers, MS Dawson 55
72. John Evelyn Wrench, *Geoffrey Dawson and Our Times*, footnote 1, p. 344
73. Entry for 1 December 1936, Geoffrey Dawson, Abdication Diary, Dawson Papers, MS Dawson 55
74. *The Times*, 2 December 1936
75. Lord Beaverbrook, *The Abdication of King Edward VIII*, p. 100
76. *The Times*, 30 November 1936
77. John Gunther, *Inside Europe*, p. 253
78. *Ibid.*, p. 254
79. Lord Beaverbrook, *The Abdication of King Edward VIII*, p. 102
80. Entry for 2 December 1936, Geoffrey Dawson, Abdication Diary, Dawson Papers, MS Dawson 55; emphasis added
81. Lilian M. Shepherd to King Edward VIII, 6 December 1936, RA, PS/GVI/ABD, Box 3
82. H. Stanley Jevons to King Edward VIII, 6 December 1936, RA, PS/GVI/ABD, Box 3
83. Press cutting [December 1936], in Brownlow Papers, BNLW 4/4/9/7/6
84. Herman Rogers to Wallis Simpson, 28 October 1936, in Michael Bloch (ed.), *Wallis & Edward Letters*, p. 209
85. Duke of Windsor, *A King's Story*, p. 362
86. Notebook kept by Lord Brownlow, Brownlow Papers, BNLW 4/4/9/1
87. Duchess of Windsor, *The Heart Has Its Reasons*, p. 256
88. Notebook kept by Lord Brownlow, Brownlow Papers, BNLW 4/4/9/1
89. Duke of Windsor, *A King's Story*, p. 370
90. Diana Vreeland, *D. V.*, p. 73
91. Notebook kept by Lord Brownlow, Brownlow Papers, BNLW 4/4/9/1
92. Diana Vreeland, *D. V.*, p. 73
93. Diary of Violet Milner, 6 December 1936, Violet Milner Papers, VM 5

8

'Tell us the facts, Mr Baldwin!'

1. Duchess of Windsor, *The Heart Has Its Reasons*, p. 253
2. Wallis to Edward, n.d. [3 December 1936], in Michael Bloch (ed.), *Wallis & Edward Letters*, p. 215
3. Frank Owen and R. J. Thompson, *His Was the Kingdom*, p. 97
4. Mrs Cecilia Melville to King Edward VIII, 8 November 1936 [but most likely 8 *December* 1936], RA, PS/GVI/ABD, Box 6

5. J. C. W. Reith, 'Broadcast over Britain', 1924, quoted in Asa Briggs, *The BBC*, p. 107

6. Martin S. Gilbert, *Winston S. Churchill*, Vol. 5, pp. 813–14

7. Letter to King Edward VIII, 4 December 1936, RA, PS/GVI/ABD, Boxes 1–6

8. From Somerset to King Edward VIII, 6 December 1936, RA, PS/GVI/ABD, Boxes 1–6

9. A. Y. C. Powers to King Edward VIII, 7 December 1936, RA, PS/GVI/ABD, Box 6

10. Mrs Mary Bishop to King Edward VIII, 3 December 1936, RA, PS/GVI/ABD, Box 4

11. Alec Roylance to King Edward VIII, 3 December 1936, RA, PS/GVI/ABD, Box 4

12. Robert Hoppock to King Edward VIII, 7 December 1936, RA, PS/GVI/ABD, Box 8

13. Fairfax M. Gifford to King Edward VIII, 4 December 1936, RA, PS/GVI/ABD, Box 8

14. Duke of Windsor, *A King's Story*, p. 361

15. Report, unsigned and undated, PRO, PREM 1/466

16. Lord Beaverbrook, *The Abdication of King Edward VIII*, pp. 70–71

17. Telegram from Prime Minister of Britain to Prime Ministers of the Dominions, 4 December 1936, PRO, CAB 21/4100/2

18. Copy of the broadcast proposed by the King, PRO, CAB 21/4100/2, file 7

19. For the Cabinet's discussion of the issue, see the minutes for 4 December 1936, PRO, CAB 23/86 Vol. LIII

20. Quoted in Iain Macleod, *Neville Chamberlain*, p. 198

21. Stanley Baldwin to King Edward VIII, 4 December 1936, PRO, PREM 1/451

22. Cabinet minutes, 4 December 1936, PRO, CAB 23/86 Vol. LIII

23. Memorandum from 'GFD' to Sir Horace Wilson, 4 December 1936, PRO, CAB 21/4100/2

24. E. A. Hughes, *The Royal Naval College Dartmouth*, p. 74

25. A. J. P. Taylor, *English History 1914–1945*, p. 402

26. Rhoda Anderson to King Edward VIII, n.d. [December 1936], RA, PS/GVI/ABD, Box 2

27. Nancy Mitford to Evelyn Waugh, 22 December 1949, in Charlotte Mosley (ed.), *The Letters of Nancy Mitford*, p. 293

28. Quoted in Hugo Vickers, *Cecil Beaton*, p. 194

29. Telegram from Prime Minister of Britain to Dominion Prime Ministers, 4 December 1936, PRO, CAB 21/4100/2

30. British Movietone News newsreel, 14 December 1936
31. Letter to King Edward VIII, 6 December 1936, RA, PS/GVI/ABD, Boxes 1–6
32. Hazel King Tillman to King Edward VIII, 8 December 1936, RA, PS/GVI/ABD, Box 8
33. Margaret Dickinson and Sarah Street, *Cinema and State*, p. 8
34. Edith Londonderry, *Retrospect*, pp. 251–4
35. Emma Taylor to King Edward VIII, n.d. [December 1936], RA, PS/GVI/ABD, Box 4
36. Olive May Neal to King Edward VIII, 4 December 1936, RA, PS/GVI/ABD, Box 2
37. Pamela Deverell to King Edward VIII, 4 December 1936, RA, PS/GVI/ABD, Box 4
38. Winston Churchill, *The Second World War*, Vol. 1, p. 218
39. Diary of John George Harmer, 4 December 1936, Acc. 6220/Box 9
40. *Hansard*, 4 December 1936
41. 'A lover of Church & State' to Mrs Baldwin, 4 December 1936, Lucy Baldwin Papers
42. Robert Graves and Alan Hodge, *The Long Week-end*, p. 363
43. Mrs Greta [?]Clench to King Edward VIII, 4 December 1936, RA, PS/GVI/ABD, Box 4
44. Dennis Wheatley to King Edward VIII, 6 December 1936, RA, PS/GVI/ABD, Boxes 1–6
45. From South Chingford, Essex, to King Edward VIII, 4 December 1936, RA, PS/GVI/ABD, Box 4
46. Margaret Chalmers to King Edward VIII, 5 December 1936, RA, PS/GVI/ABD, Box 3
47. Letter from London to King Edward VIII, 5 December 1936, RA, PS/GVI/ABD, Boxes 1–6
48. James Fenton Webster to King Edward VIII, 4 December 1936, RA, PS/GVI/ABD, Box 4
49. Gwladys M. Alexander-Williams to King Edward VIII, 4 December 1936, RA, PS/GVI/ABD, Box 5
50. A. Davies to King Edward VIII, 5 December 1936, RA, PS/GVI/ABD, Box 1
51. Diary entry for 15 December 1935, quoted in Celia Lee, *Jean, Lady Hamilton*, p. 258
52. E. J. Rendle to King Edward VIII, 6 December 1936, RA, PS/GVI/ABD, Box 1

53. William Williamson to King Edward VIII, 9 December 1936, RA, PS/GVI/ABD, Box 6

54. Letter from Trieste, Italy, to King Edward VIII, 6 December 1936, RA, PS/GVI/ABD Boxes 1–6

55. R. D. Walton to King Edward VIII, 6 December 1936, RA, PS/GVI/ABD, Box 2

56. Entry for 4 December 1936, Geoffrey Dawson, Abdication Diary, Dawson Papers, MS Dawson 55

57. E. J. Rendle to King Edward VIII, 6 December 1936, RA, PS/GVI/ABD, Box 1

58. 'The King and a crisis. Points at issue', *The Times*, 4 December 1936

59. Entry for 5 December 1936, Geoffrey Dawson, Abdication Diary, Dawson Papers, MS Dawson 55

60. Robert Skidelsky, *John Maynard Keynes*, p. 628

61. Quoted in *Ibid*.

62. From Streatham Hill, London, to King Edward VIII, 9 December 1936, RA PS/GVI/ABD, Boxes 7–9

63. Vera Brittain, *Testament of Experience*, p. 161

64. Diary entry for 9 December 1936, *The Diaries and Letters of Robert Bernays*, p. 279

65. Diary entry for 4 December, quoted in J. G. Lockhart, *Cosmo Gordon Lang*, p. 402; emphasis added

66. James Agate, Diary entry for 4 December 1936, *Ego 3*, p. 57

67. Lucy Baldwin, diary entry for 5 December 1936, Lucy Baldwin Papers

68. Diary entry, 5 December 1936, *Parliament and Politics . . . The Headlam Diaries*, p. 101

69. Evelyn Waugh, *Diaries*, 4–8 December 1936, p. 416

70. S. C. Howard [?]Fripp to King Edward VIII, 6 December 1936, RA, PS/GVI/ABD, Box 3

71. James Agate, diary entry for 5 December 1936, *Ego 3*, pp. 57–8

72. *Ibid*., p. 58

73. George Bernard Shaw, 'The King, the Constitution and the Lady', *Evening Standard*, 5 December 1936

74. Sir Charles Philips Trevelyan to Lady Mary K. Trevelyan, 8 December 1936, Sir Charles Philips Trevelyan Papers, CPT Ex 130/100

75. Diary entry, 5 December 1936, *Parliament and Politics . . . The Headlam Diaries*, p. 101

76. From Selsdon, Surrey, to King Edward VIII, 3 December 1936, RA, PS/GVI/ABD, Boxes 1–6

77. Charles Nelson Stewart to King Edward VIII, 3 December 1936, RA, PS/GVI/ABD, Boxes 1–6
78. From Cheltenham to King Edward VIII, 4 December 1936, RA, PS/GVI/ABD, Boxes 1–6
79. From Colne, Lancashire, to King Edward VIII, 4 December 1936, RA, PS/GVI/ABD, Boxes 1–6
80. A. J. Knights to Winston Churchill, 6 December 1936, Churchill Papers, CHAR 2/597-B
81. 5 December 1935, *Daily Mirror*
82. 5 December 1936, *Daily Express*
83. Telegram from Zetland to Linlithgow, 7 December 1936, Linlithgow Papers, MSS Eur/F/125.15
84. Diary entry, 7 December 1936, *The Diary of Virginia Woolf*, pp. 39–40
85. 'King and country – An anxious week-end', *The Times*, 7 December 1936
86. *Daily Mirror*, 5 December 1936
87. *Ibid.*
88. Telegram to King Edward VIII, 6 December 1936, RA, PS/GVI/ABD Box 10
89. Olwen Herbert-Jones to King Edward VIII, 5 December 1936, RA, PS/GVI/ABD, Box 3
90. J. Reeve to King Edward VIII, 4 December 1936, RA, PS/GVI/ABD, Box 3
91. Telegram to King Edward VIII, 6 December 1936, RA, PS/GVI/ABD, Box 10
92. W. Wain to King Edward VIII, 7 December 1936, RA, PS/GVI/ABD, Box 1
93. Mrs Gerald Hervey to King Edward VIII, 7 December 1936, RA, PS/GVI/ABD, Box 6

9
'Cavaliers and Roundheads'

1. Lord Beaverbrook to Roy W. Howard, 8 December 1936, quoted in Lord Beaverbrook, *The Abdication of King Edward VIII*, p. 122
2. Diary entry for 7 December, *Chips: The Diaries of Sir Henry Channon*, p. 94
3. Diary entry for 6 December, *Ibid.*, p. 93
4. Telegram to King Edward VIII, 4 December 1936, RA, PS/GVI/ABD, Box 10; Mrs R. H. Wheeler to King Edward VIII, 8 December 1936, RA, PS/GVI/ABD, Box 1

5. Letter from London to King Edward VIII, 4 December 1936, RA, PS/GVI/ABD, Boxes 1–6

6. Diary entry, 7 December 1936, *The Diary of Virginia Woolf*, pp. 39–40

7. Telegram from Zetland to Linlithgow, 7 December 1936, Linlithgow Papers, MSS Eur/F/125.15

8. Diary of Violet Milner, 3 December 1936, Violet Milner Papers, VM 5

9. Winston Churchill, 'The abdication crisis: Mr Baldwin's shrewdness', *Yorkshire Post*, 30 April 1948

10. Lord Citrine, *Men and Work*, p. 328

11. Quoted in David Cannadine, *In Churchill's Shadow*, p. 63

12. Mary Soames (ed.), *Speaking for Themselves*, p. 423

13. Hugo Vickers (ed.), *Cocktails & Laughter*, p. 68

14. Martin S. Gilbert, *Winston S. Churchill*, Vol. 5, p. 811

15. Quoted in *Ibid.*, p. 811

16. Robin Birkenhead, *Churchill 1924–1949*, p. 74

17. Martin S. Gilbert, *Winston S. Churchill*, Vol. 5, p. 812

18. *Hansard*, 3 December 1936

19. *Evening Standard*, 3 December 1936

20. Quoted in Philip Guedalla, *The Hundredth Year*, p. 276

21. Malcolm Muggeridge, *The Thirties*, p. 284

22. Martin S. Gilbert, *Winston S. Churchill*, Vol. 5, p. 814

23. Norah Thompson and D. Edwards to Winston Churchill, 6 December 1936, Churchill Papers, CHAR 2/598-B

24. F. S. Harvey to Winston Churchill, 12 December 1936, Churchill Papers, CHAR 2/598-B

25. Phyllis Bowes to Winston Churchill, 6 December 1936, Churchill Papers, CHAR 2/597-A

26. Miss M. D. Boston to Winston Churchill, 7 December 1936, Churchill Papers, CHAR 2/597-A

27. A. P. Hamilton to Winston Churchill, 5 December 1936, Churchill Papers, CHAR 2/597-B

28. Oswald Gregson to Winston Churchill, 5 December 1936, Churchill Papers, CHAR 2/597-B

29. Quoted in Martin S. Gilbert, *Winston S. Churchill*, Vol. 5, p. 814

30. 'Notes by Sir Horace Wilson, at 10 Downing Street', n.d. [late December 1936 or early 1937], CAB 127/157

31. Neville Chamberlain to Stanley Baldwin, 5 December 1936, PRO, CAB 21/4100/2

32. Martin S. Gilbert, *Winston S. Churchill*, Vol. 5, p. 814

33. *Ibid.*, p. 815

34. *Ibid.*, p. 817

35. Winston Churchill to Stanley Baldwin, 5 December 1936, PRO, PREM 1/448

36. Letter from Menston, near Leeds, to King Edward VIII, 6 December 1936, RA, PS/GVI/ABD, Boxes 1–6

37. J. Evans to King Edward VIII, 8 December 1936, RA, PS/GVI/ABD, Box 1

38. 'A Loyal Subject' to King Edward VIII, 5 December 1936, RA, PS/GVI/ABD, Boxes 1–6

39. Cabinet minutes for 4 December 1936, PRO, CAB 23/86 Vol. LIII

40. *Sydney Morning Herald*, 7 December 1936

41. Earl de la Warr to Stanley Baldwin, 4 December 1936, PRO, PREM 1/448

42. *The Times*, 5 December 1936

43. Winston Churchill to Geoffrey Dawson, 9 December 1936, Dawson Papers, MS Dawson 79, fols 52–3

44. Quoted in Iain Macleod, *Neville Chamberlain*, p. 198

45. Thomas Jones, *A Diary with Letters*, p. 291

46. 'ACD' to Geoffrey Dawson, 6 December 1936, Dawson Papers, MS Dawson 79, fol. 34

47. Quoted in Philip Ziegler, *King Edward VIII*, p. 275

48. Christopher Hibbert, *Edward: The Uncrowned King*, p. 15

49. Cabinet minutes for 6 December 1936, PRO, CAB 23/86 Vol. LIII

50. Cabinet minutes for 4 December 1936, PRO, CAB 23/86 Vol. LIII

51. Hilda Runciman diary, 11 December 1936, Hilda Runciman Papers, WR Add 10, 21 March 1936 to 26 January 1937

52. Telegram to King Edward VIII, 7 December 1936, RA, PS/GVI/ABD, Box 10

53. John Ridley to King Edward VIII, 5 December 1936, RA, PS/GVI/ABD, Box 3

54. Robert Graves and Alan Hodge, *The Long Week-end*, p. 364

55. Walton Newbold to Winston Churchill, 6 December 1936, in Martin S. Gilbert, *Companion to Winston S. Churchill*, Vol. 5, p. 460

56. Kingsley Martin, *The Magic of Monarchy*, p. 77

57. Robert Skidelsky, *Oswald Mosley*, p. 329

58. Diary of Anthony Heap, 3 December 1936, Acc. 2243/9/1

59. Kingsley Martin, *The Magic of Monarchy*, p. 77

60. Telegram to King Edward VIII, 11 December 1936, RA, PS/GVI/ABD, Box 10

61. Telegrams to King Edward VIII, December 1936, RA, PS/GVI/ABD, Box 10

62. Telegram to King Edward VIII, 7 December 1936, RA, PS/GVI/ABD, Box 10
63. *Saturday Review*, 12 December 1936
64. Kingsley Martin, *The Magic of Monarchy*, pp. 78–9
65. Ulick Alexander to *The Times*, 24 December 1965
66. Frank Owen and R. J. Thompson, *His Was the Kingdom*, p. 69
67. H. Montgomery Hyde, *The Londonderrys*, p. 238
68. Mary Finch to King Edward VIII, 8 December 1936, RA, PS/GVI/ABD, Box 1
69. Diary of David Strain, 7 December 1936, PRONI, D285/3/16
70. Letter from Sunderland to King Edward VIII, n.d. [December 1936], RA, PS/GVI/ABD, Boxes 1–6
71. 'One of *your* country men' to King Edward VIII, 6 December 1936, RA, PS/GVI/ABD, Box 3
72. *Hansard*, 8 December 1936
73. Telegram from Cloudesley Brereton to King Edward VIII, 7 December 1936, RA, PS/GVI/ABD, Box 10
74. Letter from Paris to King Edward VIII, 5 December 1936, RA, PS/GVI/ABD, Boxes 1–6
75. Letter from London to King Edward VIII, 4 December 1936, RA, PS/GVI/ABD, Boxes 1–6
76. Duke of Windsor, *A King's Story*, p. 385
77. Telegram to King Edward VIII, 3 December 1936, RA, PS/GVI/ABD, Box 10
78. M. J. Davis to King Edward VIII, 9 December 1936, RA, PS/GVI/ABD, Box 6
79. Annie E. Mead to King Edward VIII, 5 December 1936, RA, PS/GVI/ABD, Box 3
80. F. M. Toovey to King Edward VIII, 7 December 1936, RA, PS/GVI/ABD, Box 1
81. Herbert Barnes to Winston Churchill, 6 December 1936, Churchill Papers, CHAR 2/597-A
82. 'Public opinion' to King Edward VIII, n.d. [December 1936], RA, PS/GVI/ABD, Box 5
83. W. K. Leslie and H. H. Bland to King Edward VIII, 5 December 1936, RA, PS/GVI/ABD, Box 3
84. C. Bacon to King Edward VIII, n.d. [December 1936], RA, PS/GVI/ABD, Box 2
85. Letter from London to King Edward VIII, 6 December 1936, RA, PS/GVI/ABD, Boxes 1–6

86. J. A. Godley[?] to King Edward VIII, 5 December 1936, RA, PS/GVI/ABD, Box 3

87. Letter from Brighton to King Edward VIII, 3 December 1936, RA, PS/GVI/ABD, Boxes 1–6

88. H. Stanley Jevons to Winston Churchill, 8 December 1936, Churchill Papers, CHAR 2/597-B

89. Arthur Thurbon to King Edward VIII, 3 December 1936, RA, PS/GVI/ABD, Boxes 1–6

90. Marjorie Deans to Winston Churchill, 5 December 1936, Churchill Papers, CHAR 2/597-A

91. A. Jackson to King Edward VIII, 3 December 1936, RA, PS/GVI/ABD, Box 4

92. John T. Drew to King Edward VIII, 3 December 1936, RA, PS/GVI/ABD, Box 4

93. D. Howard Edwards to King Edward VIII, 3 December 1936, RA, PS/GVI/ABD, Box 4

94. J. H. Squire to King Edward VIII, n.d. [December 1936], RA, PS/GVI/ABD, Box 3

95. W. W. Hitching to King Edward VIII, n.d. [December 1936], RA, PS/GVI/ABD, Box 5

96. Herbert M. A. Richards to King Edward VIII, December 1936, RA, PS/GVI/ABD, Box 6

97. Martin S. Gilbert, *Winston S. Churchill*, Vol. 5, p. 820

98. Vera Brittain, *Testament of Experience*, p. 161

99. Diary of Florence Turtle, 8 December 1936

100. Diary entry, 7 December 1936, *The Diary of Virginia Woolf*, pp. 39–40

101. M. [?]Bland to King Edward VIII, 6 December 1936, RA, PS/GVI/ABD, Box 2

102. Duke of Windsor, *A King's Story*, p. 385

103. Gaston L. D. de Vere to King Edward VIII, 4 December 1936, RA, PS/GVI/ABD, Box 3

104. Edith Londonderry, *Retrospect*, p. 255

105. *Durham County Advertiser*, 20 November 1936, pp. 3, 7

106. Evelyn Webb Summer to King Edward VIII, 6 December 1936, RA, PS/GVI/ABD, Boxes 1–6

107. Telegram to King Edward VIII, 6 December 1936, RA, PS/GVI/ABD, Box 10

108. Letter from London to King Edward VIII, 6 December 1936, RA, PS/GVI/ABD, Boxes 1–6

109. Joan Sexton to King Edward VIII, 4 December 1936, RA, PS/GVI/ABD, Box 4
110. J. G. Lockhart, *Cosmo Gordon Lang*, p. 403

10

'Don't abdicate!'

1. Wallis Simpson to Edward VIII, n.d. [6 December 1936], in Michael Bloch (ed.), *Wallis & Edward Letters*, pp. 219–21
2. Entry for 28 January 1937, in Susan Lowndes (ed.), *Diaries and Letters of Marie Belloc Lowndes*, p. 153
3. Report, unsigned and undated, PRO, PREM 1/466
4. 'Note of interview with Mr Simpson', by the King's Proctor, 24 February 1937, PRO, TS 22/1/2
5. 'Crowded benches', *The Times*, 8 December 1936
6. Diary of Edgar Procter, 6 December 1936
7. Miss E. M. Small to King Edward VIII, 9 December 1936, RA, PS/GVI/ABD, Box 6
8. Diary of Violet Milner, 7 December 1936, Violet Milner Papers, VM 5
9. *Hansard*, 7 December 1936
10. 'Crowded benches', *The Times*, 8 December 1936
11. Beaverbrook learned this from the Lloyd George Papers: see Lord Beaverbrook, *The Abdication of King Edward VIII*, p. 78, footnote 2
12. G. M. Young, *Stanley Baldwin*, p. 242
13. J. R. O'Brien to Winston Churchill, 8 December 1936, Churchill Papers, CHAR 2/597-A
14. Francis N. Beaufort-Palmer to Winston Churchill, 8 December 1936, Churchill Papers, CHAR 2/597-A
15. Philip Guedalla, *The Hundredth Year*, p. 282
16. Duchess of Windsor, *The Heart Has Its Reasons*, p. 217
17. Philip Ziegler, *King Edward VIII*, p. 269
18. Quoted in *Ibid.*, p. 271
19. Francis Hugo Meynell, abdication journal, 112A-B
20. Alan Turing to his mother, 11 December [1936], Alan Turing Papers, AMT/K/1/50
21. Gerald Bullett to Winston Churchill, 8 December 1936, Churchill Papers, CHAR 2/597-A
22. *Ibid.*

23. Janet Trevelyan to George M. Trevelyan, 6 December 1936, Mary Moorman Papers, 2/2/9

24. B. Abbott to King Edward VIII, 4 December 1936, RA, PS/GVI/ABD, Box 3

25. Quoted in Diana Mosley, *The Duchess of Windsor*, p. 116

26. Frances Lloyd George, *The Years That Are Past*, p. 258

27. Quoted in J. Graham Jones, 'Lloyd George and the abdication of Edward VIII', p. 94.

28. Frances Lloyd George, *The Years That Are Past*, p. 258

29. Blanche Dugdale, diary entry for 8 December 1936, quoted in Martin Gilbert, *Companion to Winston S. Churchill*, Vol. 5, p. 466

30. Violet Bonham Carter to Geoffrey Dawson, 9 December 1936, Dawson Papers, MS Dawson 79, fols 48–9

31. Robin Birkenhead, *Churchill 1924–1940*, p. 78

32. Winston Churchill, *The Second World War*, Vol. 1, p. 172

33. Winston Churchill to Geoffrey Dawson, 9 December 1936, Dawson Papers, MS Dawson 79, fols 52–3

34. John Gunther, *Inside Europe*, p. 257

35. Diary entry for 9 December 1936, *The Diaries and Letters of Robert Bernays*, p. 277

36. Mrs Nellie Bagg to King Edward VIII, 9 December 1936, RA, PS/GVI/ABD, Box 5

37. Eileen Lane, Kay Dick and F. D. Lingham Burley to King Edward VIII, 9 December 1936, RA, PS/GVI/ABD, Box 5

38. Miss Edith Lowndes to King Edward VIII, 9 December 1936, RA, PS/GVI/ABD, Box 5

39. Telegram from Stanley Baldwin to the Prime Ministers of the Dominions, 4 December 1936, PRO, CAB 21/4100/2

40. 'The abdication of His Majesty King Edward VIII, Correspondence with the Dominions, Part 1', PRO, DO 114/81

41. Telegram to King Edward VIII, 4 December 1936, RA, PS/GVI/ABD, Box 10

42. Telegram from Constitutional Association of New South Wales to Winston Churchill, 7 December 1936, Churchill Papers, CHAR 2/599

43. George Fairbanks, 'Australia and the abdication crisis', p. 301

44. Telegram from Australian High Commissioner to Dominions Office, 9 December 1936, PRO, HO 144/21070

45. *Sydney Morning Herald*, 10 December 1936 (quoted in Compton Mackenzie, *The Windsor Tapestry*, pp. 494–9)

46. George Fairbanks, 'Australia and the abdication crisis', p. 302

47. *Australian Parliamentary Debates*, Vol. 152, 11 December 1936

48. 'Opinion in the Dominions', *The Times*, 4 December 1936
49. Copy of statements by Reuters to King Edward VIII, 5 December 1936, RA, PS/GVI/ABD, Box 10
50. *Ottawa Citizen*, 8 December 1936
51. Telegram to King Edward VIII, 5 December 1936, RA, PS/GVI/ABD, Box 10
52. Telegram to King Edward VIII, 7 December 1936, RA, PS/GVI/ABD, Box 10
53. *Ibid.*
54. Letter from North Vancouver to King Edward VIII, 5 December 1936, RA, PS/GVI/ABD, Boxes 1–6
55. Letter from Toronto to King Edward VIII, 11 December 1936, RA, PS/GVI/ABD, Boxes 7–9
56. Telegram to King Edward VIII, 7 December 1936, RA, PS/GVI/ABD, Box 10
57. Wallis Simpson to Duke of Windsor, 21 [January 1937], in Michael Bloch (ed.), *Wallis & Edward Letters*, p. 248
58. Duke of Windsor, *A King's Story*, p. 378
59. High Commissioner, Pretoria, to Resident Commissioners of Maseru, Mafeking and Mbabane, 5 December 1936, PRO, DO 119/1077
60. Resident Commissioner, Maseru, to High Commissioner, Pretoria, 5 December 1936, PRO, DO 119/1077
61. Resident Commissioner, Mbabane, to High Commissioner, Pretoria, 7 December 1936, PRO, DO 119/1077
62. 'The Empire', *Daily Herald*, 4 December 1936
63. Copy of statements by Reuters to King Edward VIII, 5 December 1936, RA, PS/GVI/ABD, Box 10
64. Telegram from Linlithgow to Zetland, 8 December 1936, Linlithgow Papers, MSS Eur/F/125.15
65. Report on meeting of ministers, 8 December 1936, PRO, CAB 127/155
66. Telegram from Zetland to Linlithgow, 10 December 1936, Linlithgow Papers, MSS Eur/F/125.15
67. Telegram from Governor of Bengal to Linlithgow, 8 December 1936, No. 210, Linlithgow Papers, MSS Eur/F/125.116
68. Telegram from Governor of Madras to Linlithgow, 8 December 1936, No. 210, Linlithgow Papers, MSS Eur/F/125.116
69. Governor of Punjab to Linlithgow, 7 December 1936, No. 210, Linlithgow Papers, MSS Eur/F/125.116
70. Telegram from Governor of Assam to Linlithgow, 8 December 1936, No. 210, Linlithgow Papers, MSS Eur/F/125.116

71. Telegram from Governor of Central Provinces to Linlithgow, 9 December 1936, No. 214, Linlithgow Papers, MSS Eur/F/125.116

72. Fredoon Kabraji to King Edward VIII, 4 December 1936, RA, PS/GVI/ABD, Box 5

73. Mohammed Ally Khan to Piers Legh, 6 December 1936, RA, PS/GVI/ABD, Box 1

74. Telegram to King Edward VIII, 4 December 1936, RA, PS/GVI/ABD, Box 10

75. Quoted in Philip Ziegler, *King Edward VIII*, p. 137

76. *Ibid.*

77. Telegram to King Edward VIII, 7 December 1936, RA, PS/GVI/ABD, Box 10

78. *Ibid.*

79. Copy of statements by Reuters to King Edward VIII, 5 December 1936, RA, PS/GVI/ABD, Box 10

11

'Our cock won't fight'

1. Quoted in S. M. Cretney, 'The King and the King's Proctor', p. 600, note 112

2. Lord Beaverbrook, *The Abdication of King Edward VIII*, p. 79

3. *Ibid.*, p. 80

4. Martin S. Gilbert, *Winston S. Churchill*, Vol. 5, p. 820–21

5. Lord Beaverbrook, *The Abdication of King Edward VIII*, p. 81

6. Francis Meynell, abdication journal, Francis Hugo Meynell Papers, 112A-B

7. Duke of Windsor, *A King's Story*, pp. 401–2

8. Quoted in John W. Wheeler-Bennett, *King George VI*, p. 286

9. Duke of Windsor, *A King's Story*, p. 402

10. Nancy Dugdale diary, p. 71, Nancy Dugdale Papers

11. Diary of Violet Milner, 8 December 1936, Violet Milner Papers, VM 5

12. Duchess of Windsor, *The Heart Has Its Reasons*, p. 272

13. *Ibid.*

14. *Ibid.*

15. Duke of Windsor, *A King's Story*, p. 403

16. Duchess of Windsor, *The Heart Has Its Reasons*, p. 273

17. Tom Driberg, *Ruling Passions*, p. 106

18. Entry for 8 December 1936, Geoffrey Dawson, Abdication Diary, Dawson Papers, MS Dawson 55

19. 'Constitutional crisis. Attitude of the British press', n.d. [December 1936], PRO, PREM 1/446

20. Entry for 8 December 1936, Geoffrey Dawson, Abdication Diary, Dawson Papers, MS Dawson 55

21. G. E. Buckle *et al.*, *History of The Times*, p. 905

22. John Evelyn Wrench, *Geoffrey Dawson and Our Times*, p. 336

23. Diary of Anthony Heap, 8 December 1936, Acc. 2243/9/1

24. Diary of Florence Turtle, 8 December 1936

25. Letter from Cumberland to King Edward VIII, 11 December 1936, RA, PS/GVI/ABD, Boxes 7–9

26. Mrs May Henderson to King Edward VIII, 8 December 1936, RA, PS/GVI/ABD, Box 6

27. Doreen Kendall-Bradley to King Edward VIII, 8 December 1936, RA, PS/GVI/ABD, Box 6

28. Elsa Staunton to King Edward VIII, 8 December 1936, RA, PS/GVI/ABD, Box 6

29. F. Broadbent to King Edward VIII, 8 December 1936, RA, PS/GVI/ABD, Box 5

30. Frances Horton to King Edward VIII, 7 December 1936, RA, PS/GVI/ABD, Box 5

31. Robert Spence Robertson to King Edward VIII, 8 December 1936, RA, PS/GVI/ABD, Box 5

32. Kathleen Marshall to King Edward VIII, 10 December 1936, RA, PS/GVI/ABD, Box 8

33. 'Poor working woman' to King Edward VIII, n.d. [December 1936], RA, PS/GVI/ABD, Boxes 1–6

34. R. A. Carrington to King Edward VIII, 6 December 1936, RA, PS/GVI/ABD, Boxes 1–6

35. Lord Beaverbrook, *The Abdication of King Edward VIII*, p. 89

36. Diary of Lucy Baldwin, 8 December 1936, Lucy Baldwin Papers

37. Diary of Ramsay MacDonald, 13 February 1936, PRO, PRO 30/69

38. 'Notes by Sir Horace Wilson, at 10 Downing Street', n.d. [late December 1936 or early 1937], CAB 127/157

39. Violet Milner, diary entry for 9 December 1936, Violet Milner Papers, VM 5

40. Statement by Lord Brownlow, 9 December 1936, Brownlow Papers, BNLW, 4/4/9/4

41. Telegram from Baldwin to leaders of the Dominions, 8 December 1936, PRO, HO 144/21070

42. Lord Beaverbrook, *The Abdication of King Edward VIII*, p. 118
43. 'Notes by Sir Horace Wilson, at 10 Downing Street', n.d. [late December 1936 or early 1937], CAB 127/157
44. Duchess of Windsor, *The Heart Has Its Reasons*, p. 235
45. Duke of Windsor, *A King's Story*, p. 404
46. 'Narrative of Mr Theodore Goddard, Solicitor of Mrs Simpson', July 1951, Appendix C of Lord Beaverbrook, *The Abdication of King Edward VIII*, pp. 116–20
47. Duchess of Windsor, *The Heart Has Its Reasons*, pp. 274–7
48. Diary of Nancy Dugdale, p. 75, Nancy Dugdale Papers
49. Quoted in John W. Wheeler-Bennett, *King George VI*, p. 286 (see also footnote b)
50. Quoted in R. T. E. Latham, *The Law and the Commonwealth*, Appendix: 'The abdication of King Edward VIII in Commonwealth law and convention', p. 625
51. Duke of Windsor, *A King's Story*, p. 404
52. Diary of Lucy Baldwin, 9 December 1936, Lucy Baldwin Papers
53. Francis Hugo Meynell to Lady Meynell, 11 December 1936, Francis Hugo Meynell Papers, D859/2/11/2
54. Diary of Nancy Dugdale, p. 76, Nancy Dugdale Papers
55. Diary of Cecil Scott Turner, 10 December 1936, Acc/1385
56. Diary of Edgar Procter, 10 December 1936, D222/13
57. Vera Brittain, *Testament of Experience*, p. 162
58. Notes by King Edward VIII and by Horace Wilson, n.d. [10 December 1936], PRO, PREM 1/455
59. 'Historic day in Parliament', *The Times*, 11 December 1936
60. Diary entry for 15 December 1936, *The Diaries and Letters of Robert Bernays*, pp. 279–80
61. Diary of Nancy Dugdale, p. 80, Nancy Dugdale Papers
62. Diary entry for 15 December 1936, *The Diaries and Letters of Robert Bernays*, pp. 279–80
63. Philip Guedalla, *The Hundredth Year*, p. 289
64. Diary entry for 15 December 1936, *The Diaries and Letters of Robert Bernays*, p. 279
65. G. M. Young, *Stanley Baldwin*, p. 56
66. Diary of Lucy Baldwin, 10 December 1936, Lucy Baldwin Papers
67. 'M.P.', 'Inside Westminster', *Tribune*, 1 January 1937, quoted in Michael Foot, *Aneurin Bevan*, pp. 241–2
68. *Hansard*, 10 December 1936

69. Diary entry, 10 December 1936, *Parliament and Politics . . . The Headlam Diaries*, p. 103

70. Mrs Baldwin to Nancy Dugdale, 24 December 1936, diary of Nancy Dugdale, pp. 103–4, Nancy Dugdale Papers

71. Winston Churchill, 'The abdication crisis: Mr Baldwin's shrewdness', *Yorkshire Post*, 30 April 1948

72. *Ibid.*

73. Entry for 10 December 1936, *The Diaries of Sir Robert Bruce Lockhart*, p. 361

74. Peter Gornall and Robert Bradley to Stanley Baldwin, 17 December 1936, Baldwin Papers Vol. 146

75. Dorothy M. Povah to Stanley Baldwin, 12 December 1936, Baldwin Papers Vol. 146

76. Agnes Fulton to Stanley Baldwin, 14 December 1936, Baldwin Papers Vol. 145

77. Wm J. Cooper to Stanley Baldwin, 15 December 1936, Baldwin Papers Vol. 145

78. Edith Londonderry to Stanley Baldwin, 12 December 1936, Baldwin Papers Vol. 143

79. Sir F. Maurice to Stanley Baldwin, 12 December 1936, Baldwin Papers Vol. 148

80. Diary of Hilda Runciman, 20 November 1936, Hilda Runciman Papers, 21 March 1936 to 26 January 1937

81. F. G. Watton to the Duke of Windsor, 12 December 1936, RA, PS/GVI/ABD, Box 8

82. A. G. Griffith to King Edward VIII, 5 December 1936, RA, PS/GVI/ABD, Box 2

83. British Legion, Birmingham, to King Edward VIII, RA, PS/GVI/ABD, Boxes 1–6

84. W. Graham to King Edward VIII, 4 December 1936, RA, PS/GVI/ABD, Box 4

85. G. R. Garner to King Edward VIII, Sunday [most likely 6 December 1936], RA, PS/GVI/ABD, Box 2

86. Vera Brittain, *Testament of Experience*, p. 162

87. Diary of Jan Longley, 10 December 1936, Acc. 35694/21

88. Diary of Anthony Heap, 10 December 1936, Acc. 2243/9/1

89. Diary of Mary Elizabeth King, 6 December 1936, MS 1547/15

90. Anonymous to King Edward VIII, n.d. [December 1936], RA, PS/GVI/ABD, Box 8

91. Mrs Rose Carter to King Edward VIII, n.d. [December 1936], RA, PS/GVI/ABD, Box 8

92. 'A mother' to King Edward VIII, 10 December 1936, RA, PS/GVI/ABD, Box 8

93. George A. Wright to King Edward VIII, 10 December 1936, RA, PS/GVI/ABD, Box 8

94. 'A Loyal Subject' to King Edward VIII, n.d. [December 1936], RA, PS/GVI/ABD, Box 9

95. D. D. Davies to King Edward VIII, 10 December 1936, RA, PS/GVI/ABD, Box 9

96. Letter from Kent to King Edward VIII, 10 December [1936], RA, PS/GVI/ABD, Boxes 7–9

97. Letter to King Edward VIII, 10 December [1936], RA, PS/GVI/ABD, Boxes 7–9

98. Letter to King Edward VIII, 10 December [1936], RA, PS/GVI/ABD, Boxes 7–9

99. Bernard Shaw to John G. Moore, 23 June 1937, in Dan H. Laurence (ed.), *Bernard Shaw*, p. 469

100. Lascelles to Dawson, 13 December 1936, Dawson Papers, MS Dawson 79, fol. 80

101. Edward, Prince of Wales, to Mrs Freda Dudley Ward, 28 April 1920, in *Letters from a Prince*, p. 359

102. Duke of Windsor, *A King's Story*, p. 278

103. J. Graham Jones, 'Lloyd George and the abdication of Edward VIII', p. 93

104. *Ibid.*, p. 91

105. Duke of Windsor, *A King's Story*, p. 280

106. Oliver Warner, *Admiral of the Fleet*, p. 65

107. Ross McKibbin, *Classes and Cultures*, p. 7

108. Quoted in J. Graham Jones, 'Lloyd George and the abdication of Edward VIII', pp. 89–90

109. Hazel King Tillman to King Edward VIII, 8 December 1936, RA, PS/GVI/ABD, Box 8

110. Diary of Nancy Dugdale, pp. 70–1, Nancy Dugdale Papers

111. Quoted from John Aird's unpublished diaries in Geordie Greig, *Louis and the Prince*, p. 257

112. Parliamentary Counsel, Treasury Chambers, to Sir Horace Wilson, 7 December 1936, PRO, PREM 1/466

113. Diary of Anthony Heap, 11 December 1936, Acc. 2243/9/1

114. Letter to King Edward VIII, 10 December 1936, RA, PS/GVI/ABD, Boxes 7–9

115. Letter from Kent to King Edward VIII, 10 December 1936, RA, PS/GVI/ABD, Boxes 7–9
116. Eric W. Sykes to King Edward VIII, 10 December 1936, RA, PS/GVI/ABD, Box 9
117. Letter from Tottenham, London, to King Edward VIII, 5 December 1936, RA, PS/GVI/ABD, Boxes 1–6
118. 'Miss Wales' to King Edward VIII, n.d. [December 1936], RA, PS/GVI/ABD, Box 8
119. Doris M. Devereux to King Edward VIII, n.d. [December 1936], RA, PS/GVI/ABD, Box 8
120. Geo. H. Buckland to King Edward VIII, 11 December 1936, RA, PS/GVI/ABD, Box 8
121. Harry Wild to Winston Churchill, 12 December 1936, Churchill Papers, CHAR 2/598-B
122. Note by Walter Monckton, 'Secret & Confidential', 2 November 1937, Dep. Monckton Trustees 15, fol. 313

12

'God bless you both'

1. Diary of Edgar Procter, 11 December 1937, D222/13
2. Duke of Windsor, A King's Story, p. 409
3. Martin S. Gilbert, Companion to Winston S. Churchill, Vol. 5, p. 511
4. Duke of Windsor, A King's Story, p. 409
5. J. Bryan III and Charles J. V. Murphy, The Windsor Story, p. 281
6. Lilian Shepherd to King Edward VIII, 6 December 1936, RA, PS/GVI/ABD, Box 3
7. J. Bryan III and Charles J. V. Murphy, The Windsor Story, p. 281
8. Letter to King Edward VIII, 3 December 1936, RA, PS/GVI/ABD, Boxes 1–6
9. Sibyl Colefax to Bernard Berenson, n.d. [1936], Berenson Papers, File CS 1936–1938
10. Tablet, 12 December 1936, p. 824
11. Japan Times, 'British crisis great human drama', 11 December 1936; cutting in PRO, FO, 262/1929
12. Japan Advertiser, 'Prominent women criticize decision', 12 December 1936; cutting in PRO, FO, 262/1929
13. John W. Wheeler-Bennett, King George VI, pp. 294–5
14. Letter from London to King Edward VIII, 9 December 1936, RA, PS/GVI/ABD, Boxes 7–9

15. Letter from Denbigh to King Edward VIII, n.d. [December 1936], RA, PS/GVI/ABD, Boxes 7–9

16. Letter from South London to King Edward VIII, 10 December 1936, RA, PS/GVI/ABD, Boxes 7–9

17. T. C. Vigil to King Edward VIII, 10 December 1936, RA, PS/GVI/ABD, Box 9

18. Mrs Doris M. Devereux to King Edward VIII, n.d., RA, PS/GVI/ABD, Boxes 7–9

19. Betty Williams to King Edward VIII, 10 December 1936, RA, PS/GVI/ABD, Box 9

20. Letter from Walsall to King Edward VIII, 4 December 1936, RA, PS/GVI/ABD, Boxes 1–6

21. Mrs S. Kendall to King Edward VIII, 10 December 1936, RA, PS/GVI/ABD, Box 9

22. John W. Wheeler-Bennett, *King George VI*, pp. 294–5

23. Duke of Windsor, *A King's Story*, pp. 413–14

24. Diary of Anthony Heap, 11 December 1936, Acc. 2243/9/1

25. Diary of Violet Almgill Dickinson, 13 December 1936

26. Letter from Birkenhead to the Duke of Windsor, 11 December [1936], RA, PS/GVI/ABD, Boxes 7–9

27. Reginald Ball to King Edward VIII, 11 December 1936, RA, PS/GVI/ABD, Box 8

28. Diary entry, 13 December 1936, *The Diary of Virginia Woolf*, p. 43

29. Ronald Tree, *When the Moon was High*, p. 66

30. Martin S. Gilbert, *Winston S. Churchill*, Vol. 5, p. 829

31. Quoted in *Ibid.*, p. 830

32. James Agate, Diary entry for 11 December 1936, *Ego 3*, p. 62

33. Diary of David Strain, 11 December 1936, PRONI, D2585/3/16

34. Elizabeth Perkins to King Edward VIII, 11 December 1936, RA, PS/GVI/ABD, Box 8

35. M. Gilmour to the Duke of Windsor, 13 December 1936, RA, PS/GVI/ABD, Box 8

36. E. B. Williamson to the Duke of Windsor, 13 December 1936, RA, PS/GVI/ABD, Box 8

37. 'Giovanni' to the Duke of Windsor, 12 December 1936, RA, PS/GVI/ABD, Box 8

38. Diary of Violet Milner, 11 December 1936, Violet Milner Papers, VM 5

39. Helen Hardinge, *Loyal to Three Kings*, p. 174

40. Ramsay MacDonald, diary entry for 12 December 1936, PRO, PRO 30/69, 1753

41. Diary of Cecil Scott Turner, 11 December 1936, Acc/1385
42. Diary of Florence Turtle, 11 December 1936
43. Diary of Anthony Heap, 11 December 1936, Acc. 2243/91
44. Duchess of Windsor, *The Heart Has Its Reasons*, p. 278
45. Diary notes by Julia M. Shaw for May–June 1937, Julia M. Shaw Papers, DB71/8/9/10–11
46. Wallis Simpson to Sibyl Colefax, 18 December 1936, in Michael Bloch (ed.), *Wallis & Edward Letters*, p. 222
47. Duchess of Windsor, *The Heart Has Its Reasons*, p. 278
48. Wallis Simpson to Duke of Windsor, n.d. [12 December 1936], in Michael Bloch (ed.), *Wallis & Edward Letters*, p. 231
49. Quoted in J. Graham Jones, 'Lloyd George and the abdication of Edward VIII', pp. 89–90.
50. Marc Friedman to King Edward VIII, 12 December 1936, RA, PS/GVI/ABD, Box 9
51. Margaret Case Harriman, 'The King and the girl from Baltimore', p. 366
52. Harry H. S. Phillips to the Duke of Windsor, 11 December 1936, RA, PS/GVI/ABD, Box 9
53. John Gunther to Margot Asquith, 12 December 1936, Margot Asquith Papers, MS Eng 6676
54. John Gunther, *Inside Europe*, p. 259
55. J. Bryan III and Charles J. V. Murphy, *The Windsor Story*, p. 286
56. Diary entry, 10 December 1936, *The Diary of Virginia Woolf*, p. 40
57. Diary of Nancy Dugdale, p. 74, Nancy Dugdale Papers
58. John Buchan to Edith Londonderry, 6 January 1937, PRONI, D3099/3/16/57
59. Telegram to King Edward VIII, 11 December 1936, RA, PS/GVI/ABD, Box 10
60. Telegram to King Edward VIII, 12 December 1936, RA, PS/GVI/ABD, Box 10
61. Telegram to King Edward VIII, 11 December 1936, RA, PS/GVI/ABD, Box 10
62. *Ibid.*
63. John Buchan to Edith Londonderry, 6 January 1937, PRONI, D3099/3/16/57
64. Diary of John George Harmer, 12 December 1936, Acc. 6220/Box 9
65. 'Schoolteacher' to King Edward VIII, 11 December [1936], RA, PS/GVI/ABD, Boxes 7–9
66. Telegram to King Edward VIII, 10 December 1936, RA, PS/GVI/ABD, Box 10

67. Baden-Powell to King Edward VIII, 10 December [1936], RA, PS/GVI/ABD, Box 10

68. Telegram to King Edward VIII, 11 December 1936, RA, PS/GVI/ABD, Box 10

69. Telegram to King Edward VIII, 12 December 1936, RA, PS/GVI/ABD, Box 10

70. Telegram to King Edward VIII, 10 December 1936, RA, PS/GVI/ABD, Box 10

71. Telegram from Linlithgow to Zetland 12 December 1936, Linlithgow Papers, MSS Eur/F/125.15

72. Urban District Council, Kurunegala, to Private Secretary to His Excellency the Governor, Colombo, 9 February 1937; Governor to W. G. A. Ormsby-Gore, 16 February; subject of memo by Gerald Creasy, PRO, CO 323/1522/6

73. Trinidad Citizens League to Governor of Trinidad, 25 January 1937; Governor to W. G. A. Ormsby-Gore; subject of a memo by E. B. Boyd, Colonial Office, 8 March 1937, PRO, CO 323/1522/6

74. M. G. McDonnell to King Edward VIII, n.d. [December 1936], RA, PS/GVI/ABD, Box 6

75. de Valera to Baldwin, 5 December 1936, PRO, DO 121/39

76. Telegram from de Valera to King Edward VIII, 6 December 1936, PRO DO 121/38

77. 'The abdication of His Majesty King Edward VIII, Correspondence with the Dominions, Part 1', PRO, DO 114/81

78. Winston Churchill to Geoffrey Dawson, 12 December 1936, quoted in Martin S. Gilbert, *Companion to Winston S. Churchill*, Vol. 5, p. 485

79. Buccleuch to Dawson, 10 December 1936, Bodleian Library, D, MS Dawson 79, fol. 56

80. Alec Hardinge to Dawson, 14 December 1936, Dawson Papers, MS Dawson 79, fol. 84

81. Lascelles to Dawson, 13 December 1936, Dawson Papers, MS Dawson 79, fol. 80

82. Sybil Colefax to Bernard Berenson, n.d. [1937], Berenson Papers, File CS 1936-1938

83. Geoffrey Wells, diary entry for 11 December 1936, Geoffrey H. Wells Papers, Add. 60562

84. Quoted in Martin S. Gilbert, *Winston S. Churchill*, Vol. 5, p. 825

85. Quoted in *Ibid.*, p. 820

86. W. W. Buckley to Winston Churchill, 13 December 1936, Churchill Papers, CHAR 2/597-A

87. Lord Hamilton of Dalzell to Winston Churchill, 11 December 1936, quoted in Martin Gilbert, *Companion to Winston S. Churchill*, Vol. 5, p. 481

88. Duff Cooper, *Old Men Forget*, pp. 201–2

89. Lord Harewood, *The Tongs and the Bones*, p. 17

90. Diary of John George Harmer, 10 December 1936, Acc. 6220/Box 9

91. Alan Turing to his mother, 1/2 January [1937], Alan Turing Papers, AMT/K/1/51

92. Diary of Geoffrey Wells, 12 December 1936, Geoffrey H. Wells Papers, Add. 60562

93. Letter from Manchester to King Edward VIII, 11 December 1936, RA, PS/GVI/ABD, Boxes 7–9

94. Sydney *Labor Daily*, 4 December 1936

95. Vera Brittain, *Testament of Experience*, p. 163

96. Quoted in J. Graham Jones, 'Lloyd George and the abdication of Edward VIII', pp. 89–90

97. Hugh Ross Williamson to the editor, *Time and Tide*, 19 December 1936

98. Lewis Crosthwaite to King Edward VIII, 14 December 1936, RA, PS/GVI/ABD, Box 4

99. Oliver Turpin to King Edward VIII, 11 December 1936, RA, PS/GVI/ABD, Box 8

100. Edwin Plevin to Winston Churchill, 14 December 1936, Churchill Papers, CHAR 2/598-A

101. Bernard Shaw to John G. Moore, 23 June 1937, in Dan H. Laurence (ed.), *Bernard Shaw*, p. 469

102. Tom Jeffery, *Mass-Observation*, pp. 1–3

103. Humphrey Jennings *et al.*, *May the Twelfth*, p. 302

104. *Ibid.*, p. 281

105. Thomas Jones, *A Diary with Letters*, p. 299

106. John Gunther to Margot Asquith, 12 December 1936, Margot Asquith Papers, MS Eng 6676

107. Sent with letter from Wisconsin to King Edward VIII, 3 December 1936, RA, PS/GVI/ABD, Boxes 1–6

108. *The Voice*, 12 December 1936

109. Boyd-Shannon to Sir Harry Batterbee, 13 December 1936, PRO, PREM 1/462

110. Sir Harry Batterbee to Horace Wilson, 5 January 1937, PRO, PREM 1/462

111. *Sydney Morning Herald*, 10 December 1936, quoted in Compton Mackenzie, *The Windsor Tapestry*, p. 501

112. H. V. Evatt to Winston Churchill, 12 December 1936, quoted in Martin S. Gilbert, *Companion to Winston S. Churchill*, Vol. 5, p. 487
113. 'Notes by Sir Horace Wilson, at 10 Downing Street', n.d. [late December 1936 or early 1937], CAB 127/157
114. Entry for 28 December 1936, *Diaries of Sir Robert Bruce Lockhart*, pp. 362–3
115. Quoted from Elizabeth Longford in Penelope Mortimer, *Queen Elizabeth*, p. 143, footnote
116. Diana Vreeland, *D. V.*, p. 74
117. Quoted in Christopher Warwick, *George and Marina*, p. 104
118. Janet Flanner, *An American in Paris*, p. 46
119. Diana Vreeland, *D. V.*, p. 74
120. Duke of Windsor, *A King's Story*, p. 415

13
'Rat Week'

1. *Amen, The End of a Tragic Chapter in British Imperial History*, British Movietone News newsreel, 14 December 1936
2. Diary of Mary Elizabeth King, 12 December 1936, MS 1547/15
3. Geoffrey Dawson, personal diary, 13 December 1936, Dawson Papers, MS Dawson 40
4. Robert Bernays to Lucy Brereton, 23 December 1936, *The Diaries and Letters of Robert Bernays*, p. 281
5. Diary of Florence Turtle, 12 December 1936
6. Lucy Baldwin, diary entry for 12 December 1936, Lucy Baldwin Papers
7. J. Graham Jones, 'Lloyd George and the abdication of Edward VIII', p. 96
8. Cover of *Saturday Review*, 19 December 1936
9. Diary of Geoffrey Wells, 12 December 1936, Add. 60562
10. Queen Elizabeth to Cosmo Lang, copied out by A. C. Don, Lambeth Palace, quoted in Geordie Greig, *Louis and the Prince*, p. 267
11. Philip Ziegler, *King Edward VIII*, p. 338
12. Quoted in J. G. Lockhart, *Cosmo Gordon Lang*, p. 405
13. Diary of Florence Turtle, 13 December 1936
14. Diary of Jan Longley, 13 December 1936, 25694/21
15. George M. Trevelyan to Mary C. Trevelyan, 16 December 1936, Mary Moorman Papers, 1/4/24
16. Vera Brittain, *Testament of Experience*, p. 163

17. John Gunther, *Inside Europe*, p. 263

18. J. G. Lockhart, *Cosmo Gordon Lang*, p. 404; Philip Ziegler, *King Edward VIII*, p. 338

19. Kingsley Martin, *The Crown and the Establishment*, p. 113

20. Frances Donaldson, *Edward VIII*, p. 298

21. Telegram from 'Hooper Wye Kent' to Lord Brownlow, 17 December 1936, Brownlow Papers, BNLW 4/4/9/7/10

22. Quoted in Frances Donaldson, *Edward VIII*, p. 298

23. Diary entry, 13 December 1936, *Parliament and Politics . . . The Headlam Diaries*, p. 104

24. Diary of Herbert M. Willmott, 13 December 1936, F/Wlm/16

25. Alan Turing to his mother, 1/2 January [1937], Alan Turing Papers, AMT/ K/1/51

26. Duke of Windsor, *A King's Story*, p. 331

27. Entry for 14 December 1936, *The Diaries of Sir Robert Bruce Lockhart*, p. 362

28. Winston Churchill to Duke of Windsor, 17 December 1936, quoted in Martin S. Gilbert, *Companion to Winston S. Churchill*, Vol. 5, p. 493

29. Memorandum of 15 December, quoted in J. Graham Jones, 'Lloyd George and the abdication of Edward VIII', p. 103

30. P. Thomas to Stanley Baldwin, 17 December 1936, Baldwin Papers, Vol. 147

31. Miss Annie M. Smith to Stanley Baldwin, 14 December 1936, Baldwin Papers, Vol. 147

32. Mrs Ritson Richer to Stanley Baldwin, 20 December 1936, Baldwin Papers, Vol. 147

33. Ernest [?]Baker to Winston Churchill, 16 December 1936, Churchill Papers, CHAR 2/597-A

34. Louise Thibault to Winston Churchill, 17 December 1936, Churchill Papers, CHAR 2/598-B

35. Diary of Geoffrey Wells, 13 December 1936, Add. 60562

36. Richard Hough, *Edwina*, p. 133

37. *Ibid.*

38. Diana Vreeland, *D.V.*, pp. 73–5

39. *Ibid.*

40. Lucy Baldwin, diary entry for 18 December 1936, Lucy Baldwin Papers

41. Brownlow to Cromer, 23 December 1936, Brownlow Papers, BNLW 4/4/9/6/11

42. Mrs E. Hedges to Lord Brownlow, n.d. [December 1936], Brownlow Papers, BNLW 4/4/9/7/14

43. Wallis Simpson to Perry Brownlow, 18 December 1936, Brownlow Papers, BNLW 4/4/9/5/3

44. Wallis Simpson to Duke of Windsor, 12 December 1936, in Michael Bloch (ed.), *Wallis & Edward Letters*, p. 231

45. Quoted in Greg King, *The Duchess of Windsor*, p. 249

46. Diary entry, 22 December 1936, *Chips: The Diaries of Sir Henry Channon*, p. 104

47. Elizabeth R [Queen Elizabeth] to Lady Londonderry, 31 May 1937, PRONI, D3099/3/13/26

48. Alec Hardinge to Dawson, 14 December 1936, Dawson Papers, MS Dawson 79, fol. 84

49. George M. Trevelyan to Mary C. Trevelyan, 16 December 1936, Mary Moorman Papers, 1/4/24

50. Richard Hough, *Edwina*, p. 133

51. Introduction by John Pearson to Osbert Sitwell, *Rat Week*, pp. 14-15

52. Osbert Sitwell, *Rat Week*, pp. 58-60

53. Sybil Colefax to Bernard Berenson, n.d., quoted in Kirsty McLeod, *A Passion for Friendship*, p. 149

54. Martin S. Gilbert, *Companion to Winston S. Churchill*, Vol. 5, p. 451

55. Somerset Maugham to Charles Hanson Towne, 18 March 1937, Charles Hanson Towne Papers

56. Duff Cooper, *Old Men Forget*, p. 202

57. Mary Soames, *Clementine Churchill*, p. 274

58. Winston Churchill to Clementine Churchill, 7 January 1937, in Mary Soames (ed.), *Speaking for Themselves*, p. 423

59. Diary entry for 26 February 1937, *Chips: The Diaries of Sir Henry Channon*, p. 116

60. *Time*, 21 December 1936

61. Telegram to King Edward VIII, 11 December 1936, RA, PS/GVI/ABD, Box 10

62. Telegram to King Edward VIII, 12 December 1936, RA, PS/GVI/ABD, Box 10

63. Sir Francis Floud to Malcolm MacDonald, 22 December 1936, PRO, DO 3/531/2

64. Francis Stephenson to Theodore Goddard, 14 December 1936, PRO, PREM 1/460

65. 'Notes of the evidence given at the hearing of the petition', for the King's Proctor, PRO, TS 22/1/1-2

66. Diana Vreeland, *D. V.*, p. 75

67. Wallis Simpson to Duke of Windsor, 6 February 1937, in Michael Bloch (ed.), *Wallis & Edward Letters*, pp. 256–7

68. Wallis Simpson to Duke of Windsor, n.d. [12 December 1936], in Michael Bloch (ed.), *Wallis & Edward Letters*, pp. 230–32

69. 'Note for Mr Allen. 22.12.36. Madame Tussaud's', Monckton Papers, fols 26–7

70. Wallis Simpson to Sibyl Colefax, 21 April 1937, Sibyl Colefax Papers, MS Eng c 3272, fols 19–22

71. Wallis Simpson to Sibyl Colefax, 23 April 1937, Sibyl Colefax Papers, MS Eng c 3272, fols 23–4

72. Wallis Simpson to Duke of Windsor, n.d. [14 December 1936], in Michael Bloch (ed.), *Wallis & Edward Letters*, p. 232

73. Wallis Simpson to Kitty de Rothschild, 18 December 1936, in *Ibid.*, p. 235

74. Wallis Simpson to Duke of Windsor, n.d. [late January 1936], in *Ibid.*, p. 253

75. Wallis Simpson to Duke of Windsor, 6 February 1937, in *Ibid.*, p. 257

76. Duke of Windsor to Wallis Simpson, 18 February 1937, in *Ibid.*, p. 261

77. Mrs Merryman to Duke of Windsor, 17 December 1936, in *Ibid.*, p. 237, footnote 1

78. Duke of Windsor to Mrs Merryman, 22 December 1936, in *Ibid.*, p. 237

79. Lord Brownlow to Major-General Sir Frederick Maurice, President of the British Legion, 19 March 1937, Brownlow Papers, BNLW 4/4/9/5/10

80. Charles Lambe to Perowne, 17 January 1937, quoted in Oliver Warner, *Admiral of the Fleet*, p. 72

81. J. G. Lockhart, *Cosmo Gordon Lang*, p. 406

82. John Buchan to Edith Londonderry, 15 December 1936, PRONI, D3099/3/16/56; emphasis added

83. Diary entry for 15 December 1936, *The Diaries and Letters of Robert Bernays*, p. 281

84. Quoted in H. Montgomery Hyde, *Norman Birkett*, p. 458

85. A. Millar to King Edward VIII, 3 December 1936, RA, PS/GVI/ABD, Box 4

86. Patricia Capper Parlley and Mrs S. Edward to King Edward VIII, 11 December 1936, RA, PS/GVI/ABD, Box 8

87. E. Hammond to King Edward VIII, 11 December 1936, RA, PS/GVI/ABD, Box 8

88. Andrew Thomas to King Edward VIII, 11 December 1936, RA, PS/GVI/ABD, Box 8

89. John Copeland to King Edward VIII, 11 December 1936, RA, PS/GVI/ABD, Box 8

90. J. G. Lockhart, *Cosmo Gordon Lang*, p. 407

91. Duke of Windsor to Wallis Simpson, 22 December 1936, in Michael Bloch (ed.), *Wallis & Edward Letters*, p. 235

92. Miss Frances Kemble-Harris to King Edward VIII, 6 December 1936, RA, PS/GVI/ABD, Box 3

93. Marjorie M. Wheeler to King Edward VIII, 12 December 1936, RA, PS/GVI/ABD, Box 8

94. Mrs Lily Bellis to the Duke of Windsor, 13 December 1936, RA, PS/GVI/ABD, Box 8

95. Gertrude Hall to King Edward VIII, 10 December 1936, RA, PS/GVI/ABD, Box 8

96. Quoted in Martin S. Gilbert, *Winston S. Churchill*, Vol. 5, p. 831

97. Quoted in J. Graham Jones, 'Lloyd George and the abdication of Edward VIII', p. 96

14

'We have had such happiness'

1. Miss Burke was not interviewed because she was still employed by Mrs Simpson – 'Servants still in the employ of any person owe a duty to their employer, and it is not the practice of the King's Proctor, and it would indeed be improper for him, to endeavour to get information from such servants.' Nor were servants of the royal household interviewed, 'for obvious reasons'. 'Notes of the evidence given at the hearing of the petition', for the King's Proctor, PRO, TS 22/1/2

2. For a full set of information on the challenge to the divorce and the investigation of the King's Proctor, see PRO, TS 22/1/2

3. 'Note of interview with Mr Simpson', by the King's Proctor, 24 February 1937, PRO, TS 22/1/2

4. Walter Monckton to Horace Wilson, 2 February 1937, PRO, PREM 1/460

5. 'Notes of the evidence given at the hearing of the petition', for the King's Proctor, PRO, TS 22/1/2

6. For example, Canning to Sir Philip Game, 19 December 1936, PRO, MEPO 10/35

7. D. Storrier to the Commissioner of the Metropolitan Police, 8 March 1937, PRO, MEPO 10/35

8. D. Storrier to the Commissioner of the Metropolitan Police, 28 April 1937, PRO, MEPO 10/35

9. 'Very Confidential' report by Sir John Simon, 6 January 1937, PRO, MEPO 10/35

10. Duke of Windsor to Mr J. D. Moffat, 2 June 1937, Brownlow Papers, BNLW 4/4/9/5/18

11. Sir John Simon to King George VI, 7 April 1937, PRO, PREM 1/463

12. Wigram to Sir John Simon, 12 April 1937, PRO, PREM 1/463

13. Harry Crookshank MP to Lord Brownlow, 11 May 1937, Brownlow Papers, BNLW 4/4/9/5/19

14. Nugent Hicks, Bishop of Lincoln, to Lord Brownlow, 18 May 1937, Brownlow Papers, BNLW 4/4/9/5/21

15. Quoted in typescript account by Lord Brownlow of events leading up to wedding of the Duke of Windsor, Brownlow Papers, BNLW 4/4/9/5/30

16. *Ibid.*

17. Leadbitter to Newsam, 17 March 1937, PRO, HO 144/22448

18. 'Note', Law Officers' Department, 9 April 1936, PRO, LO 3/1168

19. Cabinet minutes for 26 May 1937, PRO, CAB 23/88/1 Vol. LV

20. Sir John Simon to Neville Chamberlain, 28 April 1937, PRO, PREM 1/461

21. *The Times*, 29 May 1937

22. Jowitt to Lascelles, recalling his opinion given in 1937, 14 April 1949, PRO, PREM 8/150

23. Anthony Aldgate, *Cinema & History*, p. 139

24. Report by Metropolitan Police, 23 July 1937, PRO, HO 144/22448

25. Greg King, *The Duchess of Windsor*, p. 447

26. Winston Churchill to Clementine Churchill, 10 January 1938, quoted in Mary Soames (ed.), *Speaking for Themselves*, p. 433

27. Winston Churchill to Robert Boothby, 8 January 1939, quoted in Mary Soames (ed.), *Speaking for Themselves*, p. 446

28. Quoted in Martin S. Gilbert, *Winston S. Churchill*, Vol. 5, p. 829

29. George Allen to Mr Farrer, 10 November 1937, PRO, PREM 1/463

30. Duke of Windsor to Neville Chamberlain, 22 December 1937, PRO, PREM 1/465

31. Horace Wilson to the Chancellor, Neville Chamberlain, 10 December 1936, PRO, PREM 1/453

32. King George VI to Neville Chamberlain, 2 December 1938, PRO, PREM 1/467

33. King George VI to Neville Chamberlain, 14 December 1938, PRO, PREM 1/467

34. *Sunday Dispatch*, 8 January 1939
35. Report by Metropolitan Police, 4 September 1937, PRO, MEPO 10/35
36. Leaflet for the Octavians, printed in Barnes, n.d. [1937], PRO, MEPO 10/35
37. Leaflet by Harry Becker, printed in Twickenham, n.d. [1937], PRO, MEPO 10/35
38. R. J. Minney, *The Private Papers of Hore-Belisha*, pp. 236, 238
39. King George VI to Clement Attlee, 20 April 1949, PRO, PREM 8/150
40. Winston Churchill to Anthony Eden, 15 October 1952, PRO, PREM 11/5219
41. Leonard M. Harris, *Long to Reign over Us?*, pp. 96–9
42. *Ibid.*, p. 121
43. *Ibid.*, pp. 121–4
44. Edward Heath to Robert Armstrong, 7 November 1971, PRO, PREM 15/1184
45. Mrs E. Smith to the Leader of the House of Commons, 20 May 1972, PRO, PREM 15/1184
46. Mrs E. Roberts to the Leader of the House of Commons, 5 May 1972, PRO, PREM 15/1184
47. 'Talk at last', interview with Wallis Simpson by Adela St Johns, *Sunday Pictorial*, 15 December 1940
48. John Grigg, 'Edward VIII', p. 343
49. Lord Mayor to Mr Witney, 30 May 1972, PRO, HO 290/104
50. Speech by Mayor Jacques Chirac on the presentation of the Grande Plaque from the City of Paris, to those who have served Paris, to Mr Al-Fayed, December 1989, quoted in Hugo Vickers, *The Private World of the Duke and Duchess of Windsor*, p. 235

Archive sources

Margot *Asquith* Papers
Bodleian Library
Oxford University

Lucy *Baldwin* Papers
Private collection

Stanley *Baldwin* Papers
Cambridge University Library

Bernard *Berenson* Papers
Fototeca Berenson
Villa I Tatti
Florence

British Movietone News
British Movietone Limited
Uxbridge

Lord *Brownlow* Papers
Lincolnshire Record Office

Winston *Churchill* Papers
Churchill Archive Centre
Churchill College
Cambridge University

Sibyl *Colefax* Papers
Bodleian Library
Oxford University

Geoffrey *Dawson* Papers
Bodleian Library
Oxford University

Violet Almgill *Dickinson*: diary
Somerset Record Office

Nancy *Dugdale* Papers
Private collection

King Edward VIII: letters and
   telegrams relating to the
   abdication
Royal Archives (RA)
Windsor Castle

Government documents, including
   over a hundred files relating to the
   abdication released in January
   2003
The National Archives (PRO)
Kew

Alexander *Hardinge* Papers
Kent Record Office
Maidstone

John Kenward *Harmer*: diary
East Sussex Record Office

W. A. S. *Harris*: diary
Sheffield University Library

Anthony *Heap*: diary
London Metropolitan Archives

Mary Elizabeth *King*: diary
Birmingham City Archives

Lord *Linlithgow* Papers
Oriental and India Office Collection
British Library

London County Council Papers
London Metropolitan Archives

Edith *Londonderry* Papers
Public Record Office of Northern
  Ireland
Belfast

Jan *Longley* diary
Bristol Record Office

Ramsay *MacDonald*: diary
The National Archives (PRO)
Kew

Mass-Observation archive
University of Sussex Library
Brighton

Merthyr Tydfil: documents on local
  history
Carnegie Library
Merthyr Tydfil

Francis Hugo *Meynell* Papers
Staffordshire Record Office

Violet *Milner* Papers
Bodleian Library
Oxford University

Walter *Monckton* Papers
Bodleian Library
Oxford University

Mary *Moorman* Papers
Robinson Library Special
  Collections
Newcastle University Library

National Birthday Trust Fund archive
Manuscripts and Archives
Wellcome Library for the History
  and Understanding of Medicine
Wellcome Trust, London

Pathe Gazette newsreels
British Pathe, London
British Film Institute, London

Edgar *Procter*: diary
Liverpool University Special
  Collections

Lord *Reading* Papers
Oriental and India Office Collection
British Library

Hilda *Runciman*: diary
Robinson Library Special
  Collections
Newcastle University Library

Roy *Sambourne*: diary
Kensington & Chelsea Reference
  Library, London

Julia M. *Shaw* Papers
West Yorkshire Archive Service
Bradford

John *Simon* Papers
Bodleian Library
Oxford University

David H. *Strain*: diary
Public Record Office of Northern
  Ireland (PRONI)
Belfast

Charles Hanson *Towne* Papers
Manuscripts and Archives Division
The New York Public Library

Sir Charles Philips *Trevelyan* Papers
Robinson Library Special
    Collections
Newcastle University Library

Alan *Turing* Papers
King's College Library
Cambridge University

Cecil Scott *Turner*: diary
London Metropolitan Archives

Florence *Turtle*: diary
Kensington & Chelsea Reference
    Library, London

Geoffrey H. *Wells*: diary
Department of Manuscripts
British Library

Herbert M. *Willmott*: diary
London Metropolitan Archives

Bibliography

Adams, Samuel Hopkins, *Alexander Woollcott: His Life and His World.* London, Hamish Hamilton, 1946

[Aga Khan], *The Memoirs of Aga Khan: World Enough and Time*, with a foreword by W. Somerset Maugham. London, Cassell & Co., 1954

Agate, James, *Ego 3: Being Still More of the Autobiography of James Agate.* London, George G. Harrap, 1938

[Airlie, Lady] *Thatched With Gold: The Memoirs of Mabell, Countess of Airlie*, edited and arranged by Jennifer Ellis. London, Hutchinson, 1962

Aldgate, Anthony, *Cinema & History: British Newsreels and the Spanish Civil War.* London, Scolar Press, 1979

Altrincham, Lord [*see also* Grigg, John] and others, *Is the Monarchy Perfect?* London, John Calder, 1958

[Amery, Leo] *The Empire at Bay: The Leo Amery Diaries 1929–1945*, edited by John Barnes and David Nicholson. London, Hutchinson, 1988

Amory, Mark, *Lord Berners: The Last Eccentric.* London, Pimlico, 1999

Asquith, Lady Cynthia, *The Queen: An Entirely New and Complete Biography Written with the Approval of Her Majesty.* London, Hutchinson & Co., 1937

Attlee, Clement, *As it Happened.* London, William Heinemann, 1954

Barnes, John, and Nicholson, David, *The Leo Amery Diaries 1929–1945.* London, Hutchinson, 1988

Beaverbrook, Lord, *The Abdication of King Edward VIII*, edited by A. J. P Taylor. London, Hamish Hamilton, 1966

[Bernays, Robert] *The Diaries and Letters of Robert Bernays, 1932–1939: An Insider's Account of the House of Commons*, Studies in British History, Volume 40, edited by Nick Smart. Lampeter, Wales, The Edwin Mellen Press, 1996

Birkenhead, Lord, *Walter Monckton: The Life of Viscount Monckton of Brenchley*. London, Weidenfeld & Nicolson, 1969

Birkenhead, Robin, *Churchill 1924–40*. Bath, printed by Bookcraft, 1989

Bloch, Michael, 'Philip Guedalla defends the Duke', *History Today*, December 1979, pp. 832–44

Bloch, Michael (ed.), *Wallis & Edward Letters 1931–1937: The Intimate Correspondence of the Duke and Duchess of Windsor*. London, Weidenfeld & Nicolson, 1986

Bloch, Michael, *The Reign & Abdication of Edward VIII*. London, Bantam Press, 1990

Bloch, Michael, *Ribbentrop*. London, Bantam Press, 1992

Bloch, Michael, *The Duchess of Windsor*. London, Weidenfeld & Nicolson, 1996

Bloom, Ursula, *The Duke of Windsor*. London, Robert Hale, 1972

Bogdanor, Vernon, *The Monarchy and the Constitution*. Oxford, Clarendon Press, 1995

Bolitho, Hector, *King Edward VIII: His Life and Reign*. London, Eyre & Spottiswoode, 1937

Bradford, Sarah, *King George VI*. London, Weidenfeld & Nicolson, 1989

Brasnett, Margaret, *Voluntary Social Action. A History of the National Council of Social Service 1919–1969*. London, NCSS, 1969

Brendon, Piers and Whitehead, Philip, *The Windsors: A Dynasty Revealed 1917–2000*. London, Pimlico, 2000 [1st edn 1994, London, Hodder & Stoughton]

Brendon, Piers, *The Dark Valley: A Panorama of the 1930s*. London, Jonathan Cape, 2000

Brierley, Walter, *Means Test Man*. London, Methuen & Co., 1935

Briggs, Asa, *The BBC: The First Fifty Years*. Oxford University Press, 1985

Brittain, Vera, *Honourable Estate: A Novel of Transition*. London, Victor Gollancz, 1936

Brittain, Vera, *Testament of Experience. An Autobiographical Story of the Years 1925–1950*. London, Victor Gollancz, 1957

Broad, Lewis, *The Abdication Twenty-Five Years After: A Re-appraisal*. London, Frederick Muller, 1961

Bromage, Mary C., *De Valera and the March of a Nation*. London, Hutchinson, 1956

Bryan III, J., and Murphy, Charles J. V., *The Windsor Story*. London, Granada, 1979

Buckle, G. E., Morison, Stanley, McDonald, Iverach, *et al.*, *The History of

The Times. Part II: The 150th Anniversary and Beyond, 1912–1948, Appendix I: The Abdication. London, The Times, 1952

Burridge, Trevor, *Clement Attlee: A Political Biography.* London, Jonathan Cape, 1985

Campbell, Dame Janet, Cameron, Isabella D., and Jones, Dilys M., *High Maternal Mortality in Certain Areas: Reports on Public Health and Medical Subjects 68.* London, Ministry of Health, 1932

Cannadine, David, *The Decline and Fall of the British Aristocracy.* London, Picador, 1992 [1st edn 1990, London, Yale University Press]

Cannadine, David, *History in Our Time.* New Haven, Yale University Press, 1998

Cannadine, David, *In Churchill's Shadow: Confronting the Past in Modern Britain.* London, Penguin, 2002

Case Harriman, Margaret, 'The King and the girl from Baltimore', in Isabel Leighton (ed.), *The Aspirin Age 1919–1941.* New York, Simon & Schuster, 1949

[Channon, Sir Henry], *Chips: The Diaries of Sir Henry Channon,* edited by Robert Rhodes James. London, Weidenfeld & Nicolson, 1967

Chaplin, Charles, *My Autobiography.* London, The Bodley Head, 1964

Charmley, John, *Duff Cooper: The Authorized Biography.* London, Phoenix, 1997 [1st edn 1986, London, Weidenfeld & Nicolson]

Churchill, Randolph S., *Lord Derby, 'King of Lancashire': The Official Life of Edward, Seventeenth Earl of Derby 1865–1948.* London, Heinemann, 1959

Churchill, Winston S., *The Second World War. Volume 1: The Gathering Storm.* Boston, Houghton Mifflin, 1949

Citrine, Lord [Walter], *Men and Work.* London, Hutchinson, 1964

Colledge, Dave, *Labour Camps: The British Experience.* Sheffield, Sheffield Popular Publishing, 1989

Collis, Maurice, *Nancy Astor: An Informal Biography.* London, Faber & Faber, 1960

Cooper, Duff (Viscount Norwich), *Old Men Forget.* London, Rupert Hart-Davis, 1953

Corbitt, F. J., *Fit for a King: A Book of Intimate Memoirs.* London, Odhams Press, 1956

De Courcy, Anne, *The Viceroy's Daughters.* London, Weidenfeld & Nicolson, 2000

Coward, Noel, *Autobiography,* with an introduction by Sheridan Morley. London, Methuen, 1986

Cowles, Virginia, *Winston Churchill: The Era and the Man*. London, Hamish Hamilton, 1953

Cox, Idris, *The People Can Save South Wales!* London, Communist Party of Great Britain, n.d. [*c.*1936]

Crathorne, James, *Cliveden: The Place and the People*. London, Collins & Brown, 1995

Crawford, Marion, *The Little Princesses*. London, Cassell & Co., 1950

Cretney, S. M., 'The King and the King's Proctor: The abdication crisis and the divorce laws 1936–1937', *Law Quarterly Review*, Volume 116, pp. 583–620, 2000

Deedes, W. F., *Dear Bill: W. F. Deedes Reports*. London, Pan, 1998 [1st edn 1997, London, Macmillan]

Deedes, W. F., 'Divided we stand', *Telegraph Weekend Magazine*, 18 March 1989

Dennithorne, John, *The Unawakened World*. London, Educational Settlements Association, 1934

A Diary of the Last Days of the Reign of King Edward VIII: A Souvenir Edition. London, The Arnold-Lacy Company, n.d. [1937]

Dickinson, Margaret, and Street, Sarah, *Cinema and State: The Film Industry and the British Government 1927–84*. London, British Film Institute, 1985

Disraeli, Benjamin, *Sybil; or The Two Nations*. London, Oxford University Press, 1975 [1st edn Leipzig, Tauchnitz, 1845]

Donaldson, Frances, *Edward VIII*. London, Weidenfeld & Nicolson, 1974

Douglas, Major C. H., *Social Credit Principles*, an address delivered at Swanwick, November 1924. Belfast, KRP Publications, 1954

Driberg, Tom, *Ruling Passions: The Autobiography of Tom Driberg*. London, Quartet Books, 1978 [1st edn London, Jonathan Cape, 1977]

Duberman, Martin Bauml, *Paul Robeson*. London, The Bodley Head, 1989

Dutton, David, *Neville Chamberlain*. London, Arnold, 2001

Edwards, Cecil, *Bruce of Melbourne: Man of Two Worlds*. London, Heinemann, 1965

Eliot, Thomas H., *Recollections of the New Deal: When the People Mattered*. Boston, Northeastern University Press, 1992

Ervine, St John., *Craigavon: Ulsterman*. London, George Allen & Unwin, 1949

[Esher, Lord] *Journals and Letters of Reginald Viscount Esher, Volumes I–IV*, edited by Oliver, Viscount Esher. London, Ivor Nicholson & Watson, 1938

Estorick, Eric, *Stafford Cripps*. London, William Heinemann, 1949

The Experience of the Depression in Wales. Welsh Office, Welsh Joint Education Committee, n.d. [1990s]

Fairbanks, George, 'Australia and the abdication crisis, 1936', *Australian Outlook: Journal of the Australian Institute of International Affairs*, April 1966, Volume 20, No. 1, pp. 296–302

Feiling, Keith, *The Life of Neville Chamberlain.* London, Macmillan & Co., 1970

Fishman, Jack, *My Darling Clementine: The Story of Lady Churchill.* London, W. H. Allen, 1966

Fitzroy, Sir Almeric, *Memoirs*, Volumes I and II. London, Hutchinson & Co., n.d. [1925]

Flanner, Janet, *An American in Paris: Profile of an Interlude Between Two Wars.* London, Hamish Hamilton, 1940

Foot, Michael, *Aneurin Bevan: A Biography. Volume One: 1897–1945.* London, MacGibbon & Kee, 1962

Francis, Hywel, and Smith, Dai, *The Fed: A History of the South Wales Miners in the Twentieth Century.* Cardiff, University of Wales Press, 1998

Garside, W. R. (ed.), *Capitalism in Crisis. International Responses to the Great Depression.* London, Pinter Publishers, 1993

Gascoyne, David, *Journal 1936–37.* London, The Enitharmon Press, 1980

Gerhardie, William, *God's Fifth Column. A Biography of the Age 1890–1940*, edited by Michael Holroyd and Robert Skidelsky. London, Hogarth Press, 1990 [1st edn London, Hodder & Stoughton, 1981]

Gilbert, Martin S., *Winston S. Churchill. Volume 5: 1922–1939.* London, Heinemann, 1976

Gilbert, Martin S., *Companion to Winston S. Churchill. Volume 5: 1922–1939.* London, Heinemann, 1976

Ginzberg, Eli, *Grass on the Slag Heaps: The Story of the Welsh Miners.* New York and London, Harper & Brothers, 1942

Glendinning, Victoria, *Vita: The Life of Vita Sackville-West.* London, Penguin, 1984 [1st edn London, Weidenfeld & Nicolson, 1983]

Glendinning, Victoria, *Rebecca West: A Life.* London, Macmillan Papermac, 1988 [1st edn London, Weidenfeld & Nicolson, 1987]

Gloucester, Princess Alice, Duchess of, *The Memoirs of Princess Alice, Duchess of Gloucester.* London, Collins, 1983

Goldsmith, Barbara, *Little Gloria . . . Happy at Last.* London, Macmillan, 1980

Gordon, Peter, and Lawton, Denis, *Royal Education: Past, Present and Future.* London, Frank Cass, 1999

Gore, John, *King George V: A Personal Memoir.* London, John Murray, 1941

Graves, Robert, and Hodge, Alan, *The Long Week-end: A Social History of Great Britain 1918–1939*. London, Faber & Faber, 1940

Greene, Felix (ed.), *Time to Spare: What Unemployment Means by Eleven Unemployed, with Additional Chapters*. London, George Allen & Unwin, 1935

Greig, Geordie, *Louis and the Prince*. London, Hodder & Stoughton, 2000 [1st edn 1999]

Grigg, John [*see also* Altrincham, Lord], *Lloyd George: The People's Champion 1902–1911*. London, Eyre Methuen, 1978

Grigg, John, *Lloyd George: From Peace to War 1912–1916*. London, Methuen, 1985

Grigg, John, *The Monarchy Revisited*, W. H. Smith Contemporary Papers, No. 9. London, W. H. Smith, n.d. [1993]

Grigg, John, 'Edward VIII', in *DNB*; reprinted in Hugo Young (ed.), *Political Lives*. Oxford University Press, 2001 [page numbers quoted refer to the latter]

Guedalla, Philip, *The Hundredth Year*. London, Eyre & Spottiswoode, 1940 [1st edn London, Thornton Butterworth, 1939]

Gunther, John, *Inside Europe*, revised edition. London, Hamish Hamilton, 1937 [1st edn 1936]

Gwynedd, Viscount, Richard Lloyd George, *Dame Margaret: The Life Story of His Mother*. London, George Allen & Unwin, 1947

Hanley, James, *Grey Children: A Study in Humbug and Misery*. London, Methuen, 1937

Hannington, Wal, *Unemployed Struggles 1919–1936*. London, Lawrence & Wishart, 1936

Hannington, Wal, *The Problem of the Distressed Areas*. London, Victor Gollancz, 1937

Hannington, Wal, *Ten Lean Years*. London, Victor Gollancz, 1940

Hannington, Wal, *Never on Our Knees*. London, Lawrence & Wishart, 1967

Hardinge, Helen, *Loyal to Three Kings: A Memoir of Alec Hardinge Private Secretary to the Sovereign*. London, William Kimber, 1967

Harewood, Lord, *The Tongs and the Bones: The Memoirs of Lord Harewood*. London, Weidenfeld & Nicolson, 1981

Harris, Leonard M., *Long to Reign over Us? The Status of the Royal Family in the Sixties*. London, William Kimber, 1966

Haxey, Simon, *Tory M.P.* London, Victor Gollancz, 1939

[Headlam, Cecil] Ball, Stuart (ed.), *Parliament and Politics in the Age of Churchill and Attlee: The Headlam Diaries 1935–1951*. Camden Fifth

Series, Volume 14. London, Cambridge University Press for The Royal Historical Society, 1999

Heimann, Judith M., *The Most Offending Soul Alive: Tom Harrisson and His Remarkable Life*. Honolulu, University of Hawaii Press, 1997

Hetherington, S. J., *Katharine Atholl 1874–1960: Against the Tide*. Aberdeen University Press, 1989

Hibbert, Christopher, *Edward: The Uncrowned King*. London, Macdonald, 1972

Higham, Charles, *Wallis: Secret Lives of the Duchess of Windsor*. London, Sidgwick & Jackson, 1988

Hobsbawm, Eric, and Ranger, Terence (eds), *The Invention of Tradition*. Cambridge University Press, 1983

Hood, Dina Wells, *Working for the Windsors*. London, Allan Wingate, 1957

Horne, Alistair, *Macmillan, 1894–1956*, Volume 1. London, Macmillan, 1988

Hough, Richard, *Edwina: Countess Mountbatten of Burma*. London, Weidenfeld & Nicolson, 1983

Hughes, E. A., *The Royal Naval College Dartmouth*. London, Winchester Publications, 1950

Hughes, M. Vivian, *A London Family Between the Wars*. London, Oxford University Press, 1940

Hyde, H. Montgomery: *Norman Birkett: The Life of Lord Birkett of Ulverston*. London, Hamish Hamilton, 1964

Hyde, H. Montgomery, *Baldwin: The Unexpected Prime Minister*. London, Hart Davis, 1973

Hyde, H. Montgomery, *Neville Chamberlain*. London, Weidenfeld & Nicolson, 1976

Hyde, H. Montgomery, *The Londonderrys: A Family Portrait*. London, Hamish Hamilton, 1979

Inglis, Brian, *Abdication*. London, Hodder & Stoughton, 1966

Jackson, Stanley, *The Aga Khan: Prince, Prophet and Sportsman*. London, Odhams Press, 1952

Jackson, Stanley, *The Sassoons*. London, Heinemann, 1968

James, Lawrence, *The Rise and Fall of the British Empire*. London, Abacus, 1998 [1st edn London, Little, Brown & Co., 1994]

James, Robert Rhodes, *Memoirs of a Conservative: J. C. C. Davidson, Memoirs and Papers 1910–37*. London, Weidenfeld & Nicolson, 1969

James, Robert Rhodes, *Churchill: A Study in Failure 1900–1939*. London, Weidenfeld & Nicolson, 1970

Jameson, Storm, *Civil Journey*. London, Cassell & Co., 1939 [1st edn 1935]

Jeffery, Tom, *Mass-Observation. A Short History*, Mass-Observation Archive, Occasional Paper No. 10, University of Sussex Library, 1999

Jennings, Humphrey, Madge, Charles, *et al.* (eds), *May the Twelfth: Mass-Observation Day-Surveys, 1937*. London, Faber & Faber, 1937

Jones, J. Graham, 'Lloyd George and the abdication of Edward VIII', *National Library of Wales Journal*, Volume 30, pp. 89–105, 1997–98

Jones, Jack, *Unfinished Journey*, with a preface by the Rt Hon. David Lloyd George. London, Hamish Hamilton, 1937

Jones, Jack, *Me and Mine. Further Chapters in the Autobiography of Jack Jones*. London, Hamish Hamilton, 1946

Jones, Thomas, *A Diary with Letters 1931–1950*. London, Oxford University Press, 1954

Kaul, Chandrika, *Reporting the Raj: The British Press and India, c.1880s–1922*. Manchester University Press, 2003

Kimball, Warren F. (ed.), *Churchill & Roosevelt: The Complete Correspondence. Volume I: Alliance Emerging, October 1933–November 1942*. Princeton University Press, 1984

King, Greg, *The Duchess of Windsor: The Uncommon Life of Wallis Simpson*. London, Aurum Press, 1999

Kirkwood, David, *My Life of Revolt*. London, George G. Harrap, 1935

Latham, R. T. E., *The Law and the Commonwealth*. Reprinted from the *Survey of British Commonwealth Affairs*, Volume I; London, Royal Institute of International Affairs, 1937

Laurence, Dan H. (ed.), *Bernard Shaw: Collected Letters 1856–1950. Vol. 4, 1926–1950*. London, Max Reinhardt, 1988

Lee, Celia, *Jean, Lady Hamilton 1861–1941: A Soldier's Wife*. London, Celia Lee, 2001

Lees-Milne, James, *Another Self*. London, Hamish Hamilton, 1970

Lestrange, W. F., *Wasted Lives*. London, George Routledge & Sons, 1936

Lloyd George, Frances, *The Years That Are Past*. London, Hutchinson, 1967

Lockhart, J. G., *Cosmo Gordon Lang*. London, Hodder & Stoughton, 1949

[Lockhart, Sir Robert Bruce] *The Diaries of Sir Robert Bruce Lockhart: Volume One 1915–1938*, edited by Kenneth Young. London, Macmillan, 1973

Londonderry, Edith [Marchioness of Londonderry], *Retrospect*. London, Frederick Muller, 1938

Longford, Earl of, and O'Neill, Thomas P., *Eamon de Valera*. London, Hutchinson, 1970

Longford, Elizabeth, *The Royal House of Windsor*. London, Weidenfeld & Nicolson, 1984 [1st edn 1974]

Longford, Elizabeth, *The Queen Mother*. London, Weidenfeld & Nicolson, 1981

Longford, Elizabeth, *Elizabeth R*. London, Weidenfeld & Nicolson, 1983

Longford, Elizabeth, *Royal Throne: The Future of the Monarchy*. London, Hodder & Stoughton, 1993

[Lowndes, Marie Belloc] *Diaries and Letters of Marie Belloc Lowndes 1911–1947*, edited by Susan Lowndes. London, Chatto & Windus, 1971

McConathy, Dale, 'Mainbocher', in *American Fashion: The Life and Lines of Adrian, Mainbocher, McCardell, Novell, Trigere*, edited by Sarah Tomerlin Lee. London, André Deutsch, 1976 [1st edn New York, Quadrangle and Times Book Co., 1975]

Mackenzie, Compton, *The Windsor Tapestry*. London, Rich & Cowan, 1938

McKernan, Luke, *Topical Budget: The Great British News Film*. London, British Film Institute, 1992

McKibbin, Ross, *Classes and Cultures: England 1918–1951*. Oxford University Press, 1998

Macleod, Iain, *Neville Chamberlain*. London, Frederick Muller, 1961

McLeod, Kirsty, *A Passion for Friendship: Sibyl Colefax and her Circle*. London, Michael Joseph, 1991

McLeod, Kirsty, *Battle Royal. Edward VIII & George VI: Brother against Brother*. London, Constable, 1999

Macmillan, Harold, *Winds of Change 1914–1939*. London, Macmillan, 1966

Madge, Charles, and Harrisson, Tom, *Mass-Observation*. London, Frederick Muller, 1937

Mansergh, Nicholas, *Survey of British Commonwealth Affairs: Problems of External Policy 1931–1939*. London, Oxford University Press, 1952

Margetson, Stella, *The Long Party: High Society in the Twenties & Thirties*. Westmead, Hampshire, Saxon House, 1974

Martin, Kingsley, *The Magic of Monarchy*. London, Thomas Nelson & Sons, 1937

Martin, Kingsley, *The Crown and the Establishment*. Harmondsworth, Penguin, 1965 [1st edn London, Hutchinson & Co., 1962]

Martin, Kingsley, *A Second Volume of Autobiography 1931–45*. London, Hutchinson, 1968

Martin, Ralph G., *The Woman He Loved*. London, W. H. Allen, 1974 [1st edn 1973]

Masters, Brian, *Great Hostesses*. London, Constable, 1982

[Maugham, Somerset] *The Letters of William Somerset Maugham to Lady Juliet Duff*, edited by Loren R. Rothschild. Pacific Palisades, California, Rasselas Press, 1982

BIBLIOGRAPHY

[Merthyr Tydfil] *Report of the Royal Commission on Merthyr Tydfil*, presented by the Home Office. London, HMSO, November 1935, Cmd 5039

Middlemas, Keith, and Barnes, John, *Baldwin: A Biography*. London, Weidenfeld & Nicolson, 1969

Minney, R. J., *The Private Papers of Hore-Belisha*. London, Gregg Revivals in association with Department of War Studies, King's College London, 1991 [1st edn London, Collins, 1960]

Moore, Chris, and Hawtree, Christopher, *1936 as Recorded by the* Spectator. London, Michael Joseph, 1986

Morgan, Austen, *J. Ramsay MacDonald*. Manchester University Press, 1987

Morgan, Janet, *Edwina Mountbatten: A Life of Her Own*. London, HarperCollins, 1991

Morgan, Kenneth O., *Lloyd George: Family Letters 1885–1936*. Cardiff, University of Wales Press, and London, Oxford University Press, 1973

Mortimer, Penelope, *Queen Elizabeth: A Life of the Queen Mother*. London, Penguin, 1987 [1st edn London, Viking, 1986]

Mortimer, Penelope, *Queen Mother: An Alternative Portrait of Her Life and Times*. London, André Deutsch, 1995 [Revised edn of Penelope Mortimer, *Queen Elizabeth the Queen Mother*, 1986]

Mosley, Charlotte (ed.), *The Letters of Nancy Mitford*. London, Hodder & Stoughton, 1993

Mosley, Diana, *The Duchess of Windsor*. London, Sidgwick & Jackson, 1980

Moynihan, Maurice (ed.), *Speeches and Statements by Eamon de Valera 1917–73*. Dublin, Gill & Macmillan, 1980

Muff, Clarence, *Unbelievable, But True!* Occasional Local Papers No. 6, Bradford Libraries Division, 1984

Muggeridge, Malcolm, *The Thirties, 1930–1940, in Great Britain*. London, Hamish Hamilton, 1940

Nash, Kath, *Town on the Usk: A Pictorial History of Newport*. Gwent, Village Publishing, 1983

Nicolson, Harold, *King George the Fifth: His Life and Reign*. London, Constable & Co, 1952

Nicolson, Nigel (ed.), *Harold Nicolson: Diaries and Letters 1930–1939*. London, Collins, 1966

Nicolson, Nigel, *Great Houses of Britain*. London, The National Trust and Weidenfeld & Nicolson, 1978

Nixon, Edgar B. (ed.), *Franklin D. Roosevelt and Foreign Affairs. Volume II: March 1934–August 1935*. Cambridge, Massachusetts, The Belknap Press of Harvard University Press, 1969

Orwell, George, 'The Road to Wigan Pier Diary', in George Orwell. London, Secker & Warburg, 1980

Owen, A. E. B., 'Handlist of the political papers of Stanley Baldwin, First Earl Baldwin of Bewdley', 1973, Cambridge University Library

Owen, Frank, and Thompson, R. J., His Was the Kingdom. London, Arthur Barker, 1937

Owen, John A., and Jacob, Carolyn, The Unconquerable Spirit: Merthyr Tydfil and District in the 1930s. Merthyr Tydfil Public Libraries, 1993

Pearce, Malcolm, and Stewart, Geoffrey, British Political Decline 1867–1990: Democracy and Decline. London, Routledge, 1992

Petrie, Sir Charles, The Modern British Monarchy. London, Eyre & Spottiswoode, 1961

Pickles, Dorothy, Democracy. London, Methuen University Paperback, 1971 [1st edn London, Batsford, 1970]

Pilgrim Trust, Men Without Work. Cambridge University Press, 1938

Pope-Hennessy, James, Queen Mary 1867–1953. London, George Allen & Unwin, 1959

Prochaska, Frank, Royal Bounty: The Making of a Welfare Monarchy. New Haven, Yale University Press, 1995

Pronay, Nicholas, and Wenham, Peter, The News and the Newsreel: History through the Newsreel, the 1930s. London, Macmillan Education/The Historical Association, 1976

Ramsden, John, 'Baldwin and film', in Propaganda, Politics and Film, 1918–45, edited by Nicholas Pronay and D. W. Spring. London, Macmillan, 1982

Ramsden, John, An Appetite for Power: A History of the Conservative Party since 1830. London, HarperCollins, 1998

Report of the Committee on Cinematograph Films [Report of the Moyne Committee]. London, HMSO, 1936, Cmd 5320

Rhondda Urban District Council, Report of the Medical Officer of Health for 1934

Richards, Jeffrey, Imperialism and Music. Britain 1876–1953. Manchester University Press, 2001

Richards, Jeffrey, and Aldgate, Anthony, Best of British: Cinema and Society 1930–1970. Oxford, Basil Blackwell, 1983

Richards, Jeffrey, and Aldgate, Anthony, The Age of the Dream Palace: Cinema and Society in Britain 1930–1939. London, Routledge & Kegan Paul, 1984

Richards, Jeffrey, and Sheridan, Dorothy, Mass-Observation at the Movies. London, Routledge & Kegan Paul, 1987

[Robeson, Paul] Let Paul Robeson Sing! A Celebration of the Life of Paul

Robeson and his Relationship with Wales, a Paul Robeson Cymru Commit-tee/Bevan Foundation publication, 2001

Rolph, C. H., *Kingsley: The Life, Letters and Diaries of Kingsley Martin*. London, Victor Gollancz, 1973

Rose, Kenneth, *King George V*. London, Weidenfeld & Nicolson, 1983

Rose, Kenneth, *Kings, Queens & Courtiers: Intimate Portraits of the Royal House of Windsor from its Foundation to the Present Day*. London, Weiden-feld & Nicolson, 1985

Rowlands, Ted, *Something Must Be Done: South Wales v. Whitehall 1921–1951*. Merthyr Tydfil, ttc Books, 2000

Shaughnessy, Alfred (ed.), *Sarah: The Letters and Diaries of a Courtier's Wife 1906–1936*. London, Peter Owen, 1989

Sims, George R., *How the Poor Live, and Horrible London*. London, Chatto & Windus, 1889

Singer, H. W., *Unemployment and the Unemployed*. London, P. S. King, 1940

Sitwell, Osbert, with an introduction by John Pearson, *Rat Week: An Essay on the Abdication*. London, Michael Joseph, 1984

Skidelsky, Robert, *Oswald Mosley*. London, Papermac, 1990 [1st edn London, Macmillan, 1975]

Skidelsky, Robert, *John Maynard Keynes. Volume 2: The Economist as Saviour 1920–1937*. London, Macmillan, 1992

Slater, Leonard, *Aly*. London, W. H. Allen, 1966

Slater, Montagu, *Stay Down Miner*. London, Martin Lawrence, 1936

Smart, Nick, *The National Government 1931–40*. London, Macmillan, 1999

Soames, Mary, *Clementine Churchill*. London, Cassell, 1979

Soames, Mary (ed.), *Speaking for Themselves: The Personal Letters of Win-ston and Clementine Churchill*. London, Doubleday, 1998

[Special Areas] *Reports of Investigations into the Industrial Conditions in Certain Depressed Areas of I: West Cumberland and Haltwhistle; II: Durham and Tyneside; III: South Wales and Monmouthshire; IV: Scotland*. London, HMSO, 1934. Cmd 4728

Special Areas (Development and Improvement) Act. London, HMSO, 1934

[Special Areas] *[First] Report of the Commissioner for the Special Areas (England and Wales)*. London, HMSO, 1935. Cmd 4957

[Special Areas] *[Second] Report of the Commissioner for the Special Areas (England and Wales)*. London, HMSO, 1936. Cmd 5090

[Special Areas] *[Third] Report of the Commissioner for the Special Areas (England and Wales)*. London, HMSO, 1936. Cmd 5303

Spring Rice, Margery, *Working-Class Wives*. London, Virago, 1981 [1st edn London, Pelican, 1939]

Stevenson, John, *British Society 1914–1945*. London, Penguin, 1990 [1st edn London, Allen Lane, 1984]

Stewart, Graham, *Burying Caesar: Churchill, Chamberlain and the Battle for the Tory Party*. London, Weidenfeld & Nicolson, 1999

Stuart, Denis, *Dear Duchess. Millicent Duchess of Sutherland 1867–1955*. London, Victor Gollancz, 1982

Symons, Julian, *The Thirties: A Dream Revolved*. London, Faber & Faber, 1975 [1st edn London, Cresset Press, 1960]

Taylor, A. J. P., *English History 1914–1945*. Oxford University Press, 1975 [1st edn Oxford, Clarendon Press, 1965]

Taylor, A. J. P. (ed.), *Lloyd George: A Diary by Frances Stevenson*. London, Hutchinson, 1971

Taylor, A. J. P., *Beaverbrook*. London, Hamish Hamilton, 1972

Taylor, A. J. P. (ed.), *My Darling Pussy: The Letters of Lloyd George and Frances Stevenson 1913–41*. London, Weidenfeld & Nicolson, 1975

Taylor, Antony, *'Down with the Crown': British Anti-monarchism and Debates about Royalty since 1790*. London, Reaktion Books, 1999

Templewood, Viscount [Samuel Hoare], *Nine Troubled Years*. London, Collins, 1954

Thornton, Michael, *Royal Feud: The Queen Mother and the Duchess of Windsor*. London, Pan, 1985

Time & Tide Anthology, edited by Anthony Lejeune and André Deutsch, with an introduction by Lady Rhondda. London, André Deutsch, 1956

Tree, Ronald, *When the Moon was High: Memoirs of Peace and War 1897–1942*. London, Macmillan, 1975

Trevelyan, Julian, *Indigo Days*. London, MacGibbon & Kee, 1957

Vickers, Hugo (ed.), *Cocktails & Laughter: The Albums of Loelia Lindsay (Loelia, Duchess of Westminster)*. London, Hamish Hamilton, 1983

Vickers, Hugo, *Cecil Beaton: The Authorised Biography*. London, Weidenfeld & Nicolson, 1985

Vickers, Hugo, *The Private World of the Duke and Duchess of Windsor*. London, Harrods Publishing, 1995

Vreeland, Diana, *D. V.*, edited by George Plimpton and Christopher Hemphill. London, Weidenfeld & Nicolson, 1984

Warner, Oliver, *Admiral of the Fleet: The Life of Sir Charles Lambe*. London, Sidgwick & Jackson, 1969

Warwick, Christopher, *King George VI & Queen Elizabeth: A Portrait*. London, Sidgwick & Jackson, 1985

Warwick, Christopher, *Abdication*. London, Sidgwick & Jackson, 1986

Warwick, Christopher, *George and Marina*. London, Weidenfeld & Nicolson, 1988

Waterhouse, Nourah, *Private and Official*. London, Jonathan Cape, 1942

Watson, Sophia, *Marina: The Story of a Princess*. London, Weidenfeld & Nicolson, 1994

[Waugh, Evelyn] Davie, Michael (ed.), *The Diaries of Evelyn Waugh*, Harmondsworth, Penguin, 1979 [1st edn London, Weidenfeld & Nicolson, 1976]

Weitz, John, *Joachim von Ribbentrop: Hitler's Diplomat*. London, Weidenfeld & Nicolson, 1992

[Wells, H. G.] Smith, David C. (ed.), *The Correspondence of H. G. Wells. Volume 4: 1935–1946*. London, Pickering & Chatto, 1998

What's Wrong with South Wales? A New Diagnosis and Patent Remedy by a General Practitioner with Full Directions for the Miners' Next and Last Step, with a preface by the Rt Hon. D. Lloyd George. London, *The New Statesman and Nation*, 1935

Wheare, K. C., *The Statute of Westminster and Dominion Status*, 2nd edition. London, Oxford University Press, 1942 [1st edn 1938]

Wheeler-Bennett, John W., *King George VI: His Life and Reign*. New York, St Martin's Press, 1965

White, J. Lincoln, *The Abdication of Edward VIII*. London, George Routledge, 1937

Wilkinson, Ellen, *Peeps at Politicians*. London, Philip Allan & Co., 1930

Wilkinson, Ellen, *The Town That Was Murdered: The Life-Story of Jarrow*. London, Victor Gollancz, 1939

Williams, A. Susan, *Women and Childbirth in the Twentieth Century: A History of the National Birthday Trust Fund 1928–93*. Stroud, Sutton, 1997

Williams, A. Susan, *Ladies of Influence: Women of the Elite in Interwar Britain*. London, Penguin, 2000

Williams, Francis, *Nothing So Strange*. London, Cassell, 1970

Williams, Valentine, *The World of Action: The Autobiography of Valentine Williams*. London, Hamish Hamilton, 1938

Williamson, Philip, *Stanley Baldwin: Conservative Leadership and National Values*. Cambridge University Press, 1999

Windsor, Duchess of, *The Heart Has Its Reasons: The Memoirs of The Duchess of Windsor*. London, Michael Joseph, 1956

Windsor, Duke of, *A King's Story: The Memoirs of HRH the Duke of Windsor*. London, Prion Books, 1998 [1st edn New York, Putnams, 1947]

Windsor, Duke of, *The Crown and the People 1902–1953*. London, Cassell & Co., 1953

Windsor, Duke of, *A Family Album*. London, Cassell, 1960

[Windsor, Duke of] *Letters from a Prince, March 1918–January 1921*, edited by Rupert Godfrey. London, Warner Books, 1999

'The Woman I Love'. The Romance of Edward and Wallis, Duke and Duchess of Windsor. London, News Review Books No. 1, n.d. [1937]

Woolf, Virginia, *Three Guineas*. London, Hogarth Press, 1986 [1st edn London, Hogarth Press, 1938]

[Woolf, Virginia] Bell, Anne Olivier (ed.), assisted by McNeillie, Andrew, *The Diary of Virginia Woolf. Volume 5: 1936–41*. London, Penguin, 1985 [1st edn London, Hogarth Press, 1984]

Wragg, Arthur, *'Jesus Wept': A Commentary in Black-and-White on Ourselves and the World To-day*. London, Selwyn & Blount, n.d. [1935]

Wrench, John Evelyn, *Geoffrey Dawson and Our Times*. London, Hutchinson, 1955

Young, G. M., *Stanley Baldwin*. London, Rupert Hart-Davis, 1952

Ziegler, Philip, *Crown and People*. London, Collins, 1978

Ziegler, Philip, *Diana Cooper*. London, Hamish Hamilton, 1981

Ziegler, Philip (ed.), *The Diaries of Lord Louis Mountbatten 1920–1922*. London, Collins, 1987

Ziegler, Philip, *King Edward VIII: The Official Biography*. London, Collins, 1990

Index

Abdication Act (1936) 145, 230
Aberdare 7
Abertillery 7, 17
Abyssinia (Ethiopia) 109
Accession Council 63
Admiralty 55, 121
African colonies 204–5
Aga Khan III 54, 73, 191
Agate, James 166–7, 239
Aird, Sir John 25, 230
Airlie, Mabell, Countess of 10–11
Albert, Prince, Duke of York
   ('Bertie', Edward's brother);
   later George VI 72, 86, 137,
   170, 210
 at Naval College 157
 in the Great War 55
 health 55, 116
 and Sheila Loughborough 38
 made Duke of York (1920) 38
 proposes to Poppy Baring 38–9
 initiates Duke of York's Camps
   10
 marries Elizabeth Bowes-Lyon 40
 honeymoon at Polesden Lacey 45
 and Edward's dress 71
 friendship with Alexander and
   Helen Hardinge 87
 identifies with his parents 99

Lang visits 99–100
 told of Edward's abdication
   decision 106
 promises cooperation in the event
   of abdication 115
 personality 115, 130, 230
 readiness to be the new king 211
 see also George VI, King
Albert Victor, Prince ('Eddy') 116
Alexander, Duke of Wrttemberg
   112
Alexander, Major Ulick 69, 181,
   210
Alexandra, Queen 79
Alexandra Feodorovna, Empress of
   Russia 229
All Souls College, Oxford 61, 76
Allen, George 85, 153, 155, 181,
   210, 217, 275, 278
Aly Khan, Prince 73
Amery, Leo 108
Amritsa Bazar 205
Ancaster, Earl of 39
Anglo-French Luncheon Club
   194
appeasement period 76
Argyll House, London 44
Arlen, Michael 73
 The Green Hat 73

'Arms and the Covenant' movement 160

Asquith, Margot (Lady Oxford and Asquith) 37, 242, 251

Associated Negro Press 144

Association Better Citizenship, Inc. 109

Astor, Lady Nancy (née Langhorne) 41, 200

Astor, Waldorf 41

Astor, William Waldorf 41

Atatrk, Kemal 43

Athenaeum club, London 61

Athlone, Alice, Countess of 253

Athlone, Earl of 253

Atlantic Fleet 121

Attlee, Clement 63, 113, 176, 193, 199, 279

Australia 117, 118, 130, 166, 176, 180, 185, 201, 202–3

Australian Labour Party 202–3

Austria 233, 253, 261

Baden-Powell, Lord Robert 243

Bahamas 278

Bakewell Branch, British Legion 225

Baldwin, Lucy 100, 104, 161, 166, 194, 215, 219, 221, 222, 254–5, 261

Baldwin, Stanley 41, 63, 68, 115, 119, 143, 147, 158, 159, 172, 180, 181, 186, 187, 191, 197, 238, 248, 266
    as a businessman 61
    very worried about Edward as king 63
    and Edward's proposed North-East visit 65–67
    on Edward's relationship with Wallis 68
    discusses the royal crisis with Alexander Hardinge 74–5
    and Wallis's divorce petition 75–6, 194, 273
    discussions with Stanley Bruce 100–101
    Beaverbrook's foe 101
    meeting with Edward (16 November 1936) 102–4, 106
    and the Memorandum by Parliamentary Counsel 103
    rearmament admission 107–8
    and morganatic marriage plan 112–13, 116, 117, 118, 129–30, 161, 201, 251
    on the General Strike 121
    consults the Dominions 124, 125, 129–32, 201–4
    abdication message discussed 128
    Thomas Dugdale on 137
    and reactions to the royal crisis 139, 162, 169, 170
    pressures and bargains with Edward 145
    discusses Times leader with Dawson 148–9
    proposed speech to the nation by Edward 155, 178, 221
    broadcast speech 158–9, 161–2, 164
    Churchill confronts 173–4, 175–6, 194
    admits to Edward that wants him to abdicate 178–9
    alleged unfair treatment of Edward 182
    and foreign affairs 185
    Ernest Simpson's offer 192
    speech in the House 192–5
    defeats Churchill 195, 199

told of Edward's intention to
abdicate 209
final talk with Edward 210–11
worried Edward will change his
mind 215
breaks news of the abdication
219–22, 226
abdication as a triumph for him
222–3
receives letters regarding the
abdication 223–8
blamed for the abdication 228
and Edward's final broadcast
237–8, 239, 246
Lloyd George on 241
telegram to de Valera 245
and Lang's speech 256, 259
and Lord Brownlow 261
Balmoral Castle and estate 9, 29,
72, 86, 88, 99, 100, 115, 116,
173
Baltimore, Maryland 21
Barbados 208
Baring, Helen ('Poppy') 38–9
Barkers department store, London
144, 213, 240, 254
Barnes, Thomas 230
Barnet Urban District Council 179
Barrington-Ward, Robin 148
Basutoland 205
Batterbee, Sir Henry 124, 131,
251
BBC (British Broadcasting
Corporation) 153, 154, 156–7,
159, 235, 241
Beach House, Felixstowe 84–5
Beasley, Jack 252
Beaton, Sir Cecil 32, 45, 158
Beatrice, Infanta, of Spain 37
Beaverbrook, Lord 'Max' 114, 128,

129, 136, 147, 155, 172, 176,
200, 264
on Wallis 28
agrees to suppress news of the
Simpson divorce 86, 101
returns to Britain on Edward's
request 101
rivalry with Rothermere 112
on Edward's social interests
118–19
the Dominion prime ministers'
cables 125
feels that Baldwin is in danger
politically 139
comments on a Dawson article
148
Belton House plan 151, 192
plan for Edward to broadcast to
the nation 153
'King's men'/'Cabinet men'
remark 171
Edward urged to work with him
175
told of Edward's intention to
abdicate 209
'our cock won't fight' 210
Becker, Harry 279
Beecham, Sir Thomas 45, 260
Beefsteak Club, London 61, 169
Belgium 54, 55
Belton House, Lincolnshire 26, 151,
192, 265
Berenson, Bernard 234
Bernays, Robert 165, 200–201,
220, 221, 254, 269–70
Berners, Lord 44
'Bessie' (Wallis Simpson's aunt) see
Merryman, D. Buchanan
Bevan, Aneurin 4, 5, 15, 16, 221,
228

Biarritz 79

Bingham, Robert 50, 120

Birkett, Norman 85, 270

Birkhall, Balmoral estate 99–100, 255

Birmingham Post 134, 135

Blaenavon 13–14

Blaina 16, 272

Blenheim 239

Bletchley Park 196

Bloomsbury set 242

Blue Ridge Summit, Pennsylvania 21

Blunt, Alfred, Bishop of Bradford 134–5, 141, 142, 146–7, 148, 159, 182

Bombay 208

Bombay Chronicle 206

Bombay Sentinel 205, 206

Bonham Carter, Lady Violet 160, 199–200

Boothby, Robert 200, 209–10, 277

Boston *Record* 85

Boulogne 97

Boverton 5

Bradford, Bishop of *see* Blunt, Alfred

Bradford Diocesan Conference 134

Bradman, Donald 166

Bristol 193

Bristol, Mrs 36

Bristol cathedral 256

Britannia (royal yacht) 79

'Britannicus in Partibus Infidelium' 89–90, 141

British Embassy, Paris 78, 217

British Empire 92, 98, 106, 128, 131, 136, 138, 156, 157, 159, 162, 170, 180–82, 185, 187, 188, 203, 204, 208, 224, 228, 232, 237, 238, 244, 246, 272

British Expeditionary Force 53

British Legion 55, 56, 142, 163, 224–6, 269

British Medical Association 140

British Movietone
 Jarrow Crusade 66
 Jarrow Marchers 66
 News 159

British Union of Fascists (BUF) 179–180, 226

Brittain, Vera 64–5, 165, 187–8, 219, 226, 249

Brown, Ernest 5, 15–16, 65, 119

Brownlow, Kitty, Lady, Duchess of Buccleuch 42, 44, 99, 150, 258, 261

Brownlow, Peregrine ('Perry'), 6th Baron 18, 26, 42, 44, 99, 149–52, 192, 211, 212, 216, 217, 218, 253, 257, 261–2, 263, 265, 267, 275–6

Bruce, Mrs 100, 126

Bruce, Stanley 100–101, 114, 118, 126

Bryanston Court, Marylebone, London 23, 24, 25, 28, 33, 82, 83, 97

Brynmawr 12

Buccleuch, Duchess of *see* Brownlow, Kitty

Buccleuch, Duke of *see* Brownlow, Peregrine

Buchan, John 109, 114, 243, 269

Buchan, Susie 243

Buckingham Palace, London 5, 11, 24, 56–7, 61, 66, 69, 71, 86, 94, 95, 97, 102, 126, 139, 155, 187, 188, 237, 246, 282

Bullett, Gerald 197, 257

Burke, Mary 25, 33, 149, 152, 269

Cabinet 102, 117, 118, 119, 124,
129, 145, 155, 156, 158, 169,
175, 176, 178, 179, 183, 185,
186, 191, 212, 217, 218, 221,
276
Caernavon 2
Caf de Paris, London 73
Cain, Mary 33
Calcutta 205, 208
Caledon Shipyard Workers 142
Cambridge University 61, 121
Camrose, Lord 147
Canada 117, 124, 130, 132, 180,
201, 203–4, 266
Parliament 203
war veterans 56–7
Canadian Post 203
Canadian War Memorial, Vimy
Ridge, France 56
Canal Zone, Middle East 54
Cannadine, David 114
Cannes 150, 174, 191, 211, 216,
253, 262, 268, 274
Canning, A., Superintendent, later
Chief Constable 95–9, 126
Canterbury, Archbishop of *see*
Lang, Cosmo Gordon
Case Harriman, Margaret 242
Catholic Times 181
Cavalcade magazine 19, 20, 98
Cazalet, Victor 19
Cecil, Sir Edward 76
Cenotaph, London 51
Central Ratepayers Association,
Portsmouth 58
Ceylon (later Sri Lanka) 244
Chamberlain, Neville 14, 63, 69, 92,
102, 105, 114, 119, 147, 175,
187, 221
and Special Areas problem 62–3

and Alexander Hardinge's letter
to Edward 93
and unemployment 106
and the morganatic marriage plan
124
and proposed speech to the nation
by Edward 156
feels unsafe with Edward as King
177
on the duty of the press 212
becomes Prime Minister 276
Edward complains of his
treatment 278
appeasement period 76
Channon, Sir Henry ('Chips') 18,
32, 46, 86, 88, 118, 122, 171,
263, 265–6
Channon, Honor 86
Chaplin, Charlie 48–9, 50
Charles I, King 171, 200, 234
Chartwell, Kent 209, 233, 239
Chteau de Cand, Monts, France 274
Chesham, Lord 121
Chiang Kai-shek 24
Chirac, Jacques 282
Christianity 77, 186
Church of England 41, 61, 76,
77–8, 103, 135, 159, 227–8
Church Times 181
Churchill, Clementine 265
Churchill, Mary 265
Churchill, Randolph 275
Churchill, Sir Winston 44, 129, 168,
182, 186, 202, 264
Edward's investiture as Prince of
Wales 2
friendship with Edward 2, 29–30,
172, 175, 233–4
on Edward's relationship with
Wallis 18, 26, 37

Churchill, Sir Winston – *cont.*
 understands Edward's wish to
  marry Wallis 80
 rearmament 107–8, 109, 160
 and morganatic marriage plan
  112
 distrust of 113–14, 195
 support of Edward 128, 151,
  160–61, 172, 175, 247, 265,
  279–80
 Belton House plan 151, 192
 and idea of Edward speaking to
  the nation 153, 155
 attitude to Wallis 172–3
 confronts Baldwin 173–4, 175–6,
  194
 insists on the need for delay
  175–8, 194, 197, 200
 defeat in the House of Commons
  194–5, 198, 199, 200
 and Lloyd George 198
 and Edward's decision to abdicate
  209–10, 221–2
 on Baldwin's skilful handling of
  the abdication issue 223
 receives letters on the abdication
  crisis 231, 250, 252
 and Edward's final broadcast 239
 blames *The Times* for its role
  245–7
 and Lang's speech 258–9, 260
 on Wallis's bad press 264
 depression 265
 view of the abdication 272
 and Edward's wedding 275
 visits the Windsors 277
cinema 48, 159–60, 214–15, 246,
  266, 277
Citrine, Walter 172
Civil List 101, 263, 265

Claridges hotel, London 111,
  116
Clark, Sir William 204
Cliveden, Taplow, Berkshire 41
clover, four-leaf 270
Coldstream Guards 22, 231, 237
Colefax, Sybil, Lady 63, 127, 144,
  234, 267
 a popular social hostess 43, 44
 personality 44
 Labour supporter 44
 approves of the Edward–Wallis
  relationship 44
 on the abdication 246
 spends Christmas Day (1936)
  with Wallis 264
 Wallis's gratitude for her
  friendship 268
Collingwood, HMS 55
Commonwealth 161
Communism/Communists 109, 122,
  123, 164, 179
Conservatism 106, 107
Conservative Party 16, 49, 61, 109
Constitutional Association of New
  South Wales 202
Constitutional Crisis, The (Universal
  newsreel) 137
Cooper, Alfred Duff 42, 44, 45, 98,
  102, 129, 176, 258
 low opinion of women's abilities
  32–3
 and Edward's relationship with
  Wallis 68–9
 and the morganatic marriage plan
  116–17, 124
 efforts to keep Edward on the
  throne 128
 and the decree absolute 145
 and the abdication 247–8

Cooper, Lady Diana 42–5, 86, 98, 258
Cornish tin mines 50
Cornwall, Duchy of 14, 50, 94, 227
Corrigan, Mrs Laura 263
Court Circular 23, 37, 98, 261
Coventry 170
Coward, Noel 39, 44, 264
Cowes, Isle of Wight 5, 39
Crawshay, Captain Geoffrey 12
Crisp (Edward's valet) 252–3
Cromer, Lord 70, 261
Crystal Palace, London 56
Cumberland 65
Cumberland Terrace, London 85, 149
Cunard, Sir Bache 45
Cunard, Emerald, Lady 32, 45–6, 87, 95, 98, 195, 260, 262, 263
Cunard, Nancy 95–6
Cunard shipping line 45
Curtin, John 202–3
Cwmavon 58
Cwmbran 12–13
Cwmtillery colliery, Garn-yr-Erw 16

Daily Express 86, 101, 136, 169, 212, 213
Daily Herald 138
Daily Hindimilap 207
Daily Mail 59, 62, 66, 86, 108, 112, 136, 138
Daily Milap 207
Daily Mirror 59, 62, 65, 136, 138, 168–9, 214
Daily Sketch 136, 140
Daily Telegraph 19, 61, 86, 122, 136, 139, 147, 257
Dartmouth Naval College 157
Davis, Claude 140

Dawson, Cecilia 254
Dawson, Geoffrey 138, 158, 254
    and Edward's adoration of Wallis 40
    and the South Wales visit 61–2
    appearance 61
    member of London clubs 61, 66
    and Edward's popularity 63
    and proposed North-East tour 66
    discussions on the royal crisis 76
    the 'Britannicus' letter 89–90
    and Hardinge's warning letter to Edward 91, 93
    lengthy talk with Lady Milner 104
    and morganatic marriage plan 113
    talks with Bruce 126
    and Blunt 146–7
    'Heir Presumptive' article 147
discusses Times leader with Baldwin 148–9
    defends the Government's position 164
    hopes that Edward will abdicate 177–8
    advocates rapprochement with Germany 189
    on Canada 203
    and Wallis's offer 212–13
    role in the abdication 245, 246
Dawson, Lord, of Penn 40
de la Warr, Earl 176–7
de Valera, Eamon 131–2, 245
de Wolfe, Elsie 43
Deedes, William ('Bill') 19, 20, 59, 85–6
Democrats (US) 106
Depression (1929) 3, 4, 15, 22, 50, 106, 121

Dinas, Rhondda Valley 6
divorce, attitudes to 41–2
Dominion Federation League to
    Abolish Poverty, Ottawa 203
Dominions 117, 118, 124–6,
    128–32, 144, 145, 155, 158,
    161, 191, 194, 201–4, 216,
    245, 251, 252
Dorchester Hotel, London 28
Dowlais 111
Dowlais Aged Comrades' Choir 1
Dowlais steelworks, South Wales
    1–2, 59, 62
Driberg, Tom 212
Drinkwater, John 257
'Duck's Bill', Givenchy 225
Dudley, Lord 258
Duff, Patrick 177
Dufferin and Ava, Marquess of 261
Dugdale, Blanche 199
Dugdale, Nancy 41, 137, 218, 219,
    220, 242–3
Dugdale, Thomas 41, 137, 149,
    210, 211, 230
Duke of York's Camps 10
Dulanty, John Whelan 131
Durham, County 3, 4, 15, 58, 120
Durham Light Infantry 187
Dwyer-Gray, Mr 251

'eanum' (pet name used by Edward
    and Wallis) 26
Eden, Sir Anthony 279
Edinburgh 137, 147, 219
Ednam, Lord 78
Edward VII, King (Edward's
    grandfather) 9, 35, 79–80, 116
Edward VIII, King, formerly Prince
    of Wales, later Duke of
    Windsor

appearance 1, 29, 36, 52, 137,
    159, 267
at Naval College 157
investiture as Prince of Wales
    (1911) 2
at Oxford University 26, 51, 52,
    94, 102
tours New Zealand (1920) 228
friendship with Churchill 2,
    29–30, 172, 175, 233–4
relationship with Freda Dudley
    Ward 38, 52
relationship with Lady Furness
    23–4, 38, 44, 46
meets Wallis (1930) 23
war service in the Great War 14,
    52–5, 58, 64, 187, 223, 225,
    229, 243, 270
in love with Rosemary Leveson-
    Gower, a Red Cross nurse 78
proclaimed king (22 January
    1936) 36
planned coronation 3, 7, 74,
    76–7, 249, 271
Nahlin voyage 42, 86, 136
tour of South Wales (1936) 1–9,
    11–18, 47–8, 57–64, 94, 100,
    105, 106, 109, 111, 119, 120,
    159, 170, 185, 186, 189, 210,
    225, 227, 248–51, 254, 271–2,
    276, 281
devotion to Wallis 18–19, 26,
    46
secret affair 19–20
private language 26
Wallis's care of 35–6
Wallis's influence 37–8
popularity 52, 63–4, 100, 111,
    130, 131, 177, 184, 189,
    231–2, 242, 280

proposed tour of the North-East
65–7
dress style 71
informality 71–2
leisure pursuits 73
Hardinge's warning letter 89–94
under surveillance by Special
Branch 95, 98
meeting with Baldwin (16
November 1936) 102–4, 106
prepared to abdicate 104
attitude to Communism and
Fascism 109
morganatic marriage plan 112,
113, 116–18, 124, 128, 132,
155–6, 170
wants Parliament to be consulted
132
Blunt's reproof 134–5
letters/telegrams from the general
public 139–44, 153–5, 159,
161–4, 168, 170, 176, 183–7,
190, 201, 207, 208, 213–15,
225–8, 230–31, 234, 236–9,
241–5, 248–9, 250, 266,
270–72
Baldwin pressures and bargains
with him 145
tries to protect Wallis 148
proposed speech to the nation
155, 178, 221
compared with Charles I 171, 234
and state security 196–7
visits India (1920) 207–8
decides to abdicate 209
final talk with Baldwin 209–10
executes the Instrument of
Abdication (10 December
1936) 218–19, 226
farewell broadcast 233, 235,

237–42, 256–7, 266–7, 268,
269–70
his new name 235–6
unable to take part in politics
235–6
final meal with the royal family
253
at Enzesfeld Castle, Austria 253,
266–8, 274
told of Lang's speech 258–9
marries Wallis (3 June 1937)
274–5
his title 276–7
rest of life spent in exile 277–8,
279, 281
Governor of the Bahamas 278
loyal supporters 279
and World War II 279
death (28 May 1972) 281–2
personality 130
charm 247, 268
chivalrousness 157–8
courage 248
kindness 48–9
natural intelligence 158
obsession with weight and
exercise 29–30
sense of duty 157
sincerity 248
star quality 51, 189
sympathy with suffering 247
A King's Story 2, 25, 29, 98, 132,
188, 217, 229, 233–4, 253
Eight Hours Act 121
Elizabeth, Princess, Duchess of
York; née Bowes-Lyon; later
Queen Elizabeth, then Queen
Elizabeth the Queen Mother
137, 228, 230, 266
marries Prince Albert 40, 276

Elizabeth, Princess, Duchess of
York – *cont.*
honeymoon at Polesden Lacey 45
appearance 81
friendship with Alexander and
Helen Hardinge 87
snubs Wallis 88
George V approves of 99
Lang visits 99–100
ready for Albert to rule 211
misses last family meal with
Edward 253
writes to Lang on her new role
255
and Lady Cunard 263
and Osbert Sitwell 263–4
and Wallis's status 276
determined to keep the Windsors
out of Britain 278
refuses to meet Wallis 279
Elizabeth, Princess, later Queen
Elizabeth II 87, 100, 228, 280,
281–2
Elliot, Walter 114
Elstree Studios 186
Embassy Club, Bond Street, London
73
Embassy Theater, Times Square,
New York City 266
English Civil War 171
Enzesfeld Castle, near Vienna 253,
266–8, 274
Establishment 60–61, 67, 115, 124,
157, 189, 192, 243
Conservative 102
see also 'Society'
Ethiopia (Abyssinia) 109
Eton College 61, 121, 164
Evans, Inspector 97, 149, 274
Evatt, H. V. 252

Evening News 138
Evening Standard 3, 86, 101, 112,
137, 167, 173, 174, 258
'Londoner's Diary' 40, 139
Express Group 112

Far East 99
Fascism 109, 180, 189
see also British Union of Fascists
Federal Council of Evangelical Free
Churches 165
Felixstowe, Suffolk 84–5, 273
Fellowes, Daisy 265
Fields, Gracie 159
*50,000 Miles with the Prince of
Wales* (film) 48
Fiji islands 254
First World War *see* Great War
Fisher, Sir Warren 91–2, 93, 103
Fitzgerald, Helen 42
FitzHerbert, Lady Nora 163
FitzHerbert, Sir William 163
Flanders 54, 57, 58, 223
Flanner, Janet 35, 234, 253
Floud, Sir Francis 266
Folkestone, Kent 73, 97, 98
Fomenter, Majorca 25
Foreign Office 61
Forster, E. M. 44
Fort Belvedere, Windsor Great Park
23, 24–5, 35, 36, 75, 84, 85,
93, 96, 112, 114, 118, 128,
129, 139, 150, 159, 175, 181,
190, 192, 196, 210, 211, 212,
230, 233, 262
four-leaf clover 270
Foyle's literary luncheons 256–7
France
Great War 54, 55, 57, 78, 187,
223, 270

Wallis visits Mrs Scanlon 97–8
Wallis stays with the Rogers
    family 150, 192
the Windsors in exile 277–8
Franco, General Francisco 108
Friends of the Duke of Windsor in
    America 279
Frisco's nightclub, Soho 212
Frogmore royal mausoleum,
    Windsor 281
Front Populaire (Blum) 108
Fry, Geoffrey 177
Furness, Thelma, Lady 23–4, 38,
    44, 46, 88, 213
Fury, HMS 253

Gallipoli, Battle of 43, 54, 270
Game, Sir Philip 95, 98, 274
Garbo, Greta 159
Garn-yr-Erw 16–17
Garvey, Marcus 49, 244
Garvin, James 197–8
Gateshead British Legion and
    United Services Fund 225
Gaumont-British News 47
General Strike (1926) 120–21
George, Prince, Duke of Kent
    (Edward's brother) 99, 210,
    262, 275
    relationships with married women
        38
    proposes to Poppy Baring 39
    bisexuality 39
    addiction to cocaine 39
    marries Princess Marina 40,
        80
    at the Embassy Club 73
    personality 80–81
    told of Edward's abdication
        decision 106

witnesses Edward's abdication
    219
devastated by the abdication
    247–8
final meal with Edward 253
George III, King 178
George V, King (Edward's father) 5,
    162, 177, 263
    and the working classes 9
    as a parent 10–11
    worries about Edward's size 30
    and Sheila Loughborough 38
    and Edward's popularity 52
    fails to understand war veterans
        57
    rigid time-table 72
    love of shooting 72
    approves of Elizabeth 99
    relationship with Albert 116
    Christmas broadcasts 153, 156
    refuses to shelter the Tsar and his
        family 229–30
    personality 230
    death of 63, 68
George VI, King 266
    the new king 219, 228, 230–32,
        237–8, 246
    final meal with Edward 253
    proclaimed king (12 December
        1936) 254–5
    and Edward's wedding 275, 276
    and Wallis's status 276
    determined to keep the Windsors
        out of Britain 278, 279
    coronation 250–51, 273
    see also Albert, Prince
Germany 189, 265
Gillett, Sir George 12, 60
Glamorgan 2, 6
Glasgow 15

Globe and Mail (Toronto) 203
Goddard, Theodore 216–18, 267
Goebbels, Joseph 189
Gold Standard 121
Granard, Lord and Lady 265–6
Great War (1914–18) 5, 6, 14, 52–5,
    64–5, 73, 77, 109, 142, 187,
    223, 225, 229, 243, 270–71
Greece, King of (Georgios II) 43
Grenadier Guards 52, 53, 55, 73,
    121, 270
Greville, Mrs Ronnie 45, 189, 264
Grigg, John 51, 77
Grosvenor House, London 162
Guinness, Mr and Mrs Lee 25
Gunther, John 28, 31–2, 72, 148,
    242, 251, 257
Gwaelodygarth 7
Gwynne, 'Foxy' (later Lady Sefton)
    43, 128
Gwynne, H. A. 19–20, 128–9, 147
gypsies 244

Hailsham, Lord 105
Halifax, Lord 76, 93, 102, 105
Hall, George 119
Hamilton, General Sir Ian 54
Hamilton, Jean, Lady 40–41, 45–6,
    80, 81, 163
Hamilton of Dalzell, Lord 25, 247
Hansard's 194
Happy Valley set 39
Hardinge, Major Alexander 99,
    140, 147
  sympathy for George V's sons 10
  Edward's Private Secretary 3, 5,
    69, 74, 89, 91, 94
  South Wales royal tour 5, 94
  and Edward's interest in housing
    14

Wallis feels uncomfortable with
    the Hardinges 36
  love of shooting 72
  warns Albert that abdication is
    possible 73
  loyal to George V's court 73
  discusses the divorce issue with
    Baldwin 74–5, 194
  discusses the crisis with Lang 76
  and Alice Keppel 80
  friendship with the Yorks 87
  warning letter to Edward 89–94,
    101, 117
  and the morganatic marriage plan
    114
  the start of the new reign 246
  flourishes under the new regime
    263
Hardinge, Helen 36, 76, 79, 87, 89,
    104, 116, 152, 240
Hardinge of Penshurst, Lord (father
    of Alexander Hardinge) 5
Harewood, Earl of 248
Harmsworth, Esmond 86, 111–12,
    117, 172
Harriman, Margaret Case 242
Harrisson, Tom 250
Hartington, Lord 251
Harvey, Oliver 279
Hatfield House, Hertfordshire 76
Headlam, Cecil 68, 69, 104, 136,
    145, 166, 168, 222, 257–8
Heap, Anthony 180
Hearst, William Randolph 85
Heath, Edward 280–81
Henrietta Maria, Queen Consort
    171–2
Henry, Prince (Harry), Duke of
    Gloucester 106, 219, 253, 263
Hertzog, General 130

Hewett, Sir Stanley 230
High Court, London 74
High Lodge, Durham 58
High Wycombe, Buckinghamshire 94
Hindu newspaper 205
Hindus 206
His Master's Voice 242
Hitler, Adolf 24, 45, 108, 109, 189, 195, 196
Hoare, Sir Samuel 51, 102, 105, 116–17, 124, 221
Hobart, Tasmania 251
Hoesch, Leopold von 196
Holt, Harold 203
Holyrood Palace, Edinburgh 99
Home Fleet 51, 63, 89, 93
Hong Kong 30
Hore-Belisha, Leslie 279
Horne, Sir Robert 106
Hotel de Paris, Bray, Berkshire 85
Hotel Majestic, Cannes 212
House of Commons 64, 84, 101, 106, 119, 122, 124, 133, 158, 159, 161, 173, 174, 183, 192–5, 198, 200, 201, 217, 219, 220, 221, 226, 235, 236, 259, 281
House of Lords 78, 229, 235, 236
housing 6, 12, 14, 43, 48, 50
Houston, Lady 180–81, 255
Hughes, W. M. 176
Hunter, George 84
Hunter, Kitty 84
Hyde Park, London 57, 122, 180

Illustrated London News 121
Imperial Conference (1926) 118
India 31, 205–8, 244

Inskip, Sir Thomas 124
Instrument of Abdication 218–19, 226
Invergordon 121
Ipswich Assizes 74, 75, 84, 85, 188
Irish Free State 117, 124, 131, 132, 245
Irish Government 202
Ismaili sect 54
Italy 189, 225

James II, King 175
Japan Advertiser 235
Japan Times 235
Jardine, Reverend J. A. 275
Jarrow 66
Jarrow Crusade (British Movietone) 67
Jarrow marchers (1936) 66–7
Jarrow Marchers (British Movietone) 67
Jockey Club 71
John, Prince 80–81
Jones, Lewis 123
Jones, Thomas 114, 177, 251
Jowitt, Lord 276–7
Jutland, Battle of 55

Kaneko, Shigeri 235
Kennington, London 14, 50
Keppel, Alice 35, 79, 80, 163, 234
Keynes, John Maynard 44, 165
  General Theory of Employment, Interest and Money 164
Keynes, Lydia 165
Khan, Aly 24
Kingston, Jamaica 255
Kirkwood, David 119–20
Kit Kat club, London 73
Kitchener, Lord 53

Kurunegala Urban District Council,
    Ceylon 244

Labor Daily 249
Labour Party
    and Lady Colefax 44
    Edward's attitude to 49
    and the royal crisis 113, 249
    growing influence 122
    ruling class's fear 123
Ladbrook (Edward's chauffeur) 151
Lambe, Charles 69, 75, 94
    the South Wales visit 4, 11, 15, 16
    on Edward's devotion to Wallis
        19
    on Lady Colefax 44
    and management of the royal staff
        70
    and Wallis's divorce petition 75
    tensions in the royal household
        126
    at the Opening of Parliament 229
    in George VI's Household 263
Lang, Cosmo Gordon, Archbishop
    of Canterbury 70, 72, 76–7,
        99–100, 103, 137–8, 146,
        165–6, 169, 190, 269, 271
    'The pity of it' speech 256–60
Langcliffe Hall, Yorkshire 146
Langtry, Lillie 79
Lascelles, Tommy 66, 228
League of Nations 160, 199
Lebensraum concept 108
Leeds 170
    Peace Congress (1936) 97
Legh, Joey 4, 263
Legh, Colonel Piers 274
'Levantie' (Lavente) 225
Leveson-Gower, Lady Rosemary
    Millicent 78

Lewis, Sinclair 143
Lewis, Wyndham 264
Leyland, Morris 166
Liberal National Women's
    Committee 144
Liberal Party 49
Lincoln, Bishop of 275
Lindbergh, Colonel and Mrs 98
Linlithgow, Lord 104–5, 169,
        205–6, 207
Literary Society 40
Liverpool Disabled Ex-Service
    Men's Protection Association
        223
Llanfrecha Grange 13
Llanidloes, Mayor of 243
Llantwit Major station 2, 5
Lloyd George, David 9, 49, 54, 57,
        172, 183, 198–9, 228, 229,
        230, 241, 249, 255, 272
Lloyd George, Gwilym 249
Lloyd George, Megan 183
Lobamba Kraal, Swaziland 205
Lockhart, Bruce 40, 44, 86, 139,
        144–5, 223, 243, 252–3, 258
London County Council 243
London Irish Rifles 227
London Social Credit Club,
    Westminster, London 180
Londonderry, Charles, Lord 39, 87,
        166, 168, 182, 189
Londonderry, Edith, Lady 4, 87–8,
        127, 166, 189, 224, 263
    Retrospect 159–60, 189
Londonderry House, Mayfair,
    London 4, 87, 189
Loos, Battle of 53
Los Angeles Times 21
Lou Viei, Cannes 150, 152, 191,
        240, 265, 267

Loughborough, Lord 38
Loughborough, Sheila, Lady 38
Lowndes, Marie Belloc 32, 192
Lyons, Joseph A. 118, 126, 130,
    202

MacDonald, Malcolm 124
MacDonald, Ramsay 14, 105, 215
    annoyed at Edward's South Wales
        visit 60–61
    on courtiers' disapproval of
        Edward 69
    and Alexander Hardinge's letter
        to Edward 93
    on Baldwin's ebullience 104
    and the public's reaction to the
        royal crisis 129
    on Edward's final broadcast 240
Mackenzie, Sir Compton 123
Mackenzie King, William Lyon
    130–31, 204
McMahon, George 178
Macmillan, Harold 55, 58, 200
Macy's department store, New York
    242
Madame Tussaud's, London 267
Madison Square Gardens, New
    York 106
Magdalen College, Oxford 52, 61
Mainbocher (originally Main
    Rousseau Bocher) 32, 43, 275
Manchester Guardian 135
Maoris 130
Mare Nostrum (Mussolini) 108
Margaret, Princess 87, 100, 228
Marina, Princess, of Greece
    (Duchess of Kent) 24, 40, 73,
    80, 97, 99, 262, 280
Marlborough, Duchess of 99, 258,
    263

Marlborough, ninth Duke of 39, 99,
    258, 263
Marlborough House, London 105,
    137
Martin, Kingsley 40
Marvell, Andrew: 'An Horatian
    Ode' 233, 234
Mary, Princess 81, 105
Mary, Queen, Queen Consort
    (Edward's mother) 9, 46, 72,
    137, 158, 162, 165, 246
    as a parent 10–11
    personality 35
    dress sense 35
    and Poppy Baring 39
    teaches Edward embroidery 73
    meets Princess Marina 81
    told of Edward's decision to
        abdicate 105
    refuses to meet Wallis 105, 279
    paternal grandparents'
        morganatic marriage 112, 115
    view of morganatic plan 115
    sorry for Edward 219
    Queen Regent proposal 230
    tries to dissuade Edward from a
        farewell broadcast 233
    final meal with Edward 253
    congratulates Lang on his speech
        256, 260
    Lady Cunard ostracized 262
    and Wallis's status 276
Mass-Observation 250–51, 280
    May the Twelfth 250
Maugham, W. Somerset 264–5
Maurice, Sir Frederick 224
Mayor of Merthyr Tydfil's
    Distressed School Children's
    Fund 3
Mbabane, Swaziland 205

Means Test 122, 123

Melbourne 202

Merryman, D. Buchanan ('Bessie', Wallis's aunt) 21, 28, 33, 34–5, 93, 112, 126, 128, 150, 152, 269, 275

Merthyr Express 6

Merthyr Maternity and Child Welfare Clinic 6–7

Merthyr Tydfil 1, 6–7, 59, 111, 122

Metcalfe, Edward ('Fruity') 275

Metropolitan Police 95, 98, 273–4

Meynell, Francis 196, 210, 219

Milner, Violet, Lady 91, 101, 104, 114, 136, 139, 152, 172, 194, 211, 216, 239–40

Milwaukee Journal 251

Miners' Relief Fund 121

Miners' Welfare Institute, Garn-yr-Erw 16

Ministry of Labour 14

Ministry of Labour Home Training Centre, Gwaelodygarth 7

Mitchell, Frank 104

Mitford, Nancy 158

Mobberley Child Welfare Centre, Cheshire 214

Modern Times (film) 50

Monckton, Walter 26, 37–8, 85, 94, 95, 129, 145, 148, 173, 181, 209, 210, 216, 231, 257, 267, 273, 275

Monmouthshire 2, 4, 12, 57
    County Health Department 7

Montgomery Hyde, H. 63

Montreal Gazette 203

Moore, George 45

morganatic marriage, history and nature 112
    see also under Baldwin, Stanley;
Chamberlain, Neville; Churchill, Sir Winston; Cooper, Alfred Duff; Dawson, Geoffrey; Edward VIII; Hardinge, Major Alexander; Mary, Queen; Simpson, Wallis

Morning Post 19, 59, 61, 85–6, 129, 136, 139, 147

Mortimer, Penelope 81

Mosley, Diana (née Mitford) 28, 52

Mosley, Sir Oswald 28, 179, 180

Mount Stewart, Northern Ireland 189

Mountain Ash 7–8

Mountbatten, Edwina, Lady 39, 97, 99, 261

Mountbatten, Iris, Lady 253

Mountbatten, Louis, Lord (Edward's cousin) 69, 97, 99
    Lambe's best friend 5
    on the chemistry between Edward and Wallis 26–7
    bisexual affairs 39
    and the royal crisis 126
    aide-de-camp to George VI 263

Movietone News 47
    Amen: The End of a Tragic Chapter in British Imperial History 254

Muggeridge, Malcolm 135, 174

Muslims 206

Mussolini, Benito 24, 108, 109, 122, 189

Mydrim, India 208

Nahlin 42, 43, 85, 86, 136, 273

Nantyglo, Wales 16

National Council of Social Service 5, 57

National Government 15–16, 49,

59, 60, 63, 121, 123, 132, 179,
189
Nazi Party/Nazism 45, 189, 196,
265
New Deal 12, 24, 50, 106, 108, 236
New Statesman and Nation 15, 40,
60, 120
New York 82, 96, 150, 159, 242
Stock Exchange collapse (1929) 3
New York *Daily Mirror* 85
New York Journal 85
New York Post 143
New Yorker 242
New Zealand 117, 118, 124, 130,
180, 201–2, 228
New Zealand High Commission,
London 141
Newbold, Walter 179
Newcastle upon Tyne 66
News Chronicle 60, 136, 138–9
Newspaper Proprietors' Association
86, 111
Nicholas II, Tsar of Russia 109,
164, 229
Nicolson, Harold 41, 144–5, 169
Nonconformity 77, 138–9, 259
North Wales: Edward visits 56
North-East England 65–7
Nuremberg rallies 45

Observer 197
Octavians 279
Ogilvy, Bruce 30
Olympic Games, Winter (Munich,
1936) 189
Opening of Parliament (3 November
1936) 229
Oriental Post 207
Osborne Naval College 157
Othello (Shakespeare) 9

Ottawa Citizen 203
Owen, Frank 137, 182
Oxford 255
Oxford and Asquith, Lady *see*
Margot Asquith
Oxford University 26, 51, 52, 61,
94, 102, 121

Palestine 241
Paramount 47
Paris 78, 84, 217, 218, 274, 279,
280, 282
Paris *Daily Mail* 159
Parliamentary Counsel,
Memorandum by 92, 103
Passchendaele, Battle of 64, 225
Pathé Gazette newsreels 1, 4, 12, 56
The King Abdicates 219
The King Visits South Wales 47
Patiala State 208
Paul, Prince, of Yugoslavia 37, 81,
262
Peacock, Sir Edward 210
Peking 30, 31, 42, 150
Penrhiwceiber 7
Penrhiwceiber British Legion and
United Services Club and
Institute 225
Pentrebach Preparatory Training
Centre, Rhondda Valley 6
Penygarn housing estate, Pontypool
14, 142
People, The magazine 39
Peter Robinson department store,
London 213, 230
Philip, Prince, HRH The Duke of
Edinburgh 280
Pilkin 225
Pitman, C. E. 121
Polesden Lacey, Surrey 45

Pollitt, Harry 97, 179
Pontypool 14, 15
Poona 208
Portland 51, 89
Portsmouth 58, 253
poverty, the poor 49, 50, 57–8,
    66–7, 77, 120, 122, 123, 163,
    183, 215, 222, 224–7, 231,
    236–7, 249, 251, 271–2, 280
Press Association 74, 134
Preston, Kiki Whitney 39
Pretoria 205
Privy Council 255
Punch 172
Puritanism 259

Queen Mary 15, 213
Queen Mary's Hospital for the East
    End, London 170

Raffray, Mary Kirk 82–3, 85, 277
Rawalpindi 208
Reading, Lord 31
'Recall to Religion' campaign 77,
    103
Red Guards 229
Reith, Sir John 153, 156–7, 235,
    237, 256
Renown, HMS 30
Representation of the People (Equal
    Franchise) Act (1928) 235
Republican Government (Spain) 108
Rhedey, Claudine, Countess 112
Rhiw Park, Abertillery 17
Rhondda, Lady 146
Rhondda Valley 6
Rhymney, Wales 4, 17
Rhymney Iron Company 17
Ribbentrop, Joachim von 45, 189,
    195–6

Ritz hotel, London 234
Robeson, Paul 9, 39
Rogers, Herman 31, 42, 99, 150,
    152, 212, 265, 275
Rogers, Katherine 31, 42, 99, 150,
    152, 265
Roman Catholicism 77
Roosevelt, Franklin D. 50, 90, 106,
    108, 153, 154–5
Rosaura 25–6, 42, 273
Rosebery, Earl and Countess of 99
Rosslyn, Earl of 78
Rothermere, Lord 86, 111–12, 136,
    147, 200
Rothschild, Baron Eugene de 253,
    268, 275
Rothschild, Kitty, Baroness de 253,
    268, 275
Rothschild family 144
Rouen 151
Rowland, John 12, 59, 120
Royal Albert Hall, London 51,
    160
Royal Family 19, 60, 61, 161, 254,
    260, 275, 276, 278, 279, 280
Royal Lodge, Windsor Great Park
    219, 253
Royal Marriages Act (1772) 68, 161
Rubinstein, Artur 44
Runciman, Hilda 15, 70, 78, 115,
    179
Runciman, Walter 15, 93, 224
Russell, Bertrand 65, 256
Russia
    Five-Year Plan 108
    Edward's attitude towards 109
    trade unions 121
    and Stay in Strikes 122
Russian Revolution (1917) 164, 229
Rutland, Duke of 42

Sagan, Princesse de 79
St George's Chapel, Windsor 37, 281–2
St Giles Cathedral, Edinburgh 214
St James's Palace, London 36, 98, 139, 240
St Johns, Adela 281
St Paul's Cathedral, London 281
St Peter's Church, Blaenavon 13
Salisbury, Lord 76, 173, 256
Sandringham House, Norfolk 5, 81, 115
'Sandringham Time' 72
Sassoon, Sir Philip 73
Saturday Review 180–81, 255
Savage, Michael 130, 201
Savile Club, London 243
Scanlon, Gladys Kemp 97
Schiaparelli, Elsa 43
Schuster, Sir Claude 236
Scotland 3, 147
scouting movement 243
Seaham Weekly News 120
Second World War see World War II
Sefton, Earl of 42, 43
Shanghai 30
Shaw, George Bernard 108, 165, 228, 250, 256
  'The King, the Constitution and the Lady' 167–8
Shearer, Norma 159
Simon, Sir John 48, 74, 76, 93, 98, 105, 124, 209, 274, 275, 276
Simpson, (Bessie) Wallis (previously Spencer; née Warfield), later Duchess of Windsor 63, 114
  appearance 21, 27, 29, 31–2, 40, 81, 159, 214, 268
  background 20–21, 28

marriage to Earl Winfield Spencer 21–2, 32, 33
marriage to Ernest Simpson 22–3, 33, 34–5
meets Edward 23
Edward's devotion to her 18–19, 26, 46
a secret affair 19–20
private language 26
travels alone 30–31
death of her mother 33–4
care of Edward 35–6
influence on Edward 37–8
objectionable to the English upper class 40–42
presented at court (1931) 42
Nahlin voyage 42, 86, 136
regarded as a passport to the King 45–6, 196
divorce petition 74, 75–6, 78, 83–7, 188, 194, 216, 217, 266–7, 270, 273, 274
marriage to Ernest deteriorates 81–2
Lady Londonderry's intervention 87–8
Elizabeth, Duchess of York, snubs 88
Hardinge urges Edward to send her away 90–91, 93
under surveillance by Special Branch 95, 96–7
alleged relationship with Guy Trundle 96–7, 98–9
and the morganatic marriage plan 111–12, 155–6, 191
receives hostile letters 127
moves to Fort Belvedere 128
stays in the south of France during the crisis 149–52, 174

Simpson, (Bessie) Wallis – *cont.*
    compared with Henrietta Maria
        171–2
    and Joachim von Ribbentrop
        195–6
    Lloyd George on 199
    offers to renounce Edward
        211–14, 216, 219–20
    Wilson's view of her character
        215
    told of Edward's irrevocable
        decision 218
    listens to Edward's farewell
        broadcast 240, 241
    anxiety about Edward's future
        241
    gratitude to Lord Brownlow 262
    jealous of Edward's hostess 268
    marries Edward (3 June 1937)
        274–5
    her status 276, 277
    rest of life spent in exile 277–8
    and Edward's death 282
    her death (24 April 1986) 281,
        282
    personality
        charm 42, 88
        forthrightness 27–8
        independence 30–31, 32, 85
        intelligence 31–2
        tact 88
        warm-heartedness 33
    The Heart Has Its Reasons 25,
        27, 98, 195
Simpson, Ernest Aldrich 20, 23, 33,
        34–5, 69, 98, 266
    appearance 22
    shipping firm 22
    marries Wallis 22
    long talk with Edward 80

    marriage to Wallis deteriorates
        81–2
    and Mary Kirk Raffray 82–3,
        273, 277
    Ipswich divorce hearing 85
    under surveillance 95, 96, 98
    offer to Baldwin 192
Simpson v. *Simpson* 85, 273
Sinclair, Sir Archibald 113, 176,
        209–10
Singapore 254
Sitwell, Sir Osbert 263–4
    'Rat Week' 263, 264
Six Bells colliery, Garn-yr-Erw 16
Smiths Newspapers 202
Snatchwood Junior Instruction
        Centre, Pontypool 15
Social Credit Reformers 180
'Society' 61, 71, 87, 126, 189, 196,
        260, 262–3, 279
    see also Establishment
Somme, Battle of the (1916) 14,
        52–3, 56, 58
South Africa 117, 124, 130, 180,
        201
South America 23
South Wales
    Edward's tour (1936) 1–9,
        11–17, 47–8, 57–64, 94, 100,
        105, 106, 109, 111, 119, 120,
        146, 159, 170, 185, 186, 189,
        210, 225, 227, 248–51, 254,
        271–2, 276, 281
    seen as a flashpoint 123
South Wales Argus 11, 58, 59, 72,
        73
South Wales Miners' Federation 17
South Wales National Unemployed
        Workers Movement 123
South Wales Slave Act Special 123

Soviet Union *see* Russia
Spain: Russian influences 122
Spanish Civil War 108, 124
Special Areas 48, 60, 62, 65–6, 108, 119–22
Special Areas Commission 66
Special Areas (Development and Improvement) Act (1934) 12, 106, 121
Special Branch, Metropolitan Police 95, 97, 98, 126
Spectator 4, 8, 123
Spencer, Lieutenant Earl Winfield 21–2, 30, 32, 33, 266
Spring Hill Branch, British Legion 224
Sri Lanka *see* Ceylon
Stalin, Joseph 24, 108
Stamfordham, Lord 229
Stanley, Oliver 171, 263
Star 138, 201
Star of India 205
State Opening of Parliament (3 November 1936) 71
Statesman newspaper 205
Statute of Westminster (1931) 118, 245
Stevenson, Frances 198, 199
Stewart, Malcolm 12, 66, 106, 162, 186
Stopes, Marie 136
Stornoway House, St James's, London 153, 209
Storrier, D., Inspector 274
Strathmore, Earl of 40
Sunday Express 101
Sutherland, Duchess of 99, 258, 263
Sutherland, Duke of 78, 87, 99, 258, 263

Swazi National Council 205
Sydney 49, 202
Sydney Morning Herald 176, 202

Tablet (Catholic newspaper) 181, 234
Tasmania 251
Taylor, A. J. P. 113, 157
Tennyson, Hon. Lionel 121
Thackeray, William Makepeace: *Vanity Fair* 42
This Week 69
Thomas, Sir Godfrey 115, 156, 202, 263
Thompson, R. J. 137, 182
Time and Tide 249
Times, The 4, 40, 61, 62, 85, 91, 105, 136, 137, 144, 147, 148, 164, 165, 169, 177, 193, 194, 203, 205, 213, 220, 245–7, 256
Times of Ceylon 208
Toc H 55
Tours 274
trade unions, Russian 121
Trades Disputes Act (1927) 121
Travellers Club, London 61, 66
Treasury 164
Tredegar, Viscount 4
Tredegar House, Monmouthshire 4
Tree, Ronald 239
Trevelyan, Sir Charles Philips 168
Trevelyan, George M. 197, 256, 263
Trevelyan, Janet 197–8
Trinidad Citizens' League 244
Trinity College, Cambridge 5
Trundle, Guy Marcus 96–7, 98
Turing, Alan 20, 143, 196–7, 248, 258
Turkey 43

Tyne Improvement Commission,
  Newcastle 65
Tyneside 3, 65

unemployment, the unemployed 3,
  5, 6, 7, 9, 12–13, 15, 17, 28,
  47, 49, 50, 57–8, 59, 62, 63,
  66–7, 106, 119, 122, 123, 159,
  164, 168, 183, 185, 210,
  224–5, 227, 238, 280
Unemployment Assistance Board 3,
  122
United Australia Party 203
United French Polishers' London
  Society 60
United States of America
  exploitation of Black people 9
  New Deal 12, 24, 106, 108, 236
  British upper classes' view of
    Americans in Britain 40–41
  view of the royal crisis 89, 90
  Roosevelt elected (1936) 106
  Edward seeks an alliance 109
  cinema 159
  rumours about the significance of
    the South Wales visit 251
  Friends of the Duke of Windsor in
    America 279
Universal Films 47, 137
Universal Negro Improvement
  Association 244
universal suffrage 103
Usk 11, 18

Vanderbilt, Consuelo 39
Vanderbilt, Gloria 24
Vansittart, Lord and Lady 44
Victoria, Queen 162
Victoria Station, London 81

Vienna 43, 271, 274
Villa Mauresque 264
Vimy Ridge, France 56
Viola, Queen of the Gypsies 244
Virginia 41
Vogue 32
Voice newspaper 251
Voluntary Air Detachment 64
Vreeland, Diana 27, 33, 253, 261
Vreeland, Reed 261

Wales
  disestablishment of the Anglican
    Church 77
  see also North Wales; South
    Wales
Wales, Prince of see Edward VIII,
  King
Wall Street Crash (1929) 3, 44
Wallace, Barbara 258
Wallace, Euan 258
Walshe, Mr 131
Ward, Freda Dudley 38, 39, 52
Ward, William Dudley 38
Warfield, Alice (Wallis's mother) 21,
  33–4
Warfield family 21
Warwick, Countess of 79
Waterlow, Sir Sydney 43
Waugh, Evelyn 166
Wedgwood, Colonel Josiah 192
Wells, Geoffrey H. ('Geoffrey West')
  142–3, 246, 248, 255, 260
Wells, H. G. 61, 142, 165, 256
Welsh Board of Health 12, 59, 120
Welsh Guards 231
  Old Comrades 14
Welsh Land Settlement Society 5
Welsh Miners' Relief Fund 9
West Cumberland 3